—continued on rear outside endpaper—

EDITOR'S CHOICE

"The Small Press publishes 97% of the poetry and fiction being published in the United States today."
— Leonard Randolph, former Director of the Literature Program of the National Endowment for the Arts

"The publishing business, formerly one of the last strongholds of the independent entrepreneur, is rapidly being swallowed up by corporate capitalism...In the last 20 years, more than 300 mergers have taken place in the publishing industry...New authors find it more and more difficult to get published at all. Even established authors find most commercial publishers increasingly indifferent to a book that promises only a modest sale...Today, the censorship of ideas has entered American life through the back door. The economics of centralization and standardization threaten to achieve what could not be achieved, in a country officially committed to liberal principles, by governmental repression: uniformity of thought."
— Christopher Lasch, in *The New York Times*

1

EDITOR'S

CHOICE:

Poetry
Fiction
Essays
Graphics

with 50 pages of autobiographical notes
from the presses/magazines & authors/visual artists

Literature & Graphics from the U.S. Small Press, 1965-1977

EDITED BY MORTY SKLAR & JIM MULAC

selected from nominations by editors
of independent, non-commercial presses & magazines

The Spirit That Moves Us Press
IOWA CITY, IOWA: 1980

Acknowledgments

The publisher apologizes for any acknowledgments not made or credit not given ... we relied on the contributors to provide that information. All but a few nominations by the presses and magazines (found at the beginning of each work) are considered permission to reprint. The remaining permissions are cited below. Nominations had been made as early as Fall 1977. Further credits may be found in the author or visual artist autobiographical note section.

"from Mabel—A Story" is reprinted by permission of Marion Boyars Inc., American publisher of Robert Creeley's *Mabel—A Story*.

"So This Is Nebraska" is reprinted by permission of University of Pittsburgh Press, publisher of *Sure Signs: New and Selected Poems* by Ted Kooser. © 1980 by Ted Kooser.

"Populist Manifesto" is reprinted by permission of New Directions, publisher of *Who Are We Now?* by Lawrence Ferlinghetti. © 1976 by Lawrence Ferlinghetti.

"New York" is reprinted by permission of New Directions, publisher of *Lorca-Jimenez: Selected Poems*, translated by Robert Bly, and Agents for the Estate of Federico Garcia Lorca. All Rights Reserved.

83-01523

First Edition, clothbound & perfectbound: December 1980

Library of Congress Cataloging In Publication Data
Main entry under title:

Editor's choice

   (The Contemporary anthology series ; no. 2)
   Bibliography: p.
   1. Literature, Modern—20th century. 2. Graphic arts. I. Sklar, Morty, 1935-   II. Mulac, Jim, 1942-   III. Series: Contemporary anthology series ; no. 2
PN6014.E3   810'.8'0054   79-64861
ISBN 0-930370-05-8
ISBN 0-930370-06-6 (numbered 1-100 & signed by the editors)
ISBN 0-930370-04-X (pbk.)

THE SPIRIT THAT MOVES US PRESS
P. O. Box 1585, Iowa City, Iowa 52244
(319) 338-5569 or (319) 337-9700

Publication of this Collection Was Made Possible by

the authors, visual artists, editors and publishers

and matching grants from
the Iowa Arts Council & the National Endowment for the Arts

with matching funds by
Gannett Newspaper Foundation (thru the Iowa City Press-Citizen)

and
Senior Honorary Publishers:

Otto Mulac   Selma Sklar   Herbert Sklar & Family

and *Honorary Publishers:*

Prairie Lights Books; Norma Vogel; Isabella Gardner; Deadwood Tavern; B.J. Records; Charles L. Eble; The Best Steak House; Mace Braverman; Hamburg Inn Number 2; Hair Ltd.; Things & Things & Things; Gilda's Imports; Technigraphics; Iowa State Bank; Graphic Services; Bremer's Men's Clothing; Dorothy Huwe; Lou Ehrenkrantz; IBM,

and *further contributions from:*

Saxifrage Used Books; Norm Sage; The Sanctuary Tavern; Frohwein's; Arnie Jensen; Sheep's Head Cafe; Copper Dollar Tavern; Northwestern Bell; Bicycle Peddlers; Campus Standard; Dunton-Lanik; The Stereo Shop; Ronald Bierma; Emil Trott; Herteen & Stocker; The Hanger; Dain Bosworth; Jewel of Kashmir; Zephyr Copies; Anonymous.

Gratitude is also expressed to:

Len Fulton of Dustbooks, for information and advice,
CETA, for the employment of Stuart Mead for one year,
CAC, for the part-time employment of Shelley Sterling.

ALSO FROM THE SPIRIT THAT MOVES US PRESS

New titles:

Cross-Fertilization: The Human Spirit As Place (anthology)
The Farm In Calabria & Other Poems, by David Ray

Current titles:

The Actualist Anthology
The Poem You Asked For, by Marianne Wolfe
Riverside, by Morty Sklar

Ongoing:

The Spirit That Moves Us literary periodical (since 1975)

Other:

Poetry-With-Drawings In The Buses (two series)

Forthcoming:

New & Selected Poems, by Chuck Miller

"Let this music go from the heart to the heart."
—Beethoven

This Book Is Dedicated To

Otto Mulac
The Memory of Millie Mulac

Selma Sklar
The Memory of Jack Sklar

and
All Independent Spirits Everywhere

INTRODUCTIONS

Hello, Reader—

You have in your hands the result of an idea which crackled between my co-editor Jim Mulac and me almost three years ago. It had its source in frustration and anger which peaked in a desire to write negative reviews about anthologies claiming to be the "best" or the "greatest," and mellowed out to a commitment to do our own anthology of literature from the Small Press.

Our intentions were to 1) Collect work which resolved what we feel are two main tendencies in contemporary letters and the other arts—in fact, in most aspects of our culture: On the one hand, the gutsy, more actual expression which comes from the artist's strongest instincts and aspirations, based predominantly in the life, the living of a person; and on the other hand, the learned and the technically proficient. We realized that the skillful and thoughtful need not be dry and mental. We also realized that intense feeling may be enhanced or sustained by regard for the craft of a work *in service to* the intentions of it; 2) Make accessible to the general reading public, work from small presses and little magazines, which publish in limited editions and whose visibility is also limited by small, or no promotional budgets; 3) Offer by example, to the general reading public as well as the small and commercial presses themselves and authors and visual artists, the kind of work which we feel should be more often aspired to.

Our vision includes the political and social as well as the expressive and imaginative. We feel we've found a lot of what we looked for: works which in most cases married facts and ideas to personal, poignant expression.

It seems appropriate here to offer constructive criticism to the National Endowment for the Arts. The NEA, in its 1980 application guidelines for Small Press funding, seems to have adopted a "publish or perish" ethic: presses are now required to have published five books in the three-year period preceding the application date. From what I understand, this requirement is supposed to ensure the sincerity or commitment of the publishers. It is actually a hindrance to many sincere and committed publishers. Altho five books in three years may not appear to be a stringent requirement, it is for many. Small Press publishers for the most part do not have as a priority, quantity. They publish what they believe in and what might otherwise not see print. They might produce five books in one year, and in another year only one. *Editor's Choice* itself has been in the works, as I've said, three years. What the NEA is saying, in effect is, if you publish four books in three years—regardless of their merit and contribution to our culture—you do not deserve government funding. I'm sure the average tax-payer would support that —just as the average taxpayer supported Proposition 13 in California—one result of which has been the closing down of many small libraries, and the curtailment of purchases and services in many others. And, *most* Small Press publishers are writers themselves. They can't just publish and hold a job at the expense of their writing.

For those who would count the number of women, Blacks and other minorities in the table of contents of this anthology, and don't find the numbers they're looking for, we can only say we made every attempt to increase their proportion, short of tokenism. The response from women's and minority presses was small partly, perhaps, because some could not identify with two male caucasian editors, and partly because their representation in the Small Press community is not as great proportionally as the women and minority population is in our society.

Another frustration for us was artwork, due to the fact we often could not obtain the original work or a quality photograph or slide of it for reproduction.

I feel that most of what I have to say about this anthology has been expressed in the making of it, and so I leave you now to Jim's comments and the anthology itself. Jim and I are going to get back to where this all started—to our own writing. Happy reading!

Morty Sklar
Iowa City, Spring, 1980

When we began this project, nearly three years ago, we hoped to be as open-minded to the U.S. Small Press movement as possible. It was a monstrous thing: partially cohesive and strung together by newsletters, but largely fragmented, temporary, driven into no-man's land as editor-writer-publisher moved from Sacramento or Ann Arbor to jobs or hideouts in West Virginia or New Mexico. How would we ever find them all? Why would they trust us with their best material? And how would we face disappointing them if, in the final editing, we didn't use any of their work? It was a humbling, merely hopeful position to be in.

We decided on the time period 1965-1977 partially arbitrarily, partially with a reason. The small, alternative, literary press had existed before Hawthorne and Emerson, had grown and pulsated along with an increasing national literacy up to a minor heyday in the 1920s. It was fueled further, though partially appropriated, by the college boom of the '40s and '50s, but then in the 1960s something much greater happened. The post-college literacy and democratic activism of that decade sent inspired people to the mimeo machine and the offset printer's office as well as into the streets. Where there had once been dozens of presses and magazines there were now hundreds and eventually thousands. Probably a million people gave a stab at writing, and sent their work wherever they knew to send it or wherever they thought they'd get published. And, of course, it's still going on in 1980, bigger than ever. We wanted to stay contemporary, so 1965 seemed a good target for the '60s —not too far from the year we'd have to close.

We used the newsletters over and over again, asking people to spread the word. We used direct mailings from lists of registered presses old and new. Eventually we used the telephone, tracking people however possible. By the spring of 1978 the flow began— hundreds and hundreds of brown envelopes. In each envelope a dozen or twenty or thirty poems, plus stories, essays and graphics. Whole issues of magazines, sometimes ten-years-worth, from editors who refused to make nominations. "All our stuff is great! You pick something out." Over 400 presses in all, more than a dozen big boxes of envelopes, a mountain of material. How could we lose? How could we ever get through it?

So then the reading began—June, 1978. Twenty, forty, sometimes sixty hours a week, until your brain turned to cinders and you dreamt all night that you were reading, reading a really interesting work, following it line for line until you realized it couldn't go on, you'd never know the outcome, since it was a dream, just a dream. Wake up! I sat in my used book store and read all afternoon, then read again all evening and all through the weekend. There was no other way to get through it all—more than 50,000 pages to be read by each of us, much of it to be re-read, some as often as a dozen times over nearly two years. Naturally there were breaks, cooling off periods, new efforts on good material you feared you might have been too burned out on the first time. Give it another look. Maybe that ending's not as bad as you thought.

Everything that had even a remote chance was held back for a later reading with a fresh outlook. We forgot about names and looked at each work on its own. Quite naturally, we were inspired, deeply moved (calling each other at all hours), often bored to despair, disillusioned, stirred again, and generally educated by the task. Some of what we hoped for was rarely there, but some was much better than we'd expected, setting standards of its own that began determining "our" anthology. And, of course, technique, or techniques, were well in hand almost everywhere. We're a technically proficient country here in America. More and more you were judging and gathering something well beyond technique. You were measuring soul, breadth of personality, depth of statement, significance of philosophy, political courage, artistic "greatness"—what exactly are these things? and how did you get into this position? who in this visionary and verbal purgatory do you think you are? God? Edmund Wilson? Donald Allen? Yourself, with your own terrible and beautiful life and its blindness, its bent wisdom and patched-up readiness? Come off it, man! Just try to be objective.

How can you be objective about anything but formalist or academic art? And that's why there's so much of it, of course, so that masses of people can feel comfortable and objective, sure at last that something will last because it has the right form, the right tone, the right way of being avant-garde or traditional. You can't be objective about real art because it forgets all the rules and is totally personal. It moves you with a subtle and unprecedented jolt, just when somebody might have said it was getting sentimental, ridiculous or arcane. That's where the edges and the new center of this life are, that's the screwball music that the gods want to hear.

All this sounds, perhaps, excessive, but it's the very stuff of what we were working with, and there was plenty of it there, enough for four other books by eight other editors. So, despite our hopes, this did not become a representative anthology. Formal schools and attitudinal movements fell by the wayside and the people in each work came on through, with all their personalities, guts, mysteries and concerns. Jonas wouldn't have had it any other way, nor would Baraka, Bumpus, Chalkley, Reynolds, Bukowski, Miller, Rea, Pat Elliott or any of the others. They started to take over, and then we let them, and finally they took over completely and made it the way it is.

Jim Mulac
June 1980

TABLE OF CONTENTS

POETRY

14

FICTION

ESSAYS

GRAPHICS

POETRY

David Long / Kalispell, Montana

IN THE SUMMER OF WARREN WHITNEY

from *Porch*, Volume 1, Number 2: 1977
Tempe, Arizona
Editor: James Cervantes

I don't remember your face
except it was an old potato
you didn't shave regular
as my father who was on time
& smelled of witch hazel.
Early mornings I stared
through the stars of the windshield
& sulked into the memory of
a hard brown girl called Peachy.
Your stink ripened the cab
of the busted Chevy,
black vest & T-shirt that began
the day without sleep.
You fussed over the tools
because it killed time
& they meant no more to you
than I did & you were nothing to me
but one pain of my 17th year.
We were last to the new houses.
We rolled the humps from their soil,
busted down the fists of clay with our rakes,
broadcast seed that would wash away
in rivulets like your hair.
How many times did I listen
to how you & your brother once landscaped
that new hospital down in Lowell,
how the hills rolled rich as fur,
how they remember you.
Back of the house of a blind man
who lay in the shade with a tall white drink

I watched your stupidity drop
tree on tree until the lot was clogged
& your saw choked with blue smoke
& your fat hands shook with the power of it all.
Afternoons I waited at the empty crossroads
bearing your sour lies,
pitching stones at bottles
until the earth sparkled.
I followed you into the backrooms of the dump
& when you sent me down
into the sputtering fire I went
& brought you back iron,
loops of copper, any part of a motor,
& saw you gleam as you brushed away the black ash.
I drank bad water with you
& saw the sky swirl like a gas station toilet,
sick beside you under the hot
palms of an August noon.
I listened to you preach
the gospel of country music
through the gulley of no teeth
& honestly thought you were too corny to live.
So one morning, gassed on my impatience
I gave up waiting & drove
back into the woods to call you out
of a house I couldn't imagine.
Chickens picked at cinders between junk cars,
your daughters fluttered
in the dark windows like cloth.
Suddenly you stumbled into sunlight
this great polished fiddle stuck to your neck
& you smiled for me with all the world's
silly generosity & let loose
a terrible tune that will not die.

Liza Gyllenhaal/New York City

THE ONES YOU LOST

from *Me Too*, Volume IV: 1977
Iowa City & New York City
Editors: Mary Stroh & Patty Markert

In the morning when
everyone has gone you
turn the radio on in the kitchen.

The sun plays on the
water in the sink and
your thoughts travel like trees

across the windshield
of a speeding stationwagon.
Your husband is driving.

Children and friends are packed
inside and in the far back you can
see your father's great bald head.

From the innertube and thermos
of orange juice and gin you know
this road leads to the sea.

In the years it takes to get there
your mother-in-law slumps over her
basket on conches and angel wings

And your father sleeps with his
hands folded on one knee as
he sat for his portrait.

Sometimes in the woods
you can see running
parallel to the car

the children you lost—
in the hospital
on the stairs

in your own bed with
the television on when you
could not even look down.

Now you imagine their hair and eyes
their knees pumping through the woods
glowing like the lemons on

the windowsill like your
hands in the warm
bright water in the sink.

Amiri Baraka/Newark, New Jersey

A POEM FOR DEEP THINKERS

from *Contemporary Quarterly*, Volume 1, Number 4: 1976/77
Los Angeles
Editor: Ken Atchity

Skymen coming down out the clouds land
and then walking into society try to find out
whats happening—"Whats happening," they be saying
look at it, where they been, dabbling in mist, appearing &
disappearing, now there's a real world breathing—inhaling exhaling
concrete & sand, and they want to know what's happening. What's happening
is life itself "onward & upward," the spirals of fireconflict clash
of opposing forces, the dialogue of yes and no, showed itself in stabbed children
in the hallways of schools, old men strangling bankguards, a hard puertorican inmate's tears
exhanging goodbyes in the prison doorway, armies sweeping wave after wave to contest
the ancient rule of the minority. What draws them down, their blood entangled with humans,
their momories, perhaps, of the earth, and what they thought it could be. But blinded by
sun, and their own images of things, rather than things as they actually are, they wobble,
they stumble, sometimes, and people they be cheering alot, cause they think the skymen
dancing. "Yeh...Yeh...get on it...," people grinning and feeling good cause the skymen
dancing, and the skymen stumbling, till they get the sun out they eyes, and integrate the
inhead movie show, with the material reality that exists with and without them. There are
tragedies tho, a buncha skies bought the loopdieloop program from the elegant babble of
the ancient minorities. Which is where they loopdieloop in the sky right on just loopdieloop
in fantastic meaningless curlicues which delight the thin gallery owners who wave at them
on their way to getting stabbed in the front seats of their silver alfa romeo's by lumpen
they have gotten passionate with. And the loopdieloopers go on, sometimes spelling out

complex primitive slogans and shooting symbolic smoke out their gills in honor of something dead. And then they'll make daring dives right down toward the earth and skag cocaine money whiteout and crunch iced into the statue graveyard where Ralph Ellison sits biting his banjo strings retightening his instrument for the millionth time before playing the star spangled banjo. Or else loopdieloop loopdieloop up higher and higher and thinner and thinner and finer refiner, sugarladdies in the last days of the locust, sucking they greek lolliepops.

Such intellectuals as we is baby, we need to deal in the real world, and be in the real world. We need to use, to use, all the all the skills all the spills and thrills that we conjure, that we construct, that we lay out and put together, to create life as beautiful as we thought it could be, as we dreamed it could be, as we desired it to be, as we knew it could be, before we took off, before we split for the sky side, not to settle for endless meaningless circles of celebration of this madness, this madness, not to settle for this madness this madness madness, these yoyos yoyos of the ancient minorities, it's all for real, everythings for real, be for real, song of the skytribe walking the earth, faint smiles to open roars of joy, meet you on the battlefield they say, they be humming, hop, then stride, faint smile to roars of open joy, hey my man, what's happening, meet you on the battlefield they say, meet you on the battlefield they say, what i guess needs to be discussed here tonight is what side yall gon be on

29

Charles M. Purcell / Pasadena, Maryland
WELCOME HOME

from *Demilitarized Zones: Veterans After Vietnam*
East River Anthology, 1976: Perkasie, Pennsylvania
Editors: Jan Barry & W. D. Ehrhart

I hurtle over America's highways
Foot to the floor
Metallic scream
Steel-belted radial whine

I'm coming home

I race from west coast to east
Along America's veins and arteries
An insignificant blood cell
Among millions like myself.

Back road maniac
Midnight demon
I rush through America's guts
Stopping at scum bars
And fast food crematoriums

I'm coming home

There's a rotting smell
About this place
A smell above and beyond
The call of duty
Of cheap whiskey
And greasy food
A smell worse
Than foul streams
And deadly air
The smell of rotting flesh and

Decayed spirit

Barroom television—
Old man gets off squeezing toilet paper
Humanity shamed by ring around its collar
Nothing breaks a heart like psoriasis
Aunt Bluebelle hugs the heaviest roll
And guitar strummin'
Black clad mumblin'
Hillbilly hero
Says "love your gas station attendant"

I'm coming home

Parking lot peacocks
Flash feathers in drunken waltz
Fists smash against faces too numb
To care
I drive away over broken glass
And somebody's teeth

A tightness worse than hunger
Grips my guts like a vise
Jungle tan
Unemployed killer
Where in hell am I?

I'm coming home

There it is
It rises up behind auto graveyards
There it is
Beyond a rusting heap of scrap metal
Lying beneath the smoke and the dirt

Welcome home

I dump my exhausted car
Behind a big Ford

Jamming my bumper against his
Where a sticker proclaims
"This is My Country"
I'm happy about that
I was afraid
It might be mine

Darkness is settling over the city
Things look better in the dark
And someone is saving daylight
For a better era

A light rain begins to fall
Rivulets of dirty water
Begin to trickle from cold dark buildings

Walking toward a bright spot
I draw closer and see a movie theater
Spewing its contents onto the sidewalk
Like New Year's Eve vomit

The crowd is black
And as I pass
Someone yells
"Hey muvvuhfucka!"
I stop
Wondering who knows my name
And a big dude
Wearing bell bottoms wide enough
To hide two midgets
Strolls up to me

Peering at my face from under his wide hat
He smiles the first real smile
I've seen in three days and asks
"Whatcha lookin' for Bibbles?"
I hesitate
Undecided
Trying to remember

Why I came back
Finally I smile back answering
"I wanna score some coke."
His smile gets bigger
"All right!
All right!
I'm your man!"
And we stroll away into the darkness
Neither of us
Looking for America

Garrett Kaoru Hongo/Newport Beach, California

IN SEARCH OF THE SILENT ZERO

from *Greenfield Review*, Volume 6, Numbers 1 & 2: 1977
Greenfield Center, New York
Editor: Joseph Bruchac

for Frank Chin

On the other side of the one-way mirror,
I wait and watch, my hands
folded and cupped near my balls,
until I see pearls of sweat
grow to full maturity on his forehead.

I enter the interrogation chamber
with a prepared confession I've composed myself
and demand, "Sign it, Yank!"
with a slight trace of the soy sauce accent.

When he spits in my face
I clench my jowls and not my fists,
pull out a silk handkerchief
embroidered with purple chrysanthemums,
wipe the goo from my moustache,
which does not look like a toothbrush
treated with Clairol Grey-Away to me,
and gaze down upon the solitary finger
jutting upright from his fist.

"You will pay for this outrage!"
I shout, my voice quavering
like the last shimmers from a struck gong,
"And you will start with that finger!"

He takes the cue and tries to kick me
even though his legs are tied together

and strapped to the chair. The ingenious
Oriental knots grow tighter with struggle.

Trying to imitate Sidney Greenstreet,
I chuckle like an asthmatic accordion,
the phlegm percolating in my larynx,
and allow one eyebrow to twirl and not merely arch.
It performs a magnificent preying mantis
kung fu kata, and the audience
begins to admire my form as much as my courage.

He cowers as my aide prepares
the bamboo splint to be inserted
under the nail of his right middle finger.
"Joseph P. Martin," he murmurs, "First Lieutenant.
U. S. Army. Beachwood 4-5789."

We insert the splint.
The vein near his temple throbs,
visually echoing the vein on my own shaved head.
The cameraman is pleased.

"You have one last chance
before we ignite the splint.
Burning flesh makes an excellent
repellent for the Burmese mosquito."

He is wordless, but the soundtrack
brings strains of "God Bless America"
as the lamp above us begins to sway.
And even in this underground bunker,
we can hear the muffled sound of explosions.

He starts to laugh and sings a verse
of "Those Green Kentucky Hills"
as they cut to Spencer Tracy
piloting his Flying Fortress over the compound.

I run outside to the drill field,

shoving cowardly screaming soldiers aside.
One bursts like a water balloon as I go by him
and slowly raise my slanty eyes upward.

The flag of the rising sun,
tattered with machine gun fire and shrapnel,
ruffles in the wind and smoke behind me,
perfectly framed but in soft-focus
just over my shoulder and beside my ear.

I look into the camera,
ack-ack guns and bombs going off around me,
and stare straight into the audience
for the first time in my screen career.
I choose my words carefully,
as if giving a valedictory address:

"You have always wondered how
I speak your language so well.
I am one of you.
Have always been.
I will escape from this movie,
and, in another generation,
wear Levi's, Pendleton's, Addidas,
and pass unnoticed near military installations.
Beware.
My weapon can be a Nikon
or perhaps this poem.
And even as the whine
from the diving Flying Tiger buries my voice,
even as its anonymous pilot
sights me in his crosshairs
and thumbs the gun-button on his stick,
I am already there
beside you
while the credits begin to roll."

Edward Smith / Iowa City, Iowa
ROSIE BAKUNGAN

from *The Flutes Of Gama*
Litmus Inc., 1972: Salt Lake City, Utah
Editor: Charles Potts

smooth song
the jukebox sang
along the shore
night-long
eating sweet steamed milkfish
sucking it off the delicate
sprays of its bones
peanuts, baked bananas
drinking a case of San Miguel
with the thrumming hint of Playboy
by the marvelettes coming
at us over the mangrove
the war so far, far
away across the pond
they called the South China Sea
you called simply "dagat"
& were thrilled remembering
the smell & purring motor in the water
Naughty little girl escaping girl's chores
long ago going out in the sea with dad
& uncles, fishermen,
You sat there with me
watching the moon go down in the sea
huddle under the blanket on the sand, singing
old songs from your childhood, in Bisaya

I held you
smooth brown girl, soft wide mouth
under bushy wild eyebrows
and hair gone even more thick
& matted from the salt in the air

I thought your father must have that
ferocious look on him too.

The next day still drunk
under the daytime mild breeze
we lolled in the shallows of the lagoon
coating our bodies with black slime
like young carabaos.

I went back to hideous work
of war, bivouacs on the Bam bam River, base
alerts, over Armed Forces Radio, five A.M.
at work, the signal
"Situation Cocked Pistol for Operation Buzz Saw"
(operation bullshit, try to get off base
before they decide the army's in it)
miniatures of Gordon's gin in my gas mask container
more town, "town is good"
other girls, waking up 2 A.M.
hard iron rain on a galvanized iron roof
"another alert, you can't go back on base"
beer & benzedrine and pancit guisado
wistful letter from home
girl who sent me away
thought she wanted me back again
another letter, from saigon
written in blood (this really happened)
weekend break third class bar car to Tutuban
Sunday night first class air conditioned
with all the filthy rich Chinese back again
to other arms, other bars...

                    And you
back to other men, Jim Beam, New Year's Eve
New Kings Hotel five lays in one night
a case of clap, a trip to Olongapo
what difference does it make?
The revolution may be a long time coming
I do not know what will become of you or me,

I know we were wild and young once
& we keep it
it is not time for us to be old
I dance your silly dances in love for my wife
you make my silly faces
we give others what we first gave each other
out of mud spotted faces
ferocious eyes.

Otto Rene Castillo / 1936-1967

APOLITICAL INTELLECTUALS

from *Camels Coming*: 1967
San Francisco
Editor: Richard Morris

One day
the apolitical
intellectuals
of my country
will be interrogated
by the simplest
of our people.

They will be asked
what they did
when their nation died out
slowly,
like a sweet fire,
small and alone.

No one will ask them
about their dress,
their long siestas
after lunch,
no one will want to know
about their sterile combats
with 'the idea
of the nothing'
no one will care about
their higher financial learning.
They won't be questioned
on Greek mythology,
or regarding their self-disgust
when someone within them
begins to die
the coward's death.

They'll be asked nothing
about their absurd
justifications,
born in the shadow
of the total lie.

On that day
the simple men will come.
Those who had no place
in the books and poems
of the apolitical intellectuals,
but daily delivered
their bread and milk,
their tortillas and eggs,
those who mended their clothes,
those who drove their cars,
who cared for their dogs and gardens
and worked for them,
                  and they'll ask:

"What did you do when the poor
suffered, when tenderness
and life
burned out in them?"

Apolitical intellectuals
of my sweet country,
you will not be able to answer.

A vulture of silence
will eat your gut.
Your own misery
will pick at your soul.
And you'll be mute,
                in your shame.

translated by Margaret Randall

Lawrence Ferlinghetti/San Francisco
POPULIST MANIFESTO

from *Nitty Gritty*, Volume 1, Number 1: 1975
Pasco, Washington
Editor: Bill Wilkins

Poets, come out of your closets,
Open your windows, open your doors,
You have been holed-up too long
in your closed worlds.
Come down, come down
from your Russian Hills and Telegraph Hills,
your Beacon Hills and your Chapel Hills,
your Mount Analogues and Montparnasses,
down from your foot hills and mountains,
out of your tepees and domes.
The trees are still falling
and we'll to the woods no more.
No time now for sitting in them
As man burns down his own house
to roast his pig.
No more chanting Hare Krishna
while Rome burns.
San Francisco's burning,
Mayakovsky's Moscow's burning
the fossil-fuels of life.
Night & the Horse approaches
eating light, heat & power,
and the clouds have trousers.
No time now for the artist to hide
above, beyond, behind the scenes,
indifferent, paring his fingernails,
refining himself out of existence.
No time now for our little literary games,
no time now for our paranoias & hypochondrias,
no time now for fear & loathing,
time now only for light & love.

We have seen the best minds of our generation
destroyed by boredom at poetry readings.
Poetry isn't a secret society,
It isn't a temple either.
Secret words & chants won't do any longer.
The hour of *om*ing is over,
the time for keening come,
time for keening & rejoicing
over the coming end
of industrial civilization
which is bad for earth & Man.
Time now to face outward
in the full lotus position
with eyes wide open,
Time now to open your mouths
with a new open speech,
time now to communicate with all sentient beings,
All you 'Poets of the Cities'
hung in museums, including myself,
All you poet's poets writing poetry
about poetry,
All you poetry workshop poets
in the boondock heart of America,
All you house-broken Ezra Pounds,
All you far-out freaked-out cut-up poets,
All you pre-stressed Concrete poets,
All you cunnilingual poets,
All you pay-toilet poets groaning with graffitti,
All you A-train swingers who never swing on birches,
All you masters of the sawmill haiku
in the Siberias of America,
All you eyeless unrealists,
All you self-occulting supersurrealists,
All you bedroom visionaries
and closet agitpropagators,
All you Groucho Marxist poets
and leisure-class Comrades
who lie around all day
and talk about the workingclass proletariat,

All you Catholic anarchists of poetry,
All you Black Mountaineers of poetry,
All you Boston Brahmins and Bolinas bucolics,
All you den mothers of poetry,
All you zen brothers of poetry,
All you suicide lovers of poetry,
All you hairy professors of poesie,
All you poetry reviewers
drinking the blood of the poet,
All you Poetry Police—
Where are Whitman's wild children,
where the great voices speaking out
with a sense of sweetness and sublimity,
where the great new vision,
the great world-view,
the high prophetic song
of the immense earth
and all that sings in it
And our relation to it—
Poets, descend
to the street of the world once more
And open your minds & eyes
with the old visual delight,
Clear your throat and speak up,
Poetry is dead, long live poetry
with terrible eyes and buffalo strength.
Don't wait for the Revolution
or it'll happen without you,
Stop mumbling and speak out
with a new wide-open poetry
with a new commonsensual 'public surface'
with other subjective levels
or other subversive levels,
a tuning fork in the inner ear
to strike below the surface.
Of your own sweet Self still sing
yet utter 'the word en-masse'—
Poetry the common carrier
for the transportation of the public

to higher places
than other wheels can carry it.
Poetry still falls from the skies
into our streets still open.
They haven't put up the barricades, yet,
the streets still alive with faces,
lovely men & women still walking there,
still lovely creatures everywhere,
in the eyes of all the secret of all
still buried there,
Whitman's wild children still sleeping there,
Awake and walk in the open air.

James Magorian / Helena, Montana

THE NIGHT SHIFT AT THE POETRY FACTORY

from *Stoogism Anthology*
Poor Souls Press/Scaramouche Books, 1977: Millbrae, California
Editor: Paul Fericano

The older poets are showing the new ones
around, getting their identification
badges pinned on at the proper angle,
showing them where the cafeteria
and rest rooms are located (the short
cuts and hiding places come later).

A gray-haired laureate has a metaphor locked
in a vise and is filing off rough edges.

The foreman distributes book reviews
and then snaps a prize-money whip
over the workers' heads.

A sonneteer is at the took cage
checking out a rhyme.

"Stay on the other side
of the yellow safety lines,"
warns a cautious editor.

The grinders are run only by imagists,
and they have a special union.

A ballad-maker comes in late
with his black lunch box under
his arm and begins to sweep
broken voices out of the aisles.

"I'm only working here until I can get
enough money to be somebody else,"

mutters the epigrammatist-in-residence.

The welders are the most admired:
silent in their dark heavy masks
they put together narrative poems
and their brilliance explodes
from behind high screens.

"Is it true that the scabs get all
the foundation grants?" asks
a visiting anthologist.

The oily iron bins of scrap poems
and odds and ends of punctuation
are towed away by small tractors.

Everyone in the free verse department
just got a promotion.

"The conveyor belt broke on Assembly Line 4
and a lot of good adjectives were lost,"
sighs an inventory control inspector.

Resting under an electric sunrise,
the poets wait for the quitting bell
and think back on all the poems
they have made; outside the factory
the pale moon hangs haughtily
in the morning sky like
a cosmic rejection slip.

Cinda Kornblum / West Branch, Iowa

HEY ANIMAL—EAT THIS POPCORN

from *Me Too*, Volume II: 1975
Iowa City & New York City
Editors: Mary Stroh & Patty Markert

If you want to lead a calf
you have to know everything
about yourself—
A full skirt flapping in the wind
might threaten him
Every movement
calculated
slow
as though you are
a part of the earth
growing
imperceptibly
toward the animal

It is my hand that is feeding you daily
It is my hand you can trust

Then WHAMMO!
You and calf are at the fair
You have taught him to trust you
so he won't jump at applause
won't kick the kids who offer him popcorn
so he'll stand tall & square
when the bidding begins

Steve Jonas / 1927-1970

CANTE JONDO FOR SOUL BROTHER JACK SPICER, HIS BELOVED CALIFORNIA & ANDALUSIA OF LORCA

from *Manroot*, Number 10: 1974/75
South San Francisco
Editor: Paul Mariah

canto i

ain is located somewhere between Polk Street & Laguna Beach/
  as you cross the Oakland Bridge into Portugal/
h, that Spicer/
              he was a flamenco, that one/
                          for wld save America from
  the abuses of rime. Like Lorca (our Fedy) was 'gipsified'.
eard 'Bird's' playing & for three years
              didn't know the taste of meat. sd. he didn't know
  music had attained to it. A tear & one blue note upon yr brow, baby.
ated the east w/its glib talkin' effete
              prissy espousing test-books. sd. i was John Randolph
  of American poetry, a Spanish soul brother confused by adoption
  w/northern Europe, The American Friends & The Science & Health Book.
thankd him ("sir") for myself & for my ancestors.

he 'amen corner' is as close as we can come to cuadro flamenco.
alt Whitman's butterflys w/singed wings, all silver white
              star spangled the milky-way w/their gissem.
or then, this is Andaluz Province,
                          "cadahus
                                  en son us".
              Tradition, you can't keep it out
  nor can you lock it under box lid.
                  What is this out-cry from the dark memories,
doubt, of the caves; animal & almost human? Cante jondo.
                          Goya heard & painted it
  in all its black terror.
                  Ever hear ole Manitas ('Silver fingers')

guitarrista soul?
>>>"Ole"
>>>>"Vamos, Manitas!"
>>>>>>"Cook, baby go!"
>>poppin' their fingers (pites) & feet that won't keep still
>>(baile)
>>>>right hand for the beat like 'Jelly Roll'
>>>knockin' the box near the bridge (martillo)
or when he cuts loose with a bad jota & some sister from the corner
>>>leaps to her bravura
>>>>>>& pirouettes:
>>>>>>>>dat-dat-dat-dat
>>>>>then the abrupt halt
>>"Bien parado"!
>>>>>then the fall-prostrate on the floor.
The bull fighter is the best dancer in all Spain.
The blues came into Spain with the gypsies
>>>who joined the jews & the moors in the Holywood
>>hills back 'o El A afta the expulsion
>>>>the which might as well be Granada!
Hey, Manitas, Jack Spicer says make with Meritas Moras,
>>>& the cantaer intones the blues
>>>>like it was early one monday mornin'
>>'n i was on my way to school
>>>>& it was the mornin' i broke my muther's rule
>>"eso es cante moro!"
>>>>>this cat is *bad*
>>'cause the blues is bad
>>>>>from 'down home' southern Spain
where the gypsies cop their horse
>>>>so they can wail their romances sonambules
>>their canto jondo blues of sounds
>>>>>>—bad sounds
>>>>from the ballin' bad fartin' fuck sounds:
>>>>>>"funky", earthy.
"gumba any you peepul from the Cape"?
>>>>>>"Verde," he means.
>>>yeah, man, they made the step-over on the IN-flight
>>>>>to pick up on some Horace 'Silver-fingers' sides

then hi-taild it to New Bedford
                                    'cause their trawler wuz waitin'.
ou spick like a portageese
                        & the faint "th'eheres" go for broke.
panish? christ, i don't even speak English!
                                "ahh yeah, i got my mo-joe workin' for you."
        " 'cause ah bin to the gypsie git my fort'chun tole"
            "she say some other man come in de back way"
        "when ah leaves for wurk by de front"

picer, we want a big round sound in poetry
                        like Ammons gets from a horn,
                or Picasso's high voltage line
                        execution of a picador.
ut gone. over & done with. forget it.
ck Spicer fled Boston as Lorca fled Nueva York.
            so 'un-latin'
                    'no magic'
            saved only by Walt Whitman
                    "tu barba, llena de mariposas"
                & sleeping with his back to the Hudson.
he cantaer's voice couldn't pierce the horror of norte americano silence
                broken only by the jing-jing of the cash register.
                so Saeta
                            no cante moro
                                no blues
                                    nuthin'
ou know, us latins come to take on frightnin' implications
                confronting northern insensibility.
adopt your style, personality—deliberately a mask. "... the
                                    (only escape from
            the hatfaced bargainers & the money-changers."

        canto ii

ck Spicer says wait, don't leave, the poem's not over yet.
hey also say that Europe stops   abruptly at the Pyrenees.
picer says they mean the California-Nevada line.
ellow wind

i've seen you mount the green night
                        thru the spines of moon fleckd trees
          in the half-light.
                    "duende"
                              & yells of : "Man,
                                        he's got it"
                          & another: "he's got it"
For then this *is* Andaluz province. Spicer sd: "doan yew talk to
                                        (me about j-azz".
Flamenco came up the Mississippi afta it
                    buried its black roots under a N'Orleans cat house.
          "hey, momma gimme a taste 'o that fine ty'ass you're swingin' "
              & "yass yass yass" 'n that's tjazz
                        that's duende
                                  for they talk of nothing else
                              save "duende"
                                        "duende"
                      who's got it
                                  who aint—be it Manitas
de Plata's guitarrista
                        or Picasso's advertisements of the tribes
          & folly, as thousands roar:
                          "*Man*, he's got it"
                                        "he's got it"
            "i tell you that cat cooks"
                              "tellin' you like it is"
        "got flamenco"
                        (that's a little shit in yr blood")
Fedy (Garcia Lorca)
                      a lame, like all poets, a memory of a roar
      from the mouth of the Hudson&Harlem rivers
                                later, spat out in Havana harbor
more than likely, the bad afta taste of it all
                        but rememberd Harlem
                                where he heard some conte more,—
                                              faintly
All over America the little magazines conspired
          to board Jack Spicer up in a California Street rooming house,

for lack of space.
                        "duende"
                                "duende"
                                        —elbow nudged ribs & a wink:
                        "yeah, he's got it"
                "aw *man*, he's black with it"
                                                & "won't quit it"
                        "kno what you mean"
Miles heard it (*Sketches of Spain*) like Casals like
                        de Falla, "you kno"
                        "jes goes without saying"
            Santayana understood it "but, (hunch of shoulders)
                he's escolastico, si?" (another province, anyway)
And so it goes. Life, Death, Love, el Toro &
                                "duende"
                                        "duende"
                all they discuss
                        ones who have it
                        ones who do not
"yes, yes, yes, Senor, eso es"

When Garcia Lorca came to New York the Stock Market held firm
    & the trains ran on time as usual. The jews along 125th street
sold condoms full of gentile dreams to the black crocodiles in their
                                                (stores.
        "this cat's so bad
                he'd cut his own muther
                                        if she got on the stand".
that's black singing. "eso es canto moro"
                        negros, negros, negros, negros

        envoi
Here's to a green river
                doing a belly-crawl thru
                        yr blood thirsty sod,
                                        Andalusia
& red bells undulating the crests of yr yellow wind
                        weaving thru the green blades
                                of fixd bayonets (poor Spain)

53

                    bristling in yr geld'd landscape/by
overhead the plowd furrowd brows
                                        of darker gods hover:
                                    Toledo in a Storm
Sleep Fedy among the olive groves
                        where i imagined they planted you
                                                    "adiosito"
                    a whisper of yellow wind   rattles the dry teeth
            in the skull of a dead horse's mouth
                                        —a shudder of leaves
                            "adiosito"
        red bells thru the soft wind:
                            "adiosito"
                                        "good-nite"

Steve Jonas/1927-1970

BLACKSTONE PARK

from *Angels Of The Lyre*
Gay Sunshine Press & Panjandrum Press, 1975: San Francisco
Editor: Winston Leyland (G. S.)

Dans le vieux parc solitaire et glace

in this park of dilapidated times
    where no one comes save
        the bums & those
who love beneath the vine or the rose

winos toss empty pints
    on-to the half shell of
a no longer running fount
dry voices of castrated hopes

complain to a jagged moon
        in its final resolve
at the last bench of a row
    two shadows equivocate

they have no sex nor time
their words are witherd grasses
    beneath the shuddering night;
some old ecstasy performed for fools

who believe the words they've said
    when the wind is down
and the green innocence of death
    stalks the place

with a rattle of two elevated cars
    overhead hang-dog
and headed for the suburbs

Anselm Hollo / Sweet Briar, Virginia
AWKWARD SPRING

from *Heavy Jars*
Toothpaste Press, 1977: West Branch, Iowa
Editor: Allan Kornblum

awkward spring
has spilled its
golden ink
all over the angels' bibs

& off
the swan's soft chest
white feathers fall
into the swamp

& so forth

& i thought i was

a big & perfectly sensible dog

walking the other dog

with some dignity

thinking not of form number 0412 dash 70144

but of a city

equal to my desire

Anselm Hollo: from *Heavy Jars*

HELSINKI, 1940

exploding, shattering, burning

big lights in the sky

& this was
heaven's gate?

no no it's just the front door
same old front door you know from the daytime
& we're just waiting for a lull in the action
to cross the yard, get down to the shelter
& meet the folks, all the other folks
from all the other apartments

& there was a young woman
at least ten years older
he thought very beautiful

blankets, & wooden beams, & crackling radios & chatter

it was better than heaven, it was
being safe in the earth, surrounded by many

all of whom really felt like living

Isabella Gardner / New York City
THAT WAS THEN

from *New Letters*, Volume 42, Number 4: 1976
Kansas City, Missouri
Editor: David Ray

Union Pier Michigan. We called it Shapiro
Shangri La. People said I needed a passport.
I was the only Shicksa there Kolya Shura
Manya Tanya and Sonya, Sulya Myra and
Vera they were there. And Riva a young girl then.
Soda pop and ice cream parlors, no bars,
Delicatessens but no liquor stores.
They spoke fractured English fractured Yiddish
and fractured Russian when they did not want
their children to understand. Most husbands
drove down from Chicago fridays but mine
came to me thursdays bringing the squat green
bottles of Chilean white wine I drank
(he was angry if I forgot to buy
cucumbers) My daughter then five, now in
Bedlam, chased butterflies and thirty years
ago my infant son, now for some years
lost, was happy too. I washed his diapers
in a tub and hung them up in the sun.
Instead of a play-pen, my husband, Seymour,
called Simcha which means joy, made a paddock
for him. Dan did not like to be cooped up
(nor did Rose, my daughter Rosy; nor did she)
not then, not later, never. Dan was last
seen in Colombia South America.
Simcha little Rosy   littler Daniel
and the Shicksa we were all of us joy—
full then in Shapiro Shangri La when
we were young and laughing. On the lake beach
the women waded and gossiped. The men,

supine on the hot sand sucked in the sun
through every work and city tired pore
and on the blithe beach played chess needling each
other, "singing" they called it. The Shicksa
swam and her daughter, round pink Rosy made
castles out of sand and when the big rough
boys' unseeing feet crushed her battlements
she cried (as she would later, as she did
later, as she does now and must again
in inexorable time). Ah but then
it was different. The first summer at our
Michigan Shangri La we shared one half
a cottage with Seymour's sister Molly
Molly the matriarch and my mother
too Molly ample Yiddishe mama
bountiful heart bountiful flesh married
to tender Ben Blevitsky book-binder
and Bolshevik, not Communist though he
thought he was and paid his Party dues.
He pressed on me, a bemused fellow traveller
The Daily Worker which I occasionally
scanned. Aside from Ben's misguided fealty
to a party that betrayed his each, his
every dream, he taught the Shicksa wisdom,
ancient, Hebraic, of the heart and pulse.
This Shicksa loved him all his life. He died
attacking Zionists. In the debate
the heckling struck his heart and aged eighty two
gentle Ben Blevitsky fell down and died.
That first summer the Shicksa shared the stove
with Molly who wouldn't let her cook
a meal but did teach her to cook kugel
and fix gefilte fish. (It was only
the Shicksa's second marriage and so she
had not yet lost her appetite for cooking,
that came after the fourth marriage when
she recklessly played house with a fifth man.)
Political not pious there was not
kept, a kosher kitchen. Molly and Ben

once took the bus to Chicago saying
they'd be back saturday night for supper
saying Be well Bellotchka but don't cook!
Later Molly cheeks streaming with laughter
crowed to cronies "The Shicksa cooked a haser
for the Shabbas!" Stuck with cloves it was,
the scored cuts thumbed full of dark brown sugar
hot powdered mustard and the fresh squeezed juice
of sweet oranges and the whole ham smeared
with that luscious mixture and therewith glazed
and all ate that haser with high delight
the Blevitskys, Molly, Ben, and their Bob and Riva
Rose, Simcha and his Bellotchka—the cook
ate and ate while the infant Daniel slept.

That was then. That was then.

Gary Gildner / Des Moines, Iowa
MY FATHER AFTER WORK

from *New Letters*, Volume 44, Number 2: 1977
Kansas City, Missouri
Editor: David Ray

Putting out the candles
I think of my father asleep
on the floor beside the heat,
his work shoes side by side
on the step, his cap
capping his coat on a nail,
his socks slipping down,
and the gray hair over his ear
marked black by his pencil.

Putting out the candles
I think of winter, that quick
dark time before dinner
when he came upstairs after
shaking the furnace alive,
his cheek patched with soot,
his overalls flecked with
sawdust and snow,
and called for his pillow,
saying to wake him
when everything was ready.

Putting out the candles
I think of going away
and leaving him there,
his tanned face turning
white around the mouth,
his left hand under his head
hiding a blue nail,
the other slightly curled

at his hip, as if
the hammer had just
fallen out of it
and vanished.

Joseph Bruchac / Greenfield Center, N. Y.

FINDING A DEAD MOLE WITH MY SONS

from *Jam To-day*, Number 5: 1977
Northfield, Vermont
Editors: Don Stanford, Floyd Stuart & Judith Stanford

Together we look
at the pinprick eyes
the ears hidden slits
cut into its fur.

We learn from it
that when you go
deep into the Earth
you leave the things
which hold you back
behind.

Darcy Cummings / Cherry Hill, New Jersey
INTERPHASE

from *The Smith*, Number 21: 1977
New York City
Editor: Harry Smith

Even before the cord is cut, he seems
Angry. Flipped on my suddenly flat gut
He threatens the air with tight fists.
The polished room echoes with reproachful screams
As I slide a timid finger along his small
Wet skull, feel the fierce pulse.
His cries provoke
Green masked laughter
And a tremor in my breasts.
Weary of pain and anxious for a smoke,
I'd like to discard him until
He's cleaned up or this weakness ends,
But he screams and shudders
Until the doctor lifts him to my breast.
He nuzzles blindly.
Animal, I whisper.
The round overhead light multiplies and swings in a wide arc.
I stroke his head and whisper: son.

Chuck Miller / Iowa City, Iowa

HOW IN THE MORNING

from *The Spirit That Moves Us*, Volume 1, Number 1: 1975
Iowa City, Iowa
Editor: Morty Sklar

why always in the morning?
because you must begin your life over again every morning
you fumble for your shoes
the leather thongs stiff and cold
fumble with your fly
make sure your prick doesn't get caught in the zipper
and by then the shadows are stealing up grey and clean,
the sun a later gamble
that might make it through this hung over sky,
then the long walk out from the private shack of our
dreams, barely holding together
to the car slowly disintegrating
then if you can get it going,
drive toward the world
only just functioning on the grey edge of night
with its slouched coffee slurpers
and unconscious donut gobblers
its shoe factories stitching on soles
for the tender feet of our souls,
its bellowing trucks, posts
and positions, sinecures, backbreaking sweats
being fed the grey slimy exhausts of
constant velvet farts of our metal skins
sown onto us,
and it is all simple, grey, clear
if you don't think about it.
and there are those with their great life's works,
and those who must do these very same great life's works.
maybe Vallejo is riding with you this morning
looking for work the same as you
and he says "Understanding that he knows I love

him, that I hate him with affection and to me
he is in sum indifferent, I signal to him, he comes,
and I embrace him moved, So What! Moved . . . Moved."
and I say to him, "that was damn good Cesar
should we try the employment office today
or the toilet paper factory should we try the
donut factory once more to make that graveyard
donut shift, or maybe the mental hospital
to see if they have an opening in the laundry
I used to do the laundry thing folded sheets
off the mangle"
and Cesar is saying
"go for the pop bottles, fuck all this other stuff,
these wood bees, let's just collect pop bottles
that's the surest way"
and so the morning comes grey over the hills
and you drop the washcloth on your cold feet
and you fumble with the delicate
birds of morning
opening their cages

Chuck Miller / Iowa City, Iowa
THINGS AS THEY ARE

from *Oxides*
Seamark Press, 1976: Iowa City, Iowa
Editors: Howard Zimmon & Kay Amert

going out halfhappy
or half angry or somewhat tired
nonetheless everything in this snow
looks back directly
with a stark clearness
as i walk through this nonessential winter's day
beautiful in a way which is neither grandiose
nor too little
all the elements have announced themselves
now they break and reform
in ways that are almost recognizable

tonight stars creak
like leather harnesses
alone in the solitude
of winter rooms
feel the harness of night around your back
and belly
the icy bit in your teeth
and be pulling it
alone in the dark
know there is no way out
or through, except the long strange road ahead
in which you are the uncertain captain
of this tramp steamer your life
various companions changing through the years
like stars in the same constellation
burning intensely but too far
in their fixed orbits
and the special ones
that come terribly close

the tail of a comet passing over
your trembling body
causing strange atmospheric disturbances
pulling out great gravitational hunks
finally always coming back to the same worn self
a cave glowing darker with experience
and less comprehensible in its depths

but in summer's first fragrance
still to break off bits of the milky way
and see the evening star
rising over the dark blue drifting up from the sunset
and rejoice as though you were young once more
and saw the dawn of hope rising just beyond your reach

Cesar Vallejo / 1892-1938

THE BLACK RIDERS

from *Neruda And Vallejo: Selected Poems*
The Sixties Press, 1971: Madison, Minnesota
Editor: Robert Bly

There are blows in life so violent—I can't answer!
Blows as if from the hatred of God; as if before them,
the deep waters of everything lived through
were backed up in the soul... I can't answer!

Not many; but they exist... They open dark ravines
in the most ferocious face and in the most bull-like back.
Perhaps they are the horses of that heathen Attila,
or the black riders sent to us by Death.

They are the slips backward made by the Christs of the
    soul,
away from some holy faith that is sneered at by Events.
These blows that are bloody are the crackling sounds
from some bread that burns at the oven door.

And man... poor man! ... poor man! He swings
    his eyes, as
when a man behind us calls us by clapping his hands;
swings his crazy eyes, and everything alive
is backed up, like a pool of guilt, in that glance.

There are blows in life so violent... I can't answer!

—translated by Robert Bly

Mary Stroh / Iowa City

SETTLING IN

from *Me Too*, Volume IV: 1977
Iowa City & New York City
Editors: Mary Stroh & Patty Markert

I stock the cupboards with tomato paste,
chicken noodle soup, and just in case,
three different kinds of flour, yeast
and canned milk. I shove aside boxes
and push your toys into a closet.
I chose a small apartment
just in case we needed something
womb-like, to crawl back into.

I wrap you in extra sweaters, socks,
and we go down to the street
to see where we are living.
We find an old road
all broken in on itself
and follow it to a graveyard.
You ask so many questions.
How can I tell you
what these stones are for?
It's enough they're good
for climbing and jumping off.
I tell you dead people
are under the dirt
and you want to know
where squirrels sleep.
I almost say, we are all dead
from the beginning.
But there are trees behind us
and we go looking for nests.

T. L. Kryss / Cleveland

THE BIG ROCKS

from *Vagabond*, Number 21: 1975
Ellensburg, Washington
Editor: John Bennett

Lettering on the window:
Marble
Granite
Bronze.
Inside the ascetic little
shop, slabs
of pink and gray stone,
stuff of ages,
resting on wooden skids.
Through an open door
in the rear, a muddy yard
with two men in dusty overalls
eating their sandwiches,
handkerchiefs spread
over an unfinished tombstone
like a tablecloth,
a sleeping dog sending up one eye
like a lazy periscope,
while a white butterfly
attacks
invisible wind currents.

None of this
seems very good to me,
a shearing
of the bitter truth
to be made into coats
that anyone can wear.

My 3-year-old son
who is with me
on this dangerous mission

to the drugstore,
asks me
what the big rocks
are for.
I feel like saying
they are for
the little men,
who try
and do not try
then die.
Like some enraged insect
you keep in a jar.

Even I try.
But pretty soon
there is not much left
to understand.
All that is left
of a man's thoughts
is a creaking gate
as the storm goes
somewhere else,
dealing itself out
over an ocean,
a desert
or
a dump

RED EYES LICK THE NIGHT

from *Vagabond*, Numbers 23/24: 1976

all the words you could say
mean nothing
when you see a child
playing with a spider
on linoleum

and in the newspaper
you have a rearview photograph

of a man who lost
his face.one day
in a war somewhere
and reading on,
you learn of efforts, a plan,
to reconstruct his mouth
with metal plates
to enable him to someday
form a vowel, edge sideways
at celery

and you lay down
this item
of human interest

and note
with sinking valor
that the spider
is now playing
with the child,
inducing smiles and dances
in the sunlit crescent
of dust.

the marbled linoleum
swirls like batter
& a little cake is made
of sadness.
the child begins to talk
with his fingers
like a spider,
and you get the feeling
that somewhere
love is about to end,
the sac is about to break,
red eyes, millions,
lick the night.

Allan Kornblum/West Branch, Iowa

AWKWARD SONG FOR MY SISTERS

from *Out There*, Number 9: 1976
New York City
Editor: Rose Lesniak

Sometimes the flautist's hands
grasp the flute awkwardly.

Now and then the dancer's body moves
into, then out of a clumsy position.

Occasionally the poet stutters,
lovers sit on the bed to a loud thump.

Often one corner of the coffin
slips while lowered into the grave,

and the lurch brings
another wave of tears.

Is there a more graceful
shape than a tear,

or a more unselfconsciously
awkward gesture than weeping?

Sometimes it rains for a week, then
surprise, the sun shines bright

and every object seems to have
hard edges...colors clash...

nothing seems to soften the awkward song.
But it continues like light,

like an arm around a shoulder,

the artist adds another shadow,

the flautist a trill,
the dancer a whirl,

and soon grass will grow
over our mother's grave.

Ronald Koertge / South Pasadena, California

THE DAY ALVERO PINEDA WAS KILLED

from *Vagabond*, Number 21: 1975
Ellensburg, Washington

Editor: John Bennett

It was almost post time, the horses were
lining up. Pineda's was spooking so he
stepped off, outguessing trouble, and stood
on a little shelf in the stall of the
Puett Starting Gate.

Nobody knows what happened, but people
with binoculars saw the sudden blood. They
stared as if he had removed his helmet
to reveal a fall of thick, red hair.

The siren faded, the race went off, somebody
won. Then the announcement that he was
dead. "Boots And Saddles," a moment
of silence.

For the rest of the day we worked
the bartenders numb and heaved our money
through the windows, making everything
the favorite.

After the ninth we went home
38,000 of us
all sick
all broke

feeling lucky.

Douglas Blazek / Sacramento, California
STRAIGHTENING THE WARP

from *Poetry Now*, Volume 1, Number 2: 1974
Eureka, California
Editor: E. V. Griffith

I am shooting a game of pool
not wanting it to end
unless I am the winner.

Under the table my
dog is seemingly unaware
any game is being played, or
ever played.

Keep missing my shots because
the table has a bad warp to it.
I aim true but circumstance
keeps working against me.
This is how the days have been going.
I keep trying to make my shots with
a sledge hammer
rather than a cue stick.

I am not my dog.

In sheer exasperation I whack
the stick across the rail as if
I am severing the head of an
animal which constantly annoys me.

Even though I lose the game
I momentarily straighten the warp.

Morty Sklar/Iowa City, Iowa
RED AND BLUE NOON

from *The Night We Stood Up For Our Rights*
Toothpaste Press, 1977: West Branch, Iowa
Editors: Allan Kornblum & Cinda Kornblum

with Harlem in mind

The red and blue a property
of neon, argon,
elements amiable to bars and taverns
and other places of night,

which in daytime too
kids may enjoy at Coney Island
seeing the ascension of a balloon.
Gases most apt to be common
to Pluto, Neptune and the moons of Jupiter,
not so much shining as glowing, in the city.

Unlike the elevated train
they fit gently into the midnight of our sky.
Blue and red charged thru clear tubes of glass,
bending, twisting like a good artist's hand,
seen from many darkened streets away
by old people at their windows.

And from all directions
journeys of a few hundred feet
a few thousand,
to enter beneath
to warm exhalations of smoke,
the smell of fermented grain,
to music, strangers, and friends.

Kabir / 1440-1518

FRIEND, HOPE FOR THE GUEST...

from *Try To Live To See This*
Ally Press, 1976: Saint Paul, Minnesota
Editor: Paul Feroe

Friend, hope for the Guest while you are alive.
Jump into experience while you are alive.
Think and think while you are alive.
What you call "salvation" belongs to the time before death.

If you don't break your ropes while you're alive,
do you think ghosts
will do it after?

The idea that the soul will join with the ecstatic just because
   the body is rotten—that is all fantasy.
What is found now is found then.

If you find nothing now, you will simply end up with
   an apartment in the City of Death.
And if you make love with the divine now, in the next life
   you will have the face of satisfied desire.

Then plunge into the Truth, find out who the Teacher is,
   believe in the Great Sound!
Kabir says this:
     "When the Guest is being searched for, it is the intensity
     of the longing for the Guest
     that does all the work.
     Look at me... you will see a slave of that intensity."

               —translated by Robert Bly

Ted Berrigan / New York City
THINGS TO DO IN PROVIDENCE

from *Red Wagon*
The Yellow Press, 1976: Chicago
Editors: Richard Friedman, Peter Kostakis & Darlene Pearlstein

Crash

Take Valium   Sleep

Dream &,

forget it.

*

Wake up new & strange

displaced,

at home.

Read The Providence Evening Bulletin

No one you knew

got married
had children
got divorced
died

got born

tho many familiar names flicker &
disappear.

*

Sit

watch TV

draw blanks

swallow

       pepsi
       meatballs
       . . .

             give yourself the needle:

   "Shit! There's gotta be something
           to do
             here!"

         *

JOURNEY   Seven young men on horses, leaving Texas.
TO   They've got to do what's right! So, after
SHILOH: a long trip, they'll fight for the South in the War.
No war in Texas, but they've heard about it, & they want
to fight for their country. Have some adventures & make
their folks proud! Two hours later all are dead;
one by one they died, stupidly, & they never did find out
why! There were no niggers in South Texas! Only
       the leader,
with one arm shot off, survives to head back for Texas:
all his friends behind him, dead. What will happen?

         *

   Watching him, I cry big tears. His friends
were beautiful, with boyish American good manners,
        cowboys!

         *

Telephone New York: "hello!"

         "Hello! I'm drunk! &
           I have no clothes on!"
      "My goodness," I say.
           "See you tomorrow."

*

Wide awake all night reading: *The Life of Turner*
                ("He first saw the light in Maiden Lane")
                A. C. Becker: Wholesale Jewels
                      Catalogue 1912
             The Book of Marvels, 1934:
                    The year I was born.

No mention of my birth in here.   Hmmm.

               Saturday The Rabbi Stayed Home

               (that way he got to solve the murder)

               LIFE on the Moon by LIFE Magazine.

        *

My mother wakes up, 4 a.m.: Someone to talk with!

    Over coffee we chat, two grownups
    I have two children, I'm an adult now, too.
    Now we are two people talking who have known each other
                                  a long time,
    Like Edwin & Rudy. Our talk is a great pleasure: my mother
    a spunky woman. Her name was Peggy Dugan when she was young
    Now, 61 years old, she blushes to tell me I was conceived
    before the wedding! "I've always been embarrassed about telling yo
    til now," she says. "I didn't know what you might think!"
    "I think it's really sweet," I say. "It means I'm really
    a love child." She too was conceived before her mother's wedding,
    I know. We talk, daylight comes, & the Providence Morning Journal
    My mother leaves for work. I'm still here.

        *

Put out the cat

               Take in the clothes

off of the line

Take a walk,
buy cigarettes

*

two teen-agers whistle
as I walk up

They say: "Only your hairdresser
knows for sure!"

Then they say,

"ulp!"

because I am closer to them.
They see I am not hippie kid, frail like Mick Jagger,
but some horrible 35 year old big guy!

The neighborhood I live in is mine!

"How'd you like a broken head, kid?"

I say fiercely.

(but I am laughing & they are not one bit scared)

So, I go home.

* * * *

Alice Clifford waits for me. Soon she'll die
at the Greenwood Nursing Home; my mother's
mother, 79 years & 7 months old.

But first, a nap, til my mother comes home
from work, with the car.

*

The heart stops briefly when someone dies,
a quick pain as you hear the news, & someone passes
from your outside life to inside. Slowly the heart adjusts
to its new weight, & slowly everything continues, sanely.

*

Living's a pleasure:

     I'd like to take the whole trip

   despite the possible indignities of growing old,
 moving, to die in poverty, among strangers:

       that can't be helped.

*

So, everything, now
  is just all right.   I'm with you.

   No more last night.

*

Friday's great

10 o'clock morning sun is shining!

I can hear today's key sounds fading softly

& almost see opening sleep's epic novels.

   * * * *

Ted Berrigan / New York City

CRYSTAL

from *Chicago*, Number 6: 1973
Chicago
Editor: Alice Notley

Be awake mornings. See light spread across the lawn
(snow) as the sky refuses to be any color, today
I like this boat-ride I'm being taken for, although
It never leaves the shore, this boat. Its fires burn
Like a pair of lovely legs. It's a garage that grew up
Sometimes I can't talk, my mouth too full of words, but
I have hands & other parts, to talk lots! Light the fire
Babble for you. I dream a green undersea man
Has been assigned to me, to keep me company, to smirk
At me when I am being foolish. A not unpleasant dream.
My secret doors open as the mail arrives. Fresh air
Pours in, around, before they close again. The winds are rushing
Up off of the ocean, up Little Plains Road. Catch the Wind
In my head, a quiet song. And, "Everything belongs to me
Because I am poor." Waiting in sexy silence, someone
Turns over in bed, & waiting is just a way of being with
Now a tiny fire flares out front the fireplace. Chesterfield
King lights up! Wood is crackling inside
Elephants' rush & roar. Refrigerator's gentle drone
Imagined footsteps moving towards my door. Sounds in dreams
In bed. You are all there is inside my head.

Charles Bukowski / San Pedro, California
IF WE TAKE

from *Mockingbird Wish Me Luck*
Black Sparrow Press, 1976: Santa Barbara, California
Editor: John Martin

if we take what we can see—
the engines driving us mad,
lovers finally hating;
this fish in the market
staring upward into our minds;
flowers rotting, flies web-caught;
riots, roars of caged lions,
clowns in love with dollar bills,
nations moving people like pawns;
daylight thieves with beautiful
nighttime wives and wines;
the crowded jails,
the commonplace unemployed,
dying grass, 2-bit fires;
men old enough to love the grave.

These things, and others, in content
show life swinging on a rotten axis.

But they've left us a bit of music
and a spiked show in the corner,
a jigger of scotch, a blue necktie,
a small volume of poems by Rimbaud,
a horse running as if the devil were
twisting his tail
over bluegrass and screaming, and then,
love again
like a streetcar turning the corner
on time,
the city waiting,
the wine and the flowers,

the water walking across the lake
and summer and winter and summer and summer
and winter again.

HOGS IN THE SKY

the territory of the diamond and the territory of the
cross and the territory of the spider and the territory of
the butcher
divided by the territory of you and me
subtracted from the territory of mathematical
reality
multiplied by those tombstones in the
moonlight

just going on
is a greater gut-miracle than the life-death cycle
itself, I mean
going on against uselessness—
that's different than living,
say, the way a fly lives;
the brain gives us enough light to know
that living is only an artful sacrifice
at best. at worst, it's
hogs in the sky.

the territory of the darning needle
the territory of the mustard jar
the territory of mad dogs and love gone stale

the territory of you and me

each evening bent like the point of a thumb tack
that will no longer stick
in
each kiss a hope of returning to the first kiss
each fuck the same

each person nailed against diminishing
returns
we are slaves to hopes that have run to
garbage
as old age
arrives on schedule.

the territory of meeting and leaving
the territory of you and me
death arrived on schedule on a
Sunday afternoon, and,
as always,
it was easier than we thought
it would be.

Big John Birkbeck/Iowa City, Iowa
CUMBERLAND GAP DRIFTER

from *Me Too*, Volume II: 1975
Iowa City & New York City
Editors: Mary Stroh & Patty Markert

for Al Murphy

Them wuz the days
Them good old times
At my old Kaintucky Home
When I had myself a southern bell-style ball—

I have been:
      in and out of crockus-sack stackin
      stump-jumpin, ridge-runnin,
jug-fuggin and the U. S. Army.

Boy-howdy! Good night nurse!
Hit's going to be too wet to plow
      anyhow
      rat now
Is time to git a banjo fire started
Cross't the Big Muddy
And over into Hoss-stomp County.

I have been:
      Honky-tonkin
      High-playin
      Low lifin
      Hog callin
      Knee walkin
        DRUNK

I have squired a mighty fine lady
Or two in mah time.
I have snatched aces outta thin air.

I have passed out on the Southern Railway track
And woke up in a Yankee University.

I have been:
     Ridin' middle hoss on a merrygoround
     I have rizz up and fell back down,
I have floated a mile above the ground.
Have dreamed a team of hillbilly dreams,
Have grappled in the back-alleys of academe,
Have picked and plucked and danced and screamed.

I passed out *AGAIN* on the railroad track
And lissened all night to Johnny and Jack,
And the Foggy Mountain Breakdown gainin on my back.

I have no-dozed across a rainy night in Georgia,
Have Tennessee truck-drove a mack trip down in Mississip'
Have banjoed my way into boudoirs in Alabam',
Have Arkansawed a whole cord of knotty pine,
Have Tee-Texased the turkey trot twinkie-toed,
Have alligatored down in Luzianne,
Have Caroline'd sour mash and moonshine,
Have been carried back to both Virginnies,
Have Floridated all of Tallahassee and Jacksonville.

And I'm here to tell y'all,
When time comes for me to go,
And I cain't take it all with me,
I ain't a-goin' . . .

James Scully / Willimantic, Connecticut

CHAIN SMOKING

from *Santiago Poems*
Curbstone Press, 1975: Willimantic, Connecticut
Editors: Alexander Taylor & Judith Doyle

Having dreamed a paradise
you chainsmoke by the window

    —disarmed
except for Mao's *Thoughts*
        in Castellano. Also
a marxist handbook from the Spanish Civil War,
faded pink at the spine
        after 4 decades
    of daylight,
And one shrill, purple, unburnt copy
    of Neruda's *Nixonicide*
and Praise:
                pathetic things
now that pathos has been outlawed.

You open the balcony window, let the silence have
        the hallelujah chorus of Handel's *Messiah*
full blast: even that
backfires.
All it echoes, is
    You dreamed we would live forever
because we can't.

Cataract glare of streetlamps:
a man with his hands up
        walks the center lane
    slowly, like a man
entering a sheepfold
afraid to startle the sheep

But they're not sheep,
they're soldiers
                    who haven't got wind of him yet

Over the bookstore, the old man
half naked in an undershirt
                    lowers his blinds,
not to witness this.

You sit with the blinds up
passing a chain of embers through the night,
                    Smouldering torchlight
passed hand to hand
                    —in honor
of Quena, among others,
whose daughter
          was tortured, whose son
they shot to death in the National Stadium.
And who, now, won't shut up:
          because she wants to die, die and kill, so badly
she doesn't know what it is
she wants,

but wants less than ever
                    to be tossed and turned
on dreams of paradise.
She wants to sleep the sleep of an earth
          where Pancho grew
          boylike, watching
the children play at growing up

and close her burning eyes,
having put out the light.

Charles Potts/Walla Walla, Washington
PARA OLGA

from *Aldebaran Review*, Number 1: 1968
Berkeley, California
Editor: John Oliver Simon

ox carts
huge wooden wheels
turn
       but not smoothly

jerking th cart along
th hiway
blonde animals pull
with ther foreheads
yoked together
a team of primary love
animals and transportation
th cart man lumbers
alongside
       th mercedez-benz

busses
a diesel practical way to jump
time blocks in
el salvador
much is moving
to an older beat
th circle of love closes
a rectangular field of cotton pickers
hand pulled fiber
a generous ground
and wire retainers
at sundown

th negro boy stuffing
a gunny sack

up th rite of way
stooped
            as a gleaner
th weeds along th road
bearing as much lost cotton
as th field held naturally
blown off of trucks
and careless allotments
he gleans in th evening
a hungry smile and his nimble
fingers gather th growth
transplanted
            ther
is no sound but th vibes
from th field hands
picking ther way towards
nite

a ten year old girl tried to sell me
an armadillo
            running alongside
th car in th hills out of taxco
th armadillos feet
trussed up with string
she pleads
            viente viente

her ragged eyes on th pesos
th armadillo was not
struggling
            but hung by th string
and swayed back and forth
in th bargain

candied mangoes
rellenos and black beans

th pension galinda
and th guide who spoke english

bringing th frumpy tourist ladies
from guatemala out
to market day at
                  chichicastenango
rapped with me
about th revolution
carl
     th latvian old revolutionary

and me neophytic
listened at th sense he made
of th fires
              on th plain from th hiway

we thot they wer clearing land
by burning
              montenegro had promised
to burn th country
running as he was against
two generals from
                  humble oil
got a majority in th election
and i'v since lost track of
ther politics
                  finca
smoldering th hungry indians
th ded green berets
like an abstruse variety of
imported parrot
determined to prevent
th people from
minding ther own business
its tuff to dance
to marimba music
if u have as little rythim left
as th US tourists
that eisenhower saved th country for
from communism
one decade ago

ther dancing in th market at antigua
th ruins beneath th hand woven blouses
brown nipples of th early
flesh age
        brown lips of th babies

hungry grin
chemical terror of not enuf tortillas
bound by chords in ther mothers womb
from th lean dark penises
of ther father   land
              balls to beat down
th roman cathedrals and texaco rest rooms
into a shimmering sheet of flesh is
flesh business
        neither sold nor stolen

from contract to title
but come free to
spred legs and regard
fuck or fall back
        i love u

take each others arm in arm
th old place wher th prostitutes
tits begin
       along th rib cage
under th arm
our organs trapped
th music does not want to die
her husky voice ran chills
up my back
and up and back on my prick

i sed let me sleep with u
my frend has gone
we had only together to stay
i'v forgotten yr name

but yr fucking brown knees
deep voice
              and goodbye

my word   th american
we both knu what it meant
u sed it   i left
                    what little we have left

to prostitute
              on th left

is a staggering brown acreage
left in th skin trade
out of ther minds
brown babies   brown balls
cotton pickers   guides
labia majorica
                    pussy has made
us all free
              by birth

we claim it
              man womban

organ music
let th spirit
lift up yr clothes
and come dancing

Rainer Maria Rilke / 1875-1926

THE VOICES

from *The Voices*
Ally Press, 1977: Saint Paul, Minnesota
Editor: Paul Feroe

It's OK for the rich and the lucky to keep still,
no one wants to know about them anyway.
But those in need have to step forward,
have to say: I am blind,
or: I'm about to go blind,
or: nothing is going well with me,
or: I have a child who is sick,
or: right there I'm sort of glued together...

And probably that doesn't do anything either.

They have to sing, if they didn't sing, everyone
would walk past, as if they were fences or trees.

That's where you can hear good singing.

People really are strange: they prefer
to hear castratos in boychoirs.

But God himself comes and stays a long time
when the world of half-people start to bore him.

—translated by Robert Bly

Edward Field / New York City

THE CELEBRITY

from *Hollow Spring Review*, Number 2: 1976
Berkshire, Massachusetts
Editor: Alex Harvey

You thought the sad and lonely little boy
would go away if you ignored him

but it doesn't matter how old you get
or how famous or skilled in your art
he'll be there waiting.

Now that you've done in life
what has made you successful and adored
you find that none of it matters
and a terrible misery possesses you.
For what you were doing
was creating a false person,
that grown-up professional you are not at home in.

But the little boy doesn't want any of that.
Ask him what it is he wants.
It will not be easy to let him speak, or to listen—
he's no intellectual.
Nor will he be talked out of his feelings.

If you still have hope
that you might be rescued from this anguish you feel,
that somehow you could avoid it
by filling up your days, finding love,
it's too late for that.
Unless you deal with him at last
your life won't work.

You have to get to know him again
and take care of him,

that little boy who needs there to be a God
and who loves Lana Turner movies,
and above all, in spite of being worthless,
has a right to be loved.

All the years are falling away
with the illusion of youth that believes
we can become what we want.
Your misery is no mystery:
It's his old misery that you stifled.
You're still that little boy.

Bill Pruitt / Rochester, N. Y.

LILACS

from *Allegany Poetry*, Number 3: 1975
Olean, New York
Editors: Ford F. Ruggieri & Helen Ruggieri

after the movie, we drive down Ridge road towards home.
young people are sitting on curbs, the boys without shirts;
    a man looks at some tuxedoes
in a store window next to an x-movie show. we pick up
a hitchhiker carrying his jacket across an arm,
going to Ravine street. we pass an old department store-style building
remade into a new car showroom, rimmed with orange neon.
traffic is fast, the steam has left the streets;
men sit smoking in a dark room upstairs
    of an old brick building before an open window;
    occasionally their voices rise
    above the idling engines.
we stop at the supermarket for bandaids.   a girl with acne
       is bending over the white bread,
touching every loaf on the shelf
      before putting one in her cart.
The express checkout line is the longest,
people are buying last minute for the Memorial Day weekend:
cheese balls, rib roasts,
six packs.   the lilacs are in bloom in Highland Park,
    you can smell them a quarter-mile away.
    we get out & walk around the bushes,
    some with pink flowers, some white.
    There's no getting used to it,
    every time you inhale, it's spring.
I see a shape by a bush up ahead
& think first it's the shadow of the bush;
not far away, a small dog sitting, watching us.
we walk a little closer
& the first shape is also a dog,
lying stretched out.   I wonder if he's dead

     & the other dog is sort of guarding him.
just when I get close
the shadow dog lifts his head.
     in the full moon he saunters over to me
& lets his head down for me to rub him.
he's an old dog; I can feel his gristly skin & his boniness.
the other dog is small & walks around us,
not caring to be petted.
     you feel the back of the big dog's neck
     & tell me his heart is beating hard.
     he stretches out again beneath your hands.
        the moon is clouding over; the air is filled
              with the smell of lilacs

Ted Kooser / Lincoln, Nebraska

SO THIS IS NEBRASKA

from *Not Coming To Be Barked At*
Pentagram Press, 1976: Markesan, Wisconsin
Editor: Michael Tarachow

The gravel road rides with a slow gallop
over the fields, the telephone lines
streaming behind, its billow of dust
full of the sparks of redwing blackbirds.

On either side, those dear old ladies,
the loosening barns, their little windows
dulled by cataracts of hay and cobwebs,
hide broken tractors under their skirts.

So this is Nebraska. A Sunday
afternoon; July. Driving along
with your hand out squeezing the air,
a meadowlark waiting on every post.

Behind a shelterbelt of cedars,
top-deep in hollyhocks, pollen and bees,
a pickup kicks its fenders off
and settles back to read the clouds.

You feel like that; you feel like letting
your tires go flat, like letting the mice
build a nest in your muffler, like being
no more than a truck in the weeds,

clucking with chickens or sticky with honey
or holding a skinny old man in your lap
while he watches the road, waiting
for someone to wave to. You feel like

waving. You feel like stopping the car
and dancing around on the road. You wave
instead and leave your hand out gliding
lark-like over the wheat, over the houses.

David Ray / Kansas City, Missouri

THE LANDSCAPE

from *West Branch*, Number 1: Fall 1977
Lewisburg, Pennsylvania
Editors: Karl Patten & Robert Taylor

after photographs by Edward S. Curtis

"Long Fox led against the Sioux a war-party that captured seven
horses. He never had a vision. He married at thirty."
The wind hints at old songs. Medicine grows in weeds.
Where the Cheyenne scouts returned in high grass, their ponies
like laundry in the wind, a tin Lone Ranger's horse
draws kids to stand and squint by him, holding Tonto's
plaster hand. Trucks pull in to the truck stop,
smoke behind them, the dinosaur sign above,
drop their drivers for the coffee shop.
Out the plate glass window the semi-truck raised
on welded pipes dominates the sunset. Smog rolls
across the states. Where the tepees of Piegan Camp
raised their roof-sticks against sepia sky of Curtis,
a Winnebago gathers clouds in its plastic windows.
Inside, retired ball turret gunners have dinner
from a can, then watch a thousand *coups de grace*
and Indians on their television sets, mourning
sons and daughters, gone to the winds of China,
gone as if clawed to death by bears, gone as if
to battle, painted all the angry colors. Deep sighs,
between commercials which briefly thrill. Like circus
wagons these trailers glow, on feed lots of the nation.
Trapezes hang neglected. "Grace-notes, trills,
and shakes abound," Curtis said of that music
we did not bring, with our swords. "Pure, sustained
notes are somewhat rare." Weeds listen like the ears
of rabbits. Stones pray for change. Silver flares
in the sun. There were losers by the millions,
but the scout who seeks a winner comes back lonesome,
writes his death poem, leaves it for the waitress.

Miguel Hernandez / 1910-1942

WAR

from *The Sixties*, Number 9: 1967
Madison, Minnesota
Editor: Robert Bly

All the mothers in the world
hide their wombs, tremble,
and wish they could turn back
into blind virginities,
into that solitary beginning,
the past, leaving nothing behind.
Virginity is left
pale, frightened.
The sea howls thirst and the earth
howls to be water.
Hatred flames out
and the screaming slams doors.
Voices shake like lances,
voices like bayonets.
Mouths step forward like fists,
fists arrive like hooves.
Breasts like hoarse walls,
legs like sinewy paws.
The heart quickens,
storms, blows up.
It throws sudden black spume
into the eye.
Blood thrashes about in the body,
flings the head off,
and searches for another body, a wound
to leap through, outside.
Blood parades through the world,
caged, baffled.
Flowers wither
devoured by the grass.
A lust for murder possesses

the secret places of the lily.
Every living body longs to be joined
to a piece of cold metal:
to be married and possessed
horribly.
To disappear: a vast anxiety,
spreading, rules everything.
A ghostly procession of banners,
a fantastic flag,
a myth of nations: a
grave fiction of frontiers.
Outraged musics,
tough as boots, scar
the face of every hope
and the tender core.
The soul rages, fury.
Tears burst like lightning.
What do I want with light
if I stumble into darkness?
Passions like horns,
songs, trumpets that urge
the living to eat the living,
to raze themselves stone by stone.
Whinnies. Reverberations. Thunder.
Slaverings. Kisses. Wheels.
Spurs. Crazy swords
tear open a huge wound.

Then silence, mute
as cotton, white as bandages,
scarlet as surgery,
mutilated as sadness.
Silence. And laurel
in a corner among bones.
And a hysterical drum,
a tense womb, beats
behind the innumerable
dead man who never gets past.

—translated by James Wright,
from Cancionero y Romancero de Ausencias

Federico Garcia Lorca / 1898-1936

NEW YORK

from *The Seventies*, Number 1, 1972
Madison, Minnesota
Editor: Robert Bly

(Office and Attack)

Beneath all the statistics
there is a drop of a duck's blood.
Beneath all the columns
there is a drop of a sailor's blood.
Beneath all the totals, a river of warm blood;
a river that goes singing
past the bedrooms of the suburbs,
and the river is silver, cement, or wind
in the lying daybreak of New York.
The mountains exist, I know that.
And the lenses ground for wisdom,
I know that. But I have not come to see the sky.
I have come to see the stormy blood,
the blood that sweeps the machines to the waterfalls,
and the spirit on to the cobra's tongue.
Every day they kill in New York
ducks, four million,
pigeons, two thousand, for the enjoyment of dying men,
cows, one million,
lambs, one million,
roosters, two million,
who turn the sky to small splinters.
You may as well sob filing a razor blade
or assassinate dogs in the hallucinated foxhunts,
as to try to stop in the dawnlight
the endless trains carrying milk,
the endless trains carrying blood,
and the trains carrying roses in chains
for those in the field of perfume.

EDITORS CHOICE LIT AND GRAPH FR SMALL PR 1965 77

SKLAR

STK LOC WA

PUB COD ZTM

ACCOUNT NO 390269   TIN 32192487

INVOICE NO 040774454   P

P/P SEQ NO 00240   SUBJ CAT

CARD SEQ NO   5   1 OF 1

PLEASE KEEP THIS CARD WITH ANY BOOKS TO BE
RETURNED FOR CREDIT - THANK YOU.

04-07-83   48 SHIP

The ducks and the pigeons
and the hogs and the lambs
lay their drop of blood down
underneath all the statistics;
and the terrible bawls of the packed-in cattle
fill the valley with suffering
where the Hudson is getting drunk on its oil.
I attack all those persons
who know nothing of the other half,
the half who cannot be saved,
who raise their cement mountains
in which the hearts of the small
animals no one thinks of are beating,
and from which we will all fall
during the final holiday of the drills.
I spit in your face.
The other half hears me,
as they go on eating, urinating, flying in their purity
like the children of the janitors
who carry delicate sticks
to the holes where the antennas
of the insects are rusting.
This is not hell, it is a street.
This is not death, it is a fruit-stand.
There is a whole world of crushed rivers and unachievable
        distances
in the paw of a cat crushed by a car,
and I hear the song of the worm
in the heart of so many girls.
Rust, rotting, trembling earth.
And you are earth swimming through the figures of the
        office.
What shall I do, set the landscapes in order?
Set in place the lovers who will afterwards be photographs,
who will be bits of wood and mouthfuls of blood?
No, I won't; I attack,
I attack the conspiring
of these empty offices
that will not broadcast the sufferings,

that rub out the plans of the forest,
and I offer myself to be eaten by the packed-in cattle,
when their mooing fills the valley
where the Hudson is getting drunk on its oil.

—translated by Robert Bly

Leonard Nathan / Berkeley, California
THE RETURN

from *The New Salt Creek Reader*, Volume 6, Number 1: 1974
Lincoln, Nebraska
Editor: Ted Kooser

She has lost her innocence
and got nothing for it
but two flat glass eyes
watching sailors dance
in the blue smoke
then vanish through smoke
to lean over the rail
seeing in pure distance
the shine of hope
the other shore

she has for it a lead hand
and a rubber hand
a mouth full of greasy pebbles
a one-eyed kitten for a heart
a head of scorched grass
a robbed gas station for sex

there is no other shore
there is the one shore
twisted back on itself
where she waits in the fog
in the smoke for sailors coming
from the blue shine of hope
with strange money

she thinks she doesn't dream
but dreams sharks feeding
in her bruised waters

F. A. Nettelbeck / Santa Cruz, California
NEW STREETS

from *No Place Fast*
Rough Life Press, 1976: Inglewood, California
Editor: C. Marks

you speak with your
fingers the frightened
words of this cold
new language

spread them wide

on the motherfucker's face

the indentations of that
final anger   your hand
stamped forever   like
a gene   like a fossil

cool & lasting

like a canister of sperm
ten milleniums old slammed
against that face

you move fast & bring
the punk down

it all comes back

as you stab deeper you
create a new geography

school yards   liquor
stores   grotesque grey
buildings all fade then

vanish in the sterile
reflection on the
bloodied eight inch
blade

your legs straighten
out

you pull back

the baboons shriek
inside of your ears

you have room to move

William Wantling / 1933-1974

DON'T SHOOT!

from *Ole Anthology*
Ole, 1967: Glendale, California
Editor: Douglas Blazek

"Don't shoot!"   she
screamed, & as the dark
shadowed figure clicked
back the pistolhammer
twice I muttered Sheeeit...
I snapped off the set &
Ruthie hollored in from
the kitchen—Whatsamatter
Genius, too deep for you?
& I put Miles' *Sketches of
Spain* on the stereo & we
had popcorn that night, 7-
up, & made love on the
livingroom rug
then when Ruthie was sleeping, I read an old letter
from my first wife, wrote
a poem about her & the years
in L.A. & the narcotics, &
wondered about that old man
whose skull we had to
fracture to take his lousy
$83 that one bad sick
time, wondered if he'd
lived, if he'd ever just
loved & lived simply & with
total thanks as I had this
night...

David Hilton / Baltimore

LAST SOUTH BALTIMORE POEM

from *The Candleflame*
Toothpaste Press, 1976: West Branch, Iowa
Editors: Allan Kornblum & Cinda Kornblum

It was not 'not wanting
to get involved'—

the wino splayed
across the sidewalk

in front of the failing
shoe repairman's, on

his back, taking the
hard, slant

October sun, his nose
a red cyst, purple lesions

beneath 4-days grizzle—
because I could shake

him and rasp *mister! hey
mister!* like a kid and

so he'd just be
dead, or I could

shake him harder
and so he'd come alive—

to what difference?
I am the man, I

*suffer'd, I was
there* ... and got out.

Emilie Glen/New York City

FUN AND FUNERALS

from *Second Coming*, Volume 2, Numbers 4 & 5: 1973
San Francisco
Editor: A. D. Winans

Fun street
  Funeral street
 The brightest
  Bright as sunflowers
Fooled by the moon
   into lifting orange heads
Dark cafes in ghostly glow
  Funeral homes lighted
   bright as candy sticks
Life street
  Life and death street
The river styx must flow back there
  Darkening the cafes
While Charon entertainers
  Sing of Delia and the long black veil
   Of the hanging tree
  Of shooting a man just to watch him die
Funsters descend into caves of darkness
  Mourners enter into light

Attila Jozsef / 1905-1937

THE SEVENTH

from *Attila Jozsef: Selected Poems and Texts*
International Writing Program, 1976: Iowa City, Iowa
Editors: Paul Engle & Hualing Nieh Engle

If you set out in this world,
better be born seven times.
Once, in a house on fire,
once, in a freezing flood,
once, in a wild madhouse,
once, in a field of ripe wheat,
once, in an empty cloister,
and once among pigs in a sty.
Six babes crying, not enough:
you yourself must be the seventh.

When you must fight to survive,
let your enemy see seven.
One, away from work on Sunday,
one, starting his work on Monday,
one, who teaches without payment,
one, who learned to swim by drowning,
one, who is the seed of a forest,
and one, whom wild forefathers protect,
but all their tricks are not enough:
you yourself must be the seventh.

If you want to find a woman,
let seven men go for her.
One, who gives his heart for words,
one, who takes care of himself,
one, who claims to be a dreamer,
one, who through her skirt can feel her,
one, who knows the hooks and snaps,
one, who steps upon her scarf:
let them buzz like flies around her.

You yourself must be the seventh.

If you write and can afford it,
let seven men write your poem.
One, who builds a marble village,
one, who was born in his sleep,
one, who charts the sky and knows it,
one, whom words call by his name,
one, who perfected his soul,
one, who dissects living rats.
Two are brave and four are wise;
you yourself must be the seventh.

And if all went as was written,
you will die for seven men.
One, who is rocked and suckled,
one, who grabs a hard young breast,
one, who throws down empty dishes,
one, who helps the poor to win,
one, who works till he goes to pieces,
one, who just stares at the moon.
The world will be your tombstone:
you yourself must be the seventh.

SINCE YOU'VE BEEN AWAY

Since you've been away, things are colder here,
the pail, the milk, the handle of the axe;
split wood falls with a loud thud,
and grows white and numb as soon as it lands.

In a dull field the wind is getting dressed,
its fingers, in a flurry, stop and fumble,
and drop the branches that were pressed
to its bosom: enraged, brittle leaves tumble.

I thought I was in a mild valley,

protected north and south by your breasts,
where dawn flowers in my hair
and evening shines upon my feet...

I sit here, thin, and watch you bloom,
world, weed's flower, distant space.
In your blue petals the sky burns out.
A great grey dusk slowly bares its face.

translated by John Batki

Patricia Goedicke /Guanajuato, Mexico

LOST

from *The Hampden -Sydney Poetry Review,* Winter 1976
Hampden-Sydney, Virginia
Editor: Tom O'Grady

Miles from here, in the mountains
There is no sound but snowfall.

The wind rubs itself against the trees
Under its breath

If a crow calls it is nothing,
If a branch breaks it is nothing,

The birches look at themselves in the water,
The long white poles of their bodies waver

And bend a little,
The yellow leaves of their hair

Like pieces of far off stars come falling,
Hissing onto the lake

That is smooth as pewter, that is clear
And tranquil as an eye

Lost up here in the mountains
As if someone had dropped it, but no

The pebbles beneath the surface
Have no nerves, they are calm

If a fish leaps it is nothing
Surrounded by moss and blueberries

Flowers breathe among the rocks

So quietly you forget everything

Up here on the crusty grass
The bushes sparkle with ice

And no footprints anywhere,
If a twig snaps it is nothing

For nothing matters, once you have lost it,
Down here in the valleys among the people

The sidewalks are full of holes,
Faint memories of far off lakes

Up there in the mountains,
In the great evergreen forests

If a woodchuck whirrs it is nothing,
If a bluejay shrieks it is nothing,

Pine needles slip from the trees, silently
They pile up on the ground.

William Stafford / Lake Oswego, Oregon
ACCEPTING SURPRISE

from *The Hampden-Sydney Poetry Review*, Winter 1976
Hampden-Sydney, Virginia
Editor: Tom O'Grady

The right mistakes—that rich moment
when the rain finds you, a pinch
from a branch in the hedge that tells
you you're real, the wrong turn that
spills whole sunsets reflected and still
on a lake at a dead-end barring your road—

There are these doubled ways, returns
beyond even dreams. Mothers, Fathers,
your lives flash into pain, and out;
but maverick rainbows blind us all. I bring
you—and your children—a whole treasure:
mistakes like jewels, the hidden rush
and loss of a world that throbs
beyond control, good, good, never quite ours.

Darrell Gray / Berkeley, California

ODE TO JIBBERISH

from *North Stone Review*, Numbers 5 & 6: 1974/75
Minneapolis
Editor: James Naiden

I live in a jungle,
pull open the curtains,
and write what comes to me.

The natives are restless
in their brand new cars.
But small-pox is on the decline,
the gas stations open all night ...

What if my world,
this world
between all others,
is jibberish,
what about it then?

Bird in the bush—you
be my audience, clap
and ignite the twig-tips,
rock the worm-fed nest!

It's to you I write
now, you more than
the natives, more
than the cellophane skirts
of the girls I love.

What a crackle
of iambs! What a shower
of broken syllables,
and so many parties
to celebrate the Thud!

The streets—jibberish,
cars but a jibberish
speeded up.
I'm glad I don't own a car.
I remain a simple man,
slightly intoxicated,
surrounded by jibberish,
and dedicated to the proposition
that all propositions
are jibberish, though some
more beautiful
than others.

The sun transforms
hydrogen into light.
The purest jibberish of all!

And in the park
where my nature bids me to wander
the trees which start from the ground
so firm and definite, end
in a lacy entanglement—
a cascading jibberish of leaves.

Bronze curling leaves clog up
the Neo-Classical fountain.
And there we have a condensed
little jet of cold water, spurting
a hazy mist, taking its time.

And lovers mumbling phrases from Proust,
with cough-drops in their mouths
and looking hungry.

Ah
there are so many kinds of jibberish—
you can take your pick.
But don't be a philosopher—
dig right in

and grab a handful!
Smell it.
Taste it.
Watch it grow wings.

Oh girls,
peanuts and foxtrots,
sonnets of clouds
in the household
of the sky!
All whirling,
all red-hot
and azure-deepened—
the morning is more than
bacon and eggs,
the evening more than
a glass of wine!

Put anything into the world and soon as you leave it
it beds down with the nearest soft object
and whispers its name.

But it's of you I sing,
sweet jibberish—
language of cows and alley-cats
and infants pulled from the womb.

A cry slices the twilight
and runs away through the trees.
Anthologies fall open to admit the poem,
but it's gone—a loon's song
drunk on the lake.

I've given up trying to
perfect my form.
Why should I let my poems out-do me
at what I can't be myself?
Keep on, diabolical and fragrant mushroom
towering above the insect world below.

It's you we aspire to.
Keep on, terrifying and sugary crocodile
of the soul!

The myths are coated.
The teeth of jaguars inhabiting
narrative poems
have gone home to bed.
And you, kind listeners—
what do you have in your mouths?
Jibberish hard as a gumball
that never dissolved.

Baudelaire was right.
Proust was right.
Cezanne was right.
Bullfrogs at home in their ponds
salute us, lethargically croaking the leisure
nature affords them.

And dogs in alleys rub their backs for relief
on great compositions.
Their howls of aesthetic appreciation
piss us off in the night.

How many tongues
do you speak,
how many feet do you walk on,
how many holes do you fill?
Kant tried to trap you
in his Categories,
but you flew, star-struck,
straight in his face!

God heated you up—
you boiled,
and he ate you for breakfast,
but still you survived.
You shot out fibers

thinner than any spider's,
and entered the finite orgasm,
making it grow.

You who always knew yourself
in the close-fitting cage of the parrot,
all my words become you
but if I give you a name
you laugh at it,
change it, whirl it
till it burns my tongue

and still in the heart the blood runs away from itself,
to meet you,
and bring you back.

Lyn Lifshin / Niskayuga, New York

THE NO NEED FOR, THE COMPUTER CONCERN ERROR LETTER

from *Magazine*, Number 5, part 9: 1972
New York City
Editor: Kirby Congdon

thank you for letting us
know the computer
error error was
of course you should not
have received a bill   i'm
unable to explain or
why your name came
out as something
different   we've created
a not-you   we're
sorry sorry and don't
know but there's no
need for the records in
the office straight on
the matter of who,
we look forward
to meeting you

Street Song/North Philadelphia

MY MOMMY TOLD ME

from *Poetry Newsletter*, Number 7: 1972
Philadelphia
Editor: Richard O'Connell

My mommy told me
If I was goodie
That she would buy me
A rubber Dolly
My Auntie told her
I kissed a soldier
Now she won't buy me
A rubber dolly.

Three, six, nine
The goose drank wine
The monkey chewed tobacco
On the street car line
the line broke
The monkey got choked
And they all went to heaven in a little row boat
Clap, clap
That's that.

from a collection by Sandra McDaniel

Jim Everhard/Washington, D. C.

CUTE

from *Gay Sunshine*, Numbers 33/34: 1977
San Francisco
Editor: Winston Leyland

I was never handsome, always cute. What I lack in looks,
I make up for in personal hygiene. When you are cute
and hygienic they call you clean-cut. Unless you are
argumentative. Then they call you cute but spoiled.
I think of Rimbaud as the embodiment of the cute genius.
If you are not only cute but act as if you are cute, they
call you cute but conceited. If you are cute and with-
drawn, they call you cute but unapproachable. In other
words, you are never simply cute. But if you are handsome,
you are expected to be a little hard to get to know.
Then you become a challenge. The cute one is always
supposed to give in at the right moment. This is especially
true when the one asking you to give in is handsome. Then
you are supposed to melt. A cute person always melts when
touched by a handsome person. This is considered proper
cute etiquette. The cute person is in a constant prayerful
state. He knows he won't be cute forever though a handsome
person is always handsome. He looks even sexier with neatly
trimmed grey sideburns. He never greys any place
else unless it adds to his distinction. Handsome persons
are always masculine and cute persons are always feminine.
Handsome persons are always twenty-eight and cute persons
always eighteen. After forty a cute person usually looks
used and a handsome person looks resourceful. As I said
earlier, a cute person must always shine hygienically.
A handsome person can rough it because roughing it enhances
his masculinity. Handsome persons always get married.
Cute people are always mistresses. Handsome persons
are acutely intelligent. Cute persons without an imagination
should be good at memorizing jokes. When a handsome

person is rude, that is called style. When a cute person is rude, that is being temperamental and childish. A cute person, forever a child star, is not wanted around for very long because he reminds the handsome person that age is a real thing as the veneer of cuteness begins to sag under layers of crows feet, wrinkles and fat. The handsome person must never be reminded that he's going to get old, too. He's always prowling for someone even cuter than the cute person he's currently with. When he's got one arm around you and staring bug-eyed across a crowded room that's called setting a high standard. When a cute person is out with his handsome lover he must bask in the charisma of handsomeness or risk being labelled flighty. There are worshippers and idols. There are stars and extras. There are XKE's and Volkswagens. There are privileges and conveniences. There are peacocks and parakeets. The world is not fair. There are the fair and the fading. There is cute and handsome.

Barry Schechter / Chicago
DISCO FEVER

from *The Grand Et Cet'ra*
The Yellow Press, 1977: Chicago
Editors: Richard Friedman, Peter Kostakis & Darlene Pearlstein

for Peter Kostakis

Through hesitations, fits-and-starts; turnabouts and
vacillations, I was led here nonetheless. My life—an exercise
wheel pulled by a wagon, oblivious to halts and 'bout-faces
of my feet—dropped me under a sign commanding GET
DOWN! and I entered the life of the discos. "Hustle!"
whooped a loudspeaker. "To boogie; bestir oneself; GET
DOWN!; make haste; lose no time; scramble; make tracks;
make it snappy; get a move on; expedite; rush; bustle;
whip on! See VELOCITY! See INSTANTANAEITY!" I
gasped at limbs braiding and unraveling with the ease of
spiraling snow. My shoes, floodlit by the disco floor,
drew back in the dark like gophers. I stood there for
hours, a stick figure gawking at the third dimension.
I faced my first partners through a Junglegym of
rigid arms. Where was the escape artist to unknot me
muscle by muscle; to vanish with me in a flurry of elbows!
"Turkey!" boomed the loudspeaker. "You got a mind-
body problem. GET DOWN! devolve a bit, dig? Everything's mellow: So why you got that plumbline anchorin'
your coccyx to the center of the earth? And why
donchew cop some clothes that . . . you know . . . hustle!"
Scuttling my pig iron shoes; unbolting my hat; leaving
my coat to relive my life in semaphore, I glided back on
vast lapels. Cuffing aside a drunk who took them for
swinging doors, I sailed into the maelstrom. I performed
dance steps based on the bold advances and discreet re-
treats of the subtlest perfumes; on the spread of forest
fires; on Heisenberg's Uncertainty Principle; on the
plumbing of the Versailles palace down to the streamlet

132

trickling from a nymph's ear. More than one woman asked for an X-Ray snapshot of my bones. But I couldn't stop now. I moved in homage to swan-necked explosions arching their backs on the sun; to the partner that filled the outspread arms of Jesus. When my step synched with the beat of the strobelights, all other motion froze. The dancers stood locked in arm-and-shoulder-holds. A cocktail in mid-spill distended a glistening tongue. I had overstepped the dualities—time-space, light-dark—a shadowboxer K.O.-ing his shade. The loudspeaker screamed, "Appearing live on our dance floor: God-Man! Where flesh and spirit GET DOWN! I'm talkin' 'bout the Unmoved Mover! God, man. And who's the smartass keeps askin', how can we know the dancer from the dance!" "By the tie!" someone shouted, as I felt my grip loosen on time-dark, space-light. "The tie!"

A bucket of slop dumped by a janitor woke me on the extinguished disco floor. "We operate on the *old* geometry during closing hours," he said. "For now, the shortest distance between two points is a straight line. That puddle you're lyin' in is point A. Anyplace past that door is point B. Ergo, scram." "Yes, point A and point B," I muttered weakly. "I had forgotten." Placing one foot forward, then the other, then the other, I entered the day with its unpasteurized sounds, its oafish light falling everywhere at once.

Miroslav Holub / Czechoslovakia

NAPOLEON

from *Modern Poetry In Translation*, Number 5: 1969
Iowa City, Iowa
Editor: Daniel Weissbort

Children, when was
Napoleon Bonaparte
born? asks the teacher

A thousand years ago, say the children.
A hundred years ago, say the children.
Nobody knows.

Children, what did
Napoleon Bonaparte
do? asks the teacher.

He won a war, say the children.
He lost a war, say the children.
Nobody knows.

Our butcher used to have a dog,
says Frankie,
and his name was Napoleon,
and the butcher used to beat him,
and the dog died
of hunger
a year ago.

And now all the children feel sorry
for Napoleon.

—translation by Kaca Polackova

Celino & Steff—The Greats/Places of residence unknown.

THE INVASION OF AMERICA

from *Salted Feathers*, Number 11, or, *Miracle Finger: A Book of Works by Children*: 1975
Spokane, Washington
Editor: Dick Bakken

The sky was gray, boats outlined the shore; in the distance you could see the Nazi flag. Its red stripe stood out among the blue waves. The Americans were all asleep. The Krauts came upon the shore. Their ragged clothes and their long beards waved in the wind. The Nazi Colonel stepped off the barge. He was a tall, bald man with a wicked smile, and he was carrying a large cane in his hand. Some children were playing on the beach and they saw the invasion; they ran to tell their parents. The American army woke up and blew up the Kraut army.

Later the Americans found out the names of the Krauts who devised this plan. Their names were:

Archibald Cuboba, who lived in Krautism town.

Hugoaggogo Guperbugar, who lived in Spetzeles.

Capt. Rarrah Gabor, who was an average sour Kraut.

and Colonel Smedley VanSmidelsburger, who lived in Pakistan with his wife Ethel VanSmidelsburger; and their children

Pooper, Cutie, Egghead, and their family of cows

WE ARE GRATEFUL THAT THESE MEN
SHALL NOT HAVE DIED IN VAIN
THEY DIED TRYING TO INVADE

AMERICA

Andrew Roberts/Minneapolis
HOW TO GET A GARDEN

from *For Kids By Kids*
BkMk Press, 1977: Kansas City, Missouri
Editor: Dan Jaffe

First, you get some leaves
and spread them all over the ground
and build a house there

And you put some lights in it
then get in some paintings and books
and furniture and a sofa
then more books and records
toys and animals

And after you are there a while
you go outside
and the garden will be
right next to the sandbox

—the poet was four when this was written

Peter Wild / Tucson, Arizona

NEW STRIP

from *River Bottom*, Volume 4, Number 2: 1976
Waupaca, Wisconsin
Editor: R. Chris Halla

I see you coming toward the river, a spark
before the crowd of saints who have just picked up sherds
from the flats where old Glenton Sykes
used to play around the foundations of the bulldozed mission, where the hang gliders now land, spiralling
down full of relief from their short flights.
and sloshing across, having started this morning
almost in Mexico, the purple blossom of the sun
behind my cabbage head, shake you by both braids.
a whole year after we sat on Wasserman Peak you say
that a cup of tea and a good book are enough at night,
that last month a Peeping Tom peered in with his chicken
face through the bamboo at your daughter just stepping
from her swimming suit. I can't believe it,
no more sex. and we slog on ahead
right through the heart of town, while the others
listen to the City Engineer explain the new strip,
peered at by the dogs and goats, astounded
acolytes looking down from their sheds,
past the spring where Father Kino, escorted
by his Pima warriors, said they camped,
a hole far above our heads, scare out some bums
who run with their bedding up the bank,
inspect their neat bower in the tamarisks.
you've grown fatter around the lips
and say at forty you keep losing dates. six million
cubic feet he says to stabilize the river, enough
for years of work. but I see it bulging all in one
final wave, as I did last summer lost in the Bitterroots,
the whole horizon of the Continental Divide lurching
                              into the mean furrows of
a sunrise, then that bride, almost white, escaping from it.

Michael Lally / New York City

MY LIFE

from ZZZ: 1974
Calais, Vermont
Editor: Kenward Elmslie

I ate everything they put in front of me
read everything they put before my eyes
shook my ass, cried over movie musicals
was a sissy and a thug, a punk and an
intellectual, a cocksucker and a mother
fucker, helped create two new people,
paid taxes, voted and served four years
and a few weeks in the United States Air
Force, was courts martialled and tried
civilly, in jail and in college, kicked
out of college, boy scouts, altar boys
and one of the two gangs I belonged to,
I was suspended from grammar and high
schools, arrested at eleven the year I
had my first "real sex" with a woman
and with a boy, I waited nineteen years
to try it again with a male and was sorry
I waited so long, wrote, poetry and
fiction, political essays, leaflets and
reviews, I was a "jazz musician and a
dope dealer, taught junior high for two
weeks, high school Upward Bound for two
years, college for four years, I got up
at 5AM to unload trucks at Proctor and
Gamble to put myself through classes
at the University of Iowa, I washed
dishes and bussed tables, swept floors
and cleaned leaders and gutters, washed
windows and panhandled, handled a forty
foot ladder alone at thirteen, wrote

several novels not very good and none
published, published poems and stories
and articles and books of poems, was
reviewed, called "major", compared to
"The Teen Queens", mistaken for black,
for gay, for straight, for older, for
younger for bigger for better for richer
for poorer for stupider for smarter for
somebody else, fell in love with a black
woman at 18, kicked out of the family
for wanting to marry her at 20, I sucked
cock and got fucked and fucked and got
sucked, I was known for being a big
jerk off, a wise ass, for always getting
my ass kicked so bad neighborhood kids
would ask to see the marks, for running
for sheriff of Johnson County Iowa in 68
on the "Peace And Freedom" ticket and
pulling in several thousand votes, for
winning people to the cause with emotional
spontaneous speeches at rallies and on tv,
for being a regular guy, a romantic
idealist, a suicidal weatherman, a bomb
throwing anarchist, an SDS leader, a
communist, a class chauvinist, an
asexual politico, a boring socialist,
the proletarian man, a horny androgyne,
a junkie, a boozer, a loser, a nigger
lover, a black woman's white man, a
race traitor, a greaser, a fast man
with my hands, a hood, a chickenshit,
a crazy head, an unmarked thoroughbred,
a courageous human being, a Catholic,
a fallen away Catholic, an IrishAmerican
Democrat, a working class IrishAmerican
writer from a family of cops, a skinny
jive time street philosopher, a power
head, an underground movie star, a
quiet shy guy, a genius, an innovator,

a duplicator, a faker, a good friend,
a fickle lover, an ass lover, a muff
diver, another pretty face, a lousy
athlete, a generous cat, an ambitious
young man, a very tough paddy, a macho
hippy, a faggot gangster, a faggot,
a big crazy queen, a straight man, a
strong man, a sissy, a shithead, a
home wrecker, a reckless experimenter
with other people's lives, a demogogue,
a fanatic, a cheap propagandizer, a
fantastic organizer, a natural born
leader, a naive upstart, an arrogant
jitterbug, a white nigger, an easy lay,
a pushover, a hard working husband,
a henpecked husband, the black sheep,
a crazy mixed up kid, a juvenile delinquent,
a misfit, a surrealist, an actualist,
an Iowa poet, a political poet, an open
field poet, a street poet, a bad poet,
a big mouth, a voice of the sixties,
a pretty poet, a gay poet, a clit kissing
tit sucking ass licking body objectifying
poet, a gigolo, a jerk, a poor boy, an
old man, an assman, unsteady, immature,
charismatic, over confident, over 30,
impetuous, a rock, a pawn, a tool, a
potato lover, a great teacher, loyal
friend, concerned citizen, a humanist,
the bosses son, Bambi's old man, Lee's
husband, Matthew's ex-lover, Terry's
partner, Slater's main man, the bishop's
favorite altar boy, the landlady's pet,
the class clown, the baby of the family,
the neighborhood stranger, the hardest
working kid, with the rosiest cheeks, who
was an instigator, a trouble maker,
too smart for my own good, too soft,
too distant, too honest, too cold, too

tactless, uncommunicative, anal retentive,
self-sufficient, shameless, unsophisticated,
too butch, too skinny, too white, too
defensive, too hungry, apologetic, in-
decisive, unpredictable, I never hit a
woman or woke up gloomy, I'm a light
sleeper, an affectionate father, a bad
drinker, a city boy, paranoid, compulsive,
and a terrific body surfer, I love the
hipness in me I thought was black back
in the 50s, the vulnerability I took for
feminine in the 70s, I hate the poor kid
act I've pulled on strangers and friends
to start them out owing me, I learned to
cook and to sew, stopped chewing gum and
biting my nails, I was a weather observer,
a map maker, a printer's devil, a
carpenter's helper, a glazier, locksmith,
editor, publisher, promoter and critic,
I stopped dancing at 15 and started again
at 30, math was my best subject, languages
my worst, I've been knocked out several
times but only one black eye and one
fractured thumb, I've totalled several
cars but I'm an ace driver especially
in cities, I havent had an accident since
I stopped drinking, knock on wood, I'm
extremely superstitious, dont speak too
soon, I gave up cigarettes and coffee and
using the words chick, spade and asshole,
I've read Confucius, Buddha, Lao Tzu,
The Upanishads, The Bhagavad Gita, The
Koran, The Bible, The Prophet, Thus Spake
Zarathustra, Marx, Trotsky, Stalin, Lenin,
Mao, Che, Hesse, Proust, Firestone, Fanon,
Castaneda and Davis, I read all of Joyce
and all of Dostoevsky in translation
at least two times through on night shifts
in weather towers through 1961 and 62,

141

I love all of William Saroyan, Van
Morrison, Jane Bowles, Samuel Beckett,
Joe Brainard, and Bertold Brecht, I'm
finally getting to know and like some
"classical music", I went to my first
ballet, opera, and concert this year and
loved all of it, took my first trip out
of the country and was glad to get back
although it was great, I love the USA and
many of the people in it, I'm afraid of
my own anger, and any kind of violence,
I've been the same weight since 1957 though
I have an enormous appetite, my hair's
turning grey, I've had it cut three times
since 1966, I spit a lot and pick my nose
too much, I could buy new shoes, eat ice
cream, chicken or chocolate pudding anytime,
I'm afraid of dogs and hate zoos, I'm
known for my second winds especially
when dancing or eating, I used to think
of myself as a dreamer, I had a vision
at 9 that I'd die between 42 and 46,
the image was me doubling over clutching
my stomach, whenever I'm embarrassed I
see that in my head, some of my nicknames
have been Faggy, Rocky, Spider, Brutus,
Paddy Cat, Newark, Irish, and The Lal,
I'm a father, son, brother, cousin,
brother-in-law, uncle, record breaker,
war child, veteran, and nut about Lauren
Bacall, James Cagney, Robert Mitchum,
Bogie and Brando, "Last Tango" and "The
Conformist" are the favorite movies of
my adult life, I've fallen in love with
eyes, asses, thighs, wrists, lips, skin,
color, hair, style, movement, bodies
auras, potential, accents, atmospheres,
clothes, imaginations, sophistication,
histories, families, couples, friends,

rooms full of people, parks, cities,
entire states, talked to trees since
1956 and the wind since 52, between 56
and 59 I had few friends and a "bad
reputation" which made it difficult
to get dates with "nice girls", in 1960
and 61 I had more friends and several
lovers, I was at the SDS split in Chicago
in 1969 and didnt like either side's
position or tactics, I almost cried
when I heard John Coltrane had died,
and Ho Chi Minh, Babe Ruth, Jack
Kerouac, Eric Dolphy, Roberto Clemente,
Moose Conlon, Frankie Lyman, Fred
Hampton, Allende, Clifford Brown,
Richie Valens and Buddy Holly in that
plane crash, the four little girls
in that Alabama church, the students
at Orangeburg, the "weather people"
in the town house explosion which I
always figured was a set up, my uncle
Frank and my uncle John, my grandparents,
lots of people, I did cry when I thought
about the deaths of the Kent State and
Jackson State students, when I heard
Ralph Dickey had "taken his life" or
the first time I heard Jackson Browne
do his "Song For Adam" or when Marlon
Brando as Terry finds his brother Charley
(Rod Steiger) hanging dead on the fence
in "On The Waterfront" and before going
to get the murderers says something to
Eva Marie Saint like "And for god's sake
dont leave him here alone" or when he
talks to his dead wife in "Last Tango"
or finds out Red Buttons and his wife
have committed suicide in "Sayonara"
I've cried alot over movies especially
old ones on tv, I've never cried at a

play but I still havent seen many, the
only Broadway plays I've seen were "My
Fair Lady" and "Bye Bye Birdie", I
watched my mother die, I've paid my dues,
been through the mill, come up from the
streets, done it my way, had that once
in a lifetime thing, had trouble with
my bowels ever since I can remember
then in 72 my body became more relaxed,
I've had the clap, crabs, scabies,
syphilis, venereal warts, and unidentified
infections in my cock, my ass, my throat,
all over my body, I've been terribly
sunburned and covered with scabs from
fights and accidents, I only had stitches
once at 4 when I had my appendix out,
I've been earning money since I was 9,
supporting myself since 13, others since
22, I got "unemployment" once, been
fired several times, never paid to
get laid, I lost money gambling but
quit after I had to give up my high
school ring in a poker game at the Dixie
Hotel in Greenville South Carolina in
1962 waiting for my friend Willy Dorton
to come out from the room where he was
proposing marriage to his favorite
whore who always turned him down after
they fucked and she got most of his
paycheck from him, some of my best
friends were hookers and strippers,
postal clerks and shills, supermarket
managers and factory workers, heavy
revvies and punks, actresses and junkies,
who were and are the most difficult
of friends, art dealers and artists,
musicians and hustlers, dykes and critics,
shit workers and liberals, gringos and fags,
and honkies and bastards, queer and old

and divorced and straight and Italian
and big deals and dipshits, I know at least
six people who think they turned me on
to dope for the first time in 1960 in
New York City, in 1962 in Rantoul Illinois,
in 1964 in Spokane Washington, in 1966 and
67 in Iowa City Iowa, in 1969 in Washington
DC, I once was high on opium and didnt
want to come back, I was a recreational
therapist at Overbrook Hospital in Essex
County New Jersey in 1966 where James Moody
wrote "Last Train From Overbrook" before
he was discharged, in 1960 I had a tremendous
crush on Nina Simone, I always wanted to
name a child Thelonious, I was sure
I was an orphan at 10, I wished I was
an orphan at 18, my father's alive so
I'm still not an orphan at 32, I know
alot of orphans, I once had an
orphan for a lover, I suppose my kids
could be orphans some day, I was never
good at planning the future for more
than a couple of days, friends have
told me I always do things the hard way,
my family's response to tough times or
catastrophes was usually humor, I'm
grateful to them for giving me that,
I find cynics boring although there's
alot of the cynic in me, I find
depression dull, mine or anyone elses,
I'm no good at small talk, I feel
an undercurrent of violent tension
in most "straight" bars and on late
night city streets that intimidates
me, I find jealousy useless and
depressing, I know people who find
jealousy exciting and even rewarding,
something to live for, I'd love to
make love all the ways I havent yet

or havent thought of yet, with all
the people I havent yet or havent met
yet, although sometimes I could care
less about sex, I write everyday
and listen to music everyday and cant
imagine living without either,
libraries and hospitals intimidate me,
being around people who seem to feel
comfortable anywhere used to make me
feel insecure, I'm getting over that,
I used to feel obliged to apologize
for or defend people whose goals I
shared even though I might not like
them or their tactics, I'm getting
over that too, I've learned to love
or at least appreciate alot of things
I used to despise or ignore, I've had
trouble getting it up and trouble
keeping it down, I'm tired of alot
of things but curious about more, I'm
tired of this but that's history now.

—*March 1974*

146

Patricia Elliott/1917-1977

STUBBORN GROUND

from *Black Jack*, Number 4: 1975
Big Timber, Montana
Editor: Art Cuelho

Slow Sun.
Deep Dew.
And the time's the first of June....

Look brother! My northern bones
creak out that your weathering,
your bleaching, your havesting,
your trucking couldn't be rounded up
so soon, f'Chrisesake!
Why up here we've just had another snowstorm
hit Calgary the hardest & that's a surprise.

>   In my territory
>   Sis-Sis-Katchewan
>   (take the lazy way out
>   and spit S'Katchewan)
>   we generally get everything
>   harder, later, longer—
>   Believe it. From blizzards to floods
>   to droughts to army worms
>   to stink weed—& our summers die
>   somewhere between Medicine Hat
>   and Waskesui.

Anyways
nothing's changed—
Here it's June like down there with you
but we're still waiting—
we're standing, looking up (waiting)
waiting on the impersonal sky
until the time when my old man shouts

feel that long sun,
squint at ol' Sol he's sprouting his whiskers
spoking them down on our doubting shoulders
(the screen door slams)
today's the day, today's forever!
(the homestead shudders alive)
                  Tell your mom
                  to double the grub
                  get your lazy brother up
                  harness the horses
                  the action's gonna start!

                        2
With Spring, that's the way it is.
Waiting
        Standing
                  Wishing
Knowing nothing works in the land of russian
thistle and burnt out wives—
& then—Hope! the thing that twists like tape worm
through your gut, & at the first green sun
you're bawling for horses for tractors
(frantic trips to town)
Get nails, rivets, axle grease, binder twine,
wire, bolts, deisel oil, gas,
credit, credit, credit,
until   or if
the wheat fields survive,
turn golden bronze, cascade into elevators,
tumble three thousand miles in anxious box cars
for greedy ports &
far
        flung
                  freighters

                        3
Well, July and August we ache for rain.

We watch the grasshoppers fattening
                    prancing
            fiddling
and what's the navy-blue sky the high sky doing?
Nothing.   Not
                        one
                damn
        thing.
Not any little dust fuckin blue black
ozone thing.   just
beating out the heat waves
knocking out the shot blades
whipping my mother into the Battleford
San.
                        & my father he goes quiet
                        chalky under his tan
                        says 'Trisha we can send her
                        to her sister's in Manitoba
                        sometimes they get rain
                        ...August's bound to be better
                        (august's bound to be better)

                        4

I can't stand it
I gotta get out   I jump onto Gypsy
            (no saddle)
she's hot & she's sweating salt
& my legs are stinging
        & we tear for my one   (my only)
boy friend Lance of the *Sand Hills*
where the land is   (god's truth)
worse than ours.
                        my Gypsy's one-half race horse
                        sired by a mongrelly no-nonsense
                        stud with lots of sex drive   &
                        not one ounce of class.....
                        but she's got her mother Minto's
                        spirit, her straining for the wide

             open prairie ahead—
             no shying
             not a thought of gopher holes
             alkali sloughs   or
             shadowy, side-loping coyotes.
She starts a clip clop turn-around
settles into a drumma adrumma adrumma adrumma
pounding it out in one chestnut rock
straight to Lance's door
(dust carrying through)
                  Lance coughs around it,
                  he smiles—& all of a sudden
                  I think rain
                  I think no debts
                  I think dad's o.k.
                  I think babies   &
                  I think nights starting over...&
                  over....

                       5

Well, brother,
that long-backed horse of a horse
Minto the Mother Spirit
she's grazing in an oat-lined sky,
Gypsy's spavin'd some by now
& my cantering's been cut back from *more*
than a bridle and bit—
                  cause Lance and I did a lot of
                  layin and hayin and deep-layered
                  gazin at the rag-time stars   &
                  now I'm as low-bellied as the mare,
                  my traces are dragging
                  and all my nights are warm
                  at forty below.

                       6
So—yah—I lose track of the nights

150

but *not* the seasons.
Here I'm yelling at Lance cause it's September
we'll harvest the wheat—
to hell with everything
we're going to eat!
double the grub & double the beer
(because *maybe* the yield will be higher
than we think in this land of
always tomorrow)—by God we'll have a
bumper crop!

        that is, if the saw-fly stays away,
        the cut worm,
            the rust,
                the frost,
        o my brother from the warm south,
        pray for the nights to cloud over,
        greying the wood smoke
        singing the crickets
        under a dishraggy, sold-out moon,
        and the men working late,
        lights on their tractors
        up early again
        boots soaked with dew
        work all day
        until they're half dead
    swill their coffees... never shave...

            7

That's the way it is up here.
    I know you are dreaming of a valley,
a farther valley,
where the plains reach for the foothills
the foothills reach for the mountains
the mountains kick the sky....
        but my plains don't travel that far.
        they're flat & they're three-quarters
        frozen.
        we while away the rigid winter

                    betting fancy money on the very hour
                    the very minute!
                    when ice (slow grinding, unrehearsed)
                    breaks free of the Sis-Katchewan
                              deep   angry   waters

Through thick fingers, furred ears
we hear spring's returning arrow.
                              high
            indifferent
      colourless

We listen anyway—all stubborn—easy
in our sleeping bags for every season—
shifting dreams around—of bigger barns,
embroidered saddles—

murmuring wisdom and foolishness
wisdom and foolishness

pierced,
deep-flowering.

Michael Ventura / Los Angeles
AFTER THE SUCCESSFUL PSYCHOTHERAPY

from *Poetry &*, Volume 2, Number 4: 1977
Chicago
Editor: JoAnn Castagna

It was sometimes not more than a blemish, or a nervousness,
A fidget of the hands—sometimes not more than that—
That stood between her and an immense sameness:
So many bricks, so many legs, so many corridors, so many shoulders,
Hairstyles everywhere you look, and eyes everywhere,
Eyes that sank down to the pit of the world, if you could descend in
                                                    them—
So many pits of the world. Sometimes
Nothing more than mere, everyday tears
Would rescue her: she might collapse, but it seemed obvious
That everything else would remain. So that was something, then, her
                                                    collapse.
And so: many collapses, like leaves falling—

It's the falling, you see—into the bed, unable to move for days;
Into someone's arms (yes: they were my arms,
But that's not the point) unable to turn away; falling on the subway,
Crawling across the platform on her hands and knees—
I had to pretend I was looking for something"—
Unable to stand, unable to ask for help—do you see?
She was trying, or something was trying through her, to show us
                                                    something
Terribly important.
Do you see now, why peace was beneath her?

Everything else went on in every which way,
The traffic lights, the fashion models, the subways,
Where none of us could bear each other, and did, twice a day,
With all the world's troubles (for a nickel, and then for fifteen cents)
Folded in the crook of our arms—so her collapse, you see—

Was a genre of hope. For another world. It was faith.
She outdid the rest of us.

No, it couldn't go on. One day she entered a roomful of objects.
It could have been any room—that it's not important which room
Is the state we've gotten to, if you want to put it that way.
Who knows what finally defeated her? The vase, it may have been—
She was sentimental enough; but maybe it was
The very chair she chose, maybe the ashtray, some artifact
That shouted her down with its testimony.

Yes, an ashtray perhaps. That's likely.
It seems an accomplice, it's on your side, you reach for it,
Maybe you hold it in your lap, it's there for you—probably an ashtra

She tells her stories differently now, with a jaunty assurance.
We all of us, the defeated ones, are very assured.
She has a whole new slant on whatever went on before.
There is almost no one left to notice
The gradual atrophy
Of what had been her secrets;
Nor that her beauty has gradually turned:
It used to be one had to master oneself
To perceive her beauty. Now—
She doesn't bite her fingernails anymore,
She's really quite stunning, in the way women are now,
She's going to do just fine.

Ramon Fernandez/Casalona, Spain

TO THE SUN

from *Suction*, Volume 1, Number 3: 1973
Oakland, California
Editor: Darrell Gray

When you see me the last time,
When you finally see me,
When Nothing is added to nothing
As vine-leaves are added to sunlight
Or day to night—
When alcohol bubbles in the crevice
Of a flower, and the lamps of the city
Look sick on their poles—
Then you will know again
What you have known all along:
That our earth was found without our help
As a solitary rivulet of blood
At the heart of the universe,
Where love creates
The object that it loves.

translated by Darrell Gray

Vicente Aleixandre / Madrid, Spain

THE OLD MAN AND THE SUN

from *Twenty Poems*
The Seventies Press, 1977: Madison, Minnesota
Editor: Robert Bly

He had lived a long time,
the old man. In the evenings at sunset he used to rest
    there on the large, solid trunk of a fallen tree.
At the end of the day I'd pass that place and stop to
    look at him.
He was an old man with his face full of lines and his
    eyes dim, but not sad.
He rested on his log, and at first the sun drew close to
    him and gently nibbled at his feet—
then it seemed to curl up and rest for awhile.
Soon it rose slowly and went flowing over him, flooding
    him,
pulling him gently toward it, making him whole in its
    sweet light.
As the old man lived, as he waited, how the sun thinned
    him out!
How slowly it burned away the last wrinkles, his sad
    lined skin, the record of his misery,
how long it took, stripping and polishing everything!
In the silence the old man went slowly toward nothing,
    slowly surrendering himself,
the way a stone in a tumbling river gets sweetly abraded
and submits to the sound of pounding love.
And I saw the powerful sun slowly bite at him with
    great love, putting him to sleep
so as to take him bit by bit, so as to dissolve him with
    light bit by tiny bit,
the way a mother might bring her child very softly back
    to her breast.

I used to go by there and see him. But sometimes I

156

could see nothing but a face made of air, just the
    lightest lacework of a person.
All that was left after the loving man, the kind old man
    had passed over into light
and was slowly, slowly pulled off in the last rays of the
    sun,
like so many other things we cannot see in this world.

—translated by Robert Bly & Lewis Hyde

Rolf Jacobsen/Oslo, Norway
OLD AGE

from *Twenty Poems*
The Seventies Press, 1977: Madison, Minnesota
Editor: Robert Bly

I put a lot of stock in the old.
They sit looking at us and don't see us,
and have plenty with their own,
like fishermen along big rivers,
motionless as a stone
in the summer night.

I put a lot of stock in fishermen along rivers
and old people and those who appear after a
   long illness.
They have something in their eyes
that you don't see much anymore
the old, like convalescents
whose feet are still not very sturdy under them
and pale foreheads as if after a fever.

The old
who so gradually become themselves once more
and so gradually break up
like smoke, no one notices it, they are gone
into sleep
and light.

—translated by Robert Bly

Susan Irene Rea/Phoenixville, Pennsylvania

STROKE

from *Firelands Arts Review*, Volume VI: 1977
Huron, Ohio
Editor: Joel Rudinger

After the family dinner, language
is trivial and easy—
until you lose it entirely, Uncle,
asking for something you want
which suddenly has no name.
"Goddam," you moan, "gimme a....
All I want's a...Jesus Christ,
ain't you got one?"
The family hands you sweaters,
pills, icepicks, glasses of brandy,
knives. Nothing will do.
Afraid of empty hands,
they rush at you with objects,
determined to interpret what you've said,
afraid to name this dying
and to watch you
leave them, word by word.

Pablo Neruda / 1904-1973

FULL OCTOBER

from *Invisible City*, Numbers 16/17: 1976
Fairfax, California
Editors: John McBride & Paul Vangelisti

Little by little and also in large amounts
life happened to me
and how insignificant this business is:
these veins carried
my blood which I rarely saw,
I breathed the air of so many regions
without keeping proof of any for myself
and by the time the last returns come in
everybody knows:
nothing belongs to anyone
and the bones of our lives have only been loaned.

The beauty was in learning how not to be satisfied
either by joy or sadness,
to expect the possible from one last drop,
to demand more of the honey and the dimness.

Maybe I was punished:
perhaps I was condemned to being happy.
A steadiness stayed with me, and no one
passed by without receiving a share.

And yes I stuck my spoon in up to the elbow
in trouble that wasn't my own,
in the sufferings of others.
It had nothing to do with parties or rewards
but with a small matter: my inability
to live or breathe among such shadows,
the shadows of others like towers,
like bitter trees that buried them,
like the blows of stones against their knees.

Your own wounds can be healed with weeping,
your own wounds can be healed with singing,
but the widow, the indian, the poor man, the fisherman
stand bleeding right there in your doorway
and the miner's child doesn't know
his own father among so many scoldings.

All right, but my job
was
the soul's fullness:
a gasp of pleasure cutting the air,
the sigh of an uprooted plant,
the sum total of the action.

I enjoyed growing with the morning,
soaking up the sun, the full good fortune
of sunlight, salt, sea light and waves,
and on that unrolling of foam
my heart founded its movement:
to thrive on the deep convulsion
and to die breaking on the sand.

> —*translated by Stephen Kessler*
> *from* Memorial de Isla Negra

FICTION

E.R. Zietlow/Canada
THE BURIAL OF THE BRIDE

from *A Country For Old Men*
Lame Johnny Press, 1977: Hermosa, South Dakota
Editor: Linda M. Hasselstrom

CLAUDE had met her in front of the saloon in the little town of Pinnacle one night when he was partly drunk. Her family lived in a tent outside the town, beyond the stockyards, where the Indians always camped. She had walked up town because her father was drunk, she told him. Her name was Mary.

He had joked with her, expecting her to run away or ignore him. Instead she had giggled. That excited him, and he went up close to her. He talked some more and then started putting his hands on her, and the sensation of touch sharpened his appetite for touch, until he had her backed up against the saloon, pressing his body on hers and fondling her. She got in his car when asked, and they drove down the road. Claude looked for a place to park, but kept going until they were at his shack on the north range of the Fleming ranch. She went in with him, but there, in privacy, everything changed. He became afraid and responsible and treated her politely, keeping his hands off her. They became quite tender with each other and had something to eat. Finally, they slept together in their clothes on the bed. The shack had two small rooms.

Next day, her father came. "You take my girl!" he cried, short, fat, big-nosed, dressed in boots, Levi's, a bright red shirt and a ten-gallon hat. "You can't take my girl! First you give me ten dollars for whiskey. Then, take her. Give me ten dollar. Whiskey! Ten dollar! Whiskey!"

Claude was scared about bringing the girl home, for she looked under twenty-one. He gave the Indian ten dollars, and the Indian drove off in his broken-down Model A.

For a while, Claude wished he had sent the girl away and saved the money. Sober now, he scarcely knew how to talk to her or what to do with her. But he had paid ten dollars and, thinking it over, began to feel she was in some way his. Her idleness made him feel angry. Drawing himself up, he ordered: 'Wash the dishes!"

163

She washed the dishes.

Claude looked about the room. "Sweep the floor!"

She swept the floor. Then she began picking up his clothes and junk scattered about the room. That made him feel guilty, and he started helping. They reached for an old shirt on a chair at the same time. Both drew back, deferring to the other. They repeated the little mime in quickened tempo and suddenly were laughing. Claude caught her in his arms, hardly knowing what was happening. In a minute, they were on the bed, and he made a tremulous discovery of her body naked. Although thirty-seven, he had never had sexual contact before, and the experience, if not very successful, was amazing to him. They were in bed for hours.

When Fritz Baird, an old cowboy, stopped by and discovered Mary, Claude knew Bart Fleming would soon find out about her. Bart was on a trip, but due back soon, and Claude worried. Bart might not like his having a girl—a squaw. Maybe he (Claude) should kick her out before Fleming kicked them both out. Stewing about it over the next few days, he got very upset and abused the girl and called her a dirty Indian.

Bart Fleming had worked for Claude's parents when he first came West. They had owned a small farm that required no extra help, but Henry Keefer had known Bart's dad. They had taken Bart in to help him. Soon there was trouble. Henry felt Bart didn't do enough work and was only interested in getting things for himself. Shortly, Fleming did buy the quarter and build the shack where Claude lived. Then his holdings grew rapidly.

Claude stayed at home. His mother told him he must look after them in their old age. Marriage was out of the question. Years went by. One day, his dad bought a new car, and that very day, scarcely knowing how to drive it, he killed himself and his wife at a railroad crossing.

Claude began spending his time in the saloon. There was no one at home to tell him what to do. Soon his fields were weed-grown and his taxes delinquent. Broken machinery went unrepaired; his cows began calving in January.

In the middle of a dry summer, Bart Fleming stopped by. Claude's place had a good well. Fleming had bought out a neighboring ranch and needed water. He offered to pay the back taxes plus a few thousand dollars for the place. Claude hesitated, but

Fleming said he could live in the old shack for free. Help with the cows. Bart would let him sell a few head every year for spending money.

That was their arrangement. Claude bought a Buick, and soon most of his money was gone. Now and then, Bart singled out an old cow and scribbled off a bill of sale for her, and Claude took her to town. He helped with the branding and kept an eye on the cows on his part of the range. He was glad to be told what to do, but Fleming mystified him. Sometimes he came and talked to Claude in long monologues, complaining about his wife or worrying about money. "She whines that I don't give her nothing," he said, on more than one occasion. "Hell, what does she need? I don't have nothing. Leastwise, I don't spend no money on myself. Foolishly. Which is what she wants. Piddle it away. Women are the damnedest deal! You're lucky, living like you do. Sometimes wish I was back here."

Often he sat on the doorstep, talking on and on, apparently not expecting a response. Claude stood over him, leaning against the doorjamb, shifting now and then uncomfortably.

"Hell, you think I got a lot, huh, because I got some land and cows? Well, that ain't all there is to it. A man never knows where he is. Ain't never got it made. I come here as a young fellow thinking a herd of cows was the end of the rainbow. Lot of worry is what it is. Hell of a lot of taxes. And for what? The old lady still bellyaches day and night. Food's no better than it was when I was broke. I ate beans then. Hell, I like beans. Hardly ever get them any more. Yeah, you can count yourself lucky. Count yourself lucky!"

Other times, he bawled Claude out, reminding him of his position. "There's a critter with a horn growing into her head down there," he might complain. "Damn it, why do I have to look for things like that? I keep you around here to watch after the cows. You better remember that. You better toe the mark, by God! I'm letting you live here; I'm giving you cows to sell for your goddamned beer. Where the hell would you be if I kicked you out, huh? You couldn't make it on that place you had. Your old man, he called me a good-for-nothing, the sonofabitch! Him and that dinky place he had. He was the good-for-nothing! And you! You're just like him. I'm the one that's made something of himself, and don't you ever forget it, Keefer."

When angry, Fleming paced up and down, never looking at Claude. He was a big man, red-headed but bald. Claude was afraid of him. Alone, in the safety of the shack, he raged: "Goddamn you, Fleming, we gave you a start. You had nothing! Nothing! You were nothing!" In front of Bart, however, he was meek. He ran when Bart commanded.

Worried then that Bart might not want him to have a woman, Claude yelled at Mary. But at night he was sorry. In the darkness of the bed, she was something more than a dirty Indian, and he tried to undo what fear had compelled.

Bart, when he finally came, was not angry. Mary seemed to awe him somehow. Claude caught him watching her furtively, but he did not speak to her. Claude hadn't specially noticed before, but Mary wore no underclothes, and her dress clung over her breasts and hips.

When Bart left, Claude was puzzled and uneasy. He studied Mary secretively and concluded there was something disgusting about having tits and a wide butt. Fleming was laughing to himself. Keefer's got a squaw! Yet Claude did not want to jeopardize the night; he went no further than warning Mary: "Watch yourself around him! Look out what you do and say—the way you stand around and the way you look. He owns hundreds of cows, you know."

Claude was careful to show Bart he was looking after things. He rode fence, reported a crippled cow, drove in a bull that had broken his penis. He went to town less frequently and drank less beer.

Through the winter, they lived together. Claude saw himself differently. He kept cleaner and dressed better. Yet he rarely took Mary with him in his car. She was a source of both pride and shame, and the growth of the former accented the latter. Because of her, he began to think of owning a ranch—yet a rancher shouldn't live with a squaw. Sometimes he brooded, sometimes he cursed Bart Fleming, and sometimes he quarreled with Mary. But largely he let the days go by, and nothing came to a head.

In the spring, they discovered that Mary was pregnant. Claude hadn't given that eventuality much thought. But the fact jolted him. He rushed Mary off to the nearest court house for a license, and soon they were married.

Bart, over the months, had visited less frequently than before Mary came. But if he had not poured out his troubles to Claude, neither had he bawled him out. They saw less of each other, and Bart was reserved and sometimes a bit testy. Now, when Bart found out they were married, he stared at Claude momentarily, then dropped his eyes. "Married her, huh?" he said, as if it were an occasion for regret if not mourning.

That was all. Claude worried. He should have asked Bart whether marrying the girl was all right. Now it was too late. He blamed Mary and grew fiercely angry with her, telling her Bart didn't seem to like their being married.

"Leave then," was all she said. "Leave. Go away."

Claude fell into a morose silence. Unmanned by Bart and Mary both. The idea of a place of his own had a new appeal. Times weren't bad. Farmers and ranchers drove new trucks and tractors. But there was no way to get money—unless Bart would loan it to him. The notion caught fire. For days he turned it every which way in his mind. Sometimes he was ecstatic: Bart would give him unlimited help! Other times reason said there was no chance.

But a firmness was shaping in Mary's belly. At branding time, he would have to approach Bart. It seemed a brilliant idea: Bart would be happy because of all the calves! Get to him when he's in a good mood.

It took four days to work Bart's herd, for Bart kept the crew small and they only did a hundred head a day. Each day they finished the roundup early, driving the cattle between the V-shaped wings of a corral and separating out the cows. On the opposite end of the corral was the branding chute, beside which they built a hot fire. Bart's truck parked there provided a safe place for the vaccine and castration equipment.

On the first day, Claude did not speak to Bart about money. He watched him carefully, but sometimes Bart was in a good mood, and other times he glowered. Claude waited another day and another. On the last day, they had, in addition to the branding, a cow to dehorn. Claude realized it would be a difficult job—her horns were too wide for the chute, and they would have to tie her down. Nervous anyway because time was forcing him to act, he grew even more disturbed envisioning a struggle with the cow that would get Bart heated up.

Bart said they would leave the cow till last. Seeing what he believed to be his only opening, Claude seized the moment. "Mary's pregnant," he began. Coiling a rope, Bart froze. "She's going to have a kid!" said Claude.

Then Bart looked at him. The side of his face twitched slightly, and Claude felt a cold drench go down his body. But he had to keep on: "She wants me to get my own place. I was thinking if you could let me have a little money . . . I'd pay you back, understand!"

Bart looked at his hands, passing the coils of rope from one to the other.

"I–I–I wouldn't need much. I–I–I could borrow from the–I could–I'd still work . . ."

"Let's do the calves," Bart said quietly.

Bart did the branding, and Claude noticed that he thrust the glowing irons sharply against the ribs. Yellow smoke curling up, and the calves bawled. "Come on! Come on!" Bart snapped as Claude fumbled to get the castrating bands on and Fritz Baird scampered with the vaccine.

They ate lunch under the din of bawling calves. Yet Bart seemed to carve a bubble of silence around them. Claude's hands shook, and he dropped a bit of sandwich, and Bart noticed. Claude felt he had given himself away.

It was late afternoon when they got to the cow. Bart got a rope on her hind feet, and then Fritz roped her around the neck. They stretched her out and put one front leg in the loop to keep her from choking. Bart got a crosscut saw and some kerosene to keep flies off the horn stubs. Claude held her by the tail, and she spattered grass diarrhea over his boots.

Bart grabbed the upmost horn and began sawing. The cow gave a deep tremulous bellow. Her tongue went out into the dirt and dung of the corral. She tried to twist her head, and Bart was almost thrown off balance. He jerked the horn viciously and shouted: "Hold still, Goddamn you!"

When the horn came off, he spun it out of the corral. A tiny stream of blood spurted two yards into the air. It sprayed over Bart as the cow struggled; drops ran down his face. He tried to get the other horn in position. The cow got on her belly and looked at him. The ropes had loosened somewhat. "Step on that goddamned rope!" Bart told Claude. Claude jumped to obey. His weight controlled the cow. Bart got her turned over and began to saw on the other horn.

Again the cow gave a mournful bellow. She was not only hurt but mad. When the saw bit deeper, she wrenched herself, pitching Bart over her head so that he stumbled but didn't lose balance. Coming back, he knelt and gripped the horn, puffing, enraged, pitting his strength.

Again the cow heaved. Bart slipped; quicker than sight, her horn entered his left socket and gouged the eyeball out on his cheek. Again he recovered himself, again with sheer will, he mastered the brute strength, sawing until the horn came off. For an instant he held it, presented it—to the cow, to the men?—and then, in a gesture contemptuous even of contempt, flung it out of the corral. Once again, the blood sprayed over him, but he ignored it, putting out his hand.

Claude didn't see what he wanted, and in a moment Bart snapped his fingers sharply. "Where's the kerosene? Get the lead out of your ass! What's the matter with you? That squaw got you petered out?"

Claude scrambled. As Bart took the can, his fingers brushed Claude, leaving a sensation like a burn. Bart dashed kerosene on the stubs, dropped the can and stepped close to Claude. His dangling eye was whitish, bluish, red-streaked, and drops of blood from the cow lined his face. "Listen, Keefer," he growled, too low for Baird to hear, "don't come to me asking money for your goddamn squaw! I bailed you out on that other place, and I gave you a roof over your head. Nothing was said about moving the Reservation onto my property then. You been selling my stock! Them bills of sale don't mean shit, because you never gave me nothing for the cows. Now I let you have a squaw, so don't start gimme, gimme, gimme. You get your ass back to work, or I'll have it in jail!" Then he turned and started for the truck, as if only at this moment the pain had caught up with him.

Fritz let the cow up. "I'll drive Bart to town!" he yelled. "He's got to see a doctor!"

As the truck pulled away, Claude went to his horse. Bart's face was imprinted like a sharp flash of light on his retinas, and he felt somehow accused of the injury. **Hundreds of cows; thousands of dollars—and he's mad!** Claude whimpered as he rode. The bills of sale no good! He couldn't move away—couldn't leave or he'd go to jail. **Oh, Jesus!** Again and again the lightning went through him: **He's got me, goddamn him!** He bellowed less in rage than in fear now even knuckling under wasn't possible. Bart had all those cows, while he (Claude) was married to a squaw. He raced toward Mary, his comfort; he railed against Mary, his curse. He wanted her before him to listen to his story and see what she had done to him.

Arriving home, he turned his horse loose and almost ran to the house. Mary had just finished a bath. She stood wrapped in an old housecoat brushing her hair. The washtub, half full of water, was in the middle of the floor.

She smiled as he came in, but the smile quickly faded.

"What are you doing taking a bath?" Claude howled. "You got me in trouble with him! The critter knocked his eye out, and he told me I don't own nothing. I don't own nothing and I could be put in jail! Them cows I sold. Them bills of sale! I can't go off and get me a place—I can't even leave if he don't want to let me. He's got me! He's got me! All because of **you**! Everything was all right till you came along. I've worked for him and worked, and now he calls me a squaw man. 'That goddamn squaw got you petered out?' That's what he says to me. Eyeball out on his cheek hanging there like a dead thing!" Claude's voice was shrill and rapid. "I ain't a squaw man; I ain't never lived like no goddamn Indian. It's you that's the Indian. I never would have asked him nothing if it hadn't been for you. Now he's mad, and he's lost an eye. I don't know what he's going to do. And you're the one. I never had no trouble before!"

Across the room from her, he sat wearily and looked at the floor, sighing like a scolded boy. It came over him anew how wronged he was. "I married you!" he complained, "but what have you ever done for me? Got me in trouble! I got no one to turn to! No one gives a goddamn about **me**! I've got nothing. I'm already getting old, and I got nothing!" He wiped his eyes and stared at the floor again.

The room was still. He became aware of himself blubbering and looked up slowly at Mary. She stood across the room like a statue, watching him, nothing in her face but a searching alertness. She seemed not so much **Mary** as simply **Indian**, quietly judging. A wave of hate went through him. He snapped to his feet. **"Are you smiling at me?"** He began in a low, savage whisper that exploded into a shout: **"Are you smiling at me?** You're the one that's to blame! You're the one, goddamn you, and you smile at me?"

She clutched the housecoat and drew back against the wall.

"You goddamn Indian! You goddamn **squaw!"** Head pulled down and shoulders high, he began stalking her.

Her mouth fell slightly open and she moved along the wall.

Stabbing suddenly with a finger, he screamed: "You think you can laugh at me? You're a goddamn **Indian!** You're a goddamn **squaw!"**

He moved around the tub one way; she circled the other, tensed to spring.

He made a start. She jerked away. He showed his teeth; made another start. Again she jumped. She looked to the door, but he cut her off. A triumphant violence flooded him. He laughed without smiling, and his shoulders rippled with power. With a quick step, he got round the tub, and now she was cornered.

"Smile at me again! Go ahead, smile at me!"

She flung herself past him. He did not grab her, but stamped and shouted: "Hah!" Barefooted, she kicked the tub, splashing out soapy water. Then she limped to the wall.

Claude kicked the tub with his boot, for a moment sympathetic. But she turned defiant eyes on him. He felt an ambiguous need to catch her.

He began stalking again. "What's the matter? Scared of me? Don't be scared of **me**. Nobody's scared of **me**. I don't own nothing. I'm a squaw man. Why are you scared of me? Huh? What's the matter, can't you talk?"

She watched him, fire-eyed and silent.

"C'mere." He was sorry, and fearful of what he had done—yet ambivalent. He stalked her to catch her now; to hold her and overcome what he had made happen. She tensed visibly. He snatched the sleeve of the housecoat. Quick as a cat, she was free, springing across the room. Claude leapt after her. She rounded the tub and would be clear for the door and gone. His long grab caught a handful of flying hair just as her feet hit the spilled water. Slip and jerk together slammed her neck on the rim of the tub, and she rolled onto the floor quivering violently. After a moment, her body was still.

Claude stood beside her, arms dangling. "Hey! Hey, what's the matter? Hey, you all right? Come on, get up!" His voice grew sharp. "What you trying to do? Scare me? What the hell's the matter with you, goddamn it!" His mouth went dry and his voice broke to a whisper. "I was just kidding you a little. I didn't mean nothing." Trying to swallow, he choked. His whole body felt like a foot or arm that has gone to sleep. He felt apart from himself and heard himself mutter: "Hey"—and a recognition he had tried pathetically to conceal tricked him, mocked him—"you ain't dead, are you?" The light was fast being crowded from his eyes, and he dropped his head and hung on at the rim of consciousness. The light came back partially. Successive moments reduplicated the unmasking of reality. His sense of time was gone. But at one point, he was able to rise and get to the door. No one, nothing outside. Shooting the bolt, turning heavily, he found his strength gone, like a man in a dream who is pursued. His arms would not lift the body. Puffing, whining, he dragged it foot by foot into the bedroom and pushed and stuffed it under the bed. Panic tried to catapult him back to the tub, but his limbs refused and he lay down on the mattress. Again time was a black distance, and then he lumbered up from the bed with some strength. No one outside. He got hold of the tub and heaved it to the door. Mary had usually emptied it at the east corner, and now Claude did likewise and hung it up behind the house.

There was still water on the floor and a small spot of blood. Claude grabbed the first thing in sight—the dishcloth—and scrubbed hard. Tears flooded over his cheeks. "I didn't mean to do anything," he whimpered. "I **didn't** do anything. I didn't hurt her. It was all an accident. An accident."

Clambering up, he sped outside to check the tub. There was no blood visible on it. Nevertheless he wiped the rim several times. The sun was like a red bead on the horizon, and the evening was still and sweet. It seemed to him then that the whole thing could not have happened. Earth was calm and unaffected. Mary would come to under the bed and eventually laugh at him for putting her there. **I should have put her on top of the bed!**

Back inside, he pulled her out and began talking to her. "Come

172

on now wake up! What's the matter, huh?" He baby-talked: "Oo going to seep aw day and aw night? Tum on. Tum on. Ain't oo going to get me thum thupper?"

He patted her cheek, and the head rolled, and his whole mood inverted instantly. He jammed the corpse under the bed, flung into the other room and opened the door. No one in sight. He went to the middle of the floor and got down, studying the place, wiping it with his shirt sleeve.

Weariness overtook him there; his body almost irresistably settled to the floor. His head ached. His mind reached for sleep, trying to shut everything out. But anxiety drilled his brain. And then there was a sound—tiny, unidentifiable, but it snapped him into a crouch. **Bart was at the door!** Claude froze. The figure outside was also frozen, waiting. But there was not just one; the place was surrounded. At any moment, they might crash the door. He listened. Time was undefined, except for the thumping abandon of his heart. Finally he stood up. A sense of self-possession in surrender filled him. He opened the door, ready to explain that it had been an accident. But there was no one there. Nothing: the safety of aloneness he had hoped to escape.

It was getting dark. Claude, his nerves still a shambles, nonetheless found a simple voice of reason intact. The dead woman must be buried. He was looking absently upon a cluster of miniature buttes two hundred yards from the house. The work of rapid erosion, they had steep sides and flat tops, like great tree stumps. One in particular was well shaped and as high as his ceiling.

When the sunset had faded, Claude got his spade and went to this little plateau. He made footholds and climbed to the top. It was largely covered with prairie cactuses—an area the size of his floor, canted slightly to the east. He selected a spot near the east edge and marked out the grave in his mind, head toward the sunrise. He was aware of himself as the only strange and frightening presence.

Once underway, his labor felt good. Its purpose became secondary. Work was penance; he felt better. The night darkened around him, and then the sky was richly salted with stars. Wholly engrossed, he measured himself with the spade, and chopped out the necessary length. He removed the cactuses with a spadeful of dirt so that they could be put back—a grave covered with them would not be dug up by animals. Such practical details flowed through his mind with comfortable detachment.

When the horizon lightened and the moon rose, he was almost finished. The grave was about two feet deep. He lay down in it to check the measurement. Rest felt good—but then the dirt seemed to close in upon him. He was dead, yet alive in death and helpless to protest the smothering of his body. Suffocation sprung him out, choking for air, and he slid down from the butte, sprinting off in an incidental direction. The shadows moved; cactus and sage tangled him. He spun round, flailing convulsively. But then he froze, shivering, and the world grew quiet again; fear became fear of discovery once more.

A purposive machine took over in him now. He scurried, half-crouching, to the house and dragged the body from under the bed, wrestling it onto his shoulder with no new emotion. Getting to the butte was easy, but climbing it proved another matter. His foot slipped half way up, and the body tumbled in a knot on the dead earth, which was barren here and brightly lit. He got it again on his shoulder and heaved himself up along the difficult footholds. At the top, with puffs like sobs, he lurched to the pit just in time to get the slipping body into place. Then he straightened it on its back and sat down on the bench at the foot end, oddly comfortable in the exhaustion of his sensibility. Her face was in shadow; the misshapen moon lit the rest. Her housecoat was wrapped around her waist.

His spirit was becalmed. Nothing existed save in the focus of his eyes; nothing moved in him but the habit of desire with a restorative promise in mad and tender fantasy. Scarcely aware of his physical movement, he sank down upon her.

With the bursting of his charged excitation burst his whole spell, and in that instant, fixed foremost in his mind was an impression of a stirring in her belly. He drew back with a hoarse cry and clawed himself up onto the mound of dirt. His stomach rent itself, expelling bitter fluid. The very atmosphere was sentient now, thick with accusation. This, like his rage before, was a trick to damn him. **A Shadow! Bart!** Only an owl through the moon. But spurred by the flicker of light, the lance of terror, he snatched up the spade and whipped dirt into the pit as fast as his arms could jab. When it was full, panting, sweating , he tramped it down and then replaced the cactuses. Scarcely pausing to look again, he slid down from the butte and tore out the footholds.

Exhaustion caught up with him in the house. He fell on the bed in his clothes and was almost immediately asleep. But before dawn broke, terrible nightmares wracked him. He awoke springing upright and was unable to remember the cause of his misery. But then it came back, scorching through him like a cold fire. He felt she had come back and was under the bed to mock him. His head, when he stood, almost blinded him with pain. His balance was off, and his walk was drunken. Lighting the kerosene lamp, he got down. Nothing under the bed. But there was a spot on the floor that might be blood. He got the dishcloth and scrubbed. Then the spot stood out because it was wet and clean. So he got a pan of soapy water and lay on the floor under the bed rather than moving it, for that did not occur to him. He kept on until the floors in both rooms were finished. By that time, the dishcloth was black, but Claude did not notice and hung it on the stand where the dishes were washed. Hunger gnawed, but he hardly felt like eating.

The sun came up like a giant searchlight focused directly on him. The world was violently real. Every track, mark, disturbance was vivid, etched by the sun's brilliance. Bart would come any time to ask questions and spy around the place. **How come you washed the floor? What did you dump out here?** He had the uncanny feeling that Bart already knew. Bart would snoop around for a long time. **Left you huh? Left you?** He would keep asking about Mary. Finally he would say: **Let's go out and climb that little butte there, huh?** Bart would grunt a surly laugh the way he did when he gave Claude a cow or spoke of Claude's position with him. They would climb up the butte, and something—a badger perhaps—would have dug out a corner of the grave. That was as far as the vision went. Claude felt Bart's triumphant look, charging him with the damaged eye, smiling an open-ended threat.

In one way the fantasy was real; in another, he did not believe it and was struck by the idea that he could go away—now, and Bart would naturally think Mary had left with him. Without stopping to think it over, he got into his best clothes, locked up the house and headed for the city at a reckless speed in his old Buick. Just across the city limits, a policeman pulled him over. "Race track's the other side of town, buster." But instead of giving him a ticket, the

175

officer ultimately said: "I'll let you go, mister. Ain't never seen no one take a warning quite so much to heart."

Claude crept on down town then. The lights and traffic kept him distraught, and there seemed to be police cars everywhere. At last he found a parking place and got out, feeling conspicuous. He rushed into a dime store to lose himself, but the clerks kept asking if they could help him. Finally sheltered in a men's room, he tried to think things over. **Go on—go to the coast!** This was as far as he had ever been, and he couldn't imagine working in an entirely different area. If only there were someone to tell him what to do! Bart was the only person he could think of. At last he went into a saloon and began drinking beer. After several bottles, his mind was freer in its perspectives. He focused on the idea that Mary had died accidentally. It was true in a sense that he had participated in the accident, but hurting her wasn't his intention. They had been playing, scuffling, laughing. She had dodged away and slipped. Who would know the difference—**who would care, since she was a squaw?** He experienced a rush of relief. No one would call him guilty.

But he had buried her. Why? they would ask. Why? **What a fool!** No one would have asked about a goddamned squaw. He sat brooding, drinking more. Then he said to himself: **Hell with it! Hell with them all!** No one was going to ask about a squaw. He'd say she left. Bart would accept that. But it struck him that Bart might miss him. He wanted to be home in case anyone came snooping around—it was important to know what they saw.

He rushed from the saloon and drove back the way he had come, speeding, swearing at patrol cars that did not materialize. His mouth was dry and his body soaking with sweat as he pulled into his yard. **Bart?** His eyes searched. No one was about. No fresh tracks of horse or car. He jumped out—and a bolt went through him: ragged black buzzards circled over the little butte, flapping, dropping from sight, rising.

Claude uttered a little cry and charged out to the butte, harried, baited by the images he invented. The buzzards were not landing on it, but some distance beyond. At that spot, Claude discovered a rabbit carcass, left perhaps by a hawk or owl.

He turned away, not relieved, but with renewed guilt and a sense of foreshadowing. He clawed his way up the butte to look at the grave. It seemed not so well disguised as he had imagined in the night. There was loose dirt around it, making an outline that looked shockingly like a grave. A little rain would wash this dirt into the grass. But his hopeful glance found no clouds in the sky— only a small airplane hanging in the distance. He crouched impulsively, although it was far away.

But what if the cactuses died in a six-foot-long yellow rectangle. It would be perfectly visible from the small planes that occasionally flew over. **Carry water! Wash down the dirt! Wet the cactuses and grass so they'll root again!**

He slid down and went and got a pail of water. Carrying it up entailed scratching and kicking new footholds, and all the time he kept looking around, expecting Bart to appear suddenly beside him. Finally the well—a poor one—was dry, and still the dirt showed, and the wet cactuses showed, and the little plane droned on the horizon, going the other way now. There was nothing to do but give his efforts over to the sun. He slid down and used the bucket to scrape away the footholds. Now that side of the butte was quite scarred. Maybe a few buckets of water would harden and heal the dirt. He splashed some on as soon as the well ran in. When it dried a bit, it looked exactly as if someone had gouged a strip up the side and then splashed water on it.

Claude went to the house and sat on the step, holding his face in his hands. A realization was slowly born in him: all the trips to the butte had made a dim trail. He started up. Never had he gone to the butte before last night, and there was no admissible reason for going. **Brush out the trail with a weed!** But then the brushing would show. **Brush the whole area!** He saw himself sweeping the front yard, while Bart, having ridden up behind the house, sat on his horse and watched.

Make more trails! He sprang into action, scurrying back and forth, first out this way, then out that, always on the watch for Bart. When finished, he saw immediately that the effect was absurd. The trails went nowhere and had no excuse for being there. He sweated miserably for a while, and then a new idea struck him: **drive some cows through the yard!** Then there would be nothing but tracks. The cows never came around his buildings, but they easily might.

Claude wasted no time catching his horse in the pen out back and galloping to find some cows. It was too soon after branding for them to be easily rounded up. He ran them helter-skelter, with no conceivable reason to offer Bart if he came along. Soon Claude was weeping like a ten-year-old. But finally half a dozen cows and calves ran inadvertantly in the direction of his place, and he harried them along. Once they were in front of his house, it was not difficult to herd them back and forth. Shortly the ground was cut up with tracks.

Claude had a moment's respite and unsaddled his horse, even laughing a little although his feeling was not clear. Surveying the tracks on foot, however, he again despaired. They signified for him all his desperate antics, and surely Bart could read what was written in them. But at last he realized that there was nothing to do; that each further effort had made things worse.

On edge and unreal to himself, he hulked about, so fearful of Bart's coming that at last he began to long for it. Let it be over. An endless dialogue of questions and answers went on in his mind. Where is Mary? She got mad at me—took off. The cow tracks? He was trying to cut out one with a bad eye (there was always one with a bad eye). A spot of blood? He had shot a rabbit. All these things went through his mind in a serious rehearsal that quite engrossed him.

In the late afternoon, weary in body and spirit, he lay down on the bed. In his dozing, it seemed that Bart came, and they were in a corral with cattle. Bart was not angry, but he was dominant and full of the world. "I know," he said. "I know." And Claude got down on his knees in front of him saying: "I didn't mean it to happen. But I'll never expect anything again or ask for anything." He felt a sense of peace. But then Bart told him soothingly: "She was just a squaw." The words seemed actually spoken in the room and brought him awake with a start. Dozing had taken away his defenses, and the words felt viciously ironic. They ran through his mind: **she was only a squaw**; his guts knotted.

Soon it began to get dark. Bart would not come that day, and whereas before Claude had seen vengeance in his coming, he now read it in Bart's absence. Nothing was to be got over with. He had to wait through the night; maybe through the next day. Perhaps Bart was still in the hospital; perhaps the eye had become infected. **Oh, God, no!** That seemed the worst thing that could happen.

178

The darkness was oppressive. He tried to get supper, eat, wash up as he had done before Mary came, but it was all mechanical. When the dishes were done and the blackened dishrag wrung out and hung up, he broke into sobs—rending sobs that heaped him on the floor. Weak and ill, he stayed there, looking about the room. Every shadow was alive and had an attitude. Yet nothing would speak to him; nothing would give him the comfort of condemnation.

A scraping sound came to his ears. He could not position it or tell how loud it was. A burst of panic spun him one way and then the other. But now he spied a large beetle crawling across the floor. He caught it and put it outside.

Stretched on the bed to recover himself, he became aware of a spider dangling in the corner. There was a noise of wings past the roof. A cricket shrilled once and was silent.

Claude got his shotgun and loaded it. There was something outside the house—not Bart, not anyone. He blew out the lamp and stood very still, the gun across his belly. Silence—yet it was there. He did not know how much time passed. The presence grew less physically threatening. Claude unloaded the gun and put it away.

"All right," he said aloud, his voice husky and strange, "I'll turn her over to you. It was an accident. I buried her because I thought that was best all around. So go and do what you want to with me."

He went outside and got the spade. The moon was up. Incongruous with his present overt intention, he circled to the butte so as not to renew his trail. He chopped footholds and in a minute stood over the grave. The cactuses came out easily this time. He worked fast, but then, after several spadefuls, his thrust went deep and the blade struck something firm. A wave of nausea went over him, and reality shifted: the phantoms of his mind vanished into simple, literal facts. The body was here, concealed; no one knew; no one had to know.

Slowly then, he scraped the dirt back into the hole and replaced the cactuses. With a gut-level sense of finality this time, he turned away, descended and followed his circuitous route back to the house. Hopes of disclosure and confession were gone. He would bear the full burden of her death alone and suffer the imprisonment implicit in that freedom. He was stronger than the shadows— ever so little, yet stronger—and could not escape the fact.

Next day, Bart rode in.

He came early in the morning while Claude was making breakfast, and his knock at the door sent a drench over Claude. Bart thrust the door open after a few seconds. His appearance had changed considerably. A black patch covered his left eye and seemed to pinch his face toward that side. The other eye was bloodshot and avoided Claude's glances. "We got to get busy building that fence if we're going to have a hay crop. You only just having breakfast?" He had spoken of the fence before—it would keep the cows out of a meadow so that the grass could be cut.

Claude scurried between the stove and the table but did not answer.

Bart moved restlessly up and down the room. After a few moments, he asked: "Where's the woman?"

Claude had been waiting for the question, yet it loosed a shock wave through him. He feared for his voice. "She left—run off." The words were a croak. He faced away from Bart, expecting more questions. Bart said nothing. Claude saw his hands shaking half an inch as he served his fried eggs from the skillet. One egg almost popped onto the table.

Bart said: "Left you, huh? Well, that's a woman for you!" He grunted a mirthless chuckle. "You'll learn about them. You'll learn! Don't let it get you all rattled." Claude sat at the table. Bart watched him for a moment, then slapped him on the shoulder with his gloves and said almost sympathetically: "Figure she took all your troubles along with her, huh? Well, I might as well go back and get things together. You come on up as fast as you can, huh?"

Claude nodded.

Bart hesitated. "You ain't still figuring on pulling out on me, are you?"

"Oh, no!" Claude spattered his mouthful of egg across the table. In the same instant that he saw a door of possibility open, he heard himself close it. He glanced furtively at Bart.

Bart lingered, meeting Claude's glance now, smiling somehow awkwardly. But he favored his blinded side: it did not change; only the right half of his face smiled.

For an equivocal second, Claude wanted to retract his words, but under that look he could not.

"See you up there," said Bart and left.

Through a window, Claude saw him mount his horse, then stare at the ground. But some explanation for the tracks seemed to offer itself in his mind, for he turned the horse and rode away.

Claude had been prepared for a resolution: either Bart would know, or he would not and the worry would be ended. But nothing had happened. Claude still had an uncanny sense that Bart knew or could find out. The prospect of being indefinitely in limbo made him bellow and crash his knife and fork against the wall. Bart's smile was imprinted on his brain—two things in the same face. He couldn't finish his breakfast.

He met Bart up at the Fleming ranch, and they drove out to the meadow. Claude's job was to sit in the pickup's box and drop steel posts everytime a large measuring wheel made a full turn. Then he and Bart walked back, driving the posts in with a heavy mall. Claude gave himself almost desperately to the work, feeling a comfort and security in it.

Claude ate with the Flemings at dinnertime. Bart's wife, who was always a bit peevish, waited on them. Claude kept his eyes on his plate, and at one point Bart remarked about his being down in the dumps. "His squaw's left him!" He grunted a little chuckle. His wife said nothing, but sent a disgusted look Claude's way.

Claude's nerves were taut, yet he saw that Bart interpreted his worry as sadness over being left. The idea of this misplaced sympathy in view of the truth rent him with emotion, choked him. He had to pretend his food had gone down the wrong way.

"God, man!" said Bart genially, "don't croak yourself over it!"

Claude expected to be bullied and threatened, but as they worked that afternoon, Bart kept his voice down and even made a few jokes. He seemed to be trying to cheer Claude up. Claude managed something that sounded like a laugh now and then.

So it was in the days that followed. They built fence and repaired fence, and the work was so tiring and so steady that Claude slept well and ate well and had little time to brood. Bart was friendlier than he had ever been before. A year ago, he had either bawled Claude out or complained about his own troubles; now he talked man to man.

One day he clapped a hand on Claude's shoulder as they walked to the pickup. "Well, we're sure getting a lot of work done, huh? Guess maybe you'd like a couple of critters to sell. I ran in two dry ones last night, old devils. You might as well drive them home with you and take them to town." That evening, Bart made him out a bill of sale, drawing the words slowly with a stub of pencil.

As he drove the animals home, Claude felt pleased, but resentful of his pleasure. He was quite sure now that Bart had no inkling of where Mary had gone. Why should he (Claude) be happy about two old cows? Yet the good feeling persisted in him for a while. Next day he took the cows to market in an old trailer, he spied a new calf with its mother along the road. On an impulse, and as a kind of revenge against the gratitude he hadn't wanted to feel, he stopped and caught the calf and put it in the trailer. It was not difficult to imitate Bart's scrawl and add "one calf" to the bill of sale. Bart had only marked one price for the two cows, and that would do for the calf as well.

At the sales ring, he suffered misgivings, and afterwards drank several bottles of beer. Back home, he brooded and was depressed and experienced some physical pain in his shoulders and loins. The shack seemed unbearable, silent and empty. From now on his life would be nothing but hard work and hollow nights. No wonder Bart was smiling and slapping him on the shoulder.

He looked out at the little butte. It caused no special feeling. He went out and climbed it. The grave did not show; the grass and cactuses had rooted. For a long time he stood trying to feel his earlier anguish, testing his emotions. Only a dull, ugly emptiness fill him.

A few days later it rained. A sudden, rapid downpour washed out all traces of his scratching on the side of the butte. Like an ablution, it cleansed his world. Thereafter, Claude watched Bart carefully and grew certain that he did not suspect what had happened to Mary and would never find out. Claude discovered that he could feel contempt for Bart. He watched his boss and saw that he was a slave to fences and cows like himself. For all his money and land and herds, Bart had to sweat and listen to his wife's bellyaching.

As the summer wore on, Claude grew adjusted to the reality of the stump butte. He had had to guard himself against surprise remembering with its stab of anguish for so many weeks that control became a habit and the butte gave him a kind of power. He **knew** and had survived, while Bart did not know. Claude was able to face Bart with a feeling that there was nothing Bart could do to hurt him now. He believed that he could survive even the disclosure of his secret.

But this sense of freedom had its price: without fear his life was dull. The long agony of coming to accept what had happened, the slow inner alchemy of grace, had been a profound experience. He was no longer the Claude of early spring. He had endured his life before, but now he was bored. Yet there was nothing else that interested him, and besides, he wanted to be around to watch the butte.

Next time Bart gave him a cow to sell, Claude also loaded up two yearlings and changed the bill of sale. Another time, he loaded up two unbranded calves and forged a bill of sale.

Not long after that, Bart rode in with a 30:06 rifle in a scabbard on his saddle. His face was flushed, and the tortured quality of the left side had taken over all of it. His eye did not look at Claude. "Couple of cows with tight bags out there. Somebody got the calves. Ain't seen any goddamned Indians around, have you?"

Claude said he hadn't.

"The sonsofbitches better not be. It'll be good-bye Indian if I catch them. Are you keeping a lookout?"

"Yeah! Yeah, I been riding regular."

"You damned well better be! That's what I got you here for. I'd bet anything that good-for-nothing squaw you had up here told her relatives. There's been rustling going on for quite a while. I been missing some critters."

After Bart left, Claude realized that he had got quite shaken up. For two days there was a knot in his belly, and he worked eagerly. The third day, he became angry and sullen. **My good-for-nothing squaw, huh?** he thought. **Indians, huh?**

On a day when Bart took his wife to the city, Claude loaded a calf and drove to the Reservation. He had met some Indians at the saloon. They didn't ask for a bill of sale. One of them had a sixteen-year-old daughter, and Claude had a hard time keeping his eyes off her. Finally he returned the price of the calf and got the girl in the backseat of his Buick.

Drunk on the experience, he raced home. For days she was on his mind, until at last he got another chance to see her by giving her father money. Bringing her home, near the little butte, was out of the question, but nothing kept him from visiting her on the Reservation. He was giddy with the idea of it. **Such a young one too!**

One day, the Indian said: "Bart Fleming has a young black bull. I have a good friend called Black Bull. I want to give him that critter. We'll butcher it and have a good time. You bring me that critter, and you can have the girl anytime you want until she gets married."

Claude agreed. But once more by himself, he worried. Calves all looked alike, and Bart couldn't be sure of what happened to the odd one. However, the bull, a purebred Angus, was special. Bart might go around the Reservation asking questions. Claude sat on his step and brooded, gazing at the little butte, feeling sure that he had better not try to steal the little bull

Days passed into weeks. He worked with Bart, and sometimes in the evenings, drove to the Reservation. The Indian made fun of him: "Where's my bull, huh? What's the matter? You think I tell Bart Fleming? I don't tell Bart Fleming."

Claude watched Bart carefully. Bart was no longer so quiet-spoken with him. Things had got more as they used to be, in previous years. Bart stayed on the lookout for rustlers and always carried his 30:06. Claude thought that maybe Bart suspected him. The idea of his guilt and the idea that Fleming was in the right felt ugly in him. Fall and winter stretched boringly ahead.

Claude felt himself under tacit indictment—yet why should he be? He worked as hard as Bart. They rounded up a hundred steers to sell, and Bart shouted at him: "Come on, Keefer, get the lead out!" Bart now called him by his last name again. Sulking, calculating how many thousand dollars the steers would bring, Claude made up his mind. A sharp prickle went through his middle. He no longer felt gloomy.

A few days later, he parked the car and trailer near a corral in a little draw. Then he rode by the ranch. "Going to take a swing through the south pasture," he told Bart.

"Yeah. Good idea." Bart's eye searched him. The right side of his face was pinched now, as though the eye was pained from overuse.

Claude started out south, but over a hill, cut east. Bart's face hung before him. He was racked, vertiginous, driven. Whipping up his horse, he galloped the bull into the corral, slammed the trailer against the chute, harried the animal into it. Frantic now, panting, he dropped the endgate, bolted it, sprang around to the door of the Buick. There he froze for an instant to survey the rim of the high country that stretched westward to the ranch. In that instant, a 30:06 bullet tore away his brains.

Bo Ball/Decatur, Georgia

SIDEBURNS

from *Aura*, Volume 2, Number 2: 1976
Birmingham, Alabama
Editor: Steven Ford Brown

DWIGHT WILSON was a clever man, when cleverness meant more than knowing the capitals of the 48 states. (The way I see it, Alaska still belongs to the damn Republicans, and the moon, by God, belongs to Jesus.) A stout hairy man with burnsides as orange as wild honeysuckle, Dwight, in his prime, worked the night shift at the Red Jacket Mines near Dismal, and, by daylight, he was a rent-out farmer and the father of a dozen children. But Jesus or the devil, if they know their Deuteronomy, will take him on as an A-1 barber.

On week-ends his house was as busy as the old-timey barnbuildings that died out when the W. P. A. put people on the road. And week-end barbering meant drinking for Dwight. On a work-a-day he didn't get to talk much, going out of the hollow at 2:00 p.m., when folks were in the fields, to catch his work truck, and back up Copperhead singing "Man of Constant Sorrow" at 2:00 a.m. 8 a.m. through noon, he tilled the corn and tobacco. Those of his children that were old enough to say said he snipped a lot at them, but on Saturday, Saturday night, and all day Sunday Dwight drank his bootleg, laughed, and took a load off the heads of Straight Democrats.

When his hand clippers made their way up your neck, he'd say, if you were under the age of accountability, "This is the way a tarpin crawls to a water hole—ouu-ga-clop, ouu-ga-clop, ouu-ga-clop," and to men over 13, he'd say, "This is what you'll say after you've thanked Nanny May Presley for a little piece, 'I-got-clap, I-got-clap, I-got-clap.' "

He'd pass around the pint bottle—and we knew when to drink thin—and we'd egg him into telling about the time he cut off Press Fletcher's ear. He told that story for over thirty years and it never changed.

The scissors and clippers would slow down and he'd act out his part and Press too, showing us how Press prissed in to get a quick cut. Just flopped down in Dwight's barber chair that his wife Nadine on week days nussed whichever one was the baby in, and took the barbering sheet from the washstand and shook it three times to show he was ready. It was a Sunday afternoon and Dwight was feistier than usual since he had bought an Uncle Dave Macon record and had played "Come on Blue" over and over on his new crank R. C. A. Press just sat there and twitched his thumbs under the sheet, while Dwight listened to the record up close to get every pick and then likened his dogs—Tray, Dayshift, and Sooner—to Uncle Dave's hound Blue.

"Reckon I timed my trip bad," Press allowed, his fingers finding the knots on his knee caps.

"Now Tray, before she caught the mange and I greased her up with burnt motor oil, she'd push her way through saw-briars to get to a lizard."

"When I wake up of a morning with a side burn tickling at my ear I know it's time." Press addressed his words to the many colored hairs that peppered the sheet from Saturday's crop.

"Dayshift and Sooner just pick banjo on their fleas. Better watch out for them fleas. Getting so big they could swaller the warts on a Republican's ass." And Dwight swallowed some Early Times to show Press how the fleas stretched their adamsapples.

"Sure need to soon take that load of hair off my ears." Press dug up his 21-jewel watch from his overalls.

Dwight couldn't get no talk about dogs going with Press so he fetched his barbering gear from the mantel.

That year Dwight was heady on Al Smith. He had called him his kind of Happy Warrior. He had read somewhere that Al was Catholic and he looked the word up and read it meant a Christian who was broad in sympathies, and since Dwight was sympathetic and open to all things from a rain-crow's cry to the fast-finger picking of Uncle Dave Macon, he was heady on Al Smith.

Press was a pre-Hoover Republican. That wasn't so bad in those days—no worse than having ring-worm—but when Press started praising Republicans, Dwight let the liquor go to his head.

"That Harding, he helped get this country on the map," Press nodded, not minding the scissors that were snapping fast at his left ear.

"Coolidge sure brought a frost to my daddy's clover," Dwight allowed.

"Calvin. Christian. No Catholic." And here Press shrugged his shoulders in a dry laugh. Press knew that Dwight first paid his poll tax just to vote against John Calvin.

"I'd like to hold that Hoover up to the sun and count to see how many worms he's got in his guts," Dwight mumbled thin-lipped. He watched the slivers of hair fall to the sheet.

"That man can save this country. Money, that where hit's at. None of that cross of gold bull . . ."

But before Press could say what squoze from a bull's gut, Dwight snipped half an ear off, and Press left the nussing chair screaming that he was dead and deafened. The dogs cut to yapping and chased his heels through the ripening garden and half way out of Copperhead.

Dwight yelled after him, "You shan't crucify mankind on a cross of gold." Dwight's daddy and his six brothers had spread the Word, and Dwight, the only backslider, riled when William Jennings Bryan's text got mixed up in his head with St. James.

Press carried the word that Dwight was charitable to no-hellers, but that he'd suretogod make a Christian bleed. I guess that's why Dwight stopped getting Republican heads.

Fired by alcohol and that cross of gold speech, the first words he had heard over the wireless, Dwight told the story long after we got WSM and after Hoover brought the rickets on. When we striplings would come of a Saturday morning, not thinking that the night had been shorted for him, he'd say, "I-got-clap" and scratch his loins and laugh about that time Press Fletcher got some cartilage hung between the blades of his scissors.

I was sprouting up then and Dwight was a ways partial to me, for we talked about the Original Carter Family and the Red Jackets. I wanted to leave the farm and make me some green money. Dwight and me became what was then called hunkering buddies—he, thirty-so and me, seventeen—we'd hunker with our butts brushing the calves of our legs and we'd talk and smoke his ready-made Wings up so close that our fingers browned. Or we'd ginseng, line a bee tree, or hunt wild mushrooms. But mostly we'd hunker and talk of the old times when he had a vice on things and about the future when I would get a grip on the world when Hoover left it.

"Time's is bad," he'd say, shaking that red mane that never gave way to fashion, till necessity set in.

"But I figure we can line us up a bee tree," I'd say.

His face would flush redness from homebrew and the sun, and he'd smile a curve of recognition into his lips, and we'd unhunker and go looking for the sweetgum where we eyed yesterday's bee aim his wings for.

We got through the Hoover Times somehow, on what the earth and the store gave us, on the credit, and when the mines opened up again and John L. Lewis squinted question marks out of his eyebrows, Dwight got me on at the Red Jackets—the night shift—and he saw me through cold-dust haircuts, till my hair fell out, and through my seven daughters. We sobered for five days, and then, sure as blood pressure, we'd stop at the bootleg's for our Friday Early Times and truck out of Dismal to drink us a Friday night vacation.

But Saturdays and Sundays were for haircuts.

I remember one Saturday in particular. Drew Pearson had blackguarded Roosevelt and the New Deal, and I was low. I went to Dwight's early, before the new stretchers of denim got there. My new Ford pickup must not have sputtered I was there, for I walked up unsuspected to an open door. (Dwight never locked anything in those days.) I found him nussing Nadine in his lap and trying to teach her her letters. From a funny book. *Red Ryder and Little Beaver*, it was. I stood by the door, as mortified as if I had seen a man bleed from his bowels, and heard Dwight whisper low his A. B. C.'s, like he had just found a robin's nest with more than four eggs in it.

And Nadine, who couldn't tell A from Z, laughed the kind of purr you hope angels will gurgle when God arrives with his shirt-tail out for Gabriel's last blow of time.

I scraped a foot or two, without mud or snow, and coughed that I was standing there.

Nadine gathered her chop-sack dress out of its sprawl and boiled us up some coffee, and over my complaints about faulted chokes and burnt-out spark plugs, she clucked to the stove, "Well, I'll declare. Declare I do."

Dwight and I talked about the locust blight and about the upcoming election which looked black for the sheriff, a Democrat, who had been caught in bed with Nanny May's thirteen-year-old daughter. And Nanny Presley was the sheriff's doubled-first cousin.

Truman gave Dwight and me a fair deal. The Dismal bank let him buy a piece of land so he didn't have to go halves anymore. He humped coal by night and he and his mules and boys whipped the corn and tobacco into growing by daylight. He drank on the weekends and watched the children shoot up, not only those he planted at 3:00 a.m., but also those who came to have their heads relieved free on a Saturday or a Sunday.

Dwight smiled when Harry S. sent his two oldest boys over the waters to Korea. I helped him listen to the war on his new T. V., the first one in Copperhead. Our eyes owled in coal dust and twinkling nervously, we watched Truman's boys fight communism or My Little Margie displease her Daddy by disremembering to lock a door.

Other people started buying a box, but they kept it hidden. Dwight's R. C. A.-Victor sent out its light to anyone who had ears to hear.

Uncle Dave Macon died about the time Truman left for Independence, and Dwight cried a lot, even when we bought our pints and pretended to fish on a Friday night. He'd click his fingers against the buttons on his shirt and sing out, "Come on Blue ye rascal you, catch at possum for me an' you." He'd cough to cover up what his eyes were doing and we'd watch the fish-taut lines we didn't bother to tug.

He would have gotten over Dave Macon and Truman if Eisenhower hadn't had his name's sake and had predicted that he was as Democratic as Harry S. or Harry F., but when Dwight David changed his true nature and accepted the Republican nomination, Dwight said he couldn't tell a Democrat from a Republican by looking at their heads. The fields of corn and tobacco got smaller, inching their way up to his front porch. And the T. V. didn't show him what he wanted to hear. When Adlai E. Stevenson stubbed his toe, Dwight laid out of work a week. The T. V. stopped showing him what he wanted to hear. He got drunk over the $64,000 question—on a week night—and his lungs and liver started queasing on him.

When Davie Macon Wilson, his 12th, was delivered by Granny

Bostic for $15.00 and truck fare, he confessed to me he had done his plowing and that he was studying on letting the miners' hospital in Grundy snip a tube on his privates.

"Ever time I hang my britches on the bed post, Nadine she gets big," he told me. I kept saying for him to poke for fun, way I was doing. But I had really been trying to get a boy I could call Dwight, that was, before the Republicans claimed that name.

Then his oldest son—Woodrow Wilson Wilson—came home in a government box marked U. S. A. F. DO NOT OPEN. Before anybody could say anything, Dwight was at the miners' hospital having a doctor tie that tributary that leads to somewhere.

With his juices waylaid, Dwight didn't act natural. When he laughed, it was like graves had been pried open and he was dry-spitting at the dust. He became tender and wheezy. He started touching people, something he never did in his right body. Just reaching out and rubbing the dandruff from arms, stroking the cow-licks of children, or the black crown of my bald head as we made it home from the mines.

The last card fell when Myrnaloy Jackson let it out on her new telephone that Dwight was doing things with his twelve-year-old daughter. I won't know or believe it till we all drop our pants in that city four-squared, but the new telephone wires twanged it out loud as gospel.

Nadine, who by then had learned to sign her name, crawled to Granny Bostic's new trailer and claimed that she had caught Dwight into an Old Testament act. She wanted her to write out a warrant, but Granny was no J. P. Granny just got on her telephone and whispered to Myrnaloy Jackson Nadine's side of the story.

When Nadine left for Detroit with her six that was left at home, almost everybody shook their church heads in agreement. Dwight was coughing up now from the black lungs, and most people got shed of him, even on hair-cutting days. They went to Bascom Fincher and paid out cash money for a quick hair cut.

Dwight had already dropped out of the mines, and I didn't see him much after that. I no longer required the shears and I was busy insulating my house and what time I had for visiting I spent on the sheetrock. And traffic was getting dangerous since the State widened the road and put a white streak down the middle. People started resting up in their trailers on week-ends, watching T.V. and doing what talking they needed on the party line.

The bank at Dismal took Dwight's land back. He set up house-keeping in Pearl Ratliff's abandoned store that used to have a juke-box. Most people wouldn't have rented out to Dwight, but Pearl was deaf and didn't require a telephone.

So Dwight and the two dogs he had left moved into the shack that bore the name: MEET ME AT PEARL'S PLACE. I reckon he made his own home-brew, for what little cash he gleaned from the Union couldn't have quenched the thirst he'd worked up in forty years of Friday nights. He didn't apply for the government Give-away, though. I don't know how he got his bread stuff.

I guess the hunger finally got to him, for he took down Pearl's sign and tacked him up a new one: H.A.i.r. c.u.t.s. $1.00 C.r.e.W. c.u.t.s. $1.05.

But he didn't draw trade. He let himself go, sitting just behind the opened door at Pearl's Place so he could see the cars pass on the State Highway. You could glimpse him enough to see he was break-ing fast. His suspenders dangled like tired lassos from his shrunken sides and his orange hair grew in bushy wings, giving his lean face the look of a man that was letting a nightmare ride him in broad daylight.

I threw up my hand and blew my horn to him when I passed by, but he never acknowledged it by lifting up his hand.

He started shutting his door in daylight, and people put it out over the party line that he looked like the wild man of Borneo, that his hair was so long he could sit on it. When I'd pick up my phone and hear Lane Tee Baldwin or Myrnaloy Jackson chattering about Dwight being from Borneo, I'd give their ears a Hardshell singeing. Took my phone out last year after I quit the mines and went on pension on account of my kidneys burned my sides.

Dwight finally marked through his prices and wrote "f.r.e.e.," but only a stray Republican or two came, when they were home from Detroit to squirrel hunt, and they went away pining that you don't get nothing free no more, and swearing it was all that Catho-lic Kennedy's fault.

Then the door closed for good and something funny happened. Dwight's two hounds that lapped the State Highway for ice cream labels appeared bald as a baby's ass. It was a sight—them dogs lop-ing up and down the sides of the road without so much as a hair, not even on their tails. But it gave the school children something to throw rocks at.

When I heard about it, I thought the dogs had mange and that Dwight had shaved the hair to rub some burnt motor oil on them for their cure. But when I was going to get my government rice and cheese on Giveaway Day, I saw them and their hide was healthy. They looked like two overgrown moles Kennedy's men had brought back from the skies. On my way back from Dismal, I stopped at Dwight's to ask him did he know his hounds were bald. There was a notebook page on the door telling readers he was closed to line a bee tree. It was November—too late for bees—but I came on home before my kidneys burned a hole through my Air-Flo seat cushion.

Four days later, Sheriff Colley broke the lock on Pearl's Place to serve Dwight a warrant of peace disturbance that Myrnaloy Jackson took out on him because those two bald dogs gave her the migraines when they sniffed up to her trailer door and looked her in the eye.

Sheriff Colley put it out that Dwight had been dead longer than he should have been, for he had already turned. They said he had shaved off his bushy red burnsides, his eyebrows that look like John L.'s, and his full head of hair that had been so shimmery when the sun hit it right. Colley said Pearl's Place was wall-to-wall gray and orange hair. Nobody said what he died of, just that his face had blued all out of recognition. Young Colley, I heard it gave him an ulcer which helped to get him defeated in 1964 when he bad-mouthed Lyndon and Lady Bird.

The County Welfare buried Dwight, putting chemistry in his veins, which he never wanted. But that sorry bunch is all Republicans now, and they wouldn't let his casket be opened. They wouldn't want us old Straight Democrats congregating to politic, what with John Fitzgerald just shot and that Nixon beginning to walk cob-assed over the T.V.s again.

I went to the funeral home to put my hand on his casket. His family didn't come. Myrnaloy Jackson, her nose up everybody's ass, even long distance, reported that Nadine and the daughters couldn't take off from their work making beds in a Detroit motel, and the boys were mostly overseas fighting communism.

It was a sad funeral, if you could call it by that name. A few old Straight-Ticket Democrats passed by the closed remains and recollected how clever Dwight had been with his liquor and his shears.

"If he had a swaller on him, half of it was yourn," Abe Lockhart said, pointing a trembly finger directly at me, but meaning any man's face.

"He never ast what his country could do for him," Cowan Breeding said. Cowan beat his rubber-tipped chrome cane on the grass of the funeral home floor, greener than God ever could manufacture it.

"Who would a thought they'd a got him and Kennedy?" Gaylord Newberry wondered.

"Well, you git what ye pay for nowadays," Cowan said, reckoning, I guess, that Gaylord was meaning the coffin without a spray of plastic roses.

"Hit's them damn Republicans," Old Man Gaylord figured.

"Why didn't his people come?" Abe asked.

"All drawing checks up in Detroit. Ain't no Aunts left, and his last Uncle died off up somewhere in Ohio," I reminded him.

"You would a thought Granny Wilson would come," Old Man Newberry said.

Dwight's money had been dead for twenty years, but Old Man Newberry maybe hadn't heard.

We helped each other by the elbows up the steps and out of the main parlor to our trucks, shaking our heads yes to Old Man Newberry's mumbles: "Hit's the Republicans. Them goddamn blackguard Republicans."

I would have stopped at the new A. B. C. store in Dismal, but my kidneys were burning a hole through my sides. And them drinking times have long passed on, anyway.

Jean Thompson / Urbana, Illinois

BIRDS IN AIR

from *fiction international,* Volume 2, Number 3: 1974
Canton, New York
Editor: Joe David Bellamy

"That part of the country is, within itself, as unpoetical as any spot of the earth; but seeing it ... aroused feelings in me which were certainly poetry." —Abraham Lincoln

AN ELECTRIC fan sits on the refrigerator; it hums, rotates, billows the edge of the tablecloth. Only when it blows directly on me does it cut the heat from the stove and the heat of the day. Eat some more, says Grandma.

On her flowered tablecloth are cold ham, pickles, potato salad, tomatoes, olives, biscuits, honey, white peaches, corn, cherry pie. It is full summer and we live off the fat of the land.

You have some of the country gravy, down South they call it Mississippi butter, says Grandma.

It is thick white stuff with brown crusty bits in it. No one likes it.

It tastes bad, says my younger brother.

Hush, says my mother.

After dinner we sit, hot and overfed, in the front room. The furniture is dark wood with hard carved edges. The lamps are massive, pink-shaded, with clustered roses or shepherdesses at the base. I look through the white net curtains at the dusty trees, the leaves hanging down like tongues.

Why don't you kids do something, says my father.

It is hard to connect my father with my grandmother's old photographs. A boy in a sailor suit and Buster Brown haircut; odd, dramatic lighting.

Why don't you go to the dime store, says my father.

Where they sell wallets with little Mexican boys stamped on the leather, Souvenir of Spencer County, Ind., sneezing powder, string ties, china ashtrays consisting of a lady on a toilet, Cool Your Hot

Butt in My Old Tub.

We've been there before, says my older brother.

You could go to the Lincoln Village, my father says.

Lincoln didn't live in the reconstructed cabins, with the spinning wheels and plaques and corncob pipes and buckeyes for sale. It was north of here somewhere.

We've been there before too, says my younger brother.

Grandma's quilts are all made by hand, pieced out of cotton and linen, red stars and checks, small faded rows of daisies, candy stripes. Sewn together with good white thread, the edges bound and scalloped. In the back bedroom, shades drawn against the afternoon sun, I run my fingers over their taut surfaces and whisper the names to myself: Wreath of Grapes, Drunkard's Path, Mexican Rose, Birds in Air.

Grandma comes to the door in her long cotton slip. Too hot to sleep, she says. Too hot to do anything.

She sits next to me on the bed. Looking at these old quilts? I nod. Which one you like best?

My hand hesitates, reaches out to the Birds in Air. A pattern of triangles, like a thousand small wings, which cross and recross until they seem to lift from the cloth.

You can have it, she says, nodding. Her glasses slip and show a red nick in the skin on each side of her nose.

I think of manners, of the way my mother responds to gifts. Oh no, I *couldn't*—

I mean to will it to you, she says. I won't forget. She pats my shoulder with her brittle hand and leaves the room.

Every year there is the visit to the cemetery. Grandma sits in the front seat in her good blue dress. We drive east along the weedy road from town, slowly, my father pointing.

Here's where Lincoln might have played as a boy, he says.

There's his swing set, says my older brother.

Gray sheds and ponds and shade. The limestone cliffs along the river, chalked over with the names of high schools. Dirt roads that disappear into the green distance. I try to imagine Lincoln here. I try to imagine what was different.

We reach the brick pillars of the cemetery gates. We help Grandma from the car and her light skirt floats in the breeze.

I have no grief. I do not remember my grandfather. The sun is hot on the red clover and dandelion puffs. We stand with her a moment, not speaking. Her name is already on the stone beside his, and the date of her birth. Then the numbers 19, waiting to be rounded into four digits. On my fingers I reckon the number of years she can live without spoiling the stone. I promise myself I will never do that, never fix the limits of my life.

After a while we leave her standing there and walk on the long grass between the graves, looking for odd stones, the finger pointing upward marked Gone to Rest, the scrolls and cherubs above the infant graves. The stones are crumbling and we have a contest to find the oldest one. My mother wins with 1820. In the far corner of the lot my brothers start a game of chase.

On the way back we drive through town, the big car strange on the quiet street, the smell of its vinyl seat in our nostrils. Past the feed store and the grocery. There are roofs built out from the stores over the sidewalks, held up by poles buckling into the street. They make a narrow shade on the baked white cement. Peeling boards and black windows, the painted advertisement for a bank sinking into a brick wall.

Really, whispers my older brother, how can people stand to live here?

I frown, tell him to hush. My father is speaking.

That's the jail, he says. I remember once in a while they used to have a drunk in there and we'd sneak up to the window and try to see him. And here's where great-aunt Norma lived before she moved to Evansville. I used to work in her garden and she paid me ten cents an hour.

My older brother looks straight ahead, but I know he is talking to me: The story that he walked ten miles because he overcharged a customer five cents, is, of course, apocryphal. There are many places where Dad actually spent the night, or some historical incident occurred, but we must separate fact from legend. I mean, I'd hate to see it all get commercialized.

In the front seat my mother, father, grandmother do not move. Perhaps they have not heard. Again I try to imagine, back a hundred and fifty years when the streets were dirt, the paint fresh. Lincoln, on a hot day such as this, barefoot, riding a mule in from the back woods, thinking this a fine place, a big place, the county seat.... Now the town is full of old people. Men in overalls, with chapped pink faces, old women living in a fragile world of cats and nicked china and waterstained rugs. The whole back page of the newspaper is for obituaries. Grandma reads them carefully.

The car pulls up in front of the house. I think for dinner we'll finish off the rest of the ham, says Grandma. And maybe some beans, fresh snap beans.

Help your Grandma do the dishes, my father says to me.   I don't need any help, my grandmother says, go sit down and watch television.   No need for you to do them all yourself.   You just sit down and let me do them.   Finally I take a dish towel from the cupboard and start drying. My grandmother's hands are soft from the water, like old gum erasers, and shreds of vegetables stick under her fingernails. Her hands move in and out of the thin film of soap on the surface of the water, rinsing the bright sharp prongs of the forks. She has one bad eye, with a stripe of blood crossing the iris and the black pupil always large and vacant. The kitchen light is bug-yellow and glaring and it makes the eye water. I see a thick milky tear stream down her face and tremble on her chin.

Grandma looks up, wipes the tear away with a fierce brush of her sleeve. Now you go, she says, and pushes me away from the sink. Go watch television.

Instead I go to the back bedroom, away from the others. Here there is a picture viewer, a stereoscope, with a wire holder for the cards and a wooden hood that fits over your nose and smells of old hair. The cards are heavy and chipped around the edges. Views of Niagara Falls, Roman ruins, the Grand Canyon. The story cards are better, girls in pinafores eloping with country swains, ladies in draperies singing Only a Bird in a Gilded Cage. The two flat identical pictures on the card make one with depth and shape. Old jokes, old songs; for a moment they are almost real.

We take Grandma to see her friends. Old ladies who live in crumbling houses, as if the ivy is pulling them softly back to earth and decay. They have names like Dolly, Anna, Pearl. Bunch of old women who wear copper bracelets to keep arthritis away, says my mother under her breath. She does not enjoy these visits.

When Dolly and Anna sit inside they too use electric fans. But when they sit on the front porch they wave paper and stick fans with pictures of the American Eagle and Miss Liberty. I think Dolly's son died in the Great War because there are so many pictures of him in uniform.

They are so old, in the middle of a sentence they drift and dream. Even Grandma knows we can't stay long to talk. They wear shapeless lavender print dresses that remind me of the patches in the quilts. Their houses are full of doilies and rugs made of braided bread wrappers. Anna has saved every greeting card anyone ever sent her in the top drawer of her walnut dresser. Mistletoe and violets, angels, risen Christs For the Coming Year and In Sympathy, she spreads for our inspection, and smiles.

How pretty. Yes we will. You take care of yourselves. Good-bye Anna. Good-bye Dolly.

Back in the car my mother exhales, as if she has held her breath the whole time.

Now ain't that pitiful, says Grandma. Poor Dolly can't hardly hear. Don't walk so good either. And she's two years younger than me.

We stop for gas at Elnoe's. Elnoe, who is maybe a man or maybe a woman, I'm never sure, immense arms and chest, a sleeveless shirt and jeans, red cheeks, cropped gray hair. How you all, says Elnoe, grinning, showing two gold teeth. Elnoe's white frame house is just behind the gas pumps. The original second story now rests on the ground, a memory of the river's rising. Back home Grandma has a scrapbook of newspaper clippings about the Great Flood of nineteen thirty-something.

There are picnics on the river. From the high bluff we throw stones; they fall into the muddy edges and the great curve of shining water is unchanged. A fast-moving barge passes, blows its horn, and is gone.

My father squats beside my younger brother and his shoes skid pebbles along the riverbank.

Do you know what that is across the river?

The boy squirms at my father's hand on his shoulder. Kentucky.

That's right. Look, says my father, and his arm reaches out to the water and the haze and the fields on the other shore. Pioneers.

Indians.

Uh huh, says my brother, and he runs off to look for snakeskins and dead fish.

The sun sets and the light on the river turns opal, glossy. Grandma locks her thin arms around her knees and says to me your hair is so pretty it's like mine when I was a girl. It was my father's pride and joy, whenever company came he'd say Della show them how you can sit on your hair. And he sent off for a bottle of lotion that cost a dollar to make my hair shine.

She laughs, pats her short tight curls. I bet you can't imagine me with long hair.

I laugh and do not answer. Darkness spreads from the trees and the crickets surround us. We gather the silverware, waxed paper, pop bottles, chunks of soaked driftwood my brothers carry up from the beach. You know you could take that quilt with you when you go, whispers Grandma. I won't tell nobody.

No, I say, confused, they'd find out. . . .

I suppose, says Grandma.

You know what I'd like to do while we're here, says my father, is start a family tree.

My mother is brushing crumbs from the breakfast table. What for, she says. You think you'll find royalty?

More likely find we're all descended from John Wilkes Booth, says my older brother.

We visit Mrs. Crawford. Grandma says she knows a lot about things like that. Her parlor is dim, with old pictures hung too high on the walls. I sit in a scratchy armchair. The room smells of dust, attics, and it makes me sleepy. The tables are piled with parchment charts hand-lettered in permanent black ink. Birth certificates. The bound volumes of the County Historical Society, round-cornered books with thin, crackling pages.

Of course I knew your folks, says Mrs. Crawford. Walter's cousin George married my sister-in-law. . . . The silver eyepieces of her spectacles glint in the darkened room. The parchment scrapes as she unrolls it. She turns on a lamp. Now, she says, do you know when your grandfather was born? My father shakes his head. Together they bend over the table and their fingers trace the lines, lists, old records.

I let my eyes close. In the warm darkness their voices are small and far away.

Maybe it would be easier, Mrs. Crawford is saying, to start from the other end. Here was a settler in Virginia. If you could follow his descendants . . . .

My father takes notes on what Mrs. Crawford says, and puts them in his billfold. They will stay there until the creases of the paper grow worn and soiled. Then he will throw them away.

My grandmother still keeps a desk drawer full of toys for us. Coloring books, rubber balls, airplanes made of balsa wood, pennies in tiny glass jugs. Only my youngest brother plays with them now. It is afternoon and I am watching TV, an old *I Love Lucy* show. The screen is gauzy and flickering in the strong light from outdoors.

Grandma comes to the door and stands with her hands on her hips. She asks me if I want some pop: I got Orange Crush, Cream Soda, Root Beer. I say no thank you. Some lemonade? She'd be glad to make it. No, I'm not really thirsty.

I tell you what, says Grandma. I'm going to take you down to Lotus's shop, buy you a dress. Maybe a pretty blouse, would you like that?

I see my mother's warning face. Sure, I say.

So we walk downtown. The heat from the sidewalk wraps itself around my legs. Now you don't worry about how much things cost, says Grandma. You get anything you like.

The windows of Lotus's shop are streaked with old whitewash. A dozen shapeless, limp dresses hang on the racks. They remind me of a church rummage sale.

Lotus has a thin rouged face and lacquered hair. She pulls a stack of blouses from a shelf—can you take an eight, honey?—and watches as I look through them. They are strange prints, like kitchen wallpaper. Patterns of teakettles, vegetables, geraniums. My hands move slower as I reach the end of the pile. I think I have looked at everything in the store. I hold up the last blouse. Can I have this one?, I ask my grandmother. Can I wear it home?

The branches of trees meet overhead. The dirt road is a tunnel, scarcely wide enough for the car. You would not drive in these hills at night.

They call this Owl Town because only the owls live here, says Grandma.

Really?, asks my younger brother.

People live here too but you won't see them, says my father.

People who will never be on anyone's census or tax roll.

Children who would not know what to say to us if we met them, for they have never seen anyone outside their own family.

The air conditioning chills the back of my neck. We must keep the windows shut. I squint through the tinted glass and try to penetrate the solid green around us. We are going too fast. At the top of a hill I see a path, a fence. I look back and they are gone, the leaves covering them like water closes over a stone. We must start back. It is almost time for dinner.

The bits of thread and cloth come together into blocks, the blocks form patterns. It is hard to tell where the pattern begins and ends, for it crosses and recrosses. My grandmother dies and the telephone company buys her house. But this is not the end. She has left me the quilt. Her fingers moved along its border as mine do now, locking the stitches in place; it cannot be torn, not ever, it has been made too well.

Perhaps it ends when we are ready to leave. Everyone says goodbye to her at least twice, too loudly. My father starts the car. And she comes running after us with her apron over her face. The house is full of gas, she says, pulling at my father's arm. I smell it everywhere. He goes inside with her and the rest of us wait.

My father comes out alone and gets behind the wheel. It was nothing, he says, nothing at all. The car pulls away and although I can't see her at the window, I turn around and wave.

Ruskin Bond / Mussoorie, India
BUS STOP, PIPALNAGAR

from *The New Renaissance*, Volume 3, Number 1: 1977
Arlington, Massachusetts
Editor: Louise T. Reynolds

Some of the moving forces of our lives are meant to touch us briefly and then go their way.

I

MY balcony was my window on the world.

The room itself had only one window, a square hole in the wall crossed by two iron bars. The view from it was rather restricted. If I craned my neck sideways, and put my nose to the bars, I could see the end of the building. Below was a narrow courtyard where children played. Across the courtyard, on a level with my room, were three separate windows, belonging to three separate rooms, each window barred in the same way, with iron bars. During the day it was difficult to see into these rooms. The harsh, cruel sunlight filled the courtyard, making the windows patches of darkness.

My room was very small. I had paced about in it so often that I knew its exact measurements. My foot, from heel to toe, was eleven inches long. That made the room just over fifteen feet in length; for, when I measured the last foot, my toes turned up against the wall. It wasn't more than eight feet broad which meant that two people were the most it could comfortably accommodate. I was the only tenant but at times I had put up at least three friends— two on the floor, two on the bed. The plaster had been peeling off the walls and in addition the greasy stains and patches were difficult to hide, though I covered the worst ones with pictures cut out from magazines—Waheeda, the Indian actress, successfully blotted out one big patch and a recent Mr. Universe displayed his muscles from the opposite wall. The biggest stain was all but concealed by a calendar which showed Ganesh, the elephant-headed god, whose blessings were vital to all good beginnings.

My belongings were few. A shelf on the wall supported an untidy pile of paperbacks, and a small table in one corner of the room supported the solid weight of my rejected manuscripts and an ancient typewriter which I had obtained on hire.

I was eighteen years old and a writer.

Such a combination would be disastrous enough anywhere but in India it was doubly so; for there were not many papers to write for and payments were small. In addition, I was very inexperienced and though what I wrote came from the heart, only a fraction touched the hearts of editors. Nevertheless, I persevered and was able to earn about a hundred rupees a month, barely enough to keep body, soul and typewriter together. There wasn't much else I could do. Without that passport to a job—a University degree—I had no alternative but to accept the classification of "self-employed"—which was impressive as it included doctors, lawyers, property dealers, and grain merchants, most of whom earned well over a thousand a month.

"Haven't you realized that India is bursting with young people trying to pass exams?" asked a journalist friend. "It's a desperate matter, this race for academic qualifications. Everyone wants to pass his exam the easy way, without reading too many books or attending more than half a dozen lectures. That's where a smart fellow like you comes in! Why should students wade through five volumes of political history when they can buy a few 'model-answer' papers at any bookstall? They are helpful, these guess-papers. You can write them quickly and flood the market. They'll sell like hot cakes!"

"Who eats hot cakes here?"

"Well, then, hot chappaties."

"I'll think about it," I said; but the idea repelled me. If I was going to misguide students, I would rather do it by writing second-rate detective stories than by providing them with ready-made Answer Papers. Besides, I thought it would bore me.

II

The string of my cot needed tightening. The dip in the middle of the bed was so bad that I woke up in the mornings with a stiff back. But I was hopeless at tightening bed-strings and would have to wait until one of the boys from the tea shop paid me a visit. I was too long for the cot, anyway, and if my feet didn't stick out at one end, my head lolled over the other.

Under the cot was my tin trunk. Apart from my clothes, it contained notebooks, diaries, photographs, scrapbooks, and other odds and ends that form a part of a writer's existence.

I did not live entirely alone. During cold or rainy weather, the boys from the tea-shop, who normally slept on the pavement, crowded into the room. Apart from them, there were lizards on the walls and ceilings—friends, these—and a large rat—definitely an enemy—who got in and out of the window and who sometimes carried away manuscripts and clothing.

June nights were the most uncomfortable. Mosquitoes emerged from all the ditches, gullies and ponds, to swarm over Pipalnagar. Bugs, finding it uncomfortable inside the woodwork of the cot, scrambled out at night and found their way under the sheet. The lizards wandered listlessly over the walls, impatient for the monsoon rains, when they would be able to feast off thousands of insects.

Everyone in Pipalnagar was waiting for the cool, quenching relief of the monsoon.

III

I woke every morning at five as soon as the first bus moved out of the shed, situated only twenty or thirty yards down the road. I dressed, went down to the tea-shop for a glass of hot tea and some buttered toast, and then visited Deep Chand, the barber, in his shop.

At 18, I shaved about three times a week. Sometimes I shaved myself. But often, when I felt lazy, Deep Chand shaved me, at the special concessional rate of two annas.

"Give my head a good massage, Deep Chand," I said "My brain is not functioning these days. In my latest story there are three murders but it is boring just the same."

"You must write a good book," and Deep Chand, beginning the ritual of the head massage, his fingers squeezing my temples and tugging at my hair-roots. "Then you can make some money and clear out of Pipalnagar. Delhi is the place to go! Why, I know a man who arrived in Delhi in 1947 with nothing but the clothes he wore and a few rupees. He began by selling thirsty travellers glasses of cold water at the railway-station; then he opened a small tea-shop; now he has two big restaurants and lives in a house as large as the Prime Minister's!"

Nobody intended living in Pipalnagar for ever. Delhi was the city most aspired to but as it was two-hundred miles away, few could afford to travel there.

Deep chand would have shifted his trade to another town if he had had the capital. In Pipalnagar his main customers were small shopkeepers, factory workers and labourers from the railway station. "Here I can charge only six annas for a hair-cut," he lamented. "In Delhi I could charge a rupee!"

IV

I was walking in the wheat fields beyond the railway tracks when I noticed a boy lying across the footpath, his head and shoulders hidden by the wheat. I walked faster, and when I came near I saw that the boy's legs were twitching. He seemed to be having some kind of fit. The boy's face was white, his legs kept moving, and his hands fluttered restlessly amongst the wheat-stalks.

"What's the matter?" I said, kneeling down beside him; but he was still unconscious.

I ran down the path to a Persian well, and dipping the end of my shirt in a shallow trough of water, soaked it well before returning to the boy. As I sponged his face, the twitching ceased, and though he still breathed heavily, his face was calm and his hands still. He opened his eyes and stared at me, but he didn't really see me.

"You have bitten your tongue," I said, wiping a little blood from the corner of his mouth. "Don't worry. I'll stay here with you until you are all right."

The boy raised himself; and, resting his chin on his knees, he passed his arms around his drawn-up legs.

"I'm all right now," he said.

"What happened?" I asked, sitting down beside him.

"Oh, it is nothing, it often happens. I don't know why. I cannot control it."

"Have you been to a doctor?"

"Yes. When the fits first started, I went to the hospital. They gave me some pills which I had to take every day. But the pills made me so tired and sleepy that I couldn't work properly. So I stopped taking them. Now this happens once or twice a week. What does it matter? I'm all right when it's over, and I do not feel anything when it happens."

He got to his feet, dusting his clothes and smiling at me. He was a slim boy, long-limbed and bony. There was a little fluff on his cheeks and the promise of a moustache. He told me his name was Suraj, that he went to a night school in the city, and that he hoped to finish his High School exams in a few months time. He was studying hard, he said, and if he passed he hoped to get a scholarship to a good college. If he failed, there was only the prospect of continuing in Pipalnagar.

I noticed a small tray of merchandise lying on the ground. It contained combs and buttons and little bottles of perfume. The tray was made to hang at Suraj's waist, supported by straps that went around his shoulders. All day he walked about Pipalnagar, sometimes covering ten or fifteen miles a day, selling odds and ends to people at their houses. He averaged about two rupees a day, which was enough for his food and other necessities; he managed to save about ten rupees a month for his school fees. He ate irregularly at little tea-shops, at the stalls near the bus stop, or under the shady jamun and mango trees. When the jamun fruit was ripe, he would sit in a tree, sucking the sour fruit until his lips were stained purple. There was a small, nagging fear that he might get a fit while sitting in the tree and fall off; but the temptation to eat jamuns was greater than his fear.

All this he told me while we walked through the fields towards the bazaar.

"Where do you live?" I asked. "I'll walk home with you."

"I don't live anywhere," said Suraj. "My home is not in Pipalnagar. Sometimes I sleep at the temple or at the railway station. In the summer months I sleep on the grass of the municipal park."

"Well, wherever it is you stay, let me come with you."

We walked together into the town and parted near the bus stop. I returned to my room, and tried to do some writing while Suraj went into the bazaar to try selling his wares. We had agreed to meet each other again. I realised that Suraj was an epileptic, but there was nothing unusual about his being an orphan and a refugee. I liked his positive attitude to life: most people in Pipalnagar were resigned to their circumstances, but he was ambitious. I also liked his gentleness, his quiet voice, and the smile that flickered across his face regardless of whether he was sad or happy.

V

The temperature had touched 110 Fahrenheit, and the small streets of Pipalnagar were empty. To walk barefoot on the scorching pavements was possible only for the labourers whose feet had developed several hard layers of protective skin; and now even these hardy men lay stretched out in the shade provided by trees and buildings.

I hadn't written anything in two weeks, and though one or two small payments were due from a Delhi newspaper, I could think of no substantial amount that was likely to come my way in the near future. I decided that I would dash off a couple of articles that same night, and post them the following morning.

Having made this comforting decision, I lay down on the floor in preference to the cot. I liked the touch of things: the touch of a cool floor on a hot day; the touch of the earth—soft, grassy; grass was good, especially dew-drenched grass. Wet earth, too, was soft, sensuous and smelt nice; splashing through puddles and streams. . . . I slept, and dreamt of a cool clear stream in a forest glade, where I bathed in gay abandon. A little further downstream was another bather. I hailed him, expecting to see Suraj but when the bather turned I found that it was my landlord's pot-bellied rent-collector, holding an accounts ledger in his hands. This woke me up, and for the remainder of the day I worked feverishly at my articles.

Next morning, when I opened the door, I found Suraj asleep at the top of the steps. His tray lay at the bottom of the steps. He woke up as soon as I touched his shoulder.

"Have you been sleeping here all night?" I asked. "Why didn't you come in?"

"It was very late," said Suraj. "I didn't want to disturb you."

"Someone could have stolen your things while you were asleep."

"Oh, I sleep quite lightly. Besides, I have nothing of great value. But I came here to ask you a favour."

"You need money?"

He laughed. "Do all your friends mean money when they ask for favours? No, I want you to take your meal with me tonight."

"But where? You have no place of your own, and it would be too expensive in a restaurant."

"In your room," said Suraj. "I shall bring the meat and vegetables and cook them here. Do you have a cooker?"

"I think so," I said, scratching my head in some perplexity. "I will have to look for it."

"I'll come at seven," said Suraj, turning to go. "Don't worry, I know how to cook!"

Suraj brought a chicken for dinner—a luxury, one to be indulged in only two or three times a year. He had bought the bird for seven rupees, which was cheap. We spiced it, and roasted it on a spittle.

"I wish we could do this more often," I said, as I dug my teeth into the soft flesh of a second leg.

"We could do it at least once a month if we worked hard," said Suraj.

"You know how to work. You work from morning to evening, and then you work again."

"But you are a writer. That is different. You have to wait for the right moment."

I laughed. "Moods and moments are for geniuses. No, it's really a matter of working hard, and I'm just plain lazy, to tell the truth."

"Perhaps you are writing the wrong things."

"Perhaps. I wish I could do something else. Even if I repaired bicycle tyres, I'd make more money!"

"Then why don't you repair bicycle tyres?"

"Oh, I would rather be a bad writer than a good repairer of cycle-tyres." I brightened up. "I could go into business, though. Do you know, I once owned a vegetable stall."

"Wonderful! When was that?"

"A couple of months ago. But it failed after two days."

"Then you are not good at business. Let us think of something else."

"I can tell fortunes with cards."

"There are already too many fortune-tellers in Pipalnagar."

"Then we won't talk of fortunes. And you must sleep here to-night. It is better than sleeping on the roadside."

VI

At noon, when the shadows shifted and crossed the road, a band of children rushed down the empty street, shouting and waving their satchels. They had been at their desks from early morning, and now, despite the hot sun, they would have their fling while their elders slept on string charpoys beneath leafy neem trees.

On the soft sand near the river-bed, boys wrestled or played leap-frog. At alley-corners, where tall buildings shaded narrow passages, the favourite game was *gulli-danda*. The *gulli*—a small piece of wood, about four inches long, sharpened to a point at each end— is struck with the *danda*, a short, stout stick. A player is allowed three hits, and his score is the distance, in *danda* lengths, he hits the *gulli*. Boys who were experts at the game sent the *gulli* flying far down the road—sometimes into a shop or through a window-pane, which resulted in confusion, loud invective, and a dash for cover.

A game for both children and young men was *Kabbadi*. This is a game that calls for good breath control and much agility. It is also known, in different parts of India, as *hootoo-too*, *kho-kho*, and *atyapatya*. Ramu, Deep Chand's younger brother, excelled at this game. He was the Pipalnagar *Kabbadi* champion.

The game is played by two teams, consisting of eight or nine members each, who face each other across a dividing line. Each side in turn sends out one of its players into the opponent's area. This person has to keep on saying "Kabbadi kabbadi" very fast and without taking a second breath. If he returns to his side after touching an opponent, that opponent is "dead" and out of the game. If, however, he is caught and cannot struggle back to his side while still holding his breath, he is "dead".

Ramu, who was also a good wrestler, knew all the Kabbadiholds, and was particularly good at capturing opponents. He had vitality and confidence, rare things in Pipalnagar. He wanted to go into the Army after finishing school, a happy choice I thought.

VII

Suraj did not know if his parents were dead or alive. He had literally lost them when he was six. His father had been a farmer, a dark unfathomable man who spoke little, thought perhaps even less, and was vaguely aware he had a son—a weak boy given to introspection and dawdling at the river-bank when he should have been helping in the fields.

Suraj's mother had been a subdued, silent woman, frail and consumptive. Her husband seemed to expect that she would not live long; but Suraj did not know if she was living or dead. He had lost his parents at Amritsar railway-station in the days of the Partition, when trains coming across the border from Pakistan disgorged themselves of thousands of refugees or pulled into the station half-empty, drenched with blood and littered with corpses.

Suraj and his parents were lucky to escape one of these massacres. Had they travelled on an earlier train (which they had tried desperately to catch), they might have been killed. Suraj was clinging to his mother's sari while she tried to keep up with her husband, who was elbowing his way through the frightened, bewildered throng of refugees. Suraj collided with a burly Sikh and lost his grip on the sari. The Sikh had a long curved sword at his waist, and Suraj stared up at him in awe and fascination, at the man's long hair, which had fallen loose, at his wild black beard, and at the blood-stains on his white shirt. The Sikh pushed him aside and when Suraj looked round for his mother she was not to be seen. She was hidden from him by a mass of restless bodies, all pushing in different directions. He could hear her calling his name and he tried to force his way through the crowd, in the direction of her voice, but he was carried the other way.

At night, when the platform was empty, he was still searching for his mother. Eventually the police came and took him away. They looked for his parents but without success, and finally they sent him to a home for orphans. Many children lost their parents at about the same time.

Suraj stayed at the orphanage for two years and when he was eight and felt himself a man, he ran away. He worked for some time as a helper in a tea-shop; but when he started having epileptic fits the shopkeeper asked him to leave, and the boy found himself on the streets, begging for a living. He begged for a year, moving from one town to the next, and ending up finally at Pipalnagar. By then he was twelve and really too old to beg; but he had saved some money, and with it he bought a small stock of combs, buttons, cheap perfumes and bangles, and converting himself into a mobile shop, went from door to door selling his wares.

Pipalnagar is a small town, and there was no house which Suraj hadn't visited. Everyone knew him; some had offered him food and drink; and the children liked him because he often played on a small flute when he went on his rounds.

VIII

211

Suraj came to see me quite often, and, when he stayed late, he slept in my room, curling up on the floor and sleeping fitfully. He would always leave early in the morning before I could get him anything to eat.

"Should I go to Delhi, Suraj?" I asked him one morning.

"Why not? In Delhi, there are many ways of making money."

"And spending it, too. Why don't you come with me?"

"After my exams, perhaps. Not now."

"Well, I can wait. I don't want to live alone in a big city."

"In the meantime, write your book."

"All right, I will try."

We decided we would try to save a little money from Suraj's earnings and my own occasional payments from newspapers and magazines. Even if we were to give Delhi only a few days trial, we would need money to live on. We managed to put away twenty rupees one week, but withdrew it the next when a friend, Pitamber, asked for a loan to repair his cycle-rickshaw. He returned the money in three instalments but we could not save any of it. Pitamber and Deep Chand also had plans for going to Delhi. Pitamber wanted to own his own scooter-rickshaw; Deep Chand dreamt of a swank barber-shop in the capital.

One day Suraj and I hired bicycles and rode out of Pipalnagar. It was a hot, sunning morning, and we were perspiring after we had gone two miles; but a fresh wind sprang up suddenly, and we could smell the rain in the air though there were no clouds to be seen.

"Let us go where there are no people at all," said Suraj. "I am a little tired of people. I see too many of them all day."

We got down from our cycles, and pushing them off the road, took a path through a paddy field, and then a path through a field of young maize, and in the distance we saw a tree, a crooked tree, growing beside a well. I do not even today know the name of that tree. I had never seen its kind before. It had a crooked trunk, crooked branches, and it was clothed in thick, broad crooked leaves, like the leaves on which food is served in bazaars.

In the trunk of the tree was a large hole, and when I set my cycle down with a crash, two green parrots flew out of the hole, and went dipping and swerving across the fields.

There was grass around the well, cropped short by grazing cattle, so we sat in the shade of the crooked tree, and Suraj untied the red

cloth in which he had brought our food. We ate our bread and vegetable curry, and meanwhile the parrots returned to the tree.

"Let us come here every week," said Suraj, stretching himself
out on the grass. It was a drowsy day, the air humid, and he soon
fell asleep. I, too, stretched myself out and closed my eyes, but I
did not sleep; I was aware of different sensations. I heard a cricket
singing in the tree; the cooing of pigeons which lived in the walls
of the old well; the soft breathing of Suraj; a rustling in the leaves
of the tree; the distant drone of bees. I smelt the grass, and the old
bricks around the well, and the promise of rain.

When I opened my eyes, I saw dark clouds on the horizon. Suraj
was still sleeping, his arms thrown across his face to keep the glare
out of his eyes. As I was thirsty, I went to the well, and putting
my shoulders to it, turned the wheel, very slowly, walking around
the well four times, while cool clean water gushed out over the
stones and along the channel to the fields. I drank from one of the
trays, and the water tasted sweet: the deeper the wells, the sweeter
the water.

Suraj was sitting up now, looking at the sky.

"It's going to rain," he said.

We pushed our cycles back to the main road and began riding
homewards. We were a mile out of Pipalnagar when it began to
rain. A lashing wind swept the rain across our faces, but we exulted
in it and sang at the tops of our voices until we reached the bus
stop. Leaving the cycles at the hire-shop, we ran up the ricketty,
swaying steps to my room.

In the evening, as the bazaar was lighting up, the rain stopped.
We went to sleep quite early; but at midnight I was woken by the
moon shining full in my face—a full moon, shedding its light all
over Pipalnagar, peeping and prying into every home, washing the
empty streets, silvering the corrugated tin roofs.

IX

The lizards hung listlessly on the walls and ceilings, waiting for
the monsoon rains, which would bring out all the insects from
their cracks and crannies.

One day clouds loomed up on the horizon, growing rapidly into
enormous towers. A faint breeze sprang up, bringing with it the
first of the monsoon rain-drops. This was the moment everyone

was waiting for. People ran out of their houses to take in the fresh breeze and the scent of those first few raindrops on the parched, dusty earth. Underground, in their cracks, the insects were moving. Termites and white ants, which had been sleeping through the hot season, emerged from their lairs.

And then, on the second or third night of the monsoon, came the great yearly flight of insects into the cool brief freedom of the night. Out of every crack, from under the roots of trees, huge winged ants emerged, at first fluttering about heavily, on this the first and last flight of their lives. At night there was only one direction in which they could fly—towards the light; towards the electric bulbs and smoky kerosene lamps throughout Pipalnagar. The street lamp opposite the bus stop, beneath my room, attracted a massive quivering swarm of clumsy termites, which gave the impression of one thick, slowly revolving body.

This was the hour of the lizards. Now they had their reward for those days of patient waiting. Plying their sticky pink tongues, they devoured the insects as fast as they came. For hours they crammed their stomachs, knowing that such a feast would not be theirs again for another year. How wasteful nature is, I thought. Through the whole hot season the insect world prepares for this flight out of darkness into light, and not one of them survives its freedom.

Suraj and I walked barefooted over the cool wet pavements, across the railway lines and the river bed, until we were not far from the crooked tree. Dotting the landscape were old abandoned brick kilns. When it rained heavily, the hollows made by the kilns filled up with water. Suraj and I found a small tank where we could bathe and swim. On a mound in the middle of the tank stood a ruined hut, formerly inhabited by a watchman at the kiln. We swam and then wrestled on the young green grass. Though I was heavier than Suraj and my chest as sound as a new drum, he had a lot of power in his long wiry arms and legs, and he pinioned me about the waist with his bony knees. And then suddenly, as I strained to press his back to the ground, I felt his body go tense. He stiffened, his thigh jerked against me, and his legs began to twitch. I knew that a fit was coming on, but I was unable to get out of his grip. He held me more tightly as the fit took possession of him.

When I noticed his mouth working, I thrust the palm of my hand in, sideways to prevent him from biting his tongue. But so violent was the convulsion that his teeth bit into my flesh. I shouted with pain and tried to pull my hand away, but he was unconscious and his jaw was set. I closed my eyes and counted slowly up to seven, and then I felt his muscles relax, and I was able to take my hand away. It was bleeding a little but I bound it in a handkerchief before Suraj fully recovered consciousness.

He didn't say much as we walked back to town. He looked depressed and weak, but I knew it wouldn't take long for him to recover his usual good spirits. He did not notice that I kept my hand out of sight and only after he had returned from classes that night did he notice the bandage and ask what happened.

X

"Do you want to make some money?" asked Pitamber, bursting into the room like a festive cracker.

"I do," I said.

"What do we have to do for it?" asked Suraj, striking a cautious note.

"Oh, nothing—carry a banner and walk in front of a procession."

"Why?"

"Don't ask me. Some political stunt."

"Which party?"

"I don't know. Who cares? All I know is that they are paying two rupees a day to anyone who'll carry a flag or banner."

"We don't need two rupees that badly," I said. "And you can make more than that in a day with your rickshaw."

"True, but they're paying me *five*. They're fixing a loudspeaker to my rickshaw, and one of the party's men will sit in it and make speeches as we go along. Come on—it will be fun."

"No banners for us," I said. "But we may come along and watch."

And we did watch, when, later that morning, the procession passed along our street. It was a ragged procession of about a hundred people, shouting slogans. Some of them were children, and some of them were men who did not know what it was all about, but all joined in the slogan-shouting.

We didn't know much about it, either. Because, though the man in Pitamber's rickshaw was loud and eloquent, his loudspeaker was defective, with the result that his words were punctuated with squeaks and an eerie whining sound. Pitamber looked up and saw us standing on the balcony and gave us a wave and a wide grin. We decided to follow the procession at a discreet distance. It was a protest march against something or other; we never did manage to find out the details. The destination was the municipal office, and by the time we got there the crowd had increased to two or three hundred persons. Some rowdies had now joined in, and things began to get out of hand. The man in the rickshaw continued his speech; another man standing on a wall was making a speech; and someone from the municipal office was confronting the crowd and making a speech of his own.

A stone was thrown, then another. From a sprinkling of stones it soon became a shower of stones; and then some police constables, who had been standing by watching the fun, were ordered into action. They ran at the crowd where it was thinnest, brandishing stout sticks.

We were caught up in the stampede that followed. A stone— flung no doubt at a policeman—was badly aimed and struck me on the shoulder. Suraj pulled me down a side-street. Looking back, we saw Pitamber's cycle-rickshaw lying on its side in the middle of the road; but there was no sign of Pitamber.

Later, he turned up in my room, with a cut over his left eyebrow which was bleeding freely. Suraj washed the cut, and I poured iodine over it—Pitamber did not flinch—and covered it with sticking-plaster. The cut was quite deep and should have had stitches; but Pitamber was superstitious about hospitals, saying he knew very few people to come out of them alive. He was of course thinking of the Pipalnagar hospital.

So he acquired a scar on his forehead. It went rather well with his demonic good looks.

XI

"Thank God for the monsoon," said Suraj. "We won't have any more demonstrations on the roads until the weather improves!"

And, until the rain stopped, Pipalnagar was fresh and clean and alive. The children ran naked out of their houses and romped through the streets. The gutters overflowed, and the road became a mountain stream, coursing merrily towards the bus stop.

At the bus stop there was confusion. Newly arrived passengers, surrounded on all sides by a sea of mud and rain water, were met by scores of tongas and cycle-rickshaws, each jostling the other trying to cater to the passengers. As a result, only half found conveyances, while the other half found themselves knee-deep in Pipalnagar mud.

Pipalnagar mud has a quality all its own; and it is not easily removed or forgotten. Only buffaloes love it because it is soft and squelchy. Two parts of it is thick sticky clay which seems to come alive at the slightest touch, clinging tenaciously to human flesh. Feet sink into it and have to be wrenched out. Fingers become webbed. Get it into your hair, and there is nothing you can do except go to Deep Chand and have your head shaved.

London has its fog, Paris its sewers, and Pipalnagar its mud.

Pitamber, of course, succeeded in getting as his passenger the most attractive girl to step off the bus, and showed her his skill and daring by taking her to her destination by the longest and roughest road.

The rain swirled over the trees and roofs of the town, and the parched earth soaked it up, giving out a fresh smell that came only once a year, the fragrance of quenched earth, that loveliest of all smells.

In my room I was battling against the elements, for the door would not close, and the rain swept into the room and soaked my cot. When finally I succeeded in closing the door, I discovered that the roof was leaking, and the water was trickling down the walls, running through the dusty designs I had made with my feet. I placed tins and mugs in strategic positions and, satisfied that everything was now under control, sat on the cot to watch the roof-tops through the windows.

There was a loud banging on the door. It flew open, and there was Suraj, standing on the threshold, drenched. Coming in, he began to dry himself while I made desperate efforts to close the door again.

"Let's make some tea," he said.

Glasses of hot sweet milky tea on a rainy day ... it was enough to make me feel fresh and full of optimism. We sat on the cot, enjoying the brew.

"One day I'll write a book," I said. "Not just a thriller, but a real book, about real people. Perhaps about you and me and Pipalnagar. And then we'll be famous, and our troubles will begin. I don't mind problems as long as they are new. While you're studying, I'll write my book. I'll start tonight. It is an auspicious time, the first night of the monsoon."

A tree must have fallen across the wires somewhere, because the lights would not come on. So I lit a small oil-lamp, and while it spluttered in the steamy darkness, Suraj opened his books and, with one hand on the book, the other playing with his toes—this helped him to concentrate!—he began to study. I took the ink down from the shelf, and finding it empty, added a little rain-water to it from one of the mugs. I sat down beside Suraj and began to write; but the pen was no good and made blotches all over the paper. And, although I was full of writing just then, I didn't really know what I wanted to say.

So I went out and began pacing up and down the road. There I found Pitamber, a little drunk, very merry, and prancing about in the middle of the road.

"What are you dancing for?" I asked.

"I'm happy, so I'm dancing," said Pitamber.

"And why are you happy?" I asked.

"Because I'm dancing," he said.

The rain stopped, and the neem trees gave out a strong sweet smell.

XII

Flowers in Pipalnagar—did they exist? As a child I knew a garden in Lucknow where there were beds of phlox and petunias; and another garden where only roses grew. In the fields around Pipalnagar I had seen the thorn-apple—a yellow buttercup nestling among thorn leaves. But in the Pipalnagar bazaar, there were no flowers except one—a marigold growing out of a crack on my balcony. I had removed the plaster from the base of the plant, and filled in a little earth which I watered every morning. The plant was healthy, and sometimes it produced a little orange marigold.

Sometimes Suraj plucked a flower and kept it in his tray, among the combs, buttons, and scent-bottles. Sometimes he gave the flower to a passing child, once to a small boy who immediately tore it to shreds. Suraj was back on his rounds, as his exams were over.

Whenever he was tired of going from house to house, Suraj would sit beneath a shady banyan or peepul tree, put his tray aside, and take out his flute. The haunting notes travelled down the road in the afternoon stillness, drawing children to him. They would sit beside him and be very quiet when he played, because there was something melancholy and appealing about the tunes. Suraj sometimes made flutes out of pieces of bamboo; but he never sold them. He would give them to the children he liked. He would sell almost anything, but not flutes.

Suraj sometimes played the flute at night, when he lay awake, unable to sleep; but even though I slept, I could hear the music in my dreams. Sometimes he took his flute with him to the crooked tree, and played for the benefit of the birds. The parrots made harsh noises in response and flew away. Once, when Suraj was playing his flute to a small group of children, he had a fit. The flute fell from his hands, and he began to roll about in the dust on the roadside. The children became frightened and ran away, but they did not stay away for long. The next time they heard the flute, they came to listen as usual.

XIII

It was Lord Krishna's birthday, and the rain came down as heavily as it is said to have done on the day Krishna was born. Krishna is the best beloved of all the gods. Young mothers laugh or weep as they read or hear the pranks of his boyhood; young men pray to be as tall and as strong as Krishna was when he killed King Kamsa's elephant and Kamsa's wrestlers; young girls dream of a lover as daring as Krishna to carry them off in a war-chariot; grown-up men envy the wisdom and statesmanship with which he managed the affairs of his kingdom.

The rain came so unexpectedly that it took everyone by surprise. In seconds, people were drenched, and within minutes, the street was flooded. The temple tank overflowed, the railway lines disappeared, and the old wall near the bus stop shivered and silently fell, the sound of its collapse drowned in the downpour. A naked young man with a dancing bear cavorted in the middle of the vegetable market. Pitamber's rickshaw churned through the floodwater, while he sang lustily as he worked.

Wading knee-deep down the road, I saw the roadside vendors sal-

219

vaging whatever they could. Plastic toys, cabbages and utensils floated away and were seized by urchins. The water had risen to the level of the shop-fronts and floors were awash. Deep Chand and Ramu, with the help of a customer, were using buckets to bail the water out of their shop. The rain stopped as suddenly as it had begun and the sun came out. The water began to find an outlet, flooding other low-lying areas, and a paper-boat came sailing between my legs.

Next morning, the morning on which the results of Suraj's examinations were due, I rose early—the first time I ever got up before Suraj—and went down to the news agency. A small crowd of students had gathered at the bus stop, joking with each other and hiding their nervousness with a show of indifference. There were not many passengers on the first bus, and there was a mad grab for newspapers as the bundle landed with a thud on the pavement. Within half an hour, the newsboy had sold all his copies. It was the best day of the year for him.

I went through the columns relating to Pipalnagar, but I couldn't find Suraj's roll number on the list of successful candidates. I had the number on a slip of paper, and I looked at it again to make sure I had compared it correctly with the others; then I went through the newspaper once more. When I returned to the room, Suraj was sitting on the doorstep. I didn't have to tell him he had failed—he knew by the look on my face. I sat down beside him, and we said nothing for some time.

"Never mind," Suraj said eventually. "I will pass next year."

I realized I was more depressed than he was and that he was trying to console me.

"If only you'd had more time," I said.

"I have plenty of time now. Another year. And you will have time to finish your book, and then we can go away together. Another year of Pipalnagar won't be so bad. As long as I have your friendship, almost everything can be tolerated." He stood up, the tray hanging from his shoulders. "What would you like to buy?"

XIV

Another year of Pipalnagar! But it was not to be. A short time later, I received a letter from the editor of a newspaper, calling me to Delhi for an interview. My friends insisted that I should go. Such an opportunity would not come again.

But I needed a shirt. The few I possessed were either frayed at the collars or torn at the shoulders. I hadn't been able to afford a new shirt for over a year, and I couldn't afford one now. Struggling writers weren't expected to dress very well, but I felt in order to get the job, I would need both a haircut and a clean shirt.

Where was I to get a shirt? Suraj generally wore an old red-striped T-shirt; he washed it every second evening, and by morning it was dry and ready to wear again; but it was tight even on him. He did not have another. Besides, I needed something white, something respectable!

I went to Deep Chand who had a collection of shirts. He was only too glad to lend me one. But they were all brightly coloured—pinks, purples and magentas. . . . No editor was going to be impressed by a young writer in a pink shirt. They looked fine on Deep Chand, but he had no need to look respectable.

Finally Pitamber came to my rescue. He didn't bother with shirts himself, except in winter, but he was able to borrow a clean white shirt from a guard at the gaol, who'd got it from the relative of a convict in exchange for certain favours.

"This shirt will make you look respectable," said Pitamber. "To be respectable—what an adventure!"

XV

Freedom. The moment the bus was out of Pipalnagar, and the fields opened out on all sides, I knew that I was free, that I always had been free. Only my own weakness, hesitation, and the habits that had grown around me had held me back. All I had had to do was sit in a bus and go somewhere.

I sat near the open window of the bus and let the cool breeze from the fields play against my face. Herons and snipe waded among the lotus roots in flat green ponds. Bluejays swooped around telegraph poles. Children jumped naked into the canals that wound through the fields. Because I was happy, it seemed to me that everyone else was happy—the driver, the conductor, the passengers, the farmers in the fields and those driving bullock-carts. When two women behind me started quarrelling over their seats, I helped to placate them. Then I took a small girl on my knee and pointed out camels, buffaloes, vultures, and parriah-dogs.

Six hours later the bus crossed the bridge over the swollen Jumna river, passed under the walls of the great red fort built by a Moghul Emperor, and entered the old city of Delhi. I found it strange to be in a city again, after several years in Pipalnagar. It was a little frightening, too. I felt like a stranger. No one was interested in me. In Pipalnagar, people wanted to know each other, or at least to know about each other. In Delhi, no one cared who you were or where you came from. Like big cities almost everywhere, it was prosperous but without a heart.

After a day and a night of loneliness, I found myself wishing that Suraj had accompanied me; wishing that I was back in Pipalnagar. But when the job was offered to me—at a starting salary of three hundred rupees per month, a princely sum, compared to what I had been making on my own—I did not have the courage to refuse it. After accepting the job—which was to commence in a week's time—I spent the day wandering through the bazaars, down the wide shady roads of the capital, resting under the jamun trees, and thinking all the time of what I would do in the months to come.

I slept at the railway waiting-room, and all night long I heard the shunting and whistling of engines which conjured up visions of places with sweet names like Kumbakonam, Krishnagiri, Polonnarurawa. I dreamt of palm-fringed beaches and inland lagoons of the echoing chambers of deserted cities, red sandstone and white marble; of temples in the sun, and elephants crossing wide slow-moving rivers. . . .

XVI

Pitamber was on the platform when the train steamed into the Pipalnagar station in the early hours of a damp September morning. I waved to him from the carriage window, and shouted that everything had gone well.

But everything was not well here. When I got off the train, Pitamber told me that Suraj had been ill—that he'd had a fit on a lonely stretch of road the previous afternoon and had lain in the sun for over an hour. Pitamber had found him, suffering from heatstroke, and brought him home. When I saw him, he was sitting up on the string-bed, drinking hot tea. He looked pale and weak, but his smile was reassuring.

"Don't worry," he said. "I will be all right."

"He was bad last night," said Pitamber. "He had a fever and kept talking, as in a dream. But what he says is true—he is better this morning."

"Thanks to Pitamber," said Suraj. "It is good to have friends."

"Come with me to Delhi, Suraji," I said. "I have got a job now. You can live with me and attend a school regularly."

"It is good for friends to help each other," said Suraj, "but only after I have passed my exam will I join you in Delhi. I made myself this promise. Poor Pipalnagar—nobody wants to stay here. Will you be sorry to leave?"

"Yes, I will be sorry. A part of me will still be here."

XVII

Deep Chand was happy to know that I was leaving. "I'll follow you soon," he said. "There is money to be made in Delhi, cutting hair. Girls are keeping it short these days."

"But men are growing it long."

"True. So I shall open a Barber Shop for Ladies and a Beauty Salon for Men! Ramu can attend to the ladies."

Ramu winked at me in the mirror. He was still at the stage of teasing girls on their way to school or college.

The snip of Deep Chand's scissors made me sleepy as I sat in his chair. His fingers beat a rhythmic tattoo on my scalp. It was my last hair-cut in Pipalnagar, and Deep Chand did not charge me for it. I promised to write as soon as I had settled down in Delhi.

The next day when Suraj was stronger, I said, "Come, let us go for a walk and visit our crooked tree. Where is your flute, Suraj?"

"I don't know. Let us look for it."

We searched the room and our belongings for the flute but could not find it.

"It must have been left on the roadside," said Suraj. "Never mind, I will make another."

I could picture the flute lying in the dust on the roadside and somehow this made me feel sad. But Suraj was full of high spirits as we walked across the railway-lines and through the fields.

"The rains are over," he said, taking off his *chappals* and lying down on the grass. "You can smell the autumn in the air. Somehow, it makes me feel light-hearted. Yesterday I was sad, and tomorrow I might be sad again, but today I know that I am happy. I want to live on and on. One lifetime cannot satisfy my heart."

"A day in a lifetime," I said. "I'll remember this day—the way the sun touches us, the way the grass bends, the smell of this leaf as I crush it. ...."

XVIII

At six every morning the first bus arrives, and the passengers alight, looking sleepy and dishevelled, and rather discouraged by their first sight of Pipalnagar. When they have gone their various ways, the bus is driven into the shed. Cows congregate at the dust-bin, and the pavement dwellers come to life, stretching their tired limbs on the hard stone steps. I carry the bucket up the steps to my room, and bathe for the last time on the open balcony. In the villages, the buffaloes are wallowing in green ponds, while naked urchins sit astride them, scrubbing their backs, and a crow or water-bird perches on their glistening necks. The parrots are busy in the crooked tree, and a slim green snake basks in the sun on our island near the brick-kiln. In the hills, the mists have lifted and the distant mountains are fringed with snow.

It is Autumn, and the rains are over. The earth meets the sky in one broad, bold sweep.

A land of thrusting hills. Terraced hills, wood-covered and wind-swept. Mountains where the gods speak gently to the lonely. Hills of green grass and grey rock, misty at dawn, hazy at noon, molten at sunset, where fierce fresh torrents rush to the valleys below. A quiet land of fields and ponds, shaded by ancient trees and ringed with palms, where sacred rivers are touched by temples, where temples are touched by southern seas.

This is the land I should write about. Pipalnagar should be forgotten: I should turn aside from it to sing instead of the splendours of exotic places.

But only yesterdays are truly splendid. ... And there are other singers, sweeter than I, to sing of tomorrow. I can only write of today, of Pipalnagar, where I have lived and loved.

Raymond Carver / Tucson, Arizona

A NIGHT OUT

from *December*, Volume 12, Numbers 1 & 2: 1970
Chicago
Editor: Curt Johnson

AS THEIR first extravagance that evening, Wayne and Caroline Miller went to Aldo's, an elegant, newly-opened restaurant in the north area. They passed through a tiny, walled garden containing several small pieces of Greek statuary, and at the end of the garden they met a tall, graying man in a dark suit who said, "Good evening, sir. Madam," and swung open the heavy, polished-oak door for them.

Inside, Aldo himself showed them the aviary—a peacock, a pair of Golden pheasants, a Chinese ring-necked pheasant, and a number of smaller, indistinguishable birds that flew around the top or perched on the wire on either side. Aldo personally conducted them to a table, seated Caroline, and then turned to Wayne and said, "A lovely lady," before moving off—a dark, small, impeccable man with a soft accent.

They were both pleased with his attention.

"I read in the paper," Wayne said, "that he has an uncle who has some kind of position in the Vatican. That's how he was able to get copies of some of these paintings." He nodded at a full-sized Velasquez reproduction on the nearest wall. "His uncle in the Vatican."

"He used to be *maitre d'* at the Copacabana in Rio," Caroline said. "He knew Frank Sinatra, and Lana Turner was a good friend of his, and a lot of those people."

"Is that so?" Wayne said. "I didn't know that. I read that he was at the Victoria Hotel in Switzerland, and at some big hotel in Paris, but I didn't know he was at the Copacabana in Rio."

She moved her handbag slightly as the waiter set down the heavy, amber-colored water goblets. He poured her glass and then moved over to Wayne's side of the table.

"Did you see the suit he was wearing?" Wayne asked. "You seldom see a suit like that." In his mind he could still see the sheen and the ripple of the suit as Aldo led them to their table. "That's a three-hundred-dollar suit, as sure as I'm sitting here." He picked up his menu. In a few minutes he said, "Well, what are you going to have?"

"I don't know," she said. "I haven't decided. What are you going to have?"

"I don't know," he said after a minute. "I haven't decided either."

"What about one of these French dishes, Wayne? Or else—this. Here. Over here on this side." She held her finger under an entree, and then narrowed her eyes at him as he located it, pursed his lips, frowned, and then shook his head.

"I don't know," he said, "I'd kind of like to know what I'm getting. I just don't really know."

The waiter returned with a card and pencil and said something Wayne couldn't quite catch.

"We haven't decided yet," he said, a little irritated. He shook his head as the waiter continued to stand beside the table. "I'll signal you when we're ready."

"I think I'll just have a sirloin, you order what you want," he said to Caroline. He closed his menu and picked up his water. Over the muted voices coming from the other tables, he could hear a high, warbling bird call from the aviary. He saw Aldo greet a party of four, chat with them a minute as he smiled and nodded, and then lead them to a table near the wall.

"We could have had a better table," Wayne said. "Instead of right here in the center where everyone can walk by and watch you eat, we could have had a table against the wall. Or over there by the fountain."

"I think I'll have the Beef Tournedos," she said, ignoring him. She kept looking at her menu.

He tapped out a cigarette, lighted it, inhaled two or three times, and then glanced briefly around at the other diners, who, it seemed to him, had a serene, confidential look to them.

She was still looking at her menu.

"Well, for God's sake, if that's what you're going to have, close your menu so he can take our order." He raised his arm for the waiter, who was lingering near the back, talking with another waiter.

"There's nothing else to do but gas around with the other waiters, I guess."

"Here he comes," she said.

"Sir?" The waiter was a thin, pock-faced man in a loose, black suit and a black bow tie.

"... And we'll have a bottle of champagne, I believe. Uh, Krug, a small bottle."

"Yes, sir."

"And could we have that right away? Before the salad, or the relish plate?"

"Oh, bring the relish tray anyway," Caroline said. "Please."

"Yes, madam."

"I'm hungry," she said to Wayne.

"They're a slippery bunch sometimes," Wayne said, after the waiter had moved away. "Do you remember that guy Bruno who used to work at the office during the week and wait tables on weekends? Fred caught him stealing out of the petty-cash fund one lunch hour, and we fired him."

"Let's talk about something more pleasant," she said. "Shall we?"

"All right, sure," he said. "Here, here comes our champagne."

The waiter poured a little into Wayne's glass, and Wayne took the glass, tasted it, and said "Fine." He wasn't much of a wine drinker, but he always enjoyed this little preliminary.

"Here's to you, honey," he said, raising his glass. "Happy birthday." They clinked glasses.

"I like champagne," she said. "I always have."

"I like champagne," he said.

"We could have had a bottle of Lancer's."

"Well, why didn't you say something, if that's what you wanted?"

"I don't know," she said, "I just didn't think about it, I guess. This is fine, though. I like Krug."

"I don't know too much about champagnes. I don't mind admitting I'm not much of a ... connoisseur. Just a lowbrow, I guess," he added. He tried to laugh and catch her eye, but she was busy selecting an olive from the relish tray. "Not like the merry group you've been keeping company with lately .... But if you wan-

227

ted Lancer's," he went on, "you should have ordered it. After all—"

"Oh, shut up, will you! Can't you talk about something else?" She looked up at him then, and he had to look away. He moved his feet under the table.

After a minute he said, "Would you care for some more champagne, dear?"

"Yes, thank you," she said quietly.

"Here's to us," he said.

"To us," she repeated. They looked at each other steadily as they drank.

"We ought to do this more often," he said.

She nodded.

"It's good to get out now and then. I'll, uh, I'll make more of an effort, if you want me to."

She reached for a stuffed celery. "That's mainly up to you. It's your dice, as they say."

"That's not true! It's not me who's, who's . . ."

She looked at him.

"Ah, I don't care what you do," he said, dropping his eyes.

"Is that true?"

"No, no, you know it isn't true. I'm sorry I said that. I don't know why I said that."

The waiter brought the soup and took away the bottle and the wine glasses and refilled their goblets with ice water.

"Could I have a soup spoon?" Wayne asked.

"Sir?"

"A soup spoon," Wayne repeated.

The waiter looked amazed, and then worried. He glanced around quickly at the other tables. Wayne made a shoveling motion over his soup. Aldo appeared beside their table.

"Is everything all right? Is there anything wrong?"

"My husband doesn't seem to have a soup spoon," Caroline apologized. "I'm sorry."

"Certainly. *Une cuiller, si'l vous plait*," he said to the waiter in an even voice. He looked once at Wayne, and then explained to Caroline. "This is Paul's first night. He speaks very little English yet, but he is an excellent waiter, I believe. The boy who set the table forgot the spoon." He smiled. "It no doubt took Paul by surprise."

"This is a beautiful place," Caroline said.

"Thank you. I'm delighted you could come tonight. Would you like to see the wine cellar, and the private dining rooms?"

"Very much," she said.

"I will have someone show you around when you are finished dining."

"We'll be looking forward to it," she said.

Aldo bowed slightly, and looked again at Wayne. "I hope you enjoy your dinner," he said to them.

Wayne was furious. "That jerk," he said.

"Who?" she said. "Who are you talking about?" laying down her spoon.

"The waiter," he said. "The waiter. We would have to get the newest and the dumbest waiter in the house."

"Eat your soup," she said. "Don't blow a gasket."

"I never did care for cold soup."

"Ask for some more, if it'll make you happy. The waiter'll get you some more."

"I'll wait for the salad. How is it, though, the soup? Is it any good?"

"It's all right," she said. "It's good."

Wayne lighted another cigarette. In a few minutes the waiter arrived with their salads, took away the soup bowls, and poured more water.

When they started on the main course, Wayne said "Well, what do you think? Is there a chance for us, or not?" He looked down and rearranged the napkin on his lap.

"Maybe so," she said. "There's always a chance."

"Don't give me that kind of evasive crap," he said. "Answer me straight for a change."

"Don't snap at me, by God!"

"Well, I'm asking you," he said. "Straight out. Can I have a straight answer?"

"What do you want from me, a pledge or something? Signed in blood?"

"Maybe that wouldn't be such a bad idea."

"Now you listen to me! I've given you the best years of my life. The best years of my life, I've given to you."

"The best years of *your* life?"

"let me finish. I'm thirty-six years old. Thirty-seven years old to-night. I'm too old to make any wrong moves, any mistakes. To-night, right now, at this minute, I just can't say what I'm going to do. I'll just have to see."

"I don't care what you do," he said.

"Is that true?" she said. "You don't care?"

He didn't answer. After a few bites he laid down his fork, tossed his napkin on the table.

"Are you finished?" she asked pleasantly. "Let's have coffee and dessert in a minute or two. We'll have a nice dessert. Some-thing good." She finished everything on her plate and then picked at the remains of her salad. "I told you I was hungry," she said as Wayne stared at her.

"Two coffees," he said to the waiter. "And you wanted some dessert, Caroline?" He looked at her and then back to the waiter. "What do you have for dessert?"

"Sir?"

"Dessert!"

The waiter looked at Caroline, and then at Wayne.

"No dessert," she said. "Let's not have any dessert."

"Choc-late sundae," the waiter said, "orange sherbet, apple, ber-ry pie." He smiled, showing his teeth. "Sir?"

"I don't want any guided tour of this place, either, when we're finished," Wayne said, after the waiter moved off.

When they rose from the table, Wayne dropped a dollar bill near his coffee cup. Caroline took two more dollars from her hand-bag, smoothed them out, left them alongside the other. "It's his first night," she said.

She waited with him while he paid the check. Out of the corner of his eye, Wayne could see Aldo standing near the door, dropping grains of seed into the aviary. Aldo looked casually in their direct-ion, smiled, and went on rubbing the grain seeds getween his fin-gers as the birds collected in front of him.

For some reason he couldn't explain, it angered Wayne seeing him standing there. He'd had enough of this place, he decided. He was tired of jerk waiters who couldn't speak English, and tired of the quiet, self-satisfied air he'd felt all around him in the dining room, and most of all, he was tired of this little Aldo's superior, nonchalant attitude. He was going to cut him, by God! Give him a snubbing he wouldn't soon forget. He'd had it with this place.

As they neared the door, Aldo turned, brushed his hands, started toward them with a smile.

Wayne caught his eyes deliberately. Then, as Aldo extended his hand, Wayne looked away, turned slightly. Aldo walked right past him. When Wayne looked back an instant later, he saw Aldo take Caroline's waiting hand. Aldo drew his heels neatly together, kissed her on the wrist.

"Did you enjoy your dinner?" he asked.

"It was marvelous," she said.

"You will come back from time to time?"

"I will," she said. "As often as I can. Next time, I would like to look around a little, but this time we have to go."

"I have something for you," he said. "One moment, please." He walked over to a vase next to the cashier and came back with a long-stemmed red rose. "For you. But be careful with it! The thorns. A very lovely lady," he said to Wayne. He smiled at her again, and then turned to welcome another couple.

The doorman continued to hold open the door as Wayne and Caroline stood there a moment longer. Finally, Wayne said "Let's get out of here, all right?"

"You can see how he could be friends with Lana Turner, can't you?" she said. She felt her face still glowing, and she held onto the rose and turned it around and around between her fingers.

"Good night!" she called out to the doorman.

"Good night, madam," the doorman answered.

"I don't believe he ever knew her." Wayne said. "Don't believe everything you read."

Tony Cohan / Los Angeles

THE HUSTLER AND THE HEIRESS

from *Outlaw Visions*
Acrobat Books, 1977: Los Angeles
Editors: Gordon Beam & Tony Cohan

THERE IS a tiny farming community halfway up the Atlas mountains on the road that cuts south from Marrakech, toward the Sahara. It is a village of mud-built, flat-roofed houses, and from it you
can see the peak of the Djbal Toubkal, the highest mountain in
Morocco. A boy, Abdul, was born there, the fifth child and the second son of peasant Berbers. They were people whose origins lay
somewhere on the other side of the Maghreb, long before there was
a Morocco or an Algeria, long before the Muslim hordes swept a-
cross North Africa killing and converting, long before Caesar's
Africa Nova. Even before the Phoenecian traders ruled the port
towns from the Mediterranean's throat all the way down the Atlantic coast to Mauritania, the Berbers were there. Abdul's people
were Masmouds, mountain Berbers, their history faithfully set
down, along with those of the camel-riding desert Sanhajas and the
Zanatas, horsemen of the steppes, by the great African historian
and scribe, ibn-Khaldun, many hundreds of years ago.

The village was a strange and private place. Nobody knew how
long it had been there, or why. It was not good for farming, and
the villagers resorted to bizarre means of coaxing food to grow. If
it rained too long the farmers ploughed a corner of their fields with
a cat and a dog harnessed to a stick. If it rained too little, young
girls strolled the fields singing magic incantations.

Once someone brought a television set to the town. It was instal-
led in the village's one cafe, and every night men sat and drank
mint tea and watched the hour's transmission from Casablanca. Outside the cafe, urchins pressed against the glass, heedless of the cold,
to watch a man dressed in European clothes deliver the news in
Arabic, or a performance of French puppeteers, or film clips of
King Hassan delivering a speech from his palace in Rabat. Then
they played the national anthem. Afterwards a test pattern came

on, and everyone watched it until they got tired and went home. Abdul was one of the urchins at the window, mesmerized by the bright flickering screen.

Abdul's father, whose name was also Abdul, was a quiet, stern man who punished his second son mercilessly when he was delinquent. This was always, it seemed. From the time he could walk the boy was in trouble. As soon as he learned how to talk, he lied. Abdul's mother, a stocky, stoical woman, rued the birth of this duplicitous son, and prayed for him to no avail.

When Abdul was five his father left for Marrakech to find work. The winter had lasted far into spring and ruined the planting. There was no money. Abdul's father had provided constancy and violence in the boy's life. Now he was gone. Quickly and remorselessly, Abdul grew wild. Had he been simply another dull village boy he might have been cuffed and kneaded into shape as Berbers had done with their children for centuries. But Abdul had a sweet androgynous charm, a gift of con. And the men of the Maghreb have always been soft for a pretty boy.

Then one day, on Abdul's tenth birthday, he and a gang of boys were exploring a ravine behind the inn at the center of the village where the bus stopped. They came upon a body, lifeless and broken, lying in a ditch. The others turned to run off, but Abdul stopped them. Transfixed by his sudden authority, the boys stood still, swallowing their terror.

Abdul approached the body. It was a young man, maybe 25, a stranger. He was dressed in European clothes. There was a welt on the side of his head, and blood seeped from it. Abdul reached for his wrist. Pulling back the muddy sleeve, he saw a shiny American wristwatch with a flexible silver band. Abdul slipped it off. The hand, grey and stiff, dropped back to earth.

There was a gold ring on the dead man's left hand. Abdul took that too. The other boys watched transfixed as Abdul calmly stripped the dead man of his valuables. He burrowed into the man's pockets, caked with mud from the wet earth, and found several hundred *dirhams*. This was more than his father sent home from Marrakech in three months. He stuffed them into his own pocket.

Then Abdul saw, hanging around the man's neck on a chain, a silver hand of Fatima. It was a common charm worn by Muslims to ward off evil. Abdul had never been given one, though he had asked many times. Now he pulled urgently at the dead man's charm, trying to rip it off. The man's head bobbed up and down against the stones, widening the gash. But the chain held. Abdul lifted the body to a sitting position. The jaw dropped open, and a foul-smelling liquid ran from the mouth. Abdul slipped the chain off and let the body drop back to the ground. Then, with the calm absorption of a jeweler, he polished the charm against his shirt, and dropped it over his neck.

Grinning triumphantly, Abdul turned back to his mates. But the ravine was empty. The boys had fled in terror.

That night Abdul's older brother heard what had happened. He took everything back from Abdul and gave it to the police. The only thing he didn't get was the hand of Fatima around his brother's neck. Then he took Abdul out into a field and beat him senseless with a stick. He did it the way his father would have, silent and without mercy. Stupefied, bloodied and strangely happy, Abdul fell into an unconscious sleep.

He woke up before sunrise, bruised and aching. Without much thought he got up and limped silently down the hill and out of the village, heading for Marrakech to find his father. Whatever else might happen, Abdul knew he would never return to the Atlas.

*   *   *

Dawn breaks hard over Marrakech. Up from the East she comes, splitting the high, snowpeaked Atlas and rolling across the red plain like a Sherifian horde. She lights the tip of the ancient red Koutoubia mosque like a flame to joss, and as the tower burns downward, the *muzzein*'s dry moan spreads across the quarter.

Below in the *medina*, the old city, rooster cries echo through the alley-ways, joined by cows, a bleating sheep, a baby's lament. The sounds pump forth, wheezing and swollen, like an old organ. In a deep shadowed alley, still full of night's cold, a blind beggar, huddled against a mud wall, stirs deep inside the folds of his *djellaba*. Only his hand sticks out, frozen, even in sleep, in the supplicant's eternal gesture. His movement awakens the dark wooly-headed legless man who has fallen against him in the night. The two beggars groan and burrow deeper into their wretched robes, as the first light steals through the quarter like an assassin.

Within the *medina*'s palaces and villas, gardens of unspeakable lushness open their dripping branches to the sky. Fountains gurgle like babies, and flocks of tiny birds drop to the trees like iron filings to a magnet.

In the great Djmaa el Fnaa square, hub of the northwest Sahara, fires are built. Turbaned porters begin their day's journeys across the square and down the inscrutable alleys, bearing boards, baskets, foodstuffs and coins. Merchants of the standing booths along the walled end of the square throw open their wooden doors, rickety and heavy with leathergoods, pipes, fezes, sandals. A waterseller in red costume, laden with copper cups, stands against an earthen wall, shivering before the dawn, awaiting the daily thronged carnival of the square.

In the new city north of the walls, dawn has a different face. In rooms along the wide, orange-laden boulevards, electric clocks sound, and bodies turn beneath French sheets. In the cafes rimming the Place du 17 Novembre, Arabs and Europeans beat off the cold with coffee and buttered *baguettes*. A camel glides silently past a parked taxi whose driver snoozes within.

Marrakech: etched red against the dark, snowy Atlas, red like the sun that lights it and the soil that nourishes it. Outlaw splendor of Islam. Blood of the Maghreb. And now she stirs. For it is time, and Allah awaits the faithful.

It was on such a morning, in early summer, that the boy Abdul arrived in the city. He came from the Atlas, riding with an old Berber on the back of a donkey. The donkey was laden with bags full of nuts for the *souks*.

They reached the camel market on the eastern edge of town just after sunrise, and Abdul jumped off. The old man scratched his white stubble and looked down at him. The boy had said little ever since he picked him up by the Moulay Brahim Gorge two days earlier, only that he was coming to Marrakech to find his father. The boy was a mountain Berber like himself. Maybe he was running away. Who knows the truth? He was a pretty boy, the old man thought. The men will like him in Marrakech. The women too. But what of it? *Inch' Allah*. The boy will be alright. And so will I, God willing.

"*Shoukran*," Abdul said in thanks, looking up at the old man. Then he started to walk off.

The old man called for him to wait. He said something to his donkey, then got down. Squatting in the dust, he reached under his robe and found the ancient, stained leather bag that hung at his waist. He fished around inside and brought out three crinkled, shiny dates and handed them to Abdul. Abdul took them, saying nothing.

Abdul watched the old man reach again into his bag and pull out a long, ornately carved wood pipe stem. From another pocket he produced a tiny pink clay bowl, open at both ends and pinched in the middle so as to bend like an elbow. He worked the bowl onto the end of the stick. Then he took from his bag a goat's bladder slit at the top, and drawn together by a leather string. He dipped the pipe inside the bladder, filling the bowl with a mixture of light, finely cut green *kif* and tobacco. Then he put the pipe to his mouth and, with quiet deliberation, lit it. He took two long puffs, his hollowed, sunleathered cheeks collapsing like bellows, and let the smoke out through his nose. The *kif* in the pipe became a blackened ball. The old man turned the pipe bowl downward, and blew out the ash. It hopped out onto the dirt, glowed weakly, and expired. Then the old man was very still. His eyes grew redrimmed and warm, and filled with water.

When the man looked out again he saw that the camel market was full of men and animals. Then he remembered the boy, and looked around for him. But the boy was gone.

Abdul walked along a straight paved road into town. He passed veiled women in robes carrying shopping bags, and tall men leading their camels to market. Cars roared by, stirring the red dust at road's edge. Abdul could taste the dust on the dates the old man had given him.

As he neared the center of town, square buildings with square windows, pink and still, rose up about him, fronted by green trees heavy with oranges. He wanted to pick an orange and eat it. But everywhere there were Europeans, chattering in French and looking sickly. Abdul feared them.

Rising into the sky off to his right was the reassuring spire of a mosque. Abdul turned and walked toward it. Faces darkened again, and he knew he was nearing the *medina*, the old town.

He came to the foot of the Koutoubia tower, where a steady

stream of men entered to pray in the mosque within. Abdul stopped each one and asked him if he knew a man named Abdul.

"There are ten thousand Abduls in Marrakech," said one, laughing, and passed on. "You should go to the police," said another.

Abdul didn't want to go to the police. It was late morning, and he was hungry and tired. He wandered into a large park full of olive trees and lay down beneath one. The earth smelled of dogs and urine. The boy fell fast asleep.

Abdul awoke in the late afternoon to the sound of drumming. A deep, repetitive pattern hammered the air, carrying on its thunder a surging babble of voices. Shadowed, swirling bodies rushed past, latticing the light that poured into the boy's eyes. Overhead, the olive trees hung silver black against a hard, cloudless sky.

Abdul stood up and leaned against a tree. It was as if he had awoken in an entirely different park from the quiet, empty one where he had fallen asleep that morning. Crowds of men coursed toward the marketplace, pulled by the drums. Abdul stumbled forward to join them, tripping on the hem of his *djellaba*, buoyed from falling only by the fanatic press of the crowd toward the Djmaa el Fnaa.

The Djmaa el Fnaa: the Assembly Of The Dead, where in grislier times men had gathered to watch truant heads roll in the dust. Now it teemed with life, a bloodless but no less compelling assembly. It spread across a quarter mile, edged by dense, buzzing outdoor cafes and stalls hiding entrances into alleys that ran deep into the *medina*'s secret and tantalizing heart. Gawking country Berbers from the *bleds* to the east, eyes entranced and distant, poured into the square from buses, autos, carts and camels, and found their way to circles of men converged around a team of acrobats, an eyeless storyteller, snake charmers, ranting hawkers, sly herbalists, purveyors of mysterious charms and amulets. Grinning black Muslims from countries across the desert to the south—Senegal, Mauritania, Mali—stood proud and erect, dressed in white. From mountain, plain and desert, down from slick Casablanca and ancient Fez they came, pilgrims all, buyer and seller alike, streaming into the market to seek or offer trinkets, talismans, dentistry, cures, boys, women, wisdom and redemption. The smell of food, *kif* and incense, thick and sweet, threaded the air. The performers and patrons changed ceaselessly, but the motion never stopped. Djmaa el Fnaa: a demented blend of Tijuana and Lourdes, where sin and salvation were proffered from the same hand.

Abdul stood, a tiny boy in a sea of men, on the edge of a large circle of pilgrims where watchers gathered around a cobra on a carpet. He saw how the snake's keeper played his reed pipe, sour and imploring, then leapt up, grinning, to pass a bowl around for coins. He watched how the gleaming piles of *dirhams* grew as new onlookers gathered and the old ones moved on.

Abdul slipped to the front of another circle. A toothless mendicant recited the Qoran from memory, turban wrapped madly around his sunfurrowed head. He received fewer coins than the snake charmer, poor scholar that he was. At the center of another circle, a dozen black Mauritanian drummers, dressed in white, whipped their hide drums with hooked sticks of wood. It was the sound Abdul had awoken to, dazzling and sensuous. Their leader, a grizzled elder, sat to one side and brewed mint tea and filled the *kif* pipes, while a child Abdul's age ran around the circle collecting coins and paper money in a knitted hat.

Watching the boy, Abdul wondered what he could do to get people to give him money. It was a problem that was to occupy him for the rest of his life.

Abdul wandered now in front of the outdoor cafes, jammed with Moroccans and foreigners who sat watching the spectacle of the square or talking among themselves. Whitejacketed waiters served coffee and the sweet, steaming mint tea in glasses. Urchins gave shoeshines and hustled taxis for men leaving the cafes. Hawkers hovered at the cafe's rim, waving purses, live chickens, beads, or simply begging.

Abdul came to a cluster of small food stands. There were chick peas, dozens of varieties of dates and olives, and the hot, peppery smell of *tajin*. Abdul considered the risks of stealing a fried fish from a stand within arm's reach. Then his hunger rose up and quelled all thought. He grabbed the fish and ran. A shouting seller chased him, but Abdul slipped safely into the market's vast, anonymous sea of people.

Hidden within the pulsing life of the square, Abdul ate his fish and felt better. His thoughts turned again to the problem of finding his father. Coming to the far end of the square, he walked through an archway and descended into the labyrinthian, shadowy *souks*, the native quarter's shops and stalls. The bright sunlight gave way to the damp, earthen mood of the alleys.

Abdul wandered deeper into the honeycomb of Marrakech's quarter, searching in the face of every man he passed for his father.

* * *

(Abdul never finds his father. He moves in with an old man, a fruit-seller named Ismael. He learns English and French and starts hustling foreigners, beginning his crawl across the dim, seedless terrain of colonialism. At fourteen, he moves out from old Ismael and becomes a dancing boy in a cafe off the Djmaa el Fnaa. By the time he is seventeen Abdul is wily, adept and beautiful, and the best street hustler in Marrakech. Then one day Abdul, the angel of the medina, singes his wings.)

* * *

Just inside the northern wall of Marrakech's old city, where it parts to admit a wide boulevard, lay the city's monument to colonial splendor, the Hotel Mamounia. Its four stars unchallenged since the day it opened early in the century, the Mamounia evoked everything that the foreign experience in a colonized country would like to have been. Magnificent motifs in tile and wood ran through the vaulted interiors of the grand *salle*, the work of hundreds of artisans. French service and dining prevailed within, an oasis for the traveler, an instruction to the native, and a bold challenge to Paris' best standards.

At its rear lay an exemplary garden, rich with ordered date palms, orange groves and tall olive trees laced with bouganvilla, laid out according to Arab geometry and maintained in all its initial splendor, now with the addition of a swimming pool and tennis courts. Buffet brunches were served by the pool, and meals within in a lavish dining room by dozens of French-trained natives. An Arab restaurant featured *tajin* served in earthen dishes, the powdered delicacy of *bstilla*, and nameless delicacies of the Maghreb that rivaled the city's best. Each of the hotel's four floors was attended by a *concierge*.

At garden's end rose a wall, and beyond the wall lay the scrambled, unruly quarter, and the Djmaa el Fnaa. From dawn to dusk the cacaphony of the *medina* rose and drifted across the placid gardens of the Mamounia, offering the contemplative visitor, sitting on his porch overlooking the scene and the Atlas beyond, the safest of reflections upon the native life, their fabled restlessness properly corralled beyond the walls.

The Mamounia had survived independence. It had even survived the Americans. Now tourism buoyed it once more. Visitors from every country came to sample its legendary delights. Many French, some of them former colonists now repatriated, came for a season or a few weeks, if they could still afford it, to bask among the trappings of a finer time. For many there simply was no other place to stay in Marrakech.

The Mamounia's management was French, snobbish, and vicious to the intruder. If an unlicensed guide or hustler was caught inside the grounds, punishment was swift and unsparing. He was sent to jail for having committed the unspeakable sin of intruding upon the hotel's rigorous aura of safety and class. Independence or no independence, the Mamounia brought money to Marrakech.

The hotel's clientele were the most likely to spend money in the *souks*. Beyond the entrance, they were fair game for the hustler. So it was that the more ambitious guides converged outside the hotel's walls, seeking wealthy prey. But they had to know what they were doing, they had to be good.

Abdul stood fifty yards south of the Mamounia's wall, across the street from the entrance. It was midmorning, and the street was wide and empty. A horsedrawn carriage waited sleepily for a customer. The sky was blue and still, the mountains rising far off behind the wall, an ever-present scrim against which the city's day moved.

Tourism had invaded Marrakech: the square was alive with more Europeans than ever before. Germans, Swedes, French and American civilians wandered the town with fresh money in their pockets. It was a hustler's dream. But it afforded Abdul no sense of pleasure on this morning. The day before a rug merchant had refused to pay him for bringing a pair of customers to buy, claiming they would have purchased the rugs anyway. Abdul had spent four days softening up the tedious English couple; the commission would have been large. And he had borrowed money from a Jew, a shopowner in the *mellah*, to buy clothes on the promise of the forthcoming sale of the rugs. Now he had two irascible merchants breathing down his neck, neither of whom would hesitate to have him jailed.

Worse, Abdul had wanted to meet a German girl the evening before. But he had gone to her once before, and she was adamant about money. They must use his, not hers. She was tall and big-breasted, with long yellow hair and white skin. He was sure he could have slept with her. Abdul had ended up drinking smuggled Spanish wine in his room above the shop with a hustler friend from Tangier, listening to glamorous tales of crime, rich women and easy money. The merchant downstairs, Hrabi, had tried to seduce him later in the evening and only Abdul's drunkenness had saved him. Abdul no longer had any interest in men, if indeed he ever had, and even the thought of sleeping with them now filled him with shame.

Abdul's head was pounding. He felt depressed, irritable, put upon, the plaything of some unseen *djinn*. Bad luck was something he knew nothing of. Youth and beauty had held him in grace for as long as he could remember. This spring had been more lucrative than ever before. But he had squandered the money. Now suddenly this morning he felt the burdens of a man's problems. It left him petulant and angry.

Abdul cracked his knuckles, and glowered. The German girl had said she didn't respect him because he didn't tell the truth. One day he had told her he was going to see his family, the next that they were dead. She had caught him in the lie. Abdul darkened at the thought. What's the difference? He couldn't understand why the Europeans place so much value upon words. You said something, you said something else. What you said depended upon a lot of things. It was like painting or dancing. Words were for expressing yourself. They were not some sort of absolute vow.

Abdul held his hand up before his face and said into his palm the English word "Shit!" See, he thought, these words have no force at all. They hardly make a breeze on the hand. The Europeans were stupid sometimes, to hell with them. And the girl too. She just wanted to smoke *kif* all the time, and take a poor Moroccan's money. Abdul idly weighed the merits of taking up another profession.

A couple came out of the Mamounia and turned toward him. They were tall, sandyhaired, middle-aged, and walked briskly.

Swedes, Abdul surmised. They were accompanied by one of the city's licensed guides. The guide wore a decorated burnoose, the kind nobody wore anymore, and a knitted cap. He was short and hooknosed, with a thin moustache, his back stooped, his face drab and leathered. He was a colonial relic, a fawning man, a stoolie who guided his wards to the safest of venues to buy poor, gaudy goods, or be entertained by the town's worst dancers. For those who wanted *kif* or sex, or simply a more interesting look at the city, better to find a hustler like Abdul.

The old guide shuffled by in his *babouches*, talking a strange English that made Abdul laugh. "Marrakech is very old ... rich sultans lived here with many wives ....."

Abdul turned away, grim and bitter. Even this weasel was making money. The entrance to the Mamounia was again empty. Abdul needed a customer, he had to pay back the Jew. Then the German girl would be his. Money was everything. The sun was climbing high in the sky. Abdul considered wandering into the square to see if he could do better there. Anxiety closed in upon him, dark and fateful.

A couple emerged from the Mamounia's tall walls. They were an odd pair, even at a distance. One was a tall, pale young man with stringy blond hair that fell over his shoulders. He wore faded jeans and a Hawaiian shirt. His uncovered feet slid along in rubber shower slippers. His body was slack, without tone. With him was an older woman, much shorter, with closely clipped silver hair and the same white, boneless face as the boy. She wore a cheap green caftan of synthetic material, the folds still in it from the store. She walked slowly, laboriously, with the aid of a cane. The boy languidly slowed his step to await her.

Even in Marrakech they were a strange sight, as they came walking down the palm-lined street. Normally Abdul wouldn't have bothered with such an unlikely couple. They looked anything but rich. But his predicament left him few options. He angled quietly across the street and fell in beside them.

"It's warm this morning. Are you going to the square?"

To Abdul's surprise they seemed quite content to have him along. They didn't treat him with the usual suspicions that forced Abdul into his hustler's ploys. Abdul was disarmed. These two carried on as if they didn't care if he were there or not. Abdul, bewildered, walked slowly with them toward the *souks*.

"Are you alright, Gram?" the young man asked, looking down at the woman. "They do have taxis, you know."

"Don't be silly, Arthur," the old woman said cheerfully, her wooden cane tapping against the pavement.

"She'll make it, you'll see," the boy confided in Abdul. "She's strong as an ox."

Abdul took them around back of the square, and into the narrowing alleys that became the *souks*. He walked slightly ahead, in case police were watching. Abdul knew the alley as a stranger never could, Muslim or infidel, reading the braille of the paths' twists and turns. He guided them down a narrow passage that seemed to end nowhere, only to suddenly burst out into a blinding patch of earth, sky and sunlight, an open air *souk*, where men bartered over live chickens and geese. Gram and Arthur followed Abdul into the deepening revery of the *medina*, pausing at the shops along the way. Abdul took them past the tanners, the dyers, and the smiths, their forges soot-black, bellows hidden deep within cave-like holds off the muddy path. They passed the shoe merchants, the leather sellers, the copper merchants, the beltmakers. A symphony of craftsmen, pursuing the ancient gestures of their trade.

Abdul knew the *souks* and its people. He nodded to them as he passed, and some returned his greeting. *"Salaam aliekum."* The merchants themselves tended to ignore him, preferring to minimize the importance of the hustler. But this was just a convention. The boys who worked for the merchants greeted Abdul because he was their friend. Secretly they admired him. And secretly their bosses hoped he would bring another rich American to buy rugs or leather, or a busload of Germans to buy dozens of *babouches*.

Arthur and Gram paused at every shop and booth along the way, fascinated. But as many odd trinkets as they examined, they bought nothing. Abdul's desperation mounted as he led the pair further into the *souks*. He thought about leaving them. But there was always the chance the strange couple would suddenly make a big buy. It was a lesson Abdul had learned from the 'hippies,' who dressed like beggars but sometimes bought many hundreds of kilos of *kif*.

Abdul steered them through the *mellah*, enduring a glare from the merchant to whom he owed money, and finally arrived at the rugseller's. Arthur and Gram ascended the narrow stairs, and sat watching with intense interest as the boy pulled out rich, splendid carpets, one after the other, until he was waist-deep in rugs, his voice hoarse from talking. Gram and Arthur admired and asked questions, but showed no interest in a purchase. They thanked the boy and stood up to go. Abdul let the hawker pressure them a little further until they began to grow nervous, then led them out empty-handed. The old rugseller whispered a curse at Abdul as he passed. Abdul felt his head was about to explode.

Abdul stayed with Gram and Arthur, though he didn't quite know why. The old woman seemed to gain strength with each turn in the alley, while her vague companion drifted along nearby, gazing curiously into every booth and stall. By noon they had bought only a tiny glass bead of three *dirhams*, a commission not worth Abdul's time to collect.

Then Gram said, "Arthur, I think I'd like to go back to the hotel for lunch."

Arthur had become absorbed by a small clay drum in a *bedouin*'s music stall. He was tapping on it, a distant look in his eyes. "Why don't you go on back, Gram, and have a quiet lunch in the room? I'd like to play some of these instruments."

Arthur turned and looked at Abdul. "Abdul will take you back. Won't you?" He said it as though he and Abdul were the best of friends, and the request simply beyond discussion or refusal.

Trapped in his pose as a helpful student, Abdul had no rationale for not taking the woman back to the hotel. Maybe she would at least tip him. Certainly things couldn't get any worse.

Abdul and Gram left Arthur to his fortunes in the *souks* and emerged into the Djmaa el Fnaa. The grand market was quiet and empty at the noon hour. Desultory conversation drifted across the flat, still air from half-empty cafes. A beggar watched them pass, too enervated from the heat to bother to solicit Gram. In the sky toward the mountain Abdul saw thunderheads gathering. He knew that one of the sudden summer storms that swept down on the city was on its way. It intensified his hurry to get the woman back to the hotel and be done with her.

Abdul flagged a taxi, and helped Gram get in. Moments later they were away from the unruly square and traveling the wide, paved boulevard toward the Mamounia. Abdul, as was customary, was to be let off outside the walls of the hotel. The driver knew that. When he stopped short of the hotel to get out, the old woman offered Abdul no tip. But to his astonishment, she invited him to her room for lunch.

"You are too thin," she said, warm and scolding. "You need a good meal."

Gram seemed to be a woman completely without guile or fear. Abdul didn't know what to make of her. Without knowing quite why, he said, "Thank you. I'll be up in a few minutes. What room are you in?"

Gram told him, and Abdul jumped out of the taxi. He waited a few moments, then walked quickly to a wall that ran along the side of the hotel. He came to the gardener's entrance and slipped through. He snuck across the grounds and in a side door of the great hotel. Working his way up to the second floor, avoiding the *concierges*, he came to Gram's room, and knocked.

"I've already ordered lunch," she said cheerfully, opening the door for him. "Do come in."

Abdul immediately felt uncomfortable. The room was lavishly appointed, with tall mirrors and handwoven bedspreads. Gram's single suitcase and Arthur's rucksack sat on one bed. The newly purchased glass bead Gram had placed on a table.

"Sit down," Gram said, and Abdul did. Gram was busily fussing about the room, straightening the beds and tables, though they seemed perfectly fine to Abdul. He watched her quietly.

"Where are you from?" he asked.

"Oh, here and there, I suppose you could say," she said. "St. Louis once, along time ago. Do you know where that is?"

"No."

"It's in the middle of America. There's a big wide muddy river that rushes by, and in the winter it rains."

Abdul nodded.

"I write books, you see," Gram said. "Romantic novels. The kind women read mostly, though I write under a man's name. So traveling inspires me. I get new ideas for stories and situations. Arthur's my grandson. We travel together. We're all each of us has. Do you understand?"

Abdul felt a fear rising in him. It seemed the kinder the woman was, the more anxious it made him. He had not gotten what he wanted from her, and now this intimacy, deepened the inherent lie of the situation they were in. What was he doing here, in this place, with this woman? Suddenly, for no reason, he hated her. And his hatred extended to the hotel, to Europeans, and most of all to his own life.

There was a knock on the door.

"Lunch," Gram said.

Abdul looked up at her, pleading. "I'm not supposed to be here," he confessed.

"Well then get in the bathroom and close the door, for heaven's sake," she said impatiently, a twinkle in her eye. Abdul did what she said. When he heard the waiter leave he came back out.

On the small table at the foot of the bed was a French lunch of steak, salad, string beans and a meringue dessert. Shiny silverware sat on pressed linen napkins. Abdul could smell the food. He realized he hadn't eaten all day, and suddenly felt weak with hunger. There was a bottle of red wine, and coffee in a silver decanter.

Gram was leaning over the bed, looking for something in her purse. The purse's contents had spilled out. There were notes, kleenex, makeup—and money, lots of it, laying within reach. Abdul was able to see six or seven hundred American hundred dollar bills.

"There's something here I wanted to show you, if I can just find it," Gram was saying. "We bought it in Fez. It's a hand of Fatima, like the one you have, except it's smaller . . . " Gram chattered on, ransacking her purse for the buried treasure.

"Here it is," she exclaimed triumphantly. She straightened up and turned around, holding something in her hand. Then a look of horror crossed her face. She raised her arms in protection. The wine bottle came down, hitting her on her forearm instead of her head, sending her tumbling backwards onto the bed.

Abdul dropped the wine bottle and went for the money. He grabbed the bills and began stuffing them in his pockets. But hands were restraining him. He tried to pull loose.

"Stop it! Stop it!" The screaming voice of Arthur broke in upon him, shrill and terrified. Gram was moaning on the bed, holding her wrist. A *concierge* rushed in. An *oud* came down over Abdul's head, breaking, stunning him.

Abdul dropped the money, broke away, and ran to the balcony. It was a thirty-foot drop into the garden. Thunderclouds had filled the sky, and rain fell in thick sheets. Abdul dropped into the garden's soft soil, bruised but unhurt. He got up and ran crazily across the garden, rain-blinded, as voices from the balcony shouted after him. He reached the wall that separated the garden from the *medina*, scrambled up and dropped into the alley on the other side.

Abdul stood a moment beside the wall, shaking. His hand was stiff and bloody. He knew that Marrakech's *medina*, which had always offered him safety, would provide it no longer. Relieved at this finality, Abdul turned and stumbled on, his thoughts already turning northward.

*   *   *

Tangier is a bastard town, the most perfect model of colonial evil the march of civilizations could hope to devise. If Marrakech is red with Sherifian blood, Tangier is stained white with perfidy. Born of rape, layered with centuries of unspeakable violation by Phoenecians, Romans, Moors and Western *juntas*, she has come to offer a timeless image of corruption. She lives in a demented puberty, frozen in the first moment of defloration. No indignity remains to be visited upon her.

Still, every dawn, as the sun floods the Pillars of Hercules, she sees herself a bride in white. Teetering on the edge of the hemisphere, spilling down her hills to the bay like bouganvilla, she offers herself to every ship that passes to or from Marseilles, Naples, Athens, Beirut, Alexandria or the Red Sea. Few accept her invitation.

Abdul rode toward Tangier on a bright, cool May morning in the back of a flatbed truck, huddled inside his American windbreaker, dressed in his only set of clothes. He bounced along in the hard grooved metal bottom of the pickup, an ancient Fiat driven by a mad Rabat chicken farmer on his way to Tangier to take some money to his mother who sold cigarettes squatting in the Socco Grande. Abdul's mind was empty, like his stomach, as he watched the road roll away behind him, the red world of Marrakech crumbling like dust into the hard white stucco of the north, the road signs now in a third language, Spanish, beside the Arabic and French.

The road gradually became town's edge, fields dotted with

schools, hovels, mosques, a government agricultural building, flat
and still in the morning, as solitary plowmen, backs bent, followed
donkeys across the pebbly soil. At road's edge, old Rif women
trundled toward town in their red and white striped aprons and ter-
rycloth capes, carrying sticks and babies and nameless bound port-
age to town and market, their legs strong and placed wide like men.
Then a *rond point* where the traffic converged from all sides, a
landscaped circle of palms, cactus, bouganvilla, and Abdul knew
they were on the outskirts of Tangier.

The truck pulled over and stopped. Abdul stood up and looked
over the cab. Ahead, the road dropped downhill into the town.
Wordlessly, the driver waved Abdul out. Abdul jumped out of the
truck to the ground.

"Can't you drive me further in?"

"No," said the driver. "I turn soon."

Abdul gazed at the driver, his eyes dark and empty. "Fuck you,"
he said in English. The driver flung Moghrebi epithets at thim,
honking his horn. But Abdul didn't turn around. He walked off toward the town.

Abdul paused at the peak of the hill. Tangier lay below, the
European section running down to his right, its tall new tourist hotels, unoccupied, white and foreign, rising to the sky like ancient
dreams. And beyond, across the water, the headlands where the
bay completed its curve. Further still in the distance, through the
morning haze as it burned off across the blue straits, lay the low
mountains of Europe, close but untouchable, frozen, unreal, a
myth. Something quickened in Abdul's stomach. He gazed across
the water, standing where once lust-filled Moors had stood envisioning conquest, and later stood again, broken and in flight, must-
ering their bloodied troops. Now Abdul stood there with dreams
of his own.

The sun rose from Mecca, laying the calm harbor bare. Long
whistles blew, calling the workmen to labor. Winches groaned over
a Yugoslavian freighter, loading sardines for Dubrovnik. The morning ferry steamed silently away, making the crossing to Algeciras,
and Europe. The tide was out, the sun flat and warming.

Abdul descended the hill and turned westward, along a broad
boulevard, freshly washed and swept with sun. He came to a *plaza*
ringed with cafes. Already waiters were putting out the chairs. A

couple of hustlers sat huddled in their coats in front of the Cafe de France, stirring coffee. Abdul felt their eyes on him as he passed.

Coming to a vista, he was able to see the native quarter to the west, stitched in stone behind a crumbling wall, running crazily downhill toward the bay. Within, he knew, lay the alleys, shops and cafes he sought. As Abdul walked toward the *medina*, he recalled another time, the morning when he had arrived in Marrakech on the back of a donkey. A welling sense of destiny rose and filled him.

*   *   *

Abdul finds his way to the heart of the medina, the Socco Chico. There he picks up two Americans and a Briton, and arranges to sell them kif. But Tangier is a syndicate town, controlled by a mob, and there is no freelance hustling. Abdul is clubbed in an alley, and wakes up in a darkened room.

*   *   *

Abdul was aware of music playing. Strangely, it was music of the south, an old folk tune from the Atlas. He had grown up hearing it in his village. It had been one of the few tunes the village musicians knew how to play. He heard an oud, a drum, a mandolin and a *rebab*. The music, Abdul decided, was live. It was coming from the next room, mixed with the sound of conversation. Abdul reached up and touched a large welt behind his ear. He swooned from the pain.

A curtain parted, emitting light from the room where the music was playing. Abdul smelled *tajin*, and spicy *h'rira* soup. He decided he was in the back room of a restaurant. A figure had entered, and now stood over him. He was a street boy, one of those he had seen in the Socco Chico.

"They want to kill you. Throw you in the bay." The boy was older than Abdul. His face was pitted, his hair oily and combed back. He wore a blue French topcoat over his shoulders. The hustler sat down on a cushion next to Abdul.

"Country boy," he said quietly. "Where you from? Casa? Goulemine? Marrakech?"

Abdul struggled up onto his elbows. From the dark room he could see out through the curtain into the restaurant. There were low tables and cushions and costumed waiters. The orchestra sat on a dais in the middle of the room. One large table was full, and all the others empty. The restaurant seemed to be closed to outside business. At the table was a thin, older man in a dark suit and dark glasses. Around him were seven or eight hustlers. Some of them Abdul recognized from the Socco Chico. The two he had passed in front of the Cafe de France were there. They were telling the man in the dark glasses their hustling experiences, and laughing. Abdul watched them give him some money. He realized they all worked for the man. And he must work for somebody else.

"That's right," the boy in the room said to Abdul. "This isn't some country town, like where you come from. This is big time. It's organized here." He sat down on a cushion next to Abdul.

"They don't allow independents in Tangier," he said.

"Who doesn't?" Abdul asked, his head pounding.

The hustler smiled. "See that man in there?" He pointed to the man in the dark glasses. "That's Mustapha. See that other one?" Abdul saw that another man sat at the table, his back to him, dressed in uniform.

"Police chief," the hustler said. His quick eyes glinted in the dark. "Hotels, shops, banks. Everything's organized here."

Abdul wasn't sure he understood what he was being told. The band was playing another folk song from the south, and his head hurt. He felt overwhelmed, defeated. Dying would have been a relief.

"So, country boy," the hustler was saying. "You get up now and walk through that room out there. You keep going out the door, and you walk until you're out of Tangier. Tonight. Because if anyone sees you in the Socco Chico or the Socco Grande tomorrow they will cut off both your ears and your tongue. And maybe your penis too."

The hustler stood up and looked down at Abdul.

"Go on," he said.

Abdul rose unsteadily to his feet. His entire body was bruised and sore. He walked out into the restaurant. The room was richly tiled and carpeted, and the dense motifs dizzied him. The men at the table turned to watch. Abdul, spitting blood, stumbled across the room, past the band, past the men at the table, heading for the door. He reached it and lurched past a turbaned doorman out into the alley. He stood against the building, vomiting quietly, as the music from inside pulsed in his wound.

When he was done, he turned and lurched down the alley. Abdul had no idea where he was. It was dark, the *medina* that surrounded him a mysterious labyrinth. He knew he had to get out, but he had no idea how. Nor did he know where to go after that. In truth, he had nowhere to go.

Abdul came to a crack in the wall where water trickled from a broken pipe. He cupped his hands, and brought his face down to them. The water was icy, and brought more pain. But when he stood back up he found that he felt better. Instinctively, he took out his comb. He slicked his hair down, working gingerly around the spot where he had been clubbed.

Abdul began walking again, taking paths that led upward, toward the *casbah*, whose spire he could make out somewhere at the top of the quarter. He was afraid to pass through the Socco Chico again. And he didn't want to end up near the Pension Monaco either, for the foreigners might be waiting with revenge. Abdul thought of the American girl, of her mouth and breasts, and he felt a bleak and bitter longing. Abdul plunged on, enveloped in blackness. The *medina* had become a hallucination, devoid of space and time.

Somewhere far within the quarter, Abdul came upon a tiny cafe. Its sudden light and sound broke the *medina*'s unrelieved night. A sign said, in Arabic: *The Dancing Boy Cafe*. Abdul heard the rattling of a tambourine and the beating of a drum, and he knew that the boy was dancing. Abdul felt in his pockets. He had three *dirhams*. It would buy him mint tea. He went inside.

The cafe was small and crowded, thick with *kif* smoke and the smell of men. The customers had moved against the walls to let the dancing boy through. Abdul edged into place along the wall, and watched.

The boy was young, perhaps fourteen, and had a gold tooth. His dance parodied the Rif women, with their red striped aprons and white bandannas, a frame around his hips to make him womanly. His lips and face were rouged, his skin smooth and light. He reminded Abdul of himself, when he had danced in the El Hamra Cafe in Marrakech, off the Djmaa el Fnaa, only a few years earlier. Abdul's eyes clouded with tears at the memory.

The drum began to beat faster, and the throbbing in Abdul's head merged with the sensuous spectacle of the whirling boy. The dancer moved through the room, batting his eyes and gyrating his hips. He dared, then withdrew. He was coy like a woman, supple like a boy. Who could resist the charm of the dancing boy? And suddenly Abdul desired him, on the one hand wanting the boy himself, on the other the girl that he represented, but above all wanting the youth he had lost, the androgynous safety of adolescence, the simplicity of being admired and wanted. Abdul reached up and found the silver hand of Fatima around his neck. He fingered it and felt its weight. Then he let it go.

The dancing boy whirled by, pausing before Abdul, his eyes vacant and alluring, his gold tooth glinting beneath the cafe's bulb. He was sheathed in transparent red gauze, his lips bud-red. Abdul allowed the fantasy to overtake him, and felt the melting desire spread from his stomach down into his loins. For the first time he was not the desired, but the one who desired.

Then through the smoke and whirling clatter of the dance, Abdul saw that there was a woman, a white woman, in the cafe. He blinked, not at all sure he was really seeing her. As the dancer flickered in the space between them, Abdul watched the woman. She was sitting in between two older Arabs dressed in well-made *djellabas*. The woman looked to be in her forties, perhaps even fifty. Her hair was silver and black, her eyes grey. She wore a long plain black Moroccan cape, an expensive one. She was handsome, unusual looking. What is she doing here? Who is she? Am I dreaming this? Abdul wondered. The woman watched the dancing boy with the same entranced interest as the men, and clapped as the act reached its climax.

The dancer closed with a whirl and a bow, his tambourine shimmering. Then he ran through the room holding out his tambourine. He went to the woman first, and she gave him money. When the boy came around to Abdul he dropped in one of his three *dirhams*. Then he looked back toward the woman, transfixed. He noticed that the people in the cafe treated her with respect, almost reverence. Abdul realized she must be a habitue, known in the quarter. He heard her speak some Arabic. Yes, she was attractive. And Abdul was sure she was rich.

At that moment, in the hallucinatory ambiance of pain and desire and the whirling dream of the dancing boy, mixed with the threat of death and entrapment, Abdul began to formulate an intention. He saw the woman as the pinnacle of his aspirations. He didn't know who she was, but he knew that he could deal with the foreigner better than anyone in Marrakech, and probably in Tangier. She represented the possibility of safety. And Abdul had nowhere else to turn.

On the floor at his feet he saw a card, the cafe's advertisement for itself, with a picture of the orchestra and the dancing boy on the front. Abdul reached down and picked it up. He took a pencil out of his pocket and wrote on the back of the card: I AM VERY ATTRACTED TO YOU. WE MUST TALK. PLEASE. MY HEART IS DEMANDING IT. DO NOT REFUSE ME. Abdul completed the note. Then, as the crowd milled while the musicians took their break, Abdul walked across the room toward the woman. Abruptly one of the men with her stood up and barred his path, holding his arm. The woman looked up and saw him.

"I am sorry to disturb you. Please. I have a message for you," Abdul said imploringly, his eyes shiny with despair and the sudden elation of his act.

The woman hesitated for a moment, then told the man to let her have the card. When she looked back up, Abdul had retreated to a place near the door and stood, arms folded, in a passionate sulk, his eyes blazing. The woman watched him for a few moments, her eyes frank and unblinking. Then she put the card down on the table and turned back to her companions. Abdul's heart sunk. But he remained gazing at her, unmoving. He would melt her with the force of his passion, or turn her away from him utterly.

The woman appeared to have forgotten him. She laughed and applauded the dancing boy as he reappeared in normal costume and sat down beside her, smiling, tambourine in hand. Abdul glowered with jealousy.

Then the woman, still not looking at Abdul, turned to one of her companions, an old wizened Moor with a cavernous face, and asked him something. The man fished around inside his burnoose and came up with a pen. The woman picked up Abdul's card and wrote something on it. Then she stood up to leave. The men rose with her.

The cafe owners bowed and made a path for the woman. They

thanked her in French and Arabic. Someone else thanked her in English. "Merci, Mademoiselle. *Shoukran.* Thank you." Abdul stood by the door, mad with anticipation, his wounds and his danger forgotten.

The chorus of thanks and goodnights rose up around the priestess—for that is what it almost seemed she was, Abdul thought—as she swept toward the door. On the way out she placed the card in Abdul's hand, quickly and firmly, without looking at him. Abdul, his heart racing, took it and shoved it in his pocket.

*　　　　　*　　　　　*

Valerie Minton stood on the balcony of her castle, her villa, her prison, and looked out over the water. It was one in the morning, and she was a little drunk and a little stoned. She thought she could see Europe across the water, but it was pitch black outside, and she finally decided it was impossible, it must be the *kif* pictures in her mind. Below her fell the steep stone wall 200 feet to the beach, the wall that surrounded the *medina*, every *medina*. She could hear the water below, softly—softly not because it was far away but because the Mediterranean had taken the sting out of the hard Atlantic breakers that pounded Casablanca, Agadir, Rabat. Or for that matter New York, Miami, Brighton, Rio, Vera Cruz, Biarritz—all the cities that Valerie Minton knew. Tangier lay tucked into the Mediterranean's lip, yet still looked westward, sucked into seed and incestuous repetition like brackish Alexandria, Athens, Beirut, Naples, doomed towns fed by the tepid pond of the Mediterranean. Tangier, with its westward view, still provided the illusion of escape. Like a variety of the fruit named after it, the town was seedless. Its progeny lived in the glare of a cafe light, the immutable snapshot of money passing from hand to hand. Its people came from nowhere and were going nowhere, its children born ancient, sprung from the womb with their hand out, its old people stoned and cackling like infants.

The first day Valerie Minton had ever seen the *medina* she knew she would occupy it. She had gone to see the villa for the first time with Yakub, the old bell captain at the Hotel Minzah. Its previous owner, an old British gentleman, had called it 'the castle,' for that's what it had in fact been, a caliph's fortress, before the first foreigner had purchased it. The old chap had spoken at great length to the obviously wealthy young American girl—Valerie was twenty-five then, and that had been twenty-five years ago—about its history, the architectural splendor of its forty rooms, its stunning vistas. The British were broke, it was after the War, the gentleman had fallen on hard times. The price was a steal.

Then, as Valerie had left the villa that day with old Yacub and her entourage, she had come upon a group of tiny girls jumping rope in the narrow alley. They were dirty and poor. They couldn't have been more than five or six years old. She watched them and smiled, then gently pushed past them along the path. But the little girls ran on ahead, blocking the alley, and began jumping rope again. They were showing off. Valerie smiled and applauded, and started to pass again. The girls rushed up to her, hands out, begging for money. Valerie realized that they had been jumping rope not for fun, but to hustle money from her. She found this horrible and wonderful. When she didn't give them any money the tiny girls hit her on the back and spat at her and cursed her until the guides drove them off. As she hurried back toward the European quarter she could hear the little girls shouting after her.

The experience haunted Valerie. She had had so little experience with need, growing up in schools and estates from Madrid to Switzerland to Southampton to Santa Barbara, and the image of girls jumping rope for money overwhelmed her. She felt she had found the key to the riddle of her own *malaise*, her inauthenticity. She decided that day to buy the villa and live there. The little beggar girls would be her secret sisters.

Since then she had come back regularly to Tangier each summer for two months, and occupied the great house in the *medina*. She spent the rest of the year in other parts of the world, living in villas and hotels. Her father had made an apparently inexhaustible fortune pillaging South Africa for rubber, and left it to his only daughter. Valerie had used it to live a lavish and bohemian life.

She had wanted to be an artist, and still thought of herself as one, though it had been some years since she painted anything. She took drugs and lovers, and entertained the world's *literati* and people of unusual tastes.

She never did give a *dirham* to those girls in the alley, or their successors down through the years. She lived among the people of the quarter apart, importing most of her needs. She never felt sympathy for the *medina*'s people, never stooped for them. For this they loved her and, as years went by, considered her their own. They basked in the glow and legend surrounding the great villa in the middle of the squalid *casbah*. When independence came, nationalistic fervor seemed to have left her untarnished and uncriticized. Her villa was carefully guarded the ten months she was away by her employees and the local police. When she was here, it was as if the goddess of the *medina* had returned. Natives pointed proudly to Valerie Minton's house as if within resided a *pasha* of their own.

And when, in recent years, she began to take in young boys as lovers, the quarter offered them up gladly, like sacrifices to a deity.

Valerie lay back on a cushion, awaiting the boy from the cafe. She was glad to be back in Tangier. It had been a rough year away. Her life was not what it had always been. Friends seem to diminish as time went on. An abortive trip back to the States had ended in an IRS investigation. She had fled, leaving behind large unpaid bills. She needed to unwind, to relax into the sensuous and uncaring twilight of North Africa.

Valerie stared idly at a flower ornament on a closet door in the room. It was the first time she had noticed it since she had returned. She realized she had been moving at such a speed that she couldn't see it. It was a motif, a design, insistently repeated throughout the house. In shape, it was not unlike female genitals—set in red, articulated by gold filigree. Now, the forms that the gold spelled out suddenly came into focus.

It was a series of flower shapes, winding up from a rootless bottom, bilaterally symmetrical, forming an abstraction of flowerness, pleasing and perfect in formation, suggesting beyond the flower the red center of a woman's desire. Valerie knew that the Muslim, forbidden from depicting the human form, expressed in his motifs intricate codes of the senses and the soul. The details of the flower ornament, snaking within its vulva borders, comforted her. Valerie relaxed into languorous anticipation.

*   *   *

Abdul wound his way up the cracked and crooked alley behind the Socco Chico, the postcard in his hand. The woman had written on it instructions to her villa. A moon had come out, spilling soft, dusty light onto the alley floors.

256

In the middle of a steep path Abdul stumbled over a beggar woman, and fell to his knees. The woman, huddled in her robes, made no sound. For a moment Abdul thought she was dead. Then she stirred, wrapped her tattered burnoose around her, and scuttled back against the shadowed wall. Abdul saw that she was a Blue Person, from the desert. Tattoos ran from her forehead down to her chin, her hands stained blue with dye. She looked out at him with dark, animal eyes.

Suddenly Abdul was afraid. He scrambled to his feet and stumbled onward. The alley became steps, and the steps suddenly widened. He was in front of the wool spinner's shops, where by day boys sorted thread and yarn, standing on the steps. By moonlight Abdul could see his own shadow, long and fragmented, running diagonally across the steps. Above him the moon moved quickly over the mosque tower at the top of the quarter, throwing the mosque's shadow over him, obliterating his own. Abdul felt a bone-weary lassitude. He wished he could drop to the ground and curl up against a wall, like the Blue woman, sleep until dawn, and awake untroubled to some simple occupation, to weave his tiny piece of thread in the loom of his people's endless carpet. He wondered how he had strayed so far from his origins, and the things he knew as a child.

There on the steps of the casbah, deep in the mosque's shadow, Abdul tasted and smelled his own doom. A predator's icy lust drove him toward the rich white woman's villa to consummate his destiny and hers. And something just as deep—but no deeper—made him want to run back to the Blue Woman huddled in the alley and fall to the ground, drop his head into her lap, feel the enclosure of her mute, bottomless robes, and weep for Allah's and his mother's forgiveness. For a moment the two urges lay in perfect balance, his sudden swell of conscience poised against the magnitude of the evil that lay before him.

A cool wind from across the water, from Europe, rippled through the darkened quarter. It passed across Abdul's forehead like ice. From somewhere, an impatient cock's crow sounded. Abdul realized he was sweating, immobile, on the top step. To the right lay the wide, high entrance to the villa, gleaming blue-white beneath the moon. A tall carved door of wood stood at the end of the entranceway, intricate and formidable. A *fez*-topped guard, sleepy and large, sat on a stool in front of his door, his arms folded. He watched Abdul walk toward him with the idle interest of one trained to unleash violence at a moment's notice.

*   *   *

(Abdul and Valerie become lovers.)

*   *   *

Abdul's and Valerie's affair was predatory, joyous and evil. Their lovemaking was frenzied and imperfect, their days uneasy and idle, their fights protracted and cruel. They felt their way through the drama they had come together to play like two bantam cocks in the ring. It was colonialism's perfect romance, potent and doomed, a hustler and an heiress, history's exiles. Morocco no longer cared about its Abduls. It had its destiny set on another course. Nor did it care any longer about its Valerie Mintons, or grovel before them. Only the IRS and a few fading friends knew Valerie Minton still existed.

The news of Valerie and her new lover spread through the Socco Chico like electricity. The tawdry life of the quarter came alive around the romance. The pundits had their day, dragging out their favorite Valerie Minton jokes and stories.

But the hustlers were not happy, nor were their masters. They had been trumped by an interloper. Would the boy try to exact revenge on them? Valerie's wishes were inviolate in the quarter. What sort of influence could he have, through Valerie Minton, upon their operations?

One afternoon Valerie and Abdul walked down the path from the villa and emerged in the Socco Chico. The hustlers and storekeepers were sitting around waiting for the Algeciras ferry, and the sun was warm. Valerie had on a stylish blouse and a full skirt with clanking Moroccan jewelry, her long hair flowing behind. Abdul was dressed in a new three-piece French suit she had bought him, and dark glasses. In the middle of the square Abdul paused, took out a gold lighter and lit up a Gauloise. Then, not looking to either side, he continued on with Valerie, smiling and whispering in her ear.

It was a moment of grand theater in the life of the Socco Chico, and would nourish legends. The street boys ran to tell Mustapha about it. Mustapha swore vengeance upon the boy. When the Police Chief heard of the incident he laughed until he fell off his chair. It was the best amusement the quarter had provided in years, certainly better than the drab ritual of rounding up destitute and crazed foreigners and turning them over to their embassies, or hospitalizing them, or dumping them on the ferry. There was nothing anyone could do about Valerie Minton's affair, he said to his lieutenant, except enjoy it.

But one thing was certain. If Abdul ever fell from favor with the queen on the hill he would be devoured. The righteous and the corrupt would fight for the privilege to his flesh. Like an actor on a stage, Abdul lived bathed in light, surrounded on every side by shadows.

John Bennett / Ellensburg, Washington

THE DEFROCKING OF ALBERT DREAM

from *The Night Of The Great Butcher*
December Press, 1976: Chicago
Editor: Curt Johnson

IT WAS Mardi Gras again in New Orleans, the whole world descending upon the city in a religious fervor, distorting their faces with grease and paints and bewilderment, the grapes of wrath being pressed into Ripple Wine while Steinbeck stumbles about in the rice paddies of a lean and angry Asia, surrounded by 500,000 protective American boys all poking elbows into his old ribs and giving him the peace sign, good-humored, joshing boys, while his fingers mush through the mud of rice paddies in search of his glasses which he lost decades ago, traded them in with his soul and his vision for respectability, conservatism, and a dog named Charlie, not even knowing anymore that it's his vision he's looking for, writing underwater with a 98¢ Parker and smiling shyly at the boys, his eyes cluttered with stars and stripes and dollar signs...

Charlie, however, smells trouble and—his tail tucked securely between his hind legs—makes it for Saigon.

But back in New Orleans, Mardi Gras is gathering momentum and the church bells are pealing hallelujahs. All the drinks in all the bars are triple-priced to make you enjoy and appreciate them more. At 10 a.m. already there are solid middle-class citizens falling into the gutters, impaling themselves on their corn dogs, and vomit flows as freely as good will.

It is in the American tradition. It is sacred and sacrosanct, a preparation for Lent, and you need not confess it on Saturday evening. It's Fun Time USA, and to add spice to the festivities, every year, as dependable as the pill, a horde of narcotics agents, city cops, state troopers, representatives of the Treasury Department and the Ladies for a Sterilized New Orleans Committee descend upon the local heads and small time dealers, rounding up a good 40 to 75 of them in one night. They slap a $10,000 bail on everyone and then dump them into Parish Prison where they ceremoniously have their locks shorn by other inmates, and then are raped, set on fire and given access to more dope than they had ever dreamed of on the outside. They are held until after Mardi Gras to keep them from being a nuisance to the average good citizen who has come a long way to stagger dazed through the crowded streets. When the religious fervor finally dies down, most of the luckless heads are set free because of "lack of sufficient evidence" and given the advice: "Boy, you better *git* yor ass outa N'Orlins, hear?"

Marty O'Farrell wasn't given this advice. He was sentenced to ten years in Angola for selling to a narcotics agent.

Narcs are getting to be complex people and hard to detect, unless you're old and cynical. Marty wasn't. He was Candide, a bleeding, wild-eyed, hair to his asshole Candide with strong strains of Dostoyevsky and Jesus Christ running through him. Marty wanted to love and trust everyone. In spite of a Catholic upbringing, in spite of the Marines and Vietnam, in spite of the fact he'd been shat upon and had seen his friends go mad and babbling into oblivion under the calloused ministrations of a Mardi Gras, flag-waving, genocidal society—in spite of himself, he tended to love and trust.

He loved and trusted Albert Dream. Albert Dream was a nigger. A black nigger, although that is incidental. Albert Dream was a model poor boy who made good. (In New Orleans you eat poor boys.) Up from the slums came Albert, out of high school with a C-average, into the Air Force as a jet mechanic to keep the boys flying (quite a contrast to his later function as a narc, which was to shoot the boys down who were flying). Wife, kids. And after the Air Force, to the police department, where the G brothers told him: "Boy, we want you to be a narcotics agent and expose all the sinister and ugly gangsters who are smoking marijuana and ruining the lives of our youth and raping and molesting our children."

Albert was slightly dazed, and the "boy" that slipped in stuck in his throat a little, and it recalled visions of his father, his grey-haired old father full of the wisdom of suffering, saying, "Yassuh, mister James, yassuh. Ah won't never do it no more. Yassuh, thank ya, suh," backing out of the realtor's office with his head lowered and his crumpled hat clenched to his black breast, Albert and his brother Napoleon stumbling backward with him, clutching his tattered coat for what protection and solace it offered, eyes wide like blemished moons, stumbling backward out of the realtor's office as if a gigantic furnace blast had hit them.

"And you don't forget it, boy! You hear? You go to any authorities any more talkin' 'bout rats and high rents an' ah'll see you ain't got *no* roof over your head *no* more! Hear, *boy*?"

Albert's blood pumped heavy like cotton bales through his head. He saw a million niggers swinging from a million trees from Georgia to west Texas. He heard the white men like a host of pale angels singing "Old Black Joe." He saw the flashing steel of long razors in the lazy summer sun and heard the piercing cries of terror like splintered glass as genitals were severed. He had this vision, and it registered in the pink minds of the G brothers as hesitation.

"Albert? You hear us, Albert?"

"Yassuh," he said, and bit his tongue. He began to sweat.

"Albert, say!" And here Albert felt a heavy hand on his shoulder and found himself being offered a cigarette. "Say!" A friendly nudge in the ribs. "Here's *your* chance to kick a little ass!"

The room was full of good-natured laughter, everyone was smiling and friendly, even the comely typist was smiling and raised her skirt demurely up to her pussy, her tongue wetting her upper lip like the head of a penis...

Albert was sweating even more, and his facial muscles twitched. His blood raced through his body. It never failed.

Albert, a total unknown on the scene, laid low for a month until he could grow a mustache and a goatee. During this time he was properly briefed in the jargon and ways of narcotics users, ways which he had known about since he was old enough to walk. He was then told to dress as he thought best, and one day he came swinging through the swinging doors of the Seven Seas, a hip spade if there ever was one. He drank in the Seas and at Bonaparte's, and then he drank in Bonaparte's and at the Seas. He worked hard for his money. Once he went to LaCasa's to drink, and three bikers from L.A. threw him through the front window. He never went back. He tried to learn chess at the Seas, but it taxed his mind, and chess players didn't seem to be the type he was after anyway. He made a few friends, laid a few chicks, but everytime he said, "Hey, man, where can I score?" people always answered, "Man, I don't know. Things are tight in this fuckin' town. Narcs everywhere. You never know who's a narc." "Yeah, I know, man," he'd answer.

He was over a month on the job when he met Marty. Marty came into the Seas totally stoned on Panama Red. He was dealing. Marty was dealing like it was going out of style. It was a ritual. Every day he would arise at noon, smoke some weed, and then stuff a paper bag full of about ten lids and an assortment of Mescaline tabs and acid tabs. He would cram the paper bag into his hip pocket, and it would stick out all the way up to the small of his back. He would then trudge into the Quarter. Just off of Decatur, about a block from the Seas, he'd jam the brown paper bag into a crevice along the side of an abandoned building. Then he'd walk about like an Italian fruit vendor in New York City, practically bellowing, "Buy my wares! Buy my wares! Acid, Mescaline, good Panama Red! Buy my wares!" Marty would study a person for maybe five minutes, and if he felt the right vibes, he'd approach and bellow, "Buy my wares!" He did a thriving business, made enough to support himself and his woman Margie, who was pregnant. They were very happy and saving for the child.

Marty walked into the Seas and studied Dream. He decided he was all right. Joe Jack, the bartender, turned off the jukebox, and everyone took his place.

"Buy my wares, mister!" sang Marty, stoned as a dinosaur.

Dream was cool, and in a deep baritone sang, "Whatcha sellin', man?"

Then Marty took over the stage, bounding onto the bar. "I got soul products! I got acid to make life sweet! Grass that grows greener on the other side of the fence! An herb to hash out your problems with! I got the stones they stoned St. Stephen with, sacred relics, and they'll stone you too!"

Then Dream, he got up, and he sang deep and mellow and grave: "How I know you ain't no narc?"

Well, Dream was cool, but Marty wasn't stupid. The chorus comes in. Long hairs and legitimate spades, dock workers and artists, drunks and shop owners—they dance about waving bottles and guitars and paint brushes. They sing: "Hey! Hey! What's a narc? Noah had a narc! Narc the herald angels sing! Cool it, here comes the Narc Angel! Can't you mow your grass, man, can't you mow your grass? Chug-a-chug! Chug-a-chug! City Ordinance 513 dash says ....ohhh, I'm a hash slinger by profession, I'm a long way from home ..."

BAM. They all sit down and resume what they had or hadn't

been doing before Marty walked in. Marty finds himself walking out the door with Dream, thinking he's really got some good weed this time, some real super stuff.

The big mystery is what went on in Dream's head as he got to know Marty and Marty's friends during the six months that followed, and what must go on in his head *now* as he helps old white women across the streets and investigates broken windows and minor thefts in his new and dubious role of Patrolman Dream, his cover blown for political advantage, turned out to pasture.

Perhaps we will never know, and most of us don't care. But Marty cares. His eyes have another twist of complexity in them, and he continually asks himself—why? That's the big crime of Albert Dream: not that he got Marty busted, but that he turned the vise one full turn tighter on Marty's head, drove him one step further back into his dark cave where he someday may bash his senses out on the cold slimey walls or rush crazy out into the pink day like Christ among the money changers, his old Marine M-16 flashing white hot retribution, mowing down saint and sinner, man, woman and child alike while the $25 an hour psychiatrists thumb frantically through their Do-It-Yourself manuals looking for the answer, writing books on "The case of Martin O'Farrell, psychopathic and compulsive killer," best sellers that provide them with their European vacations.

Dream got to know Marty well. He ate at Marty's home and watched Margie grow big with child. He drank with him and met his friends. They smoked together and watched the sun rise from the Gov. Nicholls Street Wharf. Dream knew his job well, and he'd sometimes say, "Hey, man, why don't we deal some smack, make some big money?" Marty would look bewildered then and go on for hours about the countless pros and cons and perspectives involved in dealing smack; he'd relate it to people and love and responsibility, reveal a myriad of relative values, a cosmos of possibilities. Dream would laugh nervously and look sidelong at the floor or the wall or a passing car and say, "Man, you a *deep* motherfucker. You must be puttin' me *on*!" And Marty would say, "Never mind, let's do a number."

Then Mardi Gras drew near and the *NOLA Express* (the local underground paper) began to issue get-out-of-town warnings, but no one listened, no one felt guilty of any crime, no one could take it as seriously as the G brothers, and everyone got busted.

The night before they picked up Marty, Dream approached him with a gun. They had just finished supper at Marty's, Margie had cleared the table and was in the kitchen doing the dishes, and Dream took out the gun and laid it on the table.

"Let's kill that nigger," Dream said. Marty had gotten burned for $200 in a deal with a black guy from across town.

Marty's head spun. Tommy was there too, and he had never trusted Dream. Now he felt sick and cautious. Marty and Tommy looked at each other and they said a lot of things with their eyes that the suddenly impatient Dream could not understand, things the G brothers could not teach him.

"Come on, man, we'll blow the bastard away!" Dream said, rubbing the seasoned revolver, a somber 38 automatic. It was supposed to work. The G brothers said it would work. They said that all the heads were vicious anarchists and had to be eliminated. But something went wrong with the final touches. Marty and Tommy rowed off in a small skiff across a moat of strange ideas, and Dream felt his grip on them slipping.

He told all this to the G brothers the next day as they made ready for the big bust that night. The G brothers said he had handled it wrong, and Dream said he didn't think so, said he didn't think there was any way to make Marty do it, and then the room fell silent. Dream was losing his grip on everything, it seemed, and he vaguely wondered if he had ever had a grip on anything to begin with. The sweat ran down his muscular flanks and made dark musty beads in the springy hair of his arm pits. The second hand on the wall clock moved relentlessly down toward the six, scanning the face of time like radar. They were all waiting.

"Ah guess you're right," Dream said, looking at the area of floor between his imported Italian shoes.

Everyone exhaled, the second hand moved past the six and began climbing slowly up toward the twelve, and the room was full of laughter and joking again. One of the G brothers offered Dream a cigar, saying, "Take it! Come on, *boy*, take it!" The comely secretary pulled her dress up and came and sat on his lap, straddling him with her white thighs and rubbing the moist warmth of her panties against his enormous erection. The cigar in his mouth had been lit and a thousand hands were pounding him on the back. The room resounded with laughter, deep, red-throated laughter. He did not move, did not dare move, sat motionless like a hare in a thicket as the sound of the hunters and the dogs came closer. He smiled contortedly, pleadingly, his huge eyes darting from one to the other of the faces that swirled above him in the smoke. He wished he could make his erection go away, but it grew and swelled larger, and he felt the warm waves of climax vibrating through him.

He came in great twitching spurts, and the room went red with terror. Stereophonic angels stretched away as far as the eye could see, and the world became the sound of their singing; "Old Black Joe" drove him like a cat-o-nine-tails back to where he became Little Black Sambo in endless flight from tigers, back through history, back to where he came from. The church bells pealed their victory from Saint Louis Cathedral, and the tourists stripped themselves of their clothing and swam naked in a sea of Dixie Beer. New Orleans erupted time and again like a volcanic orgasm, hot lava gurgling from her lips, rolling into the sea like bright-orange billows of cloud. All the fleets were called back from the Seven Seas, and the sun set on the Union Jack. The largest bomb in the world exploded in the basement of City Hall, and everything went black.

They threw a glass of water into his face, and he sat up too abruptly, feeling that warm, burning pain up through his neck and into the back of his skull. He shook his head like a dog coming out of water and felt between his legs for his genitals. They were still there.

"What happened?" he mumbled.

"You went an' fainted on us, boy," said one of the G brothers. "Why ah believe you been workin' too hard!" There was a polite murmur of laughter, and the comely secretary smiled at him from behind her typewriter. "Listen, you go home an' git some sleep, hear? Come on back about ten tonight for the pictures."

Outside it was cold. The sweat on his body dried, leaving white deposits of salt on his black skin. He drove home without turning on the radio, and he slept on the couch fully dressed.

While Dream slept, Marty and Margie made love. They lay on the couch after supper stroking each other and whispering, and then they went to their large bed and sat naked, smoking. They sat kissing on the edge of the bed like children. Their hands began to seek each other out, to fondle breasts full with mother's milk and smooth curving skin, napes of neck and genitals and thighs and their tongues hot on each other. He pulled her over on him and she rocked there like the rocking horse of lost childhood, pressing his child against him to give him solace and ease his bruised mind. He entered her and they moved together. She sat high on him and thrust her head back, letting all her rich dark hair flow, her hands behind her resting on his strong legs for support. He moved with her and his hands raced gently over her swollen breasts and her great protrusion of child. She cried softly as they made love, and she could not define her tears. Their rhythm became faster and his hands shifted to her buttocks. They came together in a prolonged climax, and she collapsed against him, her tears wetting his neck and chest, his face and the great beard. He held her and wanted to tell her it would be all right, but he couldn't, he could only stroke her hair and her back, press her to him, press their child gently between them.

The next day was trash day, and about midnight, Marty gathered the large brown paper bags and went down the stairs to place them on the curb. He placed them on the curb, but before he could get back inside, three men grabbed him and shoved him against the wall. He did not struggle, because he knew by their clothes and their eyes that they were police and would beat him if he resisted. He acknowledged that he was Martin O'Farrell, and they cuffed his hands in front of him. Margie opened the window and called, but he yelled, "Get back! Don't come down here!" and they hit him. One officer asked her if she was with him, but it had been foreseen, this moment, and she said no and closed the window, going immediately to the phone to call Tommy.

Marty was taken to Central Lock-up, and at Central Lock-up were all Marty's friends, all cuffed and shackled, some of them stoned, some of them straight and full of bitterness and hate. They were all gathered outside, herded together on a large concrete courtyard. There were bright floodlights for the occasion, and newsmen standing about smoking cigarettes and joking; there were TV cameras and officers of the law and the handful of narcs who had made it all possible; and among them was Dream, his eyes puffy, shivering from the cold. Flash bulbs exploded in Dream's eyes, and questions were fired at him by articulate newsmen. He stammered and stuttered and scuffed his feet, looking down with his hands jammed into his pants pockets as he had done all his life whenever the Man drew him into focus. His father's face fluttered through his mind like a bat. He kept trying to remember something, something important, something that would give him back his grip on things. But before he could find it, they were leading him across the courtyard past moaning children and grim-faced men, leading him past the great cargo of humanity to the side of Martin O'Farrell, the man of cosmic thought with whom Dream had stood at sunrise on the shores of the Mississippi. Martin O'Farrell who had stood on the battlefields of Vietnam and on the battlefields of Baltimore and New York and New Orleans. Martin O'Farrell who had searched across this great land for love. Dream approached him, haggard and finally civilized.

Marty stood before him in a ragged pair of jeans, no shoes, no shirt, the hair swirling on his naked chest. Dream scuffed his feet and looked intently at the hard concrete. The reporters fired questions at him.

"Hey, Dream, this is your big fish, right?"

"How'd you get him, Dream?"

"Were you ever in danger?"

"Did your family suffer?"

"Stand beside him, Dream, give him a 'that'll learn ya' look!"

Laughter, laughter, joshing, good-humoured American boys, laughter and chains and blood and hate, all without roots, the 200-year American tradition... *oh America, it is not your blood-stained hands that horrify, it is the childlike way you wield the axe...*

"Look at him, Dream! *Look at him!*"

But Dream had no stomach for it, not until Marty raised his cuffed hands and shook them and the thick vessel bulged in his neck. "*Nigger!* he yelled. "*Nigger!*"

Dream froze.

"You are a nigger to the human race!" Marty yelled, and the courtyard fell silent.

It was then that Dream felt the full brunt of the shame, and only the suffering and pride of 200 years gave him the strength to raise sullen eyes to lock with Martin O'Farrell's.

The photographers captured it for the front page the next day, and that glance is all the public knows of the 1969 Mardi Gras bust, all they have to form their opinions by. There were no cameras or ears to capture Marty's soft, "Why, Dream? Why?"

It is a one-dimensional world we live in, and for the time being, all three-dimensional beings must suffer. But it is a universe of countless dimensions, and the bells of Mardi Gras toll just for you.

Robert Creeley / Buffalo, New York

from MABEL: A STORY

from *Unmuzzled Ox*, Number 13: 1976
New York City
Editor: Michael Andre

THINK OF the good times...Jo's commodious nature, sprawled amply at base of tree trunk wet extensive night somewhere in Wales. Being young, of course, room for it all possibly. Girls then to women, subtle but inevitable transfer. 'Thirty years on this case...'

And you wanted to be *good*, however you defined it for yourself, *fitting*, appropriate to the occasion. It's about all that's left of that way of thinking of it, 'shape up...'

Built up resentments inevitably also, also not to be avoided. Bitterness. Anger. Frustration of being stuck with it, part now of the history. 'Fucking isn't everything...' Slapped face.

So you got stuck with it too, trying to please the ladies—and why weren't they pleased. Histories of shifting discontent, maladjustments, *try again.*

You put them where you thought they were, in your head, you saw them as a partial contest, of yourself, by some circumstance you had no information of otherwise. You considered them, possibly, to be the best judges, etc.

Again and again, 'it isn't really the point, that I come, that isn't what fucking's about, for me...' You thought. But could never really accept it as true, and how would you tell the others, if you thought to, and sometimes you did, that they didn't. Didn't what? They said.

Stuck with wanting to win, to prove it. Given world as destructive quicksand you had to find some purchase in, point of—struggling to get to mythic elsewhere was here all the time. Just lie down for once, simple enough.

The jungle's casual, good lord! Eighteen yet. In the middle or edge of the *second* world war. You'd heard enough about the first from your uncle, who lived unhappily next door. He even rode a motor-cycle, in capacity of dispatch rider, through bombs bursting in air to immaculate completion of his appointed rounds. Touch of chlorine gas, attractive occasional cough—ah hero...

Whereas you hung on in the chaos to funked-out drunks and weird-os, the *men*—got hauled one night from water barrel you were sharing with several floating up-ended dead cats you were too stoned to realize were there too. Bothering the world again. But laughing.

Confusion, compulsion to stay in that company, freaked horror, minimal, at mode of coercion Murphy uses to 'get girls for us,' friend King from San Diego riding shotgun, you in back seat of truly careening jeep. Take the boss man of this charming village for a ride! Trees so huge, so steamy, they look like parboiled fingers coming out of the earth. 'This is Burma, buddy. I see you're back.'

Give the head man a drink, friend. Sits in unconfident dignity as jeep plows on and on, bullock tracks, miles from home now, gentle man in some consternation as to how return shall be accomplished. Explains that the kind of women you have in mind are not persons of the town. Another five miles, he's reconsidered. So three, for you three, are presented once you have given him back to his people. Three relaxed maidens, hopefully, yours the small sort of vigorous one, giggles. In jeep, as you drive back to base, her hands are busy about proud young body, much to your thoughtful dis-may, you think. In camp you separate from the friends, crawl into back of your ambulance with newly acquired companion, let back flap fall.

The world's smallest room. Or vice versa. You don't share a lang-uage, like they say. Few cultural pursuits in common. Just one of each. Amazing how factually and persistently it works out. Thuds, shudders, grunts of body's delight. She is *pleased*, she is *happy*, she is *laughing*! No joke. Later, leaving, you give her carton of cigarettes *in memoriam*. She breaks up!

Fumbling around world in subsequent years, head full of plans and patterns, you remember wistfully that clandestine affair. If you could just get it together again, of course no gun at the temple this time, no flooring the car just to prove the point. These are more thoughtful people presently your company. They tell you a lot about yourself that otherwise you would never have known.

Animal body with wired up head. Back tracking through maze of knotted kite strings. If you could just get it clear of that one branch up there, it might come down. Elsewise whiff of pleasing sweat stench, gutsy chuckles. Won't they let you out anymore to play?

Sadly they don't dig you anymore. Got to face up to that. You land too much on their heads, breaks the rhythm. Who wants to hear about the dead and dying or the terms of the new job, with their hands in yours, put it. Can't you shut up and let them go to sleep. How many have you got in there.

Fantasies of past present improvements possible. Remember the lady who used to change you into Dostoyevsky? You spent a lot of time with that one, flattered no doubt. But she finally switched authors.

So a few times you dance in the rain, telling the neighbors for days after what a great place you live in because you can be naked in your own backyard. Gee whiz. Next time you should have a party. You come so close, as it is.

Possibly it's over, hairy greying old person. Pull up a chair and get that load off. Your feet. Surely life had it's moments in spite of you. And you saw the point—dazzling, clear, *open*—even as you missed it. Closer than most. And next time you'll know better.

When that head gives up, and that skin's finally gone, and the old bones have been kicked around, and it's mouldy and natural and quiet, you'll have done well enough. There'll be another Jo's broad bottom, flat on that moist luxurious earth, and the humming generous darkness, you old tree, you. And for once you won't care she isn't listening.

Jerry Bumpus / San Diego, California

LOVERS

from *Vagabond*, Numbers 23/24: 1976
Ellensburg, Washington
Editor: John Bennett

PENNY leaped the Morgans' back yard fence—she knew that would
stop all of them but Danny. The rest of the children had to run up
the fence and crowd through the gate. As she turned between the
Morgan house and the Dunlap house she heard feet pounding behind her, and, turning the corner of the Dunlaps', she glanced over
her shoulder and let out a trilling shriek when she saw Danny right
behind her. She dodged around the corner, behind the shrubberies,
and lost Danny for a moment. But when she ran from the shrubs,
Danny lunged for her and they fell across the sidewalk, over the
little wire fence, and into a deep bed of petunias.

The rest of the children came squealing around the corner,
swarming through the shrubberies, and piled onto Penny and
Danny, and they were all of them rolling around, giggling, touching Penny, their sweaty faces big-eyed, gleeful, when the screen
door banged open and Mrs. Dunlap charged onto the porch, her
bushy gray hair seeming to stand on end as if she were beholding
wild animals in the act of seizing control of the neighborhood.

She came to the edge of the porch, faltered, her large mouth
hanging open. Then she clenched a fist and struck her forehead.
"Jesus God," she whispered.

One of the kids giggled. Penny and Danny scrambled to their
feet.

Then it hit—but Penny was moving fast. She jerked one of the
really little ones to his feet, and she didn't catch all Mrs. Dunlap
was saying. But she caught the tone. Mrs. Dunlap was temporarily
out of her mind—and she repeated that several times: "You've just
plain driven me out of my mind, for God's sake."

They all climbed over the little wire fence and retreated to the
street—expecting that at any moment Mrs. Dunlap would grab an
arm, or the back of the neck, which was much worse; they all knew
Mrs. Dunlap would go for the back of the neck.

But when they reached the middle of the street they turned and saw Mrs. Dunlap wasn't chasing them. Down in the flower bed on her hands and knees, Mrs. Dunlap was crying.

Penny giggled. But stopped. All the kids, even Danny, were very serious when they saw the woman down like that.

They stood there, and Penny felt the entire length of the block on both sides of the street hush with an awful intensification of the already somber quiet of dusk. She was glad her mother wasn't home.

"Why, oh why?" Mrs. Dunlap wept. "My lovely petunias. Why my *petunias*?"

"We're sorry, Mrs. Dunlap," Penny said.

"And *you*," Mrs. Dunlap said, slowly looking up from the trampled flowers, and Penny wished she had kept her mouth shut. "*You!* You little ..." She stopped herself. Penny wanted her to go on. She wanted very much to know what Mrs. Dunlap almost called her.

"Tell me," Mrs. Dunlap said, getting to her feet and coming across the yard to stand on her sidewalk, her fists on her wide hips. "Just tell me why you lead these little children to *do* such things as this. Why do you *play* with them? *Look* at you." The kids crowded around Penny. Danny turned and stared at Penny. She wanted to look down, but didn't. She just blinked her eyes once. "How old are you, young lady?"

"Thirteen."

"Thirteen years old. And you're all the time playing with these little tiny kids. Why *look* at them. They're five and six years old and you're *playing* with them."

Danny's eleven, Penny wanted to say, but didn't.

"There must be something wrong with you. Why don't you play with children your own age?" She waited. "You're disgusting. You're *all* disgusting, running around after her like a pack of ..." Mrs. Dunlap jerked her head to the side. For the rest of it, her railing at the kids for all their other crimes—beating down her grass and the grass of all the other yards in the neighborhood—Mrs. Dunlap avoided Penny's eyes. And Penny noticed that and she was puzzled, and it was funny—she laughed. When she did, the other kids laughed.

"This is *not* a laughing matter," Mrs. Dunlap said. She told them she was going into the house right this minute and call their parents.

275

"And when your mother gets home, young lady," she said, looking at Penny again, "I'll be right over and the three of us will have this out *once and for all*."

But that didn't worry Penny—her mother wouldn't be back till tomorrow afternoon. But the threat worked on the little kids—most of them went straight home.

Penny and Danny, and Danny's little brother Mike, went up and sat on Penny's porch steps. They watched Mrs. Dunlap, in the flowerbed again, pick up the limp corpses of her petunias and lay them in a pile. Mr. Dunlap came out and stood at the side of the porch. Penny could hear them talking low, though she couldn't hear the words. She watched Mr. Dunlap, bald and short, and she thought maybe he would look across the street at her, but he didn't. He only looked at her when he didn't think she would see him—and when she caught him, he would look away quickly. She always said, "Hello, Mr. Dunlap," when she happened to be out front as he backed his car out of his driveway, or when he was alone in his front yard, and he always answered her, but low, his head down, not looking at her, as if he didn't really mean it when he said hello.

Penny, Danny, and Mike rode Danny and Mike's bikes for a while, Penny and Danny riding double, Penny behind Danny on the long banana seat, her large, smooth legs straddling Danny's narrow hips.

Then they sat on the porch again, talking, and Mike went home. After a while Danny followed Penny into her house.

James Morgan, from his window in the second floor of the house across the street, watched them go inside and then there was a heavy, dull blank.

He was unable to know what she was thinking when he couldn't see her. When she was playing in the street or in one of the yards, he could merely look at her closely—seldom blinking his eyes, hardly breathing—and inside himself he could hear her, hear every word she whispered to Danny, every thought that passed through her mind.

James knew what they did when she and Danny went inside her little house. First they went to the kitchen. Penny's mother worked at the A & P and she brought home big boxes of cookies. She and Penny ate gingersnaps and cream-fills all the time. So Penny and

Danny went into the kitchen and ate some cookies, and then they came out to the front room and listened to the Beatles on Roy's stereo. Roy was Penny's mother's fiance. Then sometimes they went into Penny's tiny bedroom, crowded with stuffed rabbits and giraffes, and Penny would take off her clothes, all but her bikini panties and bra, and she would lay on her bed, stretched out, and while Danny sat in the little rocking chair by the bed, Penny would tell him about men and women.

But James could only see them. He couldn't hear Penny, no matter how hard he stared at the house and the pink and white curtain, always closed, over the window in Penny's bedroom.

James waited, hoping Penny and Danny would come out again, but once they went into the house, they would stay for a long time, and when the front door eventually opened, Danny would come out alone.

But James could hear Danny and know what he was thinking no matter how far away he went. When Danny and Mike and some of the other boys went up to the park to play, James always knew where they were and exactly what they were doing—he could listen closely and hear what Danny was thinking as he played baseball or as he swam when they all went to the pool.

Danny came Tuesday afternoons to visit James. They played checkers and sometimes Fascination or Monopoly. James' favorite was Monopoly, but Danny didn't like it—it took too long. "There's going to be a new fourth grade teacher next year," Danny said. "My aunt knows her. She just got out of college. It's your move."

They were playing checkers and James played slowly, being careful with his moves.

"Miss Wilson is going to California. She's going to live with her mother," Danny said. "Can you imagine being that old and going someplace to live with your mother?"

James moved. Danny moved quickly and again waited for James.

"They had to make Miss Wilson quit. There's something wrong with her. It's your move. Probably being a teacher is what did it to her. Always fighting with me and Rodney Pearson and George Getz. Your move."

James moved. Danny quickly moved one of his kings, and as soon as he did James jumped that king and another, leaving Danny just one man on the board to James' five. "Geez," Danny said, shaking his head, his handsome face grimaced into a wrinkled imitation of his father's.

"Let's play another one," James said.

"Uh huh," Danny said, shaking his head, not looking at James. "I got to go."

"You just got here. It's just twenty after one and you got here at five minutes till one."

"I don't care. I got to go. I'm supposed to meet some guys."

"Who?"

Danny acted as if he hadn't heard. Then he glanced at James and said, "What?"

"Who are you going to meet?"

"Some guys. You don't know them. They don't live around here. I'm going to meet them up at the park. We're starting up a league." He looked out the window at the sun, bright on the maple tree below James' window.

James' mother tried to get Danny to stay a little longer, play another game of checkers and have some cake—the icing was cooling on a chocolate cake, it had probably set long enough, she would go down and cut them both a piece . . . But Danny couldn't stay. Sorry. He had to meet those guys, and he didn't look at James as he pushed the table back. And he pushed the table too far—it jolted James' bed, making a strange, hollow *koong*, and Danny looked away, embarrassed.

While James ate a piece of the chocolate with ice cream, he looked out the window. In a few minutes Danny came down the sidewalk with Mike. They had their baseball gloves, and both wore new red baseball caps. They crossed the street to Penny's. Danny knocked and they talked when she came to the door, barefooted and wearing cut off jeans and a tight sweater. Danny was asking Penny to go with him and Mike to play baseball, and James knew Penny was glad he asked her, for it meant that someday he would ask her to marry him and they would live in this block and have children who would ride their bikes up and down and play bounce ball until they were big enough to go to the park and play real baseball and . . .

Penny went into the house and Danny and Mike waited on the porch, talking, Danny socking his fist into his glove. Then Penny came out. She was still barefooted, but she had changed to tight red shorts and a white halter. They headed up the street, and by the time they reached the corner five or six little kids were tagging along.

And James lay back and with his eyes half closed, staring out the window at the top limbs of the maple tree bobbing slightly in a breeze that seemed to touch only some, not all, of the leaves, he was with Penny, Danny, and Mike, and when they got to the park the other guys were already there.

The baseball diamond and the swimming pool, at opposite ends of the park, were separated by picnic tables and benches scattered under enough trees to make a forest when the kids needed one, and two stone toilets where last summer Penny had taken off all her clothes and let some of the kids look at her, and where with lipstick she had drawn a picture of a naked woman on the wall and under it written her name and the phone number of the police station.

The other guys knew Penny. They were in the same grade with her and they didn't like her—over a year ago they nicknamed her Pigpen Penny. But since today was the first day of the new league, they needed some extra players so they let Penny play, and they also let a couple of the little kids play in the outfield, even though they didn't have gloves.

Penny and Danny weren't on the same side, and while Danny sat waiting his turn at bat he tried not to watch Penny—this was baseball and he had to pay attention to what his team was doing. But he couldn't help but look at her now and then. Playing second base, she stood on the bag with one foot, the other leg bent and its bare foot pressed against the calf of the other leg, and she took off Danny's glove and tossed it into the air and caught it without losing her balance. The other guys were watching her too. Now she was giving little tugs to the tight legs of her shorts. Suddenly she became very interested in the game. She started chattering, hopping around second base, barking encouragement to her teammates. Then the kid at bat hit a line drive at her and she turned and ran. The ball hit her on one of the round soft cheeks of her butt. Everyone laughed. They laughed so hard they fell down and rolled around. When they stopped, her team's pitcher motioned in one of the little kids from the outfield. The pitcher took Danny's glove from Penny and gave it to the little kid, and sent Penny out to right field.

But Penny got bored in right field and wandered off to the girls' toilet and they were able to forget about her for a while. Then as if from very far away they heard her, her voice high and cool.

"Oh Danny. Yoo hoo. Dannnnn-y."

He tried to ignore her, but everyone, even the little kids, got mad and started telling him to make her shut up.

"Shut up," he yelled.

But she kept it up. "Dannnnn-y. Yoo hoo."

Until his face was red and wrinkled, and he yelled so loudly he could have been heard clear to the swimming pool, "Shut up, damnit. Leave me alone. You're a big fat stupid pig. I hate you."

And suddenly she was as cold as the stone walls of the girls' toilet. She stood looking straight ahead at the walls, the names, faces, the dirty words, the pictures of wonderful, horrible men and gaping witches, and she put on her clothes.

When she came out of the toilet she didn't look at them, but headed the other direction, through the forest, where she felt the same strange coldness, as if winter lurked here in the woods, watching the children. She walked to the swimming pool and some of the little kids came over to talk to her. But they were just little kids.

James was waiting for her when she came down the sidewalk, looking at the house as she walked along. It was a strangely silent afternoon, the only sound the whisper of the water sprinklers. She sat on the porch of the little house where she lived, and once she glanced up at James' window. And as she looked into his eyes, though she couldn't see him, James stared back at her, unblinking, and knew that for the first time in her life Penny was lonely: she knew as completely as she ever would that she would be a woman all her life, and she was stunned.

They played baseball all summer and they even got uniforms—polo shirts with numbers which their mothers sewed on. Danny—number 3—was the pitcher for one of the teams, and he pitched every game. At the height of the season they played four, five, games a day, starting early in the morning and sometimes not stopping until suppertime—and then, likely as not, there was a game after supper.

And James and Penny were alone. She played bounce ball with

the little kids in the block and rode double with them on their bikes, and sometimes she babysat Mrs. Clark's twins. At night Danny and Mike occasionally played hide and seek with Penny and the little kids. One night when they were playing, some junior high boys came around and Penny stopped playing and went down to the corner and talked to them. When they left and Penny came running back, Mike was still playing hide and seek, but Danny had gone home.

A tall, gaunt boy with long black hair—James never learned his name—came to see Penny about every night for a week. He played hide and seek with her and the little kids. He laughed a lot and Penny laughed at everything he said. And then one morning he came to see Penny and they went into her house. James knew what they did was what Penny had done with Danny, except James knew Penny didn't take the tall, gaunt boy into her bedroom and she didn't take her clothes off and let him look at her.

One afternoon Danny was up at the park playing baseball and a kid on the other team started talking about Penny and the tall, gaunt boy. They had got in her bed with their clothes off. The baseball game stopped and they listened. When the kid had told everything—and some parts twice—they all stood in silence. How had he heard it? The tall, gaunt kid, who would be a sophomore in high school next year, had told a bunch of guys, and now anybody in high school who wanted to could go over to Penny's and do it to her.

The game resumed. Danny pitched, concentrating, leaning into every pitch, sweating, not thinking, his team ahead 8-4, the endless afternoon safe from time, a fine dust and the smell of fresh-cut grass floating on the air, the sun high in the perfectly blue sky ...

He turned from the batter, dropped the ball, and walked off the mound.

"Hey."

"What's the matter?"

He shook his head.

Several of them trotted after him.

He walked straight through center field, hearing now very clearly the kids at the swimmin pool, and it occurred to him that never before when he was playing ball had he heard the kids at the pool, and he looked up at the sky, clear blue, blank.

Danny walked down the sidewalk, tossed his glove onto the
front porch as he passed his house, and James from his window
watched him coming down the street in his red shirt with number 3
in front, his faded red cap, his arms tanned smooth like dark stone.
He walked not fast, not slow, as if he were on his way to the grocery store, but James knew, and in front of Penny's, Danny turned
up the sidewalk, swinging his arms, not looking up, and he went up
the steps, crossed the porch, and he didn't knock but opened the
door and went in, shutting it slowly behind him with a quiet, lumi-
nous click that James heard as he closed his eyes.

All the blinds were pulled and the house was dark. It had the
smell of cigarettes and sour clothing. The front room was very
small—smaller than Danny had ever noticed—and the ceiling
seemed strangely low. The walls were brown, nearly black, and the
chairs and lumpy sofa hunkered against the walls. As he passed
through to the tiny hall joining the front room with the other three
rooms of the house, he heard a drawer open, then close.

Wearing shorts and a sleeveless yellow blouse, Penny was coming
out of her bedroom. Her mouth fell open, but she didn't speak.
They stared at each other, the hall, the entire house, narrowing to
the tight lines of their staring, and Danny moved first, going toward her like a ship slowly turning to sea. "What ... ?" she started,
and he stopped her, his face in hers, and he smelled her, and smelled her mouth, and saw deep into the slow swirl of her eyes, leaning
forward until he was falling away, he was already into her and
rising like gray smoke from the little boys' prison of innocence into weather that blew him toward life.

James watched the pink and white curtain of the bedroom. Once
he believed it moved very slightly. But if it did, it didn't move again
until it came down several months later when Penny's mother
moved herself and Penny out with the help of a new fiance with a
pick-up truck, and for years James watched the house and that
window, sometimes covered by curtains, sometimes by blinds, and
once the window had nothing over it and James could see in the
narrow room a table piled with cardboard boxes.

In time he lost interest in the neighborhood and what they were
thinking: he knew them too well. James spent most of his time
watching television, soap operas, baseball in the summer, and for a

year or so he avidly watched the wrestling matches. Now when he looked out the window it was either to watch for the newspaper boy, late in the afternoon, even after dark in the winter, or it was to look out at the sky through the limbs of the maple tree.

Phillip Lopate / New York City

GETTING A CAT

from ZZZZZZ: 1977
Calais, Vermont
Editor: Kenward Elmslie

AFTER SEVEN years of living alone, I broke down and got a cat.

I really didn't want a cat. Once I was in Jungian therapy and the therapist said to me, "You should get a cat." He was a very decent man, I got a lot from him, I listened respectfully to everything he said, except when he gave me practical advice like this. "You should try it," he said. "You'll learn interesting things about yourself...." And then he slid away into his mysterious smile. One might almost say, a Cheshire cat smile.

I didn't feel I was ready for it. You can't imagine how many people have been offering me their superfluous cats and kittens over the years, how many times I have had to say say, in a friendly way, no. Why was everyone so eager to give me a cat? I saw them all smiling, rubbing their hands: "Ah, he'll get a cat, very good, it's a good sign, means he's settling down."

I don't understand the logic of this. By what Darwinian fluke was I supposed to graduate from one to the other? Maybe I was to start with a cat; then I would go on to a sheepdog, next a pony, then a monkey, then an ape, then finally a Wife.... It was far more likely that, if I got a cat, I would stop there. What annoyed me was this smug assumption that because I live alone, there was something barren about me. I needed to start making "commitments" to other living creatures, to open up my heart to them and take on that responsibility. As far as I can piece it together, the idea seems to be that we should commit ourselves to something in this howling, senseless black hole of a universe. We should make an effort to join the Association of fellow creatures, and rub our shoulders against them for warmth. Now, "commitment" comes in when belief in love starts to slide. They're not so sure any more, the experts, the theologians, that there is such a thing as love. So they tell you you should build up to it—practice. Throw your arms around a tree. Myself, I still believe in love, what do I need commitment for? So this was one reason for my not getting a cat. Plus my apartment is too small; there are no doors between the rooms; and I sometimes have to travel at the spur of the moment. I could keep piling on reasons. Most important was, I didn't feel I needed a cat.

Very well, you might ask; how did it happen that you got a cat?

It was partly a misunderstanding. I was in the country one weekend, where one is always more fragiley prone to sentimental longings and feelings of incompleteness. That's why I stay out of the country as much as possible. But I was visiting a friend; and there was an old man staying at the house, a respected old writer, a lovely man, we'll call him Claude. Because I've always like that name—Claude Rains is one of my favorite actors. This old man is very handsome: his hair is beautiful silky white, he moves with graceful modesty, slight of build and wearing threadbare sweaters with holes in them, not because he can't afford any better but because he has already passed over to the other side, where one stops caring about making an impression. He lives alone and seems wonderfully self-sufficient, except for his cats. He and I were standing in-side the threshold of his bare room and bending over a box where the mother cat was sleeping with her four kittens. The children were all sleeping head to foot, with their mouths in each other's tails, so that together they looked like one big cat.

They made, I had to admit, a cute effect. I was trying to get a suitably fond expression into my face; and he was explaining about their delivery.

"There was a lot of hard labor involved. Usually she likes me to be around—some cats don't. There has to be a box ready. She knew just what to do. She ate the umbilicus, and the afterbirth, which is supposed to be good for them. Then she licked off the first kitten and was ready for the next. Each kitten comes in a different sack...they're not like humans that way."

"Hm," I said, impressed. Each kitten had a different coloration: one grey, one black, one cinnamon-orange, and one whitish. A Mendelian demonstration. I liked the grey cat, because he was so common and straightforward, your basic alley-cat. I was also drawn to the milky-orange one but distrusted her because she was *too* pretty.

Claude's hand, which was large and sensitive, pale-veined with brown spots—I shook it every chance I got—descended to stroke each of the cats along its furry back.

"What are you going to do with all the kittens?" I asked idly.

"I'll give away as many as people want, and let her keep one to raise; and the rest will have to be taken to the vets to be killed. That's the difficult part," he said. The fold above his eye twitched as he talked, and he turned his face for a moment deliberately toward me, with a politeness and candor which showed he was not afraid to look his listener in the eye. "But she isn't willing to do it," he said, "and so I have to. I don't need more than one cat, you see."

I was so taken with this, with his acceptance of the world as it was, that I wanted to have one of his cats. I spoke up impetuously, and offered to take a kitten. He looked at me with a kind, piercing gaze, and asked if I was positive I wanted one. I said I was absolutely sure, trembling at what his look of examination might have told him about me. For awhile he pretended I hadn't made the offer at all, in order to let me gracefully off the hook. But I kept forcing myself into a firm statement that I wanted one of his kittens—the grey one probably. Although the cinnamon-orange one was pretty too.... And suddenly I became horribly torn between these two animals, as between two ideals. If I took the grey alley-cat, I would be opting for everything that was peasant stock, lower-middle-class, slugging away, maybe not dazzling but a hard worker—in short, myself. If I rejected the orange one, I would be turning my back on beauty. I stood over the box, wondering if I should be ruled by glamor—a flash of prettiness: the feminine, the graceful, the mysterious, the gamine, the treacherous, as I had done so often in my life, to my regret—or whether, in embarking on this new stage in my life, I should rather choose a cat with sturdier virtues. In the end I did pick the grey, only because I would have felt too guilty to have gone back on my promise to him, after noticing a new, more fetching piece of fur.

Two or three days later, back in the city, grimly contented, cool-headed, myself again, I realized I had made a bad mistake. I didn't want a cat, I wanted to be this old man. I wanted to grow up more quickly and be done with my idiotic youth and literary ambitions and sexual drives which bossed me around, and—I wanted to be Claude, gentle, pure. I must have just fallen in love with his white beard and his hands; and under the spell of his life, in that charmed propinquity, I had somehow gotten the idea that I wanted a cat. Whatever he had warmed with his glance that day, I probably would have coveted. Fortunately it was only a cat!

I had to find a way to tell him that there had been a misunderstanding. For a long while I did nothing. I sat on my hands, waiting for the decision to sift down to them. Finally I wrote him a card saying that I hadn't forgotten, that I hoped he was keeping the grey for me—but maybe it was the orange one I really wanted, I couldn't make up my mind....It was a scatterbrained, sloppy note, and I hoped it would convey the impression of an irresponsible young man who is not to be believed in anything he says. You may be amazed at this subterfuge: but it was the closest I could get to honesty; I simply couldn't face his judgment of me as someone who would go back on my word.

In any case he did not get the hint. Like the Grim Reaper coming to call, Claude telephoned me once he was back in New York, and said it was time for me to stop by and collect my kitty.

With a heavy heart, I rode down in the taxi with the Black Maria by my side, the metal carrying box which friends had loaned me. I had already provisioned my apartment with the supplies that Claude, in a moment of doubting me, had called to remind me to have ready as soon as the cat should enter its new home. I climbed the stairs to Claude's loft, wondering how this old man managed them every day. He opened the door with an impish smile.

I wanted to get this over with as quickly as possible. "Hello, kitty," I said, bending down to pet the grey kitten.

"No, that's not your cat. I gave that to someone else. Here's your cat," he said. "There she is—she was under the bed! She's a very timid creature. Not like her brother Waldo, the grey. *There* she is! *There* she is," he held her in his arms, and poignantly gave her over to me, as though he no longer had any right to her.

I need not say how grateful I was that it was the orange one. She was warm in my hands, and gorgeous, obscenely pretty. Old Claude must be some student of the human heart, I thought.

The rest was odds and ends, formalities of transfer of property. She had already had her first distemper shot but I was to take her again in four months. I would be better off not giving her too much milk at first. She liked Purina Tuna most of all the brands he'd tried. She was a good jumper—a first-class jumper; but as she had been up to now in the shadow of her brother Waldo, she seemed retiring. That would probably change. He had noticed that sometimes happened with girls, when they had brothers, that the boy kittens would be very active at first and dominate them. A good thing was to get an empty crushed pack of Winstons, which she liked to play with. Did I smoke? he asked. No, I said.—"Well then get your smoking friends to save them for you. She also likes to play with a little toy ball, and I'll give that to you." He located the ball, and his last empty cigarette pack, and gave me a box of dry catfood and would have piled on several cans of tuna if I had not stopped him and said I had plenty at home. "Very well," he said, simply and with loss. "I guess that's it."

I felt like a mother coming to take away her child from a foster-mother after a long court battle. Though Claude and I had been barely even acquaintances before this, we were caught in such an emotional moment that I wanted to throw myself into his arms and comfort him, or be comforted myself. Instead, I shook his hand, which was always a good idea.

"Goodbye, *****" he said, calling her something like Priscilla, or Betsy. I didn't want to hear; I should have stopped up my ears. I wanted her named existence to begin with me. "You're going off to your new home," he said. "Have a good time."

"Won't she be lonely for her brother and her mother?" I asked.

"Yes...but that's life," he replied, smiling at both the thread-bareness of the phrase and the truth of it.

I nodded my head. He walked me to the door and stood at the top of the stairs with me. "If you have any questions, ask people who have cats for advice. They'll be more than happy to give it to you, and most of it will be wrong—but that's all right, they'll all have dozens of tips. And of course you can call me any time you want if you're having problems with her. I know very little but I can hold your hand."

2

And so I settled down to my comfortable married life. After she had overcome her first shyness, the girl began to demonstrate her affectionate nature. She would take my finger in her mouth and lick it, and move on to the next finger, and the next.... Her little pink tongue, rough as a washcloth, would sand away at my skin

288

until it became sore. Then I would push her away, and pick up my book.

But a little while later, I would try to entice her back. "Come here, Milena," I would say. She would look uncertainly, mistrustfully up at me. I would wave my hand in the air, a gesture that hypnotized her each time, and wiggle my fingers until she jumped at them. Then I'd *catch* her and clutch her to me and squeeze her. She didn't like to be squeezed, or even petted; she would immediately turn around and start licking the hand that had moved to stroke her.

In the evening she would curl up on my lap and close her eyes; and make that motor-running, steady breathing sound. I didn't have the heart to move with her on my lap, purring like that. Moreover, she held her paw on my wrist, as if to detain me and keep me immobile. How could I reach for my pencil?

When she had first come to my house, she had investigated every corner of it, going around the perimeters of the livingroom into the bedroom, the kitchenette, and finally into the bathroom, where she took note of her catbox. I was wondering when she would begin to use the box. The first day passed, and the pebbles were unruffled. Then another day came and went without commission; and I thought she might be so nervous from the move that she was constipated. On the third day I sat down on the couch; something was wrong. My nostrils opened. Right next to me on the sofa was the most disgusting pile of shit. I could barely control myself from throwing up. I cleaned it off distastefully and dropped a piece of it in the catbox, so that she would know that was the proper place for it. Then I lowered her into this same catbox and she dropped out of it more quickly than if she had got an electric shock. This was too much. Claude had assured me that she was toilet-trained! I sprayed the sofa with lysol disinfectant. She kept returning to the spot like the criminal she was, and sniffing the upholstery, trying to puzzle out the two different smells, and backing away, bewildered.

That afternoon I called Claude, to get the exact name of the kitty litter he'd been using. I told him what she had done. He said, "Oh, dear, that must be disagreeable; I'm so sorry to hear it..." Never mind, I thought, just tell me the name of your kitty litter. It turned out to be another brand; so, hoping this would make the difference, I went from supermarket to supermarket until I had found the preferred gravel, I lugged twenty pounds of it home with me and poured a deep, cloud-releasing stratum in her box.

That night I couldn't sleep. I was so disgusted with the image of finding that bundle on the couch, I felt almost as if my house had been broken into. Why had I gotten a cat? That night my dreams were full of unpleasant surprises.

In the morning I awoke to the smell of a stack of her shit on the white brocade armchair. This could go on for weeks....My work was suffering, I couldn't concentrate, I couldn't do a thing until I had "broken in" that cat and shown her who was master. I bet she knows that's her box, I thought, but she just prefers taking a crap on a nice comfy armchair or a sofa surrounded by pillows. Wouldn't we all? She must think I'm a total sucker, or a bigger one than Uncle Claude!

I went back to routines: sponged the chair, sprayed it with lysol, deposited a piece of her droppings in the catbox. Then I grabbed her by the neck, not so gently, and dropped her into the gravel. She jumped out like a shot. I caught her and put her in again. She hopped out, whining. I threw her in again. Romance of education: she was the wild child, Helen Keller, I was the stubborn tutor, Annie Sullivan, wearing her down. I was willing to treat it like a game: you jump out, I'll throw you back. She bounded, I caught her. My arm was stuck out like a fence to grab her as soon as she escaped. Each time she grew a little slower in leaving the box, a little more pensive and frustrated. Staring at me with her big victimized pussycat eyes. "That look is wasted on me," I told her. She fell in the gravel, defeated. She seemed to chew over the situation for half a minute. Then she sat up in the posture of evacuating, and lowered her bottom ever so gradually. She got off of it (it was a little pee) and carefully kicked some pebbles over the spot.

I have never been happier to see anyone take a piss.

After that we had no more surprise "bundles." Life fell back to normal, or let us say, my new normal, which was nothing like the old normal, since it seemed to consist in spending my days running to the store for cat food and Hartz litter, and buying a vacuum cleaner to swoop up cat's hairs so that my allergic friends could visit me, or finding the right scratching-post before it was too late. Milena had found the under-guts of a chair and was taking clumps of stuffing out of it for sport. In fact she was doing nightmarish things to all the furniture. Since I live in a furnished apartment, I was terrified of what would happen if my landlady ever came snooping in. My landlady is not fond of signs of life in any form. I had been too afraid to ask her permission in the first place; and had sneaked in the cat on my favorite principle of the *fait accompli*. You see, if I had asked her she would have said no; this way she would either have to accept it or start costly eviction proceedings. One afternoon, as I was walking up the stoop of my house, where she lives also, unfortunately, directly beneath me, she told me that "there was someone knocking" at my door. I thought this was odd; but then I noticed the more than usually scowling, misanthropic expression on her pudgy face and the two tufts of dirty-blondish hair sticking angrily out of her ears (God, she looked like a bulldog!), and via this animal association I realized that she was referring in her elliptical way to my cat. As I waited for her next volley, she followed this statement about someone-at-my-door with "No cats, Mr. Lopate. We can't have cats here, you understand?"

I said nothing, and proceeded past her into my apartment and closed the door, trembling with anger. I was ready to fight her to the bitter end. I turned to Milena, all innocent of the threat against her. "Don't worry," I said. "I won't let her throw you out. We'll move first." So our destiny was sealed. "But you must," I said, "you must control your destructiveness. We live in this woman's house, don't you see; this is her furniture! If you go tearing large holes in everything it will cost me a fortune. Look, I bought you a scratching-pad; can't you bring yourself to use it?"

In the meantime, something had to be done. I consulted friends: some advocated declawing; others were aghast at the idea, with a foaming passion that made you suspect they were talking about something else. Anyhow, someone said, a kitten her age was too young for the operation. When I learned that it was indeed an "operation," that she would have to go to the hospital for it, I gave up the project indefinitely. Instead I clipped her toenails and coaxed her to try the new scratching-post (I had exchanged the cardboard stand for one made of fabric). The man in the pet shop said, "If you put some catnip around the base she'll be sure to like it." I bought a container of fresh catnip—anything for my baby-girl. I spread the leaves up and down the scratching-post. She did love the smell; she licked at the catnip and slept on the fabric base when she needed a rest from her more exhausting vandalisms.

<h2 style="text-align:center">3</h2>

After that, a strange sullen period began for us. At times I thought I loved her, at other times I would be completely indifferent to her. I would kick her off the bed when she tried to sleep with me, because I wanted to be alone, and not worry about rolling onto her. But always when I had almost forgotten she was there, she would crouch into my vision.

She had the annoying habit of trying to stop me when I dialed the phone, as if jealous of my speaking to anyone else. She would smudge the dialing circle with her paw, forcing me to dial the same number as many as four times. We often got in each other's way. She and I competed for the bright red armchair—the one I considered my "writing chair." Milena always seemed to be occupying it just as I was getting ready to lower myself. I either had to squeeze onto part of it, or shoo her off, which made me the bad guy.

Sometimes I would come home and find her sleeping on that chair, a lazy housewife. She would blink her eyes as I turned on the light.

When I totally ignored her, she began knocking down my clay animals. Or she would tear through the house. It felt to me like she was taking over the living space and squeezing me into a small, meaningless corner. How I resented her when I smelled her all over my apartment! At my typing desk, in the kitchenette, there was that warm, cloying offensively close odor from her shed hairs. And I wanted to vomit when she kept crapping all the time, more than it seemed necessary, and leaving the results uncovered in her box. I got very cross at her for not raking under her shits. Cats were supposed to be "fastidious creatures" and do that instinctually—it seemed a violation of the contract.

I was looking for violations, I suppose. I kept thinking in the back of my mind that I could send her away. It was so hard for me to grasp the idea that I was going to have to care for her permanently. At least until one of us died.

Claude called from time to time, "to hold my hand," as he put it. He was very sweet. I was delighted to have the chance to talk

292

more often with him, even though our conversations were rather specialized. Once he suggested that I spread baking powder through the kitty litter to cut the smell. Not a lot on the top surface—she wouldn't use it if you did that—but a little throughout the mixture.

All this lore of cats! It was too much to take in; and it was only the beginning. As Claude had predicted, everyone had instructions for me.

It so happens there are four things I can't stand to hear people going on about: one is their pets, two is their coincidences, three is their favorite restaurants and meals, and four is their dreams. I've been relenting a little on the last, if they're not told in too-meticulous detail. But as for cat discussions, spare me. And I never did like going over to a friend's house and in the middle of an intense conversation watching the friend's eyes turn senile with fondness as he interrupts to draw my attention to the cute position his cat has gotten herself into.

Now that I had this cat, every visitor started off with fifteen minutes of reaction to Milena. I don't suppose, in a circle of friends such as I belong to, composed of articulate, inquisitive and easily-apprehensive individuals, that an event such as one's getting a cat could pass without commentary. Women-friends, particularly, made much of Milena. Judy commented that it was rare to find an orange female. Most orange cats she had seen were male. Sandra said the cat was so elegant that she herself felt "under-dressed" around her.

Edie, the woman I was going out with, remarked: "Your cat is so gentle. She's exquisite! I can't get over how delicate—how attuned she is!"

Really? It was news to me. I couldn't help thinking the description applied more to this woman than to the cat.

"Oh, she's so exquisite," she went on, sighing. "She's gentle the way cats are talked about as being but so rarely are."

I felt abashed for not having perceived this extra-special "thing" in Milena. From my point of view she was doing a kitten's job adequately, she was holding down the role, earning her can a day, but not setting any box office records. They all seemed to want to find something unique about her; whereas I, on the contrary, liked Milena precisely because she was just a cat. True, she had an appealingly pathetic stare: those black pupils with two concentric circles of olive around them....But I resisted, I fought their flattery, which seemed to me of the delusional baby-worshipping kind. I had no idea how much I had given secretly into it until I came up against a non-believer.

My friend Jennie remarked, without having seen her: "She's not as nice as my cat, is she?" and assured herself no, as if it were self-evident. I was furious. Not that my cat is so great, but why should hers be better? Jennie was my model of the delusional cat-owner. She had theories about how her cat knew her moods better than anyone, stayed away from her when that was the right thing to do, comforted her when she was done, was totally independent, intuitively kept her claws in—a miracle of a domestic cat that didn't need to be declawed, spayed or altered or anything else cats usually need to be, because it was so considerate and discreet. Her cat was an Edith Wharton novel. Often, people hurt Jennie with their rudeness or selfish insensitivity, but her cat—never. Her cat sets the standard, I thought sardonically, that all of us, her friends, must chase after raggedly and fall short of. When Jennie shuts the door on her last visitor of the night, she curls up with her kitty cat, the understanding one.

This would never happen to me, I vowed.

Why? Because I had already given up the fantasy that Milena could understand me. Neither could I understand her. We were one of those couples who were destined to live side by side without ever being able to stare into the other's soul. How could we, when our interests were so different? I had known this about us from the very beginning. Nevertheless, it did not prevent me from linking myself to her. We are entirely different, Milena and I. We have separate hobbies, separate yearnings. Still, this is the most serious relationship I have had with a woman in years.

I don't pretend to guess her secrets. I watch her. That is the best I can do.

There she is, chasing a fly.

Now she knocks a spoon off the table, a magic marker from the desk, and starts kicking it about. Everything is a toy to her. In this way we differ passionately, also. She drags her booty through a square hole she has scratched in the white brocade armchair. I don't know how to stop her from gouging the seatcovers. This one tear-hole particularly has a use in her play. What does it mean to her? Someone said to me, "Kittens have such imaginations. They think they're in the jungle!" Is that it? Are you thrashing through the Amazon chasing enemies? Milena, you have your toy, you have that rubber ball with chimes inside. But to you, all the world is your plaything! Being a worker myself, I disapprove of that attitude. But, since play is children's work, as Piaget maintains, I suppose the same is true for kittens. Who am I to deprive a creature of her meaningful work?

Milena can do all kinds of tricks. She can tear a paper towel into shreds and strew it all over the apartment. She can stand on her hind legs and turn on the lamp. It's the truth! She's fascinated by light.

When I go into the bathroom she likes to come in with me and make at the same time. But even when I shut the door she manages to squeeze inside. She crawls into her cat box and makes a little pee and then steps aside and inspects the wet. I love the way she buries her shits, and then sifts through at a later time to see if they are still there. They're her property, her valuables in the safety deposit box. You're like a rich old dowager, Milena, with your orange and white mink coat and your jewels.

Then I come out of the bathroom with my robe on and she starts squeaking. She wants to eat! Take your time, you'll get it. She's so eager that she doesn't let me scoop out all her canned food. She gets in the way so that I can't even put the rest on her plate—a clump of it drops on her head. You see that? if you'd only let me...

Now the cat is quiet. She has gotten what she wants to eat, her tuna. She sits in a pool of sun. The days are getting shorter and shorter. Winter is coming, Milena. I explain it to her.

ESSAYS

Louise T. Reynolds / Arlington, Massachusetts

THE AGE OF MEDIOCRITY:
APPLYING GRESHAM'S LAW TO LITERATURE

from *The New Renaissance*, Volume 3, Number 1: 1977
Arlington, Massachusetts
Editor: Louise T. Reynolds

WITH good literature as rare as a literate person (i.e., one familiar with the world of letters) and mediocre books as commonplace as an ignorant one (i.e., unknowing, unlearned), Gresham's law might be re-stated as bad literature driving good literature out of circulation. Even a casual study of publishers' lists these past 10 years will indicate this is happening. Yet it does not represent an abrupt change in the reading patterns of the American people nor a sudden decline in their cultural priorities but is rather the insidious and inevitable result of levelling down to the lowest common denominator in the name of pragmatic democracy. The pace of the decline was quickened in the 1920s when the citizen emerged in his new role as consumer; after the mid-1940s, it became his chief role. Because the artist, along with the intellectual and the person of culture, was able to perceive other options, he clogged up the machine of democracy which favored the identical response. What this country has been producing for the last 50 years has been a people of similar mediocrity who march, along with whatever group they've attached themselves to, like trained fleas, although with the advent of the television generation, the word "trained" becomes an overstatement.

The Oxford Universal Dictionary on Historical Principles defines mediocre as "Of middling quality; neither bad nor good; indifferent. (e.g.) *It is thus that mediocre people seek to lower great men*—Carlyle." In an age rife with mediocrity, conformity, and shoddiness in both products and in attitudes, we find ourselves constantly flattered, and not only by politicians, as a "good, great and generous" people. Any modern gadfly who tells the people not what they want to hear but what they need to hear—that they are becoming as standardized as computer forms—will not only be considered troublesome but "negative" and will not only be listened to, will be disliked. Too many of us are unwilling not to be liked and since our opinions or emotions aren't deep-seated, they are easily discarded for whatever opinion will make us acceptable to our fellows. It's as if we were compelled to believe in the group imperative, that this time is the best of times, that the opinion of today's majority is the best and only opinion. Our credulous belief in the inevitable and continual progress of each decade over the previous one cuts us off from the stream of mankind which studies, honors, and accepts its past. From deTocquerville, in 1840, ("Thus not only does democracy make every man forget his ancestors, but it hides his descendants and separates his contemporaries from him; it throws him back forever upon himself . . . .") to Sir Harold Nicolson in 1933 ("I say that not only have they (Americans) no sense of the past: they have no sense of the future. They do not plant avenues for their great grandchildren. This gives them not merely an absence of past roots but of future roots also. It gives a ghastly feeling of provisionality: 'Chicago's ever-changing skyline.' "), the inability of Americans to accept their past and bequeath it, along with their present, to the future has been criticized, mostly by foreigners. This sense of impermanence justifies our emphasizing the moment and everything that is accepted in that moment. "The past's relation to the artist or man of culture," Randall Jarrell observed,[1] "is almost the opposite of its relation to the rest of our society. To him the present is no more than the last ring on the trunk, understandable and valuable only in terms of all the earlier rings. The rest of our society sees only that great last ring. . . ." The artist's separation from society began to disintegrate in the 1950s, however, and by the mid-1960s, he no longer was the independent loner but a member of the group. Mr. Jarrell, who saw where this grouping was taking us, quoted[2] Goethe: "Mediocrity . . . may often give us unqualified pleasure; it does not disturb our self-satisfaction, but rather encourages us with the thought that we are as good as another. . . ."

The mediocre writer has produced books that have stunted our growth, shrunk our hearts, and atrophied our minds. Where writers once astounded us and enlarged our sympathies, we now have the writer-as-a-groupie anxious to appease those in power and desiring above all else the security of a forum. It has not been difficult to produce a generation which finds unacceptable good and great works—it is only required that you catch them early enough to train them in peer adjustment; for more than 25 years we have had teachers who, with their rudimentary knowledge of psychology and their total lack of spiritual insight and imagination, could conceive of no higher goal than adjustment to the group. Several years ago when talking to the family cat, I told her I put up with her tricks and her ways (she was then ignoring me to study a front paw) only because I loved her. My cousin, then in high school and a witness to the scene, immediately took exception: "you can't love anything that can't love you back" he quoted; the cat, a creature incapable of emotions, was tied to me on a strictly needs basis and no other and vice versa; I was deluding myself if I thought I "loved" her. I told my cousin he had a regrettable tendency toward literal mindedness, but he couldn't take credit for the dictum as it had recently been declared in an English class. Citing his teacher as authority, he enumerated some of the other things one couldn't love: the flag, country, cities, towns, houses, music books, theatre, architecture, dead writers, ideas, and so on.

This incident reveals how the sensibilities and imaginations of pupils have in the last 25 years been shaped and stifled by teachers who, in line with the reigning philosophy of their day, armed children against the cheap emotionalism that pervades the hack work of writers, visual artists, movies, etc. C. S. Lewis in *The Abolition of Man*[3] claimed that such educators had apparently conceived of school children as being inundated by emotional propaganda and, remarking that in his own experience, the contrary was true, added, "For every one pupil who needs to be guarded from a weak excess of sensibility there are three who need to be awakened from the slumber of cold vulgarity.... By starving the sensibility of our pupils we only make them easier prey to the propagandist when he comes. For famished nature will be avenged and a hard heart is no infallible protection against a soft head."

The generation which had initiated this philosophy against emotionalism (graduates of college from 1920 through 1936) actually had experienced a surfeit of 19th century stock pathos and, in grafting their reactions and ideals onto the curriculum of another generation, were pioneering a different kind of education, a "progressive" one, devoted to the development of the "whole person" rather than to mastery of the 3 Rs. Their students, the second group (graduates of college from 1940 to 1956), were disinclined to make waves and although not themselves subjected to the same kind or degree of sentimentality as their teachers, nonetheless accepted, refined, and promulgated their value system. In turn, their students, the third group (in high school from the mid-1950s through 1970 and in college until the late 1970s) were the first of television's children and this medium by fostering an early cynicism, a short attention span, and a reluctance to do personal research, re-enforced their teacher's warnings against emotionality and their exhortations to be practical about results and idealistic about aims. Not surprisingly, the pragmatism of the television generation broke into rebellion on all fronts: against their parents and inherited value system; against their culture and their country; and, finally, against western civilization. Their idealism combined with cynicism turned into a naivete toward their own and a disillusionment with their elders. At college where, switching majors, dropping in and out, they prolonged their dependency status, they emerged with Masters or PhDs but whereas the first group had worked within the system to reform it and the second group worked to implement those reforms, the television generation stayed with their own, outside the system (which after all couldn't love them back). Since they hadn't been disciplined and since their studies emphasized the immediate present, they lacked the inheritance of a liberal art background and relied on their own feelings, on identifying with peers or idealistic themes, and on justifying actions by intentions. Unaccustomed to self-criticism and self-examination, they are illiterate in a totally new way but they're protected from that realization by college degrees, areas of specialization, easy successes, and not infrequent capitulations by society to their demands. C. S. Lewis[4] lamented that the purpose of modern education has been the production of what may be called "Men Without Chests", for he claims that only by his emotional sensibility and magnanimity is man man "for by his intelligence he is mere spirit and by his appetite mere animal." Rollo May in *Love and Will* put it more clinically: that since modern man is without a heart, he has nothing between his head and genitals and is therefore more schizoid than cool. Duncan Williams picking up on Lewis's theme deplored[5] the tendency of modern writers (and other artists) to see mankind merely through its generative and ex-cretory functions. And like Christopher Booker (in *The Neophiliacs*) he found the television generations's "love of the new" alarming since it entails ignoring the past.

The first contingent of the television generation has been out of college for more than a decade and later editions are coming off college and university conveyor belts in greater numbers every year. During this time the interest in the traditional arts (symphonies, operas, ballets, museums, all long-time recipients of the largess of the rich) has declined so steadily that, without government funding to sustain them, the programs of this group would become as errat-ic as revolutionary art. Other art forms (jazz, dance, serious theatre) which had verged on being self-supportive, are among the needy mainly because government and private funding gives them too lit-tle too late. It is small wonder, then, that the most private and least generous art—literature—the one beholden to no government or pa-tron, stands threatened to the point of favoring the pop arts and other schlock that wouldn't qualify as *kitch* in the Fourth World, has rendered traditional art obsolete unless gimmicked up (elec-tronic Bach) or slanted to their generation (mod-versions of *Hamlet, Romeo and Juliet, The Dolls House*); reading, outside of cult figures and interests, isn't their thing. They are not only un-able to read the good and great writers of the past, they are unable to read the good and near great writers of contemporary times. As the endurance of western civilization has depended upon each gen-eration communicating with the next by studying the achieve-ments of their great thinkers and creative writers of the past, both of which are now under the cloud of irrelevance, the question—can a democracy support the arts?—ceases to be hypothetical. Trade publishing, now largely the least important division of giant con-glomerates, has been abdicating its commitment and responsibility to literature and this void, the non-commercial small presses and cooperatives are trying to fill. But while the multiplicity of publish-ers are ensuring that more books will be published—in itself unfor-tunate, since much coeterie, incompetent, and tyro writers will be accepted—the exposure of books will become more limited and the encouragement to promising new writers (in the form of sales or critical recognition) will pass from the general public and reviewers to small pockets of special-interest groups. In such a parochial atmosphere, where readers and writers are interchangeable, writers will be isolated from the rest of humanity; writing will become a purer art form, focusing on techniques and styles, and the general reading public, what is left of it, that is, will be in the same situation as the jazz audience 15 years ago when jazz got so cool it was understood only by musicians. To an extent, this has already happened in poetry and in some types of "literary" novels.

None of this, however, is the official word. Propagandists, sociologists, psychologists, educators, and media commentators insist that art and culture are flourishing as never before in the U. S., and they point with pride to the ever-increasing budgets of the National Endowment For The Arts, and state art councils; to the wide public response to programs sponsored by federal, state, and independent agencies; to the proliferation of little magazines; and, finally, to the large number of practicing artists including writers. It is rarely noted that while inflation has contributed to the larger budgets, they are nevertheless retrenchments. Nor has it been admitted that much of the public response to artistic programs has come from artists themselves, their teachers and pupils as well as from those generally associated with the arts, sometimes as administrators, sometimes as dilettantes. As for the multiplicity of little magazines, most have little or nothing to do with literature but, instead, serve as proselytizing or advocacy efforts for groups such as women's liberation, gay or lesbian rights, black civil and social rights, Marxist and other revolutionary activists. And the large number of writers instead of being a cause for celebration is a cause for alarm for large isn't synonymous with good or deserving. James Farrell in an interview[6] considers this phenomenon: "I went to a party recently at which there were 80 poets in one room. How in hell can there be 80 poets in one city, in one room?" Obviously only by accepting the "poets" at their own evaluation, by equating the mediocre poet with the good or true poet. And if we continue encouraging our grade school children to "express yourself through art", we will soon have 280 poets in one room, in one city, each emboldened by that glorious moment when, at the age of eight, his Arts-in-the-School Poet/Teacher singled out, in a recital or book, his "genuine poem". By the time such "poets" reach 28, their "careers" will have been over, leaving them only their memories

and their pretensions. Yet the apologists of the status quo claim
that since more and more people participate in the creative arts, a
cultural explosion is upon us. The slogan "More is better" applied
to the arts befits a country that has always equated quantity with
quality. Yet nothing flourishes here like our own cherished myths
and for the past decade no myth has been received more reverently
than the one that runs something like this: "The current generation
is the best educated, most informed, most creative generation in
the history of our country."

That this statement can be made in the face of evidence which
reveals that high school graduates are unable to write a simple de-
clarative sentence or that they can't figure out what money is due
them on an exchange involving addition, subtraction, and/or mul-
tiplication, exposes our self-delusions and our insecurities. And it is
not only high school graduates who qualify as the new illiterates as
the escalating remedial courses in colleges, in reading, grammar,
math, history—despite the camouflage that they are offered primarily to the "disadvantaged" (a bureaucratic non-word)—attests to
the failure of urging college upon all. Even with examinations gear-
ed to multiple-choice questions, matching columns, and fill-ins;
even with automatic passing grades, automatic promotions and
graduations, all of which have been designed to conceal the depth
of our illiteracy, the truth is surfacing. But it will not be faced
while the staggering number of undergraduate and graduate students continues to convince us, if not the rest of a skeptical world,
of a literacy our lives belie.

College graduates who can write a readable and interesting essay
are vanishing as their numbers increase. And if they can barely
write, we dare not question their reading habits—or non-reading
habits, to be exact—for the answer would mean redefining civilization to include those who have been programmed to polarized re-
sponses, who produce to order, who are unaware of what the
world's great literature consists; who can barely read, write, or
speak their native language. Remember that "the best educated,
most informed, most creative generation" bought *Love Story* with
its infantile theme, "Love is never having to say you're sorry"; who
idolize cult figures such as Vonnegut, Kesey, Hesse, Heller, and
others who fade in and out every seven to ten years (the new
"generational" span.) To take exception to this lack of taste which

doesn't amount even to bad taste merits the charge to end all charges—elitist. Besides, the champions declare, and with truth, that the intentions of the television generation are good, their enthusiasms sincere, their ideas relevant. When the conceptions are hazy, performances faulty, ideas puerile, emotions confused, that's the time to bring in red herrings.

Because a frame of reference in language, its importance, meanings, and usage is lacking, discussing differences in ideas and in literature leads nowhere. Diction has become an esoteric subject even for writers; dictionaries and usage books offer reportage, not guidance. After all, why should philologists, lexicographers, or etymologists think they know more than the man in the street? Underneath this attitude lies not only fear of ridicule and a suspicion of any judgment but one's own, but, more important, an indifference to all meanings whether in language, in literature, or in life. John Simon in an intriguing essay *Pop Goes The Word*[7] says, "The word . . . is the father of logic and the mother of style; it has given birth to both philosophy and literature, the very things that the non-intellectual ignores and the anti-intellectual rebels against." In his opinion, the decline of language might be traced to rock music and its "unintelligible and unintelligent" lyrics. The banality and repetitiousness of rock account for sloppiness in language, but the decline of culture might be more comprehensively traced to that great experiment of the U. S. —education for one and all. When this concept was introduced, the only education going was an Americanization of liberal arts (the "education of a free man"; an education for living the good life instead of what we have now—an education for making a good living) which stressed Greek, Latin, logic, metaphysics, philosophy, history, and literature. It didn't take long to discover that everyone could no more master this kind of learning than he could love his neighbor. Rather than admit the non-democratic obvious—that some are more equal than others—the educators restructured the system, adding vocational, technical, business, and civic courses, which Mortimer Adler calls the "dirty water" of education. But even here, where students played at work, home, or citizen projects, it has been difficult, especially since there are no consequences, to inspire the unmotivated, the uninterested, the incapable. Yet compulsory education demands that schools keep and struggle with the child with zero interest in learning rather than turn him out; thus the average child is held back by the dull one and the bright child is bored instead of challenged. Mr. Adler has argued that those of limited capacities ("half-pint containers") be given the same "cream" of liberal arts education that the intellectually superior ("gallon containers") receive but in lesser amounts. With democracy glorifying the ever-lowering average, the idea of there being a "gallon container" went against the American grain long before the cant of "elitism". There are signs that the pendulum may be swinging back, for some educators, perhaps alarmed at the dullards with degrees, are proposing a return to the 3 Rs and are revealing that long-suppressed or unavailable studies of schools without audio-visual aids, labs, gyms, rest-and-recreation areas, stadiums, etc., schools considered underprivileged, by concentrating on the 3 Rs, have produced children with superior skills; there is also talk of grading students according to their mastery of subjects rather than automatically advancing them through graduate school; Mr. Silber, President of Boston University, has gone so far as to suggest that only those with aptitudes for learning be admitted to the halls of higher education. Although he is already netting a volley of abuse for this stand, at least the idea is out in the open.

Jean Stafford in a recent book review[8], commenting on a time "when folks knew something" discusses Randall Jarrell's essay "The School of Yesteryear (A One-Sided Dialogue)."[9] Since its subject is pertinent to the theme of mediocrity in our time and literacy two generations and more ago, it is worth examining.

Uncle Wadsworth's singing "School days, dear old golden rule days" is interrupted by his nephew Alvin who remarks, "that's just nostalgia. ..." When Uncle continues, "Readin' and ritin' and 'rithmetic", Alvin interrupts with "What a curriculum! Why, it sounds like it was invented by an illiterate.... No civics, no social studies, no hygiene; no home economics, no manual training, no physical education! And extra-curricular activities—where are they?" Uncle goes on: "Taught to the tune of a hick'ry stick' " and Alvin shouts, "Stop! ... Imagine having to *beat* poor little children. ... Thank God those dark days ... are over, and we just appeal to the child's better nature, and *get him to adjust.* ..." (italics, mine). This leads to Uncle's showing Alvin, *Appletons' Fifth Reader* with its frontispiece quote from *L'Allegro*, the entire poem having been memorized by Uncle and his schoolmates. "But Uncle Wadsworth, you don't mean to say they had Milton in a Fifth Reader!" Alvin relates how his class, when sophomores in college, spent "two whole days on that poem and on—you know, that other one that goes with it. ... and there were two football players that were juniors, and believe me, it was all Dr. Taylor could do to get us through that poem." Uncle reads the names of writers in that Fifth Reader: Addison, Bishop Berkeley, Bunyan, Byron, Coleridge, Carlyle, Cervantes, Defoe, DeQuincy, Dickens, Emerson, Fielding, Hawthorne, George Herbert, Hazlitt, Jefferson, Dr. Johnson, Shakespeare, Shelley, Sterne, Swift, Tennyson, Thoreau, Twain and some simpler writers: Scott, Burns, Longfellow, etc. Alvin, in turn, reads from *his* Fifth Reader: Fletcher D. Slater, Nora Burglon, Sterling North, Ruth G. Plowhead, Ruth E. Kennell, J. Walker McSpadden, Merlin M. Taylor & others of the same ilk, plus "Three Boy Scouts." Apropos this last, Uncle remarks, "An Indian, no doubt. ... Never heard of him." "Them," says Alvin, "There're three of them." "Three? Thirty! Three hundred! They're all Boy Scouts!" Warming to his theme, Uncle quotes from Appleton's a paragraph on *Don Quixote* to which Alvin can only ask, "If I'd gone to school, then, I'd have known what that means in the *fifth grade*?" Or you wouldn't have seen the sixth grade, Uncle says. Now a junior in college, Alvin wouldn't have seen the sixth grade. He asks, "But how did things like Shakespeare and Milton and Dickens ever get in a Fifth Reader?" Uncle replies, "Alvin, they've always *been* there. Yesterday, here in the United States, those things were in the Fifth Reader; today, everywhere else in the world, those things or their equivalent are in the Fifth Reader; it is only here in the United States, today, that the Fifth Reader consists of *Josie's Home Run* by Ruth G. Plowhead and *A Midnight Lion Hunt* by Three Boy Scouts. ... The child who reads and understands the Appleton Fifth Reader is well on the way to becoming an educated, cultivated human being. ..." Convinced, Alvin joins in a chorus of "School days".

Miss Stafford[10] says that vast numbers of the population, "brainclogged" in school, "don't know *anything* and don't give a damn that they don't." To illustrate "the lower depths to which writers and editors have sunk", she cites a recent Viking Press novel for adolescents, *I Know You, Al* by Constance C. Greene and quotes: " 'You two are old enough to read Damon Runyon,' my grandfather said. 'He wrote a book of pieces about some very interesting characters. He called it *You Know Me Al*. Give it a whirl. You might like it.' " Miss Stafford cannot resist commenting: "If these stories hit the girls between the eyes, they may be inspired to go on to such other Runyon stories as 'Haircut' and 'The Maysville Minstrel'; . . . perhaps they will come on Ring Lardner, who is best remembered for 'Guys and Dolls'. . . . Wouldn't you think that somebody at Viking . . . would have caught such a terrible boner? Not so very many years ago, if it had slipped through the editorial offices because everybody was suffering from ambulatory encephalitis, it might still have been caught at the printing concern—by the shop steward, say, for in the good old school days, the good old golden-rule days, even blue-collar workingmen read. . . ." As Viking is the firm that invited Mrs. Jacqueline Onassis to join its staff to acquire manuscripts for the Viking list from her "wide circle of social, political, and international contacts"—jet-set celebrities apparently requiring the inducement of a jet-set editor before signing the lucrative contracts that publishers in any case are anxious to offer them, complete with collaborator of their choice, any boner that Viking's editorial staff make isn't likely to embarrass them as long as the stuff sells. As for the lower echelons at Viking, if it has as many members of the television generation as other publishers, the expectation that these young people would recognize Ring Lardner from Saki or Sherwood Anderson from Kipling, has long since passed. They may intend to read just as they may intend to do good works for the poor but, if it's on an individualized and not a programmed basis, with this generation, one must be satisfied with intentions.

But while celebrities may be sought after in the land of equality, it is only on the basis of their fame, not their knowledge, abilities, or talents. If they possess these qualities, they may not be celebrities at all but just editors, thinkers, or writers in which case they are expendable. Egalitarians have a fascistic appreciation of power, money, prestige, only the true superiority of others rankles them. "The claim to equality, outside the strictly political field," says C. S. Lewis,[11] "is made only by those who feel themselves in some way inferior. . . . No man who says I'm as good as you believes it. He would not say it if he did."

With each ensuing decade democracy had been turning out more and more non-entities, but World War II, possibly by a full generation, finished off the liberal arts education by eliminating, at first cautiously, then courageously, the fixed requirements for college; open admissions and students dictating the curriculum followed as a matter of course. Television came along at the psychological moment to scatter the remains by substituting a common background of situation comedies, detective, medical, and cowboy series, and game shows instead of the classics. But whereas a classical education lasted one century to the next, a TV series mightn't last through the season and, except for Ed Sullivan's vaudeville acts, even the most successful program doesn't last a decade. This is one reason why the television generation relates so well to its exact age group and less well with those of different memories, those four or more years older or younger. For more than 25 years, we have been told about the "great promise" of enlightenment and illumination that television would bestow; but for every hour of enlightenment we've been given a 100 hours of *I Love Lucy, Perry Mason, Mission Impossible*, and the like. The illusions of those who had imagined that given the choice, people would want the good over the bad, have been shattered. The advertisers knew better and by shrewdly applying H. L. Mencken's precept that nobody ever went broke underestimating the intelligence of the American people, they grew rich. When it comes to 95% of television programming, aesthetic and intellectual judgment must be suspended, for to search for merit in that medium is like searching a 100-ton dung heap for a 10-karat gold piece. Now, after a generation of congratulating American ingenuity for presenting us with the labor-saving instant and conveniece food, nutritionists are discovering that roughage may be vital to the digestive system and bodily health. When will educators and the FCC discover that roughage is equally vital for mental and emotional health? In the 1950s, Marya Mannes wrote an article with a title like *The Case of the Orange Oranges*[12] in which she contrasted the harmful effects of orange dye on the human body with the less obvious but more dangerous effects of junk fiction on human sensibilities. Although the United States has never lacked the lone dissenting critic, it has always preferred to listen to the roar of the crowd which in a democracy passes for the voice of the people asking for more of the same. In that way, no one is really responsible for what's being published and what isn't; for what's being dramatized on stage, screen or TV and what isn't; for what's being discussed on radio or in magazines or newspapers and what isn't, ad infinitum. We can then concentrate on the more popular question—what's in it for us?

Identification with a group is essential if one is not to be as powerless as the dissenters. Although the latter is encouraged to join the crowd, if the offer should be rejected they are treated with scorn and disdain; if that doesn't bring them to heel, they find themselves as shunned as lepers in ancient times. The methods of bringing those who are different to compliance are discussed by C. S. Lewis: [13] "You remember how one of the Greek Dictators ... sent an envoy to another Dictator to ask his advice about the principles of government. The second Dictator led the envoy into a field of corn, and there he snicked off with his cane the top of every stalk that rose an inch or so above the general level. The moral was plain. Allow no pre-eminence among your subjects. Let no man live who is wiser, or better, or more famous, or even handsomer than the mass. Cut them all down to a level; all slaves, all ciphers, all nobodies. All equals. ... (but) No one need now go through the field with a cane. The little stalks will of themselves bite the tops off the big ones. The big ones are beginning to bite off their own in their desire to Be Like Stalks." The person who rocks the boat because he sees life's experiences through his own eyes and not through the mirror of his time is recognized by society for what he is—a critic who makes it look foolish. Conformity has gone beyond acceptability to desirability; rather than be cast aside, those who are different latch on to a larger group which at least gives them the semblance of dissent. While the rhetoric of individuality can be encouraged, honored, even recommended, individuals themselves must be discouraged, discredited, despised.

A widespread conformity has silenced the voices of individuality in all phases of contemporary life including writing where two major forces have emerged: the academics and the scribblers, [14] both largely mediocre. The academics have studied the technique and substance of the giants of 20th century literature and adeptly interpret and refine those techniques. But whereas the giants were unstable, bohemian, iconoclastic, the academics are, in Sinclair Lewis's telling phrase, dullness made god. They are respectable, reasonable, intelligent to the point of intellectuality, serious, and secure in their twofold careers: professors, assistant professors, heads of creative writing departments, writers-in-residence, *and* writers regularly published by the university or literary reviews. Unfortunately their writings are more often than not the deliberate chronicling of trivia and their style so studied and so derivative that it reads like the uniform printout sheet of a computer. If you remove the title and author's name from the individual stories, you can read through one after another, in one review after another, coming up with the equivalent of a short novel, before a personalized voice breaks the pattern of sameness.

The scribblers, on the other hand, are spontaneous, uncritical, undisciplined members of the counterculture or, at least, the non-establishment. Though inclined to self-indulgence and self-pity, some show considerable promise which, in light of their regular acceptances by their you-scratch-my-back, -I'll-scratch-yours peers, may never be developed. A similarity of style and/or subject pervades their writing too, but unlike the academics, individuality runs higher among them since they are often outsiders, more likely to be jack-of-all-trades, part-time workers, or unemployed, than respected members of the community.

Still, it is outrageous that these two groups, both in-bred and intolerant, should control non-commercial writing just as it is outrageous that lawyers should control the three branches of both the federal and state governments and also assume advisory roles to virtually every profession and trade, interpreting their brethren's laws and finding loopholes for their clients'; their ubiquitous presence has made our society restrictingly legalistic. In a similar way, with academics and scribblers dominating the non-commercial outlets and their partisans controlling the reviewing in the media, writing that has a content, statement, or style which is unfashionable is passed over or condemned out of hand, thereby restricting its availability. Arthur Conan Doyle's observation [15] "Mediocrity knows nothing higher than itself but talent instantly recognizes genius" is proving truer each succeeding decade. Jane Heap, commenting on the critical neglect of *Ulysses* when it was appearing in

The Little Review, said that some critics wouldn't recognize the pyramids outside of Egypt. Now we're in danger of having an in-group of reviewers and critics who don't even know what pyramids are and who, if they come across them, would find them irrelevant.

The higher may stand with the lower but the reverse is not true. Even when good literature is recognized for its worth, it may be passed over with the excuse that it would interest only a few; when you're playing this kind of numbers' game, *TV Guide* and *Readers' Digest* with their better-than-18 Million circulation, are the tops and anything less than 1 Million, about ½ of 1% of the U. S. population, isn't in the running. So pressing is the majority view that it behooves even the Coordinating Council of Literary Magazines to focus on the prevailing opinion among litmags. In a 1973 brochure, the CCLM, recapitulating the "difficult editorial questions" that were discussed during the (Tempe) Arizona Conference, asked: "Is it elitist for editors to make quality decisions about the contents of their magazines or irresponsible not to? ... Does everyone have a right to be published? ... Should editors publish manuscripts because, like mountains, they are there?" If this emphasis on egalitarianism weren't so dangerous, it would be ludicrous. Elitism is usually defined as "the best or choicest" (The Oxford Universal Dictionary defines it as "The choice part or flower (of society, etc.)") and although in the current climate of shoddiness even "good" is suspect, elite isn't used in a denotative sense but purely as an incantation to denounce anyone with the temerity to judge the work of anyone else. But this opinion ignores the fact that artists, whatever their social or financial status, aren't egalitarians; their dreams compel them to strive for the best and their sensibilities enable them to see more sharply, more deeply than others. To incite the ignorant to believe that elitism implies legal and political injustice is self-defeating for any artist, however justified it may be for communists, socialists, and other revolutionary forces. In this century, social, legal, economic, and political inequalities have been practiced most frequently by those major powers with the loftiest intentions, the People's Republic of China, The Soviet Union, The United States, all of which think heaven on earth not improbable.

In *The Writer's Demotion to Solid-Citizen Status*,[16] John Aldridge says, "The idea of the writer as an exceptional man is uncomfortable, perhaps because so seldom demonstratable, at the present time. Yet it is a measure of just how far we have fallen, that in the great period of modernism the idea was not simply taken for granted: it was a concept of such liberating force that from it the movement derived much of its creative confidence and authority." Citing Margaret Anderson's [17] remarkable productivity and fervor during the 1920s, he restates her belief as ". . . the artist, to the extent that he is a genuine shaper of consciousness, is in fact an exceptional man, superior to other men by virtue of his talent and intelligence and would necessarily be anti-bourgeois in his attitude and values, if only because bourgeois society is the enemy of artistic freedom, is corrupted by materialism and hypocrisy and exists in a state of spiritual paralysis, which is a form of death."

The wonder isn't that we have so few good writers or so few exceptional people but that we have any at all. Even the television generation is contributing, in low numbers, of course, unique individuals to our culture. But the pressures to conform are unending and the opportunities for corruption unlimited. Our educational system has reared us not only to be faceless but gutless. When pressure mounts, we crack up or give up. But there are times in every country's history when only collective heroism will suffice— individual acts are not enough to stop a cultural, political, economic, or legal decay. In the last several years we have been barely able to come up with an individual hero; in the MaiLai massacre, for instance, it seemed as if only the prosecuting attorney spoke for humanity. On an average Sunday, in the tiny book review sections of our leading cities' newspapers, friends and cronies review, with glowing praise, each other's books which are presented to the duped public as impartial commentary. At social and literary luncheons, lackeys don't dare defend either a friend or a genuine talent if such a one has been placed beyond the pale by that set's literary lion. When *Esquire* accepts a subsidy from a giant American corporation for a rather dubious project the enormity of their compromise repels only a few. Talented writers join literary coeteries not just to "make it" but not to make enemies of the "right people". And in our everyday social life, the list of betrayals is endless. A South Boston parent who doesn't oppose busing (or Negroes) had better not make his views known or he could get more than his tires slashed. A Negro should think more than twice before breaking the wall of black solidarity by sounding off about the violence, and the casual obscenity in the black community. A teacher would be foolish to be publicly honest about her small charges' failings. And so on and on and on. Between the Philistines who wouldn't know the real thing if they saw it and who mouth whatever they're conditioned to, and the Pharisees who know but who choose not to be committed, the difference lies in intentions, not in ends. But when the ends themselves are unworthy, as Djilas said, nothing can sanctify the means. Hypocrites realized that conviction won't insure the success that sycophancy will.

Just as the nation's knee-jerk reaction to the MaiLai massacre disclosed a gap between our words and deeds so does the toadyism of the literary set reveal the sordidness of our cultural life. It is the ultimate decadence to leave "undone those things which we ought to have done; and to have done those things which we ought not to have done". Corruption seeps in slowly, in seemingly small insignificant ways but we pay for it in large ways: we don't just lack individual or collective integrity, we lack greatness and the appreciation of greatness. Mediocrity has done more than merely enshrine the third-rate among us: it has made cowards of us all.

---

[1] Title essay from *A Sad Heart at the Supermarket* (1962)
[2] "Poets, Critics, and Readers", ibid.
[3] Chapter 1, "Men Without Chests"
[4] Op. cit.
[5] *Trousered Apes*
[6] *Newsart*, Spring 1975, The Smith, N.Y.C.
[7] *The New Leader*, June 19, 1974
[8] *The New Yorker*, December 1, 1975
[9] Op. cit.
[10] Op. cit.
[11] *Screwtape Proposes A Toast and other Pieces*; title essay
[12] Published in *The Reporter* but not reprinted in her collections *More in Anger* (1958) or *But Will It Sell?* (1964)
[13] *Screwtape Proposes A Toast*, ibid.
[14] I am referring throughout this essay to "serious" literature and not to "popular" literature.
[15] *The Valley of Fear*
[16] *Saturday Review*, September 18, 1971
[17] Editor and founder of *The Little Review*

John F. Adams / Pullman, Washington
VINEGAR PIES, AIR-TIGHT DUMPLINGS,
AND OTHER NORTHWEST FAVORITES

from *South Dakota Review*, Volume 15, Number 4: Winter 1977
Vermillion, South Dakota
Editor: John Milton

IF the cost of living is beginning to make a well-provisioned cook shack appear more attractive than a split-level ranch style, perhaps it's time to begin looking at some cook shack recipes. If a cook shack meal doesn't always turn out to be particularly cheap, that's largely because many of them can't conveniently be reduced to serve fewer than a round-up crew. That does, of course, make them agreeable prospects for company meals, particularly if a real western theme can be justified for the occasion. For certain of the recipes, the name alone might be enough to perfectly well satisfy a pretty robust appetite. Recipes for Southwestern cooking are in general rather well-known. However, what was served up by Northwestern ranch cooks ("gut robbers" or "belly-cheats" by affectionate designation) tend to be virtually unknown outside of their place of origin.

Begin with one of the all-time western favorites, and a perfect jewel of a main course for an authentic western soiree, and a dish quite suitable for outdoors cooking. Although the name was sometimes refined or ameliorated, properly it was always called a "son of a bitch stew." By the odd quirks of chance and fortune, nowadays the ingredients are probably more easily come by in a large city than out on the range itself. So while nothing was dearer to the voracious appetite and iron constitution of the old time cowboy than a good son of a bitch, it's rare today to find a man who has tasted it. The recipes are varied, and the modes of preparation sometimes highly individual, but the essential ingredients were always the same.

The stew requires heart, liver, tongue, sweetbreads, brains, tenderloin, and marrow gut of a young veal. The "marrow gut" requires a word of explaining. Actually it consists of the tube connecting the first and second stomach of a ruminant, and in a young calf secretes digestives necessary in the assimilation of milk. In an older animal it ceases to provide these secretions, and it is no longer suitable for the stew. All of these ingredients (even the marrow gut on a special order) can be obtained through a specialty butcher shop. You can scour the stores in the range country, though, and today could seldom come up with more than half of the ingredients. For the most part the modern range people dourly reject as food any part of a cow that is not muscle.

The cooking pot—it must be of substantial size—is put on to heat with about a quarter of a pound of chopped veal suet. When the fat is well rendered, remove the "cracklings." Cut the heart into small cubes, and add to the grease. Skin the tongue, cube it, and stir in with the simmering heart. These ingredients, being the toughest, should be cooked slowly until they begin to become somewhat tender, about an hour. Cube about two pounds of veal tenderloin, half a pound of liver, and the sweetbreads, and slowly add them to the mixture, stirring and browning as you add them. Slice the marrow gut into thin rings (do not scrape the "marrow" out of the marrow gut, or the whole point is lost), and add to the other ingredients, stirring for a few minutes while they brown in the mixture. Cover the whole stew with water, and simmer for about two hours. Now cook about two pounds of calves brain in a greased skillet, stirring in a little flour until it thickens, then add to the stew. Salt and pepper, and add half a pound of small onions— "skunk eggs," as the cowboys called them. Allow the stew to simmer for another hour and serve hot with a minimum discussion of its ingredients.

By way of euphemism, the son of a bitch stew is of course sometimes referred to as a "son of a gun." Sometimes it is also referred to by the name of the current president or any politician, or by the name of anyone else you don't feel particularly amiable towards. No one seems to know the origin of the name of the stew any more than the origin of the stew itself. Today, however, the stew—if not the name-sake—is approaching extinction.

If you cook up a son of a bitch, you no doubt will have guests in to share it, and a company meal should always be followed by a suitable and appropriate dessert. There are a couple of good choices in this department that are bound to be received with appreciation after the main dish. A sure pleaser, and welcomely sim-

ple after the preparation of the stew, would be "air-tight dumplings." Actually the name has nothing to do with the physical characteristics or construction of the dish, but applies only to the principal ingredient, canned peaches. In western parlance, any canned
goods went by the name of *air-tights*, but since the cowboy appetite abominated all canned vegetables but tomatoes, and all canned
fruits but peaches, the name became interchangeable with those
two commodities. Since pies were never made of tomatoes, by simple elimination an air-tight dumpling was made with canned
peaches.

The air-tight dumpling is a variety of fried pie, and the usual
crust was biscuit dough. They are actually better made with regular pie dough, if you care to trouble, but ranch cooks seldom did.
Simply cut a circle from biscuit dough rolled to pie crust thickness,
about the bigness of the mouth of a lard (or shortening) can, which
was usually what the dough was cut with. Sprinkle it liberally with
sugar and place several sections of peach on one half of the circle,
and dust a teaspoon of sugar over them. Turn the other half of the
dough across the filling, and pinch the edges. Fry in a hot well-
greased pan until brown on the bottom; turn, and fry until the
other side is brown. Of course several may be cooked at one time.
They are good either hot or cold, and were sometimes served as a
treat with breakfast. Some cooks preferred frying them in deep fat.
Using the same technique, they may be prepared with any dried
fruit (stewed first, or at least soaked), fresh berries, and are quite
fine made with applesauce, especially if well sprinkled with cinnamon. If prepared with any filling other than canned peaches, the
pastry is called simply fried pie. The other fillings, except applesauce, require considerably more sugar.

Cowboy desserts tended to be very simple and make-shift, dictated to more by what was possible than what might be desireable.
Regular closed-topped pies were possible; even when an oven was
not available they could still be baked by the fire in a Dutch oven.
They could not, in general, require eggs or fresh milk, and naturally
had to be apple pies. There was, however, an "un-natural" version,
going by the unexciting name of *vinegar pie*. By stretching credi-
bility, it might be called an ersatz lemon pie. Mix a half cup of vinegar with a cup of water, and add enough sugar to sweeten. Melt a
quarter of a cup of lard (or beef tallow) in a frying pan, and when

it is melted, stir in flour until it thickens like gravy. To this add the vinegar slowly, stirring over the heat until the whole mixture thickens. Cool slightly and add to a pie crust. Top with strips of rolled pie dough and bake.

The cowboy vernacular maintained a precise distinction between adequate and palatable food and border-line or subsistence fare. The former was called chuck; the latter, *bait*. It was only when the services of a professional cook were available that the cowboy could expect chuck, and such culinary elegance as a son of a bitch stew or vinegar pie. In the line shack, those lonely little outpost accommodations far from the home ranch where a couple of cowboys might fare alone for several months, fending off hunger was their own responsibility, and the diet which sustained their existence was strictly *bait*. The ideal to be strived for in cooking under those conditions was something that had to be prepared only once, and thereafter remained forever, making no further demands than to be heated and eaten, like provender from the magic porridge pot in the fairy story.

Never has that old fairy story come closer to actualization than in the line shack's "perpetual mulligan." The chief difference between a mulligan and a stew, if there is indeed a difference in the west, is that in a mulligan everything has been so thoroughly cooked that all individual distinction or recognizable characteristics are lost. The secret of the mulligan's perpetuity of course was no fairy gift; eternality required simply that as much new substance must be added each day as was eaten. The substance added day by day to mulligans became a part of the western folk lore, and line-shackers exercised terrifying ingenuity in contriving how to splice out the lives of their mulligans with the least expenditure of cooking effort. Actually most mulligans, at least in their infancy, were pathetically simple and bland—boiled beef or venison, potatoes and onions, plus salt and pepper. An occasional handful of dried beans were sometimes added to sustain the consistency and avoid the bother of actually cooking a batch of beans. But stories told about mulligans always climax with the particular ingredient that snuffed out their charmed life: "and then I added a hawk I had shot, and we finally had to throw the damned thing out," or "I threw in a bunch of grouse eggs, only it turned out they were close to ready to hatch, and . . . ." Sometimes biscuit dough might be dropped on top of the stew to make dumplings. When dumplings were made, the necessity of bread baking was eliminated, and so the preparation of the whole meal was confined to a single pan, and one that didn't need washing, at least not until someone inadvertently killed the mulligan.

Even though they might not want to expend it washing dishes, the men in the line shacks would have a considerable amount of time on their hands. Liquor of any kind was—and is—usually completely forbidden for ranch hands on the job. But if the line shack was lonely, it was also private, and free from prying supervising eyes. A very simple but serviceable still was easily improvised from the materials to be found in even the most primitive line shack. Needed was a medium sized funnel and a can into which it could be slipped, bottom-side down. Then a goodly quantity of solder (if necessary it could be salvaged from the seams of old tin cans) was dropped alongside the funnel where it rested on the bottom of the can, and the can heated until the solder melted and spread, forming a seal between the funnel and the inside of the can. When it cooled, a large hole was cut in the bottom of the can, freeing an opening up into the sealed-in mouth of the funnel. This contrivance was placed with exacting care on top of a can of the same size, into which had been poured whatever was to be distilled. Together the two cans were set on top of the stove, and a pan of cold water (or ice, if it was winter) balanced on top, more or less loosely seal-it off. As the mixture in the first can heated, the steam rose through the hole in the bottom of the second can, through the funnel, and vented through the spout against the bottom of the can of cold water. This caused it to condense, and the liquid trickled down the neck of the funnel and collected in the bottom. After simmering on top of the stove long enough to extract all or most of the alcohol, the cold water pan was removed, the liquor poured off from the second can, and a fresh batch set on to heat.

This process was not particularly fast, but with a little patience it could make booze considerably faster than even the most determined cooks could drink it. The metal salts liable to be assimilated into the liquid from a still made of these materials could not have been healthy, but to a physical constitution seasoned by participating in the demise of several perpetual mulligans it cannot have posed much of a hazard. What the cowboy distilled in his still, like what he put in his perpetual mulligan, depended upon what was available. If there was grain to feed the horses, of whatever kind, it would be cooked and fermented, with or without sugar. Sugar was not often in long supply, but if available a simple solution of plain sugar water was fermented and distilled. Sometimes molasses, "larrup," or "lick," as the cowboy called it, would be mixed with water or cooked grain and fermented. Molasses was cheap, and consequently in fairly liberal supply, chiefly to be added to beans or eaten with hotcakes or sourdough bread. With a little sacrifice, much could be liberated for the distillery. More rarely dried fruit was available, and when it was, either alone or as a blend found its way into the fermentation crock. And of course in season wild berries were frequently fermented into wine and drunk while the juice was still bubbling. With his preference for strong spirits, however, the majority of ferments went the route of the funnel.

Another treat that was dear to the cowboys' appetite, but requiring the attentions of a professional cook, was "bear sign." It takes its name from the striking resemblance of its form to the shape and configuration of bear-droppings, or *bear sign*. For the uninitiated, bears leave their droppings in plump neat crescents, frequently taking the form of almost perfectly round closed circles. That is exactly the shape of this delicacy, a closed circle. The recipe for it can be found in any all-purpose cookbook under the less pungent name of *doughnut*.

It is one of the paradoxes of the American cattle industry, at least as it was practiced in years past, that milk was almost totally lacking in the ranch diet. The explanation for this seeming anomaly is quite simple: beef cattle are notoriously scant milk producers, which when coupled to the fact that the cows were not trained to be milked and the cowboys were not trained to be milkers, there just was no fresh milk. But there was little call for milk, and that small demand was amply satisfied by canned milk. A story so old that it's almost new again tells of a rancher's wife who answered an advertisement on the label of a condensed milk can to submit a jingle for a contest, extolling that brand of milk. She wrote:

Carnation milk is the best in the land—
It comes to the table in a little red can.
She sent this jingle to town with one of the hands, asking him to

buy a stamped envelope and mail it for her. Some weeks passed, and she received a letter from the milk company, saying her entry was hands down the most original of all submitted, but unfortunately its language was totally unsuitable for printing and it had therefore been disqualified. Burning with embarrassment, she asked the hand if he had tinkered with her submission. Finally she wrung from him the admission that he had read it, deciding it was a little pallid he had added a couple of lines. With his corrections, her contest entry had read:

> Carnation milk, the best in the land—
> It comes to the table in a little red can:
> No teats to pull, no [manure] to pitch,
> Just punch a hole in the son of a bitch.

Like his counterpart in the Southwest, the Northwestern ranch cook prepared lots of beans, or "strawberries," as they were almost universally known. Their preparation was simple enough that they were often an important item of bait in the line shack. The taste in the Northwest was for beans which were quite bland. Chili and other seasonings were rarely used. By a process of cow-country snobbery, in the ill-logic only a cowboy would be capable of, heavily spiced dishes were associated with Mexican and Basque sheepherders; hence eating such fare tended to suggest one might have at one time functioned as a sheepherder, carrying untold and unredeemable loss of caste. Therefore white, red, or pinto, the beans were cooked about the same, and with very little spicing. The first step is to "look" the beans. Spoiled, molded, or otherwise suspicious appearing beans were located and discarded. Inevitably small lumps of dirt and even small rocks may be present, and can be eliminated only by hand-sorting. After an overnight soaking, the beans are drained, rinsed again and again drained, then put in a Dutch oven or pot well covered with water. Salt pork, cut up, is added, the beans covered, and cooked slowly all day. No salt is added, if at all, until an hour or so before serving. In the long slow cooking the beans absorb nearly all of the fat from the pork, and although they are quite bland by Southwestern standards, they are in their own mild way quite delicious. Seldom is molasses added to the beans before cooking, as in baked bean recipes, but often individuals would liberally lace their plate of beans with molasses before eating them. Sometimes raw onions, sliced or chopped, lots of them, would be spread over the top of the beans, or a large help-ing of them eaten with the beans as a side dish. Not infrequently the beans were served liberally spread over the tops of sourdough biscuits or soda biscuits broken in half on the plate. It's very heavy, but very good if eaten before it has time to get soggy.

There is another classic ranch dessert that a western cookout particularly ambitious for authenticity should consider, although it is almost never made today. In appearance it resembles the classic nursery rhyme illustration of a Christmas pudding. Its name, how-ever, does not. Again exploiting the westerner's favorite epithet, it goes by the name of a "son of a bitch in a sack." The matrix of the pudding was hardened, crumbled biscuits mixed with a little dough, or rarely biscuit dough alone. This bread crumb filler was liberally sweetened, spiced with cinnamon and nutmeg, and stirred with suf-ficient canned milk to soften the crumbs. To this was added a little molasses, plus a liberal blending of raisins, stewed prunes (pitted), and dried apples and apricots if available (soaked and chopped, of course). When the ingredients were thoroughly mixed and blended together, it was poured out into a cotton sack, and the opening twisted and tied, making a spherical pudding about eight inches in diameter. Any larger and it becomes difficult to get it cooked all the way through.

The sack is suspended above a pot of boiling water and allowed to steam for several hours. Hence it is a dish which is very easy to cook outdoors where a fire had to be kept going anyway to cook a pot of beans or whatever, and a pole or rack can easily be assem-bled to suspend the sack from. But for the same reason, it is fairly difficult to contrive a convenient way to prepare it in the conven-ience of a modern kitchen. Nevertheless, on the occasion of an out-door barbecue, it might be quite easily managed and quite worth the trouble. It is served sliced (or spooned, if the consistency is soft) and topped with a lacing of condensed milk and/or molasses.

There is no doubt that "native" cookery in the Northwest is a poor step-relative of the rich and varied Southwestern ranch fare. It lacked subtlety of seasoning, and often of preparation, and its kind and quality supposed physical conditions more primitive and make-shift than that to be found on a century old Spanish ranch. It is unlikely to ever spawn a style of cooking, or inspire a specialty restaurant, but including a dish or two might insure that an outdoor barbecue will be remembered for longer than the next invitation.

Robert Bly / Madison, Minnesota

LEAPING IN POETRY

from *The Seventies*, Number 1: 1972
Madison, Minnesota
Editor: Robert Bly

LOOKING FOR DRAGON SMOKE

1

IN ANCIENT times, in the "time of inspiration", the poet flew
from one world to another, "riding on dragons", as the Chinese
said. Isaiah rode on those dragons, so did Li Po and Pindar. They
dragged behind them long tails of dragon smoke. Some of that dragon smoke still boils out of Beowulf. The Beowulf poet holds tight
to Danish soil, or leaps after Grendel into the sea.

This dragon smoke means that a leap has taken place in the
poem. In many ancient works of art we notice a long floating leap
at the center of the work. That leap can be described as a leap
from the conscious to the unconscious and back again, a leap from
the known part of the mind to the unknown part and back to the
known. In the epic of Gilgamesh, which takes place in a settled
society, psychic forces suddenly create Enkidu, "the hairy man"
as a companion for Gilgamesh, who is becoming too successful.
The reader has to leap back and forth between the white man,
"Gilgamesh" and the "hairy man". In the *Odyssey* the travellers
visit a Great Mother island, dominated by the Circe-Mother, and
are turned into pigs. They make the leap in an instant. In all art derived from Great Mother mysteries, the leap to the unknown part
of the mind lies in the very center of the work. The strength of
"classical art" has much more to do with this leap than with the
order that the poets developed to contain, and, partially, to dis-
guise it.

As Christian civilization took hold, and the power of the spiritual patriarchies deepened, this leap occurred less and less often in
Western literature. Obviously the ethical ideas of Christianity in-
hibit it. From the start Christianity has been against the leap.
Christian ethics always embodied a move against the "animal

instincts"; Christian thought, especially Paul's thought, builds a firm distinction between spiritual energy and animal energy, a distinction so sharp it became symbolized by black and white. White became associated with the conscious and black with the unconscious. Christianity taught its poets—we are among them—to leap *away* from the unconscious, not *toward* it.

The intellectual Western mind accepted the symbolism of white and black, and far from trying to unite both in a circle, as the Chinese did, tried to get "apartheid". In the process, some weird definitions of words developed.

If a European avoided the animal instincts and consistently leaped away from the unconscious, he was said to be living in a state of "innocence". Children were thought to be "innocent" because it was believed they had no sexual, that is, animal, instincts. Eighteenth century translators like Pope and Dryden forced Greek and Roman literature to be their allies in their leap away from animality, and they translated Homer as if he too were "innocent". To Christian Europeans, impulses open to the sexual instincts or animal instincts indicated a fallen state, a state of "experience".

Blake thought the whole nomenclature insane, the precise reverse of the truth. He wrote *The Songs of Innocence and Experience* about that. In that book he reversed the poles. He maintained that living open to animal instincts was precisely "innocence"; children were innocent exactly because they moved back and forth between the known and unknown minds with a minimum of fear. To write well, you must "become like little children". Blake, discussing "experience", declared that to be afraid of a leap into the unconscious is actually to be in a state of "experience". (We are all experienced in that fear.) The state of "experience" is characterized by blocked love-energy, boredom, envy, and joylessness. Another characteristic is a pedestrian movement of the mind; possibly constant fear makes the mind move slowly. Blake could see that after eighteen hundred years of no-leaping, joy was disappearing, poetry was dying, "the languid strings do scarcely move! The sound is forced, the notes are few." A nurse in the state of "experience", obsessed with a fear of animal blackness (a fear which increased after the whites took Africa), calls the children in from play as soon as the light falls:

When the voices of children are heard on the green

> *And whisp'rings are in the dale*
> *The days of my youth rise fresh in my mind,*
> *My face turns green and pale.*

> *Then come home, my children, the sun is gone down*
> *And the dews of night arise;*
> *Your spring and your day are wasted in play*
> *And your winter and night in disguise.*

The nurse in "The Songs of Innocence" also calls the children in. But she is not in a state of "experience", and when the children say:

> *"No, no, let us play, for it is yet day*
> *And we cannot go to sleep;*
> *Besides in the sky the little birds fly*
> *And the hills are all cover'd with sheep."*

She replies:

> *"Well, well, go and play till the light fades away*
> *And then go home to bed."*
> *The little ones leaped and shouted and laugh'd*
> *And all the hills echoed.*

She enjoys their shouts. They leap about on the grass playing, as an "innocent man" leaps about inside his psyche.

My idea, then, is that a great work of art often has at its center a long floating leap, around which the work of art in ancient times used to gather itself like steel shavings around the magnet. But a work of art does not necessarily have at its center a single long floating leap. The work can have many leaps, perhaps shorter. The real joy of poetry is to experience this leaping inside a poem. A poet who is "leaping" makes a jump from an object soaked in unconscious substance to an object or idea soaked in conscious psychic substance. What is marvellous is to see this leaping return in poetry of this century.

So far the leaps tend to be fairly short. In "Nothing But Death" Neruda leaps from death to the whiteness of flour, then to notary publics and he continues to make leap after leap. We often feel elation reading Neruda because he follows some arc of association which corresponds to the inner life of the objects; so that anyone sensitive to the inner life of objects can ride with him. The links are not private, but somehow bound into nature.

Thought of in terms of language, then, leaping is the ability to associate fast. In a great ancient or modern poem, the considerable distance between the associations, the distance the spark has to leap, gives the lines their bottomless feeling, their space, and the speed of the association increases the excitement of the poetry.

2

Sometime in the thirteenth century poetry in Europe began to show a distinct decline in the ability to associate powerfully. There are individual exceptions, but the circle of worlds pulled into the poem by association dwindles after Chaucer and Langland; their work is already a decline from the Beowulf-poet. By the eighteenth century, the dwindling had become a psychic disaster. Freedom of association had become drastically curtailed. The word "sylvan" by some psychic railway line leads directly to "nymph", to "lawns", to "dancing", so to "reason", to music, spheres, heavenly order, etc. They're all stops on some railroad. There are very few images of the Snake, or the Dragon, or the Great Mother, and if mention is made, the Great Mother leads to no other images, but rather to words suggesting paralysis or death. As Pope said, "The proper study of mankind is man."

The loss of associative freedom showed itself in form as well as in content. In content the poet's thought plodded through the poem, line after line, like a man being escorted through a prison. The "form" was a corridor, full of opening and closing doors. The rhymed lines opened at just the right moment, and closed again behind the visitors.

By the eighteenth century the European intellectual was no longer interested in imagination really. He was trying to develop the "masculine" mental powers he sensed Socrates stood for—a demythologized intelligence, that moves in a straight line made of tiny bright links, an intelligence dominated by linked facts rather than "irrational" feelings. The European intellectual succeeded in developing that rationalist intelligence and it was to prove useful. Industry needed it to guide a locomotive through a huge freight yard, or to guide a spaceship back from the moon through the "re-entry corridor".

Nevertheless, this careful routing of psychic energy, first done in obedience to Christian ethics, and later in obedience to commercial needs, had a crippling effect upon the psychic life. The process amounted to an inhibiting of psychic flight, and as Blake saw, once the child had finished European schools, he was incapable of flight. He lived the rest of his life with "single vision and Newton's sleep".

Blake took the first step: he abducted the thought of poetry and took it off to some obscure psychic woods. Those woods were real woods, occult ceremonies took place in them, as they had in ancient woods. In Germany, Novalis and Holderlin abducted a child, also, and raised it deep in the forest. All over Europe energy in poetry began to come more and more from the unconscious, from the black side of the intelligence. Freud pointed out that the dream still retained the fantastic freedom of association known to us before only from ancient art. By the end of the nineteenth century, both the poem and the dream had been set free: they were no longer part of the effort to develop Socratic intelligence. The poets then began to devote their lives to deepening the range of association in the poem, and increasing the speed of association.

It is this movement that has given such fantastic energy and excitement to "modern poetry" in all European countries. The movement has been partly successful; after only a hundred years of effort, some of the psychic ability to fly has been restored. So this issue will concentrate on leaping poetry, and try to give some examples of it.

SPANISH LEAPING

IT'S ODD how seldom American poets or critics mention association when they talk of poetry. A good leap is thought of as a lucky strike if it appears in the poem, wonderful; if not, no one thinks the worse of it. The leaps in a man like Patchen are never talked of; instead people think of him as an angry poet or a social poet. The absence of association leads to no conclusion either. We accept tons of dull poetry, and no one looks for an explanation of why it is dull. We are not *aware* of association. The content of a poem is thought to be important, and rapid association is a "device" or "technique" (as A. M. Rosenthal calls it), which can be applied or not, depending on what school you belong to!

But it is possible that rapid association is a form of content. For example, a poem on the Vietnam war with swift association and a poem with dull association have two different contents, perhaps even two different subject matters.

The early poems of Wallace Stevens are some of the few poems in English in which it is clear that the poet himself considered association to be a form of content. Often in *Harmonium*, his first book, the *content* of the poem lies in the *distance* between what Stevens was given as fact, and what he then imagined. The farther a poem gets from its initial worldly circumstance without breaking the thread, the more content it has. In *The Emperor of Ice Cream*, for example, the chances are he is watching a child put together a funeral for her doll. That is the worldly fact. He begins to associate:

> Take from the dresses of deal,
> Lacking the three glass knobs, that sheet
> On which she embroidered fantails once
> And spread it so as to cover her face.
> If her horny feet protrude, they come
> To show how cold she is, and dumb.
> Let the lamp affix its beam.
> The only emperor is the emperor of ice-cream.

That's a wonderful leap there. Yet the odd thing is that if he had described the play funeral directly, that is, with dull association, the poem would have had no content. As *"On The Manner of Addressing Clouds"* begins, I suspect he is watching a Yale commencement. This comes out:

> Gloomy grammarians in golden gowns,
> meekly you keep the mortal rendezvous,
> eliciting the still sustaining pomps
> of speech which are like music so profound,
> they seem an exaltation without sound.

At the end, he suggests that the "pomps of speech" are important, if the grammarians in the drifting waste of the world are to be accompanied by more than "mute bare splendors of the sun and moon."

About the old banal American realism *a la* Bret Harte, he says:

> Ach, Mutter,

> *this old black dress,*
> *I have been embroidering*
> *French flowers on it.*

The flowers are French because the French poets were the first, as a group, to adopt underground passages of association as the major interest. We hide all that by calling them symbolists, but poet after poet through several generations gave his entire work to exploring these paths of association—Gerard de Nerval, Lautreamont, Aloysius Bertrand, Baudelaire, Mallarme, also Poulet, whom Wallace Stevens, in some *Harmonium* poems, resembles fantastically. Eliot too entered association through a French poet.

But the Spanish poets of this century—much greater than the French in my opinion—loved the new paths of association even more than the French. They considered them *roads*. Antonio Machado says:

> *Why should we call*
> *these accidental furrows roads? ...*
> *Everyone who moves on walks*
> *like Jesus, on the sea.*

Machado noticed that fear of sinking prevents many men from association, or "walking":

> *Mankind owns four things*
> *that are no good at sea.*
> *Anchor, rudder, oars,*
> *and the fear of going down.*

Machado says:

> *It doesn't matter now if the golden wine*
> *overflows from your crystal goblet,*
> *or if the sour wine dirties the pure glass ...*

> *You know the secret corridors*
> *of the soul, the roads that dreams take,*
> *and the calm evening*
> *where they go to die ....*

Machado's calmness comes from the fact that he *does* know the secret roads. He has positively abandoned the old poetry, which we described as following association railways. Much of the hysteria of contemporary American poetry, especially of the 40's poets, comes from the poet's intense longing to use the old railroads of association; but when he does so he finds they didn't lead anywhere. This is the hysteria that underlies Lowell's *Notebooks*. Anne Sexton's recent work points to some such discovery on her part also.

Machado abandoned them. He is calm because he *knows* that something new has happened to the western mind, at least it happened to his! (he can't tell if it only happened to him or also to many others). In any case the change makes him joyful:

> While dreaming, perhaps, the hand
> of the man who broadcasts the stars like grain
> made the lost music start once more
> like the note from a huge harp,
> and the frail wave came to our lips
> in the form of one or two words that had some truth.

Juan Ramon Jimenez, who made marvellous gifts to the opening of wider association, has a powerful image for the discovery of new associative depths to the mind:

> ### OCEANS
>
> I have a feeling that my boat
> has struck, down there in the depths,
> against a great thing.
>
>   And nothing
> happens! Nothing...Silence...Waves...
>
> Nothing happens! Or has everything happened,
> and are we standing now, quietly, in the new life?

The "new" at the end could be the new life, or the new association, or the new depth, or the new spirituality—he refuses to be specific. In a late poem called "Dawn Outside the City Walls" he makes an interesting distinction between true joy and false joy:

> You can see the face of everything, and it is white—
> plaster, nightmare, adobe, anemia, cold—
> turned to the east. Oh closeness to life!
> Hardness of Life! Like something
> in the body that is animal—root, slag-ends—

with the soul still not set well there—
and mineral and vegetable!
Sun standing stiffly against man,
against the sow, the cabbages, the mud wall!
—False joy, because you are merely
in time, as they say, and not in the soul!

So much of the experience of the ecstatic widening of association has been denied to us, because poetry in Spanish is still under-
rated and underread. The American poets of the 40's and 50's did
not read the Spanish poets. The poets didn't read them, and so
they didn't translate them. Instead translations were done by professors and scholars. When these men and women, with good will
on the whole, translated the leaping Spanish poets, they changed
the great Spanish leaps back into the short plodding steps we were
used to, they translated wild association into dull association. The
translators of Rilke—Leishman, the worst—did the same thing. It's
wrong to blame them—they couldn't do anything else, but the reason they are not poets is precisely because they can only take the
leaps that have already been taken many times before. The only
way out then is for the American poets themselves to translate the
Spaniards.

A second thing that has kept us from being aware of association
as the core of a poem is the grudge American critics and university
teachers have always had against surrealism. Philip Lamantia,
Robert Duncan and others write of, and to some extent, out of,
Breton surrealism, and regarded French surrealism as far superior
to other sorts; but all through the fifties and sixties we didn't have
a single important surrealist magazine in the United States. A
small magazine has recently been started in San Francisco, *Anti-
Narcissus*, which is devoted to French surrealism and it is good.
We still don't have a magazine to represent Spanish surrealism, to
say nothing of German, or Greek.

American poetry faltered in the 40's and 50's: we can make a
generalization: if the Americans do not have European poets to re-
fresh their sense of what association is, their work soon falls back
to the boring associative tracks that so many followed through the
Kenyon Review times and the dull political landscapes of the
Partisan Review.

The American poets are now turning to Lorca, Vallejo and
Neruda for help. Lorca and the South Americans learned swift associations from Quevedo, Goya, Becquer, Juan Ramon. Vallejo especially is a genius in association. Eshleman worked hard, but he lacks
all sense of joy, and his Vallejo translations once more transform
ecstatic leaps back into dull association. So I have printed here a
few newly translated poems of Vallejo, from *Poemas Humanos*, to
indicate his swiftness. Neruda doesn't move as fast, but he puts his
feet down with great firmness.

WILD ASSOCIATION

ONE DISTINCTION between Spanish surrealism and French surrealism is that the Spanish "surrealist" or "leaping" poet often enters into his poem with a heavy body of feeling piled up behind
him as if behind a dam. As you begin the Spanish poem, a heavy
river rolls over you. Vallejo's poem "What if after so many words
..." is a good example of this. And what an incredible poem it is!

French surrealism and Spanish surrealism both contain wonderful leaps, but whereas French surrealism often longs for the leaps
without any specific emotion—many believe that the unconscious
does not *have* emotions—the Spanish poets believe that it does.
The poet enters the poem excited, with the emotions alive; he is
angry or ecstatic, or disgusted. There are a lot of exclamation
marks, visible or invisible. Almost all the poems in Lorca's *Poet in
New York* are written with the poet profoundly moved, flying.
Powerful feeling makes the mind associate faster, and evidently the
presence of swift association makes the emotions still more alive; it
increases the adrenalin flow, just as chanting awakens many emotions that the chanter was hardly aware of at the moment he began
chanting.

When the poet brings to the poem emotions from his thought-
life and his flight-life, emotions which would be intense whether
the poem were written or not, and when he succeeds in uniting
them with the associative powers of the unconscious, we have something different from Homer or Machado; a new kind of poem
(apparently very rare in the nineteenth century) which we could
call the poem of "passionate association", or "poetry of flying".

Lorca wrote a beautiful and great essay called "Theory and

331

Function of the Duende", available in English in the Penguin Lorca. "Duende" is the sense of the presence of death, and Lorca says:

> *Very often intellect is poetry's enemy because it is too much given to imitation, because it lifts the poet to a throne of sharp edges and makes him oblivious of the fact that he may suddenly be devoured by ants, or a great arsenic lobster may fall on his head.*

Duende involves a kind of elation when death is present in the room, it is associated with "dark" sounds, and when a poet has duende inside him, he brushes past death with each step, and in that presence associates fast (Samuel Johnson remarked that there was nothing like a sentence of death in half an hour to wonderfully clear the mind). The gypsy flamenco dancer is associating fast when she dances, and so is Bach writing his Cantatas. Lorca mentions an old gypsy dancer who, on hearing Brailowsky play Bach, cried out, "That has duende!"

Lorca says:

> *To help us seek the duende there is neither maps nor discipline. All one knows is that it burns the blood like powdered glass, that it exhausts, that it rejects all the sweet geometry one has learned, that it breaks with all styles ... that it dresses the delicate body of Rimbaud in an acrobat's green suit: or that it puts the eyes of a dead fish on Count Lautreamont in the early morning Boulevard.*

> *The magical quality of a poem consists in its being always possessed by the duende, so that whoever behold it is baptized with dark water.*

What is the opposite of wild association then? Tame association? Approved association? Sluggish association? Whatever we want to call it, we know what it is—that slow plodding association that pesters us in so many poetry magazines, and in our own work when it is no good, association that takes half an hour to compare a childhood accident to a crucifixion, or a leaf to the I Ching. Poetry is killed for students in high school by teachers who only understand this dull kind of association, while their students are associating faster and faster.

The Protestant embarrassment in the presence of death turns us into muse poets or angel poets, associating timidly. Lorca says:

> *The duende—where is the duende? Through the empty*
> *arch comes an air of the mind that blows insistently over the*
> *heads of the dead, in search of the new landscapes and unsuspected*
> *accents; an air smelling of child's saliva, of pounded*
> *grass, and medusal veil announcing the constant baptism of*
> *newly created things.*

HOPPING

EUROPEAN POETS led and still remain the leaders in poetry of association. They began it in 1780 while our ancestors in the United States were still a few Puritans dressed in black and white, frightened by the black forests west of them. Some European painters made as great leaps as the poets did, perhaps greater. Max Ernst's leaps are oceanic, and full of distance. Perhaps he's better than any modern French poet, though we remember how close the connection in any event was between poets and painters in France, and Lorca's admiring friendship in the thirties with Dali. In America, the painters and poets have had little in common, and that has contributed to the American poets' unawareness of leaping as a principle in art. Poets like Nims or Shapiro simply do not grasp association, and we notice we never think of them in connection with painting at all. Frank O'Hara had a deep interest in painting in general, especially in French painting, and so does John Ashbery. So we have a link of sorts there. Ashbery has real leaping in his work.

The poets who came out of Ashbery, the St. Mark's and Bolinas group, retain his affection for painting, but unfortunately have no more relation to the intense Spanish poetry than Karl Shapiro has. They leap, but without that "head of emotion" that gives such power to many Spanish works of art. They do not approach the poem with passion at all. That great head of water which Lorca and Vallejo back up over the poem before they set down a word is simply absent (except perhaps in O'Hara's poem for Billie Holiday). O'Hara and Berrigan, to name two extremely talented poets, are both for the most part poets of pleasure, a very different thing from being a poet of emotion. The St. Mark's poets are very aware of that distinction—this is nothing new to them—and some actually prefer the poetry of pleasure to poetry of intense emotion, and they like the eighteenth century poetry precisely for that reason. Surely in a brutal, job-ridden, Puritanical, Billy Grahamized America, poetry of pleasure, describing the six or seven lovely things you did that day, is a victory of sorts.

The trouble with all that is that the pleasures Berrigan, for instance, describes, tend to be pleasures of the conscious mind and not of the unconscious. Occasionally we find the poets in bed with a girl, but we get little feeling of the mystery of that pleasure. Usually it takes place quickly just before the girl goes off to work. Most of the pleasures they describe are of an even more rational sort, like finding the Sunday Times on the doorstep, then throwing it out, or seeing a good movie with Lon Chaney in it, or eating marshmallows in a Chinese restaurant. All of these are what Snyder calls "the pleasures of the educated mind". I think some of Ashbery's poems are great poems, but the generations of these poets clearly make some sort of diminishing tunnel—in each generation the poems of the school get smaller. Tom Clark, Lew Warsh, Anne Waldman, Larry Fagin all suffer from a lack of growth so far—of that group Ted Berrigan and Peter Schjedahl have grown the most—and I think it's partly because this "New York" poetry, though it appears to leap, actually leaps about inside one room of the psyche only. The poems are not flying from the intellect to the sea, from Denmark to the unconscious, they are not going anywhere; in other words, it is not leaping so much as hopping. It's fun to hop—I enjoy watching these poets avoid standing in the same place, keeping their feet in the air. But Max Ernst does a lot more than that.

The St. Mark's poets learned from Creeley to stay in one cave of the mind; but they are not far enough back in that room. There is an agony in Creeley's work, which means he is living far back in the archaic part of his cave. The intensity comes from that, and it is the intensity that makes his best poems give off light. The St. Mark's poets always have a leisure class mood about them; they are essentially the products of a rich country, who see nothing to fight for, and never fight. In a way, they are consumer poets. They refuse to consume cars and steaks, but they consume subtler things—like poetic pleasures.

This is not to say I hate their poetry; on the contrary, I enjoy it, but they long too much to stay in one part of the psyche, a fairly well-lit part, as Hemingway called it, and the result eventually has to be boring. They treat their adopted style as if it were content, but it's only a style. There is nothing sacred about a style. Lorca says duende "rejects all the sweet geometry one has learned, it breaks with all styles...".

THE THREE BRAINS

SOME RECENT brain research throws light I think on what we've been talking about. I'll sum up some of the conclusions and speculations made by the American neurologist, Paul MacLean. I first ran into his ideas in Koestler's book, *The Ghost in the Machine*, where he gives about six pages to MacLean's theories, and refers to the neurological journals in which MacLean publishes. The gist of MacLean's thought is that we do not have one brain, but three. MacLean's map of the head isn't psychological, as Freud's Ego, Id and Superego, but geographical—the three brains are actually in the head, and brain surgeons have known for a long time what they look like. MacLean's contribution has been to suggest that each of these brains is to some extent independent. During evolution, the body often re-shaped the body—fins, for example, in us, turned utterly into arms, but the forward momentum in evolution was apparently so great that the brain could not allow itself the time to reform—it simply added.

The reptile brain is still intact in the head. Known medically as limbic node, it is a horseshoe shaped organ located in the base of the skull. The job of the reptile brain appears to be the physical survival of the organism in which it finds itself. Should danger or enemies come near, an alarm system comes into play, and the reptile brain takes over from the other brains—it takes what we might call "executive power". In great danger it might hold that power exclusively. It's been noticed, for example, that when mountain climbers are in danger of falling, the brain mood changes—the eyesight intensifies, and the feet "miraculously" take the right steps. Once down the climber realizes he has been "blanked out". This probably means that the reptile brain's need for energy was so great that it withdrew energy even from the memory systems of the mammal and new brains. The presence of fear produces a higher energy input to the reptile brain. The increasing fear in this cent-

335

ury means that more and more energy, as a result, is going to the reptile brain: that is the same thing as saying that the military budgets in all nations are increasing.

MacLean himself speculated, in a paper written recently for a philosophical conference, that the persistent trait of paranoia in human beings is due to the inability to shut off the energy source to the reptile brain. In a settled society, if there are no true enemies, the reptile brain will imagine enemies in order to preserve and use its share of the incoming energy. John Foster Dulles represented the reptile brain in the fifties.

When the change to mammal life occurred, a second brain was simply folded around the limbic node. This "cortex", which I will call here the mammal brain, fills most of the skull. The mammal brain has quite different functions. When we come to the mammal brain we find for the first time a sense of community: love of women, of children, of the neighbor, the idea of brotherhood, care for the community, or for the country. "There is no greater love than that of a man who will lay down his life for a friend." Evidently in the mammal brain there are two nodes of energy: sexual love and ferocity. (The reptile brain has no ferocity: it simply fights coldly for survival.) Women have strong mammal brains, and probably a correspondingly smaller energy channel to the reptile brain. They are more interested in love than war. "Make love, not war" means "move from the reptile brain to the mammal brain". Rock music is mammal music for the most part; long hair is mammal hair.

The Viking warrior who went "beserk" in battle may have experienced the temporary capture of himself by the mammal brain. Eye witnesses reported that the face of the "beserk" appeared to change, and his strength increased fantastically—when he "woke up", he sometimes found he had killed twenty or thirty men. The facial expression is probably a union of the concerns of all three brains, so if one brain takes over, it is natural that the shape of the face would change.

What does the third brain, the "new brain", do? In late mammal times, the body evidently added a third brain. Brain researchers are not sure why—perhaps the addition is connected to the invention of tools, and the energy explosion that followed that. In any case, this third brain, which I shall call here the new brain, takes the form of an outer eighth inch of brain tissue laid over the surface of the mammal brain. It is known medically as the neo-cortex. Brain tissue of the neo-cortex is incredibly complicated, more so than the other brains, having millions of neurons per square inch. Curiously, the third brain seems to have been created for problems more complicated than those it is now being used for. Some neurologists speculate that an intelligent man today uses 1/100 of its power. Einstein may have been using 1/50 of it.

The only good speculations I have seen on the new brain, and what it is like, are in Charles Fair's new book, *The Dying Self*, Wesleyan University Press. Fair suggests that what Freud meant by the "Id" was the reptile and mammal brain, and what the ancient Indian philosophers meant by the "self" was the new brain. His book is fascinating. He thinks that the new brain can grow and that its food is wild spiritual ideas. Christ said, "If a seed goes into the ground and dies, then it will grow". The reptile and mammal brains don't understand that sentence at all, both being naturalists, but the new brain understands it, and feels the excitement of it. The Greek mystery religions, and the Essene cult that Christ was a member of, were clear attempts to feed the new brain. The "mysteries" were the religion of the new brain. In Europe it was at its highest energy point about 1500, after knowing the ecstatic spiritual ideas of the Near East for 700 years. Since then, "secularization" means that the other two brains have increased their power. Nevertheless a man may still live if he wishes to more in his new brain than his neighbors do. Many of the parables of Christ, and the remarks of Buddha evidently involve instructions on how to transfer energy from the reptile brain to the mammal brain, and then to the new brain. A "saint" is someone who has managed to move away from the reptile and the mammal brains and is living primarily in the new brain. As the reptile brain power is symbolized by cold, and the mammal brain by warmth, the mark of the new brain is light. The gold light always around Buddha's head in statues is an attempt to suggest that he is living in his new brain. Some Tibetan meditators of the 13th century were able to read books in the dark by the light given off from their own bodies.

2

If there is no central organization to the brain, it is clear that the three brains must be competing for all the available energy at any

moment. The brains are like legislative committees—competing for
government grants. A separate decision on apportionment is made
in each head, although the whole tone of the society has weight on
that decision. Whichever brain receives the most energy, that brain
will determine the tone of that personality, regardless of his intelligence or "reasoning power". The United States, given the amount
of fear it generates every day in its own citizens, as well as in the
citizens of other nations, is a vast machine for throwing people into the reptile brain. The ecology workers, the poets, singers, meditators, rock musicians and many people in the younger generation
in general, are trying desperately to reverse the contemporary
energy-flow in the brain. Military appropriations cannot be reduced until the flow of energy in the brain, which has been moving for four or five centuries from the new brain to the reptile
brain is reversed. The reptile and the new brains are now trying to
make themselves visible. The reptile brain has embodied itself in
the outer world in the form of a tank which even moves like a reptile. Perhaps the computer is the new brain desperately throwing
itself out into the world of objects so that we'll *see* it; the new
brain's spirituality could not be projected, but at least its speed is
apparent in the computer. The danger of course with the computer is that it may fall into the power of the reptile brain. Nixon is
a dangerous type—a mixture of reptile and new brain, with almost
no mammal brain at all.

3

We do not spend the whole day "inside" one brain, but we flip
perhaps a thousand times a day from one brain to the other. Moreover we have been doing this flipping so long—since we were in the
womb—that we no longer recognize the flips when they occur. If
there is no central organization to the brain, and evidently there is
not, it means that there is no "I". If your name is John there is no
"John" inside you—there is no "I" at all. Oddly, that is the funda-
mental idea that Buddha had thirteen hundred years ago. "I have
news for you", he said, "there is no 'I' inside there. Therefore trying to find it is useless." The West misunderstands "meditation" or
sitting because being obsessed with unity and "identity", it as-
sumes that the purpose of meditation is to achieve unity. On the
contrary, the major value of sitting, particularly at the start, is to

let the sitter experience the real chaos of the brain. Thoughts shoot in from all three brains in turn, and the sitter does not talk about, but *experiences* the lack of an 'I'. The lack of an 'I' is a central truth of Buddhism (Taoism expresses it by talking of the presence of a "flow"). Christianity somehow never arrived at this idea. At any rate, it never developed practical methods, like sitting, to allow each person to experience the truth himself. Institutional Christianity is in trouble because it depends on a pre-Buddhist model of the brain.

4

Evidently spiritual growth for human beings depends on the ability to transfer energy. Energy that goes normally to the reptile brain can be transferred to the mammal brain, some of it at least; energy intended for the mammal brain can be transferred to the new brain.

The reptile brain thinks constantly of survival, of food, of security. When Christ says, "The lilies do not work, and yet they have better clothes than you do," he is urging his students not to care so much for themselves. If the student wills "not-caring", and that "not-caring" persists, the "not-caring" will eventually cause some transfer of energy away from the reptile brain. Voluntary poverty worked for St. Francis, and he had so little reptile brain paranoia the birds came down to sit on his shoulders.

If energy has been diverted from the reptile brain, the student, if he is lucky, can then transfer some of it to the mammal, and then to the new brain. Christ once advised his students, "If someone slaps you on the left cheek, point to the right cheek." The mammal brain loves to flare up and to strike back instantly. If you consistently refuse to allow the ferocity of the mammal brain to go forward into action, it will become discouraged, and some of its energy will be available for transfer. Since the mammal brain commits a lot of its energy to sexual love, some students at this point in the "road" become ascetic and celibate. They do so precisely in order to increase the speed of energy transfer. The women saints also, such as Anna of Foligno, experience this same turn in the road, which usually involves an abrupt abandonment of husband and children. Christ remarks in the Gospel of St. Thomas that some men are born eunuchs; and some men make themselves eunuchs in

339

order to get to the Kingdom of the Spirit. However if a man is in the reptile brain at the time he begins his asceticism, then the result is a psychic disaster, as it has been for so many Catholic priests and monks.

The leap from the reptile to the new brain cannot be made directly; the student must go through the mammal brain. St. Theresa's spiritual prose shows much sexual imagery, perhaps because the mammal brain contributed its energy to the spiritual brain.

"Meditation" is a practical method for transferring energy from the reptile to the mammal brain, and then from the mammal to the new brain. It is slow, but a "wide" road, a road many can take, and many religious disciplines have adopted it. The orientals do not call it meditation, but "sitting". If the body sits in a room for an hour, quietly, doing nothing, the reptile brain becomes increasingly restless. It wants excitement, danger. In oriental meditation the body is sitting in the foetal position, and this further infuriates the reptile brain, since it is basically a mammalian position.

Of course if the sitter continues to sit, the mammal brain quickly becomes restless too. It wants excitement, confrontations, insults, sexual joy. It now starts to feed in spectacular erotic imagery, of the sort that St. Anthony's sittings were famous for. Yet if the sitter persists in doing nothing, eventually energy has nowhere to go but to the new brain.

Because Christianity has no "sitting", fewer men and women in Western culture than in oriental civilizations have been able to experience the ecstasy of the new brain. Thoreau managed to transfer a great deal of energy to the new brain without meditation, merely with the help of solitutde. Solitude evidently helps the new brain. Thoreau of course willed his solitude and he was not in a reptile city, but in mammal or "mother" nature. Once more the truth holds that the road to the new brain passes through the mammal brain, through "the forest". This truth is embodied in ancient literature by the tradition of spiritual men meditating first in the forest and only after that in the desert. For the final part of the road, the desert is useful, because it contains almost no mammal images. Even in the desert, however, the saints preferred to live in caves—perhaps to remind the reptile brain of the path taken.

To return to poetry, it is clear that poets, like anyone else, can be dominated by one of the three brains. Chaucer is a great poet of the mammal brain; clearly St. John of the Cross and Kabir are great poets of the new brain. The reptile brain seems to have no poet of its own, although occasionally that brain will influence poets. Robinson Jeffers is a man with an extremely powerful mammal brain, in whom, nevertheless, the reptile brain had a slight edge. His magnificent poems are not warm towards human beings. On the contrary, he has a curious love for the claw and the most ancient sea rocks. Every once in a while he says flatly that if all human beings died off, and a seal or two remained on earth, that would be all right with him.

Bach makes music of new brain emotions; Beethoven primarily out of mammal brain emotions. Blake is such an amazing poet because he talks of moving from one brain to another. His people in "the state of experience", after all, have been pulled back into the reptile brain.

> The invisible worm
> That flies in the night,
> In the howling storm,
> Has found out thy bed
> Of crimson joy,
> And his dark secret love
> Does thy life destroy.

When we are in a state of "innocence", Blake says we are feeling some of the spiritual ecstasy of the new brain. The industrialists, as Blake saw clearly, are in a state of "experience", trapped by the reptile brain.

I think poetry ought to take account of these ideas. Some biological and neurological speculations are marvellous, and surely that speculation belongs in literary criticism as much as speculation about breath or images or meter. A man should try to feel what it is like to live in each of the three brains, and a poet could try to bring all three brains inside his poems.

Lorenzo Thomas/Houston, Texas

BARAKA IN NEWARK: GATHERING THE SPIRITS

from *Hoo-Doo*, Number 6½: 1977
Galveston, Texas
Editors: Ahmos Zu-Bolton & Jake Massa

COMING out from New York, you suffer the Hudson Tubes on the train or else you drive through interminable marshes, the flatness broken here and there by the transmitter tower of an easy-listening New York FM radio station, onto the iron Pulaski Skyway with its dull view and noxious swamp gas industrial fumes. I took the motor route once with Sun Ra, band members and friends jiving and doing Dozens in the car. We were going out to visit Baraka, which was really—in those days—the only sane reason to be going to Newark.

Newark, New Jersey is, at any time, something less than you would expect. In the mid-60s, the city was a combination of smoldering opposites. On the surface, Newark was a dull industrial city run by an exceedingly corrupt "sausage machine" (Polish and Italian Democrats); and it was also a city with a predominantly Black population whose urban lifestyles continued, distorted, and disguised Southern smalltown folkways in an entirely predictable way. A town where you could always buy a half-pint on Sunday if you knew where to go. Who to ask . . . cousin or "hometown." Even now, Newark ain't like New York City. New York has vice, indeed, but it has never developed that old-fashioned neighborhood bootlegging tradition.

Nathan Heard's *Howard Street* (1968) succinctly described Newark's hard-core innercity ghetto in suitably hard language:

> Two blocks bisected by Howard Street are bordered by Court, Broome, and West Streets, and Springfield Avenue. Dark little Mercer Street crosses Howard between Court Street and Springfield Avenue. From Court to Mercer is a long block with two trees (birch) fighting valiantly but vainly to stay alive. . . .
>
> The short block between Mercer Street and Springfield

Avenue is something so different as to be classed
almost as another world. While laborers and domestics
—poor but respectable people—live in the long block,
the short one is as wild and rowdy as Dodge City or
Tombstone ever was, with no Hickok or Earp in evidence. It also has the strange, but familiar and inevitable, combination of religion mixed in with every
conceivable vice.[1]

Heard earned his understanding of those streets the hard way. He
came up hard and spent his time behind the walls before writing
his novel and assuming a teaching career. Heard has been attacked
by critics, perhaps impatient with his naturalistic approach, who
are dismayed by his downbeat portraits of Black folks; but these
critics are missing an important point. Anybody who presumes to
understand the dynamics of Black Newark, from the good-doing
Black politicians on down to the junkie nodding in the balcony at
RKO Proctor's, by reading Black Power essays or the militant
newspaper *Unity and Struggle*, had better also read Heard. For
good or ill, disrespectful of Black folks though he may be, Nathan
Heard tells another side of the story: Newark was (and is) a bitch.

In the 1960s, Newark was still the kind of town where a white
traffic cop in his ridiculous Day-glo armor would call Ishmael
Reed, Steve Cannon, and me "boys" when we asked for directions.
Well. Actually, we weren't so old then, and the cop was but a mere
whit older so we convinced ourselves to be indignant anyway.

After riding the Hudson Tubes, anything can make one indignant ... most specially a rookie cop with international orange
creeping up his neck.

Newark was also where you could listen to the futuristic fantasy
music of Sun Ra's Arkestra at Art Williams' Jazz Art Study
Society (JASS), a "revolutionary" cramped basement concert hall
near Springfield. On another evening you could lay dead in Art's
basement and hear drummer Eric Brown literally play his ass off ...
falling off his stool after treating the universe to a blur of hands
and body cymbals snare tom-tom and bass drum ... heralding the
advent of "new music." Newark, in such transcendant moments,
was an exciting place.

One Christmas Eve, Reed and I went bar hopping in Newark and stopped at the Blue Note, a typical Howard Street type bar. A sissy in slightly outdated pimpish clothes and gold dangling earrings eased Charles Brown's "Merry Christmas Baby" out of a tired piano and the assorted drinkers in the club nodded their heads and said "yessss" and drifted and drifted outward inward toward more beautiful space than the club could otherwise afford.

We broke the weird and sentimental spell and wandered down the street, on Reed's money, in a taxi. We found ourselves at the local Urban League/NAACP good-doing brothers' hangout which was a private house, cattycorner to the Father Divine hotel, with a plush red-lighted bar inside. All of the upandcoming cats were there. In dim suits and flaming ties under the red bulbs, they were busily hustling on their level. The conversations were subdued and "significant."

—Well, just um give me a call on Chewsday ... um hmm ... like that.

—I'm sure we can put a little something together.

—Mine host, lay another Cutty on my man here.

And so forth. Same old jive. The music was canned, subtly spinning from somewhere beyond us, lacking the painful intensity and truth of the cat nodding over the Blue Note's piano.

We split from there, too. We walked through the cold quiet streets a few blocks to a union hall or community center sort of place where Amiri Baraka was reading feverish political poems to a handful of cheerful working-class Black folks. Same kind of folks we had left in the Blue Note, but these were their mommas, sisters, little brothers, and wives. Cousins, nieces, nephews of the big-talkers in the red-lit private bar.

Baraka was dressed in a flowing big-sleeved danshiki and a Morrocan knit cap. He was shouting and singing his poems. One of them was a severe but lyrical *j'accuse* aimed at the horde of colored political hacks sucking up behind Hugh Addonizio, the Newark mayor who later went to jail for extortion. The poem was cold. Baraka cynically employed images from popular literature, the doxology, and street slang in a skein of tight words stitched in acid:

We have a nigger in a cape and cloak. Flying above
the shacks and whores.
he has just won an election. A wop is his godfather.

Praise Wop from whom
all blessings flow. The nigger edges sidewise in the light
    breeze, his fingers
scraping nervously in his palms. He has had visions. With
    visions. With commercials. Change
rattles in his pockets. He is high up. Look, he signals.
    Turns, backup, for
cheers. He swoops. The Wop is waving. Wave Wop.[2]

The audience, just like a church congregation, said "Amen" when the poem was finished.

Ishmael Reed and I sat there with our eyes bugged out, wondering if the nigger was mad. Talking like that. Talking that talk.

Reed at that time was editing the *Advance*, a Black weekly in Newark, drawing upon his early experience as star investigatives reporter on the insanely social activist Buffalo *Empire Star*.[3] After a few weeks of Reed's badmouth articles on Buffalo's city government, that paper began losing most of its ads. Editor Joe Walker (later New York bureau chief for *Muhammad Speaks*) allowed Reed to continue and by the time both of them finally quit, the *Empire Star* had lost *all* of its advertising revenue. Obviously, they'd been printing the truth.

The last straw had been drawn when Mr. Walker and Mr. Reed presented an interview with Malcolm X on WUFO in 1960. Yes, they got phonecalls, cards, and letters coming in ... many of which carried the traditional *bon voyage* message: "Get outta Dodge!" Or words to that effect.

Reed's constructive muckraking eventually produced much the same result in corrupt New Jersey as it had earlier in corrupt upstate New York. While the Newark *Advance* gave him an opportunity to bring some of his new-fangled journalistic ideas to reality, his most notable success in the stylistic area was in inspiring art director Walter Bowart and poet Allen Katzman to publish the *East Village Other* in New York City. *EVO* very quickly became the stylebook for the influential "counterculture/underground press" movement of the Vietnam-haunted '60s.

As for hometown Newark, Reed ran up against the usual fatlip small town/small mind going nowhere negroes. From these encounters he did manage to salvage the inspiration for his bitingly satirical first novel, *The Freelance Pallbearers*.[4] It's understandable, that Reed (knowing the Newark scene) was worried when Baraka returned from Harlem in 1966 and set up the Spirit House on Stirling Street in the very heart of the ghetto/saint home. And, worse yet, the nigger come talking like that! Talking about the political machine.

> Black people!
>
>   What about that bad short you saw last week
> on Freylinghuysen, or those stoves and refrigerators,
>   record players
> in Sears, Bambergers, Klein's, Hahnes', Chase, and the
>   smaller joosh
> enterprises? What about that bad jewelry, on Washington
>   Street, and
> those couple of shops on Springfield? You know how to get
>   it, you can
> get it, no money down, no money never, money don't grow
>   on trees no
> way, only whitey's got it, makes it with a machine, to
>   control you.[5]

"No money down, no money never?" The people were saying "yeah, uh huh" laughing and bopping their heads. Like in church. In this undecked hall.

I was amazed at what the poems were doing. Baraka was *home.*

There was, in fact, really no reason we should have worried. Newark is, of course, Baraka's hometown. You've got to figure that the brother understands the place. At the time, many of the literary folk in New York had the feeling that, following the personal disappointments and headline notoriety surrounding the closing of the Harlem Black Arts Repertory Theater/School, Baraka had fled to Newark to lick his wounds. Far from it. If anything, his rhetoric escalated and carefully particularized his social and political concerns.

Baraka's connection to this city was both practical and sentimental. In his studio at the old lower East Side apartment on Cooper Square he had kept a large street map of Newark tacked up next to his desk. It may have served his research needs for *The System of Dante's Hell* (1965), but the map was also a sort of spiritual reminder, a *yantra* focusing the energies of his earliest personal awareness of the world and connecting him, at any remove, to the environs of his immediate ancestry. He possessed a profound understanding of the place and its people, which he later put to use in political organizing that helped elect Kenneth Gibson the first Black mayor of Newark. Baraka also established a powerful Black nationalist organization, the Committee for a Unified Newark (CFUN), which later figured prominently in both national and Pan-African politics and in the development of the Congress of Afrikan People (CAP).

The embryonic stirring of these energies rocked the bare, but joyful hall that cold Christmas Eve. Baraka read on with strength and apocalyptically urgent brilliance. Yet though the production was humble, the people's response held intimations of power. Baraka was treading the boards of a larger stage.

It was strange, alright. And it is interesting to try to analyze the source of the energy that Baraka was then uncoiling.

Most Americans tend to think of any location in the Northeast as "the big time," "the fast track." It's a national media myth. Baraka described that idea in his story "The Screamers"; as heard through the grapevine of touring musicians: "... Newark had a bad reputation. I mean, everybody could pop their fingers. Was hip. Had walks. Knew all about The Apple."[6] Sure they did. But there are small towns up that way, too. There are even parts of the major cities that breed the drives and sensibilities that we have so long associated with growing up in Nebraska. In a certain sense, Baraka suffered such urges. Like any ambitious Midwesterner, he also went to New York—just across the river on the Hudson Tubes—and conquered it; a young "literary lion" in Greenwich Village, he had a full-length play, *A Recent Killing*, scheduled for Broadway when he blew it all off and headed for Harlem and the Black Arts notion.

In a very real sense, Baraka's return to Newark was the return of a prodigal son grown wiser for his sojourn in the cruelest core of the Big Apple. He'd seen the fast tracks both uptown and down. Returning home, he was one up on his neighbors. He knew exactly who and what they were, and he knew also what was going to happen elsewhere. Baraka returned to Newark with ideas that were incredibly advanced by any standards, but definitely far beyond the Newark he had left in the '50s. Or even the city of turmoil to which he had returned.

These energies of ambition and social consciousness were intensified by Baraka's peculiar racial alienation. From his earliest days, Baraka had nurtured a desire to "fit in" to the Black community. The frustration of this desire in his youth is chronicled in *The System of Dante's Hell*, the earlier stories in *Tales* (1967), and poems such as "Letter to E. Franklin Frazier" (written in 1963). The trouble was that Baraka was attracted to the dark and desperate glamour of Howard Street-style negroes in whom he detected an urgency of life and genuine feeling that was denied by both White society and its Black "middle class" shadow.

Having himself come from that shadow "middle class" (which does *not* share economic parity with the White middle class), there was no place for Baraka on Howard Street and his yearning for an impossible involvement there made him suspect in his own environs. In *Tales*, he wrote: "Our house sat lonely and large on a half-Italian street, filled with important Negroes. (Though it is rumored they had a son, thin with big eyes, they killed because he was crazy.)" And he admits his contempt for the "carefully scrubbed children of my parents' friends," his own peers who "fattened" on washed-out imitations of real jazz and blues music, studiously imbibing the White value system "until they could join the Urban League or Household Finance and hound the poor for their honesty."[7] The irony of contempt, of course, comes from the writer's knowledge that he is much like these others. In the early poem "Hymn for Lanie Poo,"[8] Baraka complains that his own sister, a government social worker in those days, had fallen into such bourgeois wrong-headedness. The portrait he draws of her is strikingly reminiscent of daughter Beneatha in Lorraine Hansberry's *A Raison in the Sun* (1959). Indeed, the social identity problem that beset aspiring young Blacks in the '50s is central to both Hansberry's and Baraka's writings; the difference is that, while Hansberry (after carefully exposing Beneatha's naive illusions) reconciled herself —and her characters—to the expected behavior and long-faced hair-trigger patience demanded of her class, Baraka persisted in his love affair with the hard streets. "You see," he wrote in *Tales*, "I left America on the first fast boat."

Obviously, as James Baldwin periodically testifies, one does not flee America quite so easily. Baraka did not actually vanish into the ghetto; rather, he assumed the role of an intellectual, though he tempered it with the rebellion of bohemianism. But he did not completely abandon his yearning to find a place in a vital Black community, away from the tawdry void of White society. The same desire, experimented with on a higher and more meaningful level and again frustrated by the Harlem experience, was succeeded by Baraka's perception and acceptance of a leadership role in Newark's Black community.

He wasted little time. Spirit House, established at 33 Stirling Street, was a direct application of the new ideas about art and society that he had attempted to work out in Harlem, but activities here were consciously structured to avoid the tensions and conflicts that had destroyed the Black Arts theater. Spirit House was a happy place, decorated in bright neo-African color scheme, full of neighborhood children. The order of the house seemed to be a disciplined determination, not a desperate survival motion. In "Stirling Street September," Baraka wrote:

> We are strange in a way because we know
> who we are. Black beings passing through
> a tortured passage of flesh[9]

Clearly, the way through was to be accomplished by the exercise of a higher spiritual consciousness. Revitalization began with a self-knowledge that would lead to actual, tangible power in the sense of self-determination. Meaningful art and useful instruction. Organization. And a mayor!

The resident company, called the Spirit House Movers and Shakers, was to be a sort of model of cooperation on which, later, the United Brothers and its successor, the Committee for a Unified Newark, would be based. The entire program was designed as an exercise in organization to achieve clearly defined goals.

Poet Sonia Sanchez, visiting the house, was impressed by the healthy energy there and wrote a lovely poem comparing the place to the depressed ghetto environment recorded by Nathan Heard:

> if each one of us moved to a
>   howard street
> and worked hard like they do on
>   stirling street
> wudn't be no mo howard sts at all[10]

Spirit House was much more than a theater; it was also a social and political movement, and what began to happen there in 1966 changed the municipal government of Newark and changed the entire aesthetic of Amiri Baraka's work.

The first work to emerge from Spirit House was the play *Black Mass* (1967). Based on the Honorable Elijah Muhammad's teaching about Jacoub's creation of the White race, *Black Mass* was an important and disturbing production which provides the key to understanding Baraka's subsequent directions. "Yacub's creation," wrote critic Larry Neal, "is not merely a scientific exercise. More fundamentally, it is the aesthetic impulse gone astray. The Beast is created merely for the sake of creation. Some artists assert a similar claim about the nature of art. They argue that art need not have a function. It is against this decadent attitude toward art—ramified throughout most of Western society—that the play militates."[11] Baraka's art, from the very first, certainly had a function ... social change in its most mundane and immediate form, *and* the higher spiritual development of Black people. Later he realized that even artists who claimed to work purely "for art's sake" invariably produced work marked with its own social utility. "Poetry," Baraka wrote in 1975, "is apologia for one particular class or another and that class' views, needs and visions."

Baraka's own early alienation among the conflicting motives of the Black bourgeoisie, his later religious searching, and the self-assumed "hopped-up witchdoctor" phase in which he accomplished the work of "gathering the spirits" to the Black Arts movement in Newark and elsewhere led, eventually, to a new stance in which he seemingly has abandoned those spirits in favor of "scientific socialism."[12] He's been quite straightforward about it. His own earlier militant poems, Baraka says now, "came from an enraptured patriotism that screamed against whites as the eternal enemies of Black people, as the sole cause of our disorder + oppression. The same subjective mystification led to mysticism, metaphysics, spookism, &c., rather than dealing with reality ..." Reality, he feels, would have been the recognition of his movement's innocent adherence to "an ultimately reactionary nationalism that served no interests but our newly emerging Black bureaucratic elite and petit bourgeois, so that they could have control over their Black market." It may be, then, that Baraka's current disenchantment with mainline Black municipal politics, his split with Mayor Gibson and the National Black Political Caucus, reflects his dismay

with the recent influence of the same Black middle-class consciousness that his earliest poems and stories satirized.

It may sound like the consolation of hindsight to the blind but
in my opinion, all of these developments could have been read in
the roots of Baraka's lifelong involvement with Newark, in the social reality of the city itself, or in the casual experience of anyone
who has ever been there.

Today, and from now on, Baraka's critics and readers will have
to deal with *all* of this "motley of experience." New poems such as
"Remembering Malcolm" (1977) represent Baraka's own attempt,
from his new "scientific socialist" viewpoint, to grasp the actual
meaning of the turnings of his road; and the new tone is much
more humble than *The Dead Lecturer*'s confession:

> I am a man
> who is loud
> on the birth
> of his ways. Publicly redefining
> each change in my soul, as if I had predicted
> them[13]

The new sense of humility has not necessarily diminished his
power—his purpose may even be stronger—but the close reader of
Baraka's recent work may sense a certain diffusion. It is not that
the flame is not still burning "full up," but that the damper may
not be all the way down. Some of Baraka's readers will still feel a
draft either from excessively extra-literary concerns or from "new"
political influences that have more than once proven to be inappro-
priate to the real issues of Black people here in the United States.
While the works of Lenin, Amilcar Cabral, and Enver Hoxha are
still essential reading, I'm certain that Baraka's apotheosis of Josef
Stalin is more than distasteful to Black activists of our parents' generation who suffered first-hand from the expediencies of Soviet
politics as filtered through the pre-World War II American Communist Party. With Stalin, I'm afraid, Baraka has been taken in by the
mystique of "the man of action" without carefully scrutinizing
what those actions were.

While the socialist ideology may be different, the rhetorical man-
nerisms of *Hard Facts*, Baraka's first collection of poems since
Black Magic Poetry (1969), sometimes seem repetitious of earlier

and often better written) works. Even so, the polemical invective of poems like "Niggy the Ho" and "Gibson"—wherein, after the unified front "honeymoon", Newark mayor Kenneth Gibson is bitterly satirized in the dramatic monologue mode perfected by Robert Browning—is effective and arrestingly entertaining. No one can doubt that Baraka remains a master at dozens; when he gets on somebody's case he can be as cuttingly funny as Oliphant or Gary Trudeau, and his rhetoric can be as outrageous as the "double punishment" so-called diplomatic notes Mao's emissaries used to hand-carry to Kruschev and Ike. Baraka's talent for clever signifying is impressive in the poem "History On Wheels":

> negroes world wide, joined
> knees, and shuffled heroically
> into congress, city hall, the
> anti-p program, and a thousand
> penetrable traps of cookstove
> america, a class of exploiters,
> in black face, collaborators,
> not puppets, pulling their own
> strings, and ours too, in the
> poor people's buck dance, w/o
> the bux[14]

Take that, Andrew H. Young! Heh heh heh. As the beboppers of my daddy's Harlem days would say: "Take it easy, greasy ... you got a long way to slide." And Baraka is right to remind us.

My point is that Baraka's sense of balance (which, in his early Greenwich Village days, he claimed to have learned from Charles Olson and others of the William Carlos Williams school) seldom betrays even his most ideological pronouncements into mere didacticism. Beyond that, his earlier training in "talking that talk" guarantees that, no matter what the matter is, Baraka's statements will never be boring. Annoying, perhaps—when you disagree with him, or when it is painfully obvious that he has gotten caught up in one of his own fashions and is not thinking—but never irrelevant or boring.

Amiri Baraka's work—the work he has been able to accomplish in a various career during a troubled time—repays a reader's interest with confusion. Toni Cade Bambara complained that, ideologically, Baraka seems to believe that he must personally re-live every historical moment, "If you can read," she said, "seems like you could learn something out of a book ... like, you don't have to do *everything* yourself!"

Others might say that we, as a group, must be sophisticated enough today to do without self-appointed pioneers and martyrs. It was not always so, and this might be a point of foolish pride. Still, too many other men done gone and we really do need to hold on to what we got. This is not specifically a literary concern; but then, Baraka's own works and personality make purely literary questions seem small.

Baraka has, through all his personal and ideological changes, already achieved a lasting place in the history of the Afro-American struggle, and has influenced that struggle with his own concerns. It was he, Calvin Hernton wrote, "who first assaulted the white world with what he called the Black Arts, The Black Theater of Cruelty." In those turbulent days, Baraka declared:

> We are the witchdoctors and the assassins
> But we will make a path for the true scientists[15]

Many are not convinced by his current notion of science. For good and bad reasons. Baraka, as critic Ezekiel Mphalele (otherwise one of our most alert readers) has consistently failed to understand, is best as a poet of intense reflection; which is exactly why he always appears to us in the prophet's sackcloth of social activism. Literally, he does not have time to be himself. But, were he given the time, who (as he himself eloquently ponders in his poems) would that self be? In this way he speaks to us in our lostness, striving, and misery and we are habituated now to the eager anticipation of his own subsequent interpretations of each current guise.

Because Baraka's metamorphoses continue, and because they have always been so momentous, you may guess that I am hesitant about ending this essay, fearful that by the time it sees print it will conclusively brand its author a fool. I will conclude nothing, except to note that Baraka has offered great consolation to Black America simply because we know that he will always dare to go farther than the rest of us, and that he will come back and break it down for us, consolidate, before heading out there again. He is a valuable scout ... a leader in the real sense of the word. I suspect, however, that there are many who will feel, upon reading his new poems, that his journey suggests there is yet another dimension of the parable of Yacub that might stand a reexamination even by Baraka himself. Baraka is, after all, a master in these things; not no apprentice. Long ago now, it was he who first gathered the spirits.

1 Nathan Heard, *Howard Street* (New York: New American Library, 1968), p. 20.

2 LeRoi Jones, "Election Day—2," *Black Magic Poetry 1961-1967* (New York: Bobbs-Merrill Company, 1969), pp. 213-214.

3 The Buffalo *Empire Star*, credited by some as "the nation's first black daily," had a colorful history even before the coming of Walker and Reed. The paper was founded in 1932 by Andrew J. Smitherman who had started out as a lawyer and publisher in Tulsa, Oklahoma. Both his home and newspaper office were burned to the ground in the 1921 Tulsa "race riots." Smitherman died in Buffalo in 1961, and the *Empire Star* died with him. See Ronald E. Wolseley, *The Black Press, U. S. A.* (Ames: Iowa State University Press, 1972), p. 50.

    After leaving the *Empire Star*, Joe Walker became New York editor of *Muhammad Speaks* newspaper. Ishmael Reed also moved to New York City and became one of the prominent members of the Umbra Workshop.

4 See Joe David Bellamy, *The New Fiction: Interviews with Innovative American Writers* (Urbana: University of Illinois Press, 1974), pp. 132-133.

5 Jones, "Black People," *Black Magic Poetry*, p. 225. It was this poem, in its first publication in *Evergreen Review*, that influenced a Newark judge to hand down an unusually severe prison sentence for Baraka's alleged involvement in the Newark riots of 1967. Baraka was later acquitted on appeal. See "Poetic Justice," *Newsweek* (January 15, 1968), p. 24 and "Jones Is Acquitted of Weapon Charge in Newark Retrial," New York *Times*, July 3, 1969, p. 18. See also Eugene B. Redmond, *Drumvoices: The Mission of Afro-American Voices* (New York: Anchor Press, 1976), pp. 352-353.

6 LeRoi Jones, "The Screamers," *Tales* (New York: Grove Press, 1967), p. 77.

7 Jones, *Tales*, p. 74.

8 LeRoi Jones, "Hymn for Lanie Poo," *Preface to a Twenty Volume Suicide Note* (New York: Totem Press, 1961).

9 Jones, "Stirling Street September," *Black Magic Poetry*, p. 177.

10 Sonia Sanchez, "a ballad for stirling street," *We a BaddDDD People* (Detroit: Broadside Press, 1968). See Bernard W. Bell, *The Folk Roots of Contemporary Afro-American Poetry*, Broadside Critics Series No. 3 (Detroit: Broadside Press, 1974), p. 53, for an interesting analysis of this poem.

11 Larry Neal, "The Black Arts Movement, "*Tulane Drama Review*, XII (Summer 1968), 29-39.

12 Baraka's catalytic importance in the period prior to the current socialist stance cannot be underestimated. His sojourn in California in the late 1960s (augmented by the visitations or migrations of Sonia Sanchez, Ishmael Reed, Sarah Webster Fabio, Askia

Muhammad Toure, David Henderson, and others) helped determine the tone of the Black Power consciousness that swept the entire country in the early 1970s. The ideas of the Black Arts movement spread far beyond the Harlem theater. A rather poor film, *Black Spring* (Jihad Productions, 1969) documents this period.

Many of those who were swept up in that movement reacted harshly to Baraka's and the Congress of Afrikan People's turn toward a Marxist ideology; an example of such reaction is Haki R. Madhubuti's incoherent *Enemies: The Clash of Races* (Chicago: Third World Press, 1976). A more intelligent, informative, and reasoned discussion of the new developments is Ronald Walters' "Marxist-Leninism and the Black Revolution," *Black Books Bulletin*, V: 3 (Fall 1977), pp. 12-17, 63. Baraka attempts to clarify his position in his introduction to *Hard Facts, 1973-75* (Newark: Congress of Afrikan People, 1976).

[13] LeRoi Jones, "The Liar," *The Dead Lecturer* (New York: Grove Press, 1964), p. 79.

[14] Amiri Baraka, "History on Wheels," *Hard Facts*, p. 12.

[15] Calvin Hernton, "Blood of the Lamb and a Fiery Baptism," *Amistad 1*, ed. John A. Williams and Charles F. Harris (New York: Vintage Books, 1970), p. 218.

Merritt Clifton/Richford, Vermont

ON SMALL PRESS AS CLASS STRUGGLE

from *Aspect,* Number 69: 1976 & *Samisdat,* Volume XI, Number 4: 1976
Somerville, Massachusetts & Richford, Vermont
Editors: Ed Hogan & Merritt Clifton

TIME WAS, until under twenty years ago, that 'small press' stood virtually synonymous with 'private press'. Whether publishing books, chapbooks, or little magazines, the small pressman typically was a hobbyist, typically a letterpressman if he did his own printing, and in consequence typically worked slowly, as the artistic spirit moved him. Priding himself on his amateur status, he more often than not reprinted established authors, producing keepsakes of old favorites rather than first volumes of the new. Leonard and Virginia Woolf might, on their Hogarth Press, help introduce themselves, Robert Graves, James Joyce, T. S. Eliot, and others; Harry and Caresse Crosby might, on their Black Sun Press, bring out Hart Crane's first book; Robert McAlmon's Transition Press might do Ernest Hemingway's first; and James and Blanche Cooney, handsetting *The Phoenix*, might introduce Henry Miller to American readers. By and large, however, unless running a magazine printed outside, the small pressman sought no unsolicited submissions. Like James and Hilda Wells, of Slide Mountain Press, Connecticut, who published Robert Frost ephemera; S. A. Jacobs, of Golden Eagle Press, New York, who published odd items by E. E. Cummings and Stephen Crane; or Valenti Angelo, of Peter Pauper Press, New York, who also did Stephen Crane items, he had money, had leisure, and had a love of fine books—but not, necessarily, fine literature. Among the longest-lived and most representative efforts of the private press era was the Trevillion Private Press, 1908-1937, conducted as a hobby by Violet and Hal Trevillion, Herrin, Illinois. Their eighteen-title list includes ephemera by Oscar Wilde, Robert Louis Stevenson, and others, a few items by friends, a few self-publications, collected sentiments, and precisely nothing of lasting significance. A corresponding magazine would be *The Lariat*, 1923-1929, published by Colonel E. Hofer of Portland,

Oregon, printed outside, and filled mostly with polite verse from confessed dilettantes.

Small pressmanship was in short a plaything. It might become an obsession, especially in magazines, as with Margaret Fuller and *The Dial*, 1840-1842; Harriet Monroe and *Poetry*, 1912-1935; or Margaret Anderson and *The Little Review*, 1914-1929. As such, it might in time have to become self-supporting. Nonetheless, most small press people—distinguishing editors and publishers from authors—did not have to be. Frequently they did skip to other diversions relatively quickly. Even Fuller and Anderson quit while young. Authors did often have to seek alternative outlets, at least at first. Edgar Allen Poe, Stephen Crane, and Ezra Pound jobbed their first books, hoping to win future capital support. Walt Whitman, Carl Sandburg, and Anais Nin printed their own, envisioning future freedom from the publishing process. Significantly, these and most other major small press discoveries did achieve commercial publication within just a few years.

Until recently, therefore, the small press did not challenge the publishing status quo. With Alan Swallow a rare exception, the small pressman did not try to combine quality literature with economic self-sufficiency. To authors, small presses and little magazines served either as an apprenticeship toward commercial viability, or as an outlet for what they themselves did not take seriously. In general small pressmanship like the rest of literature belonged mostly to the upper ten percent, the minority privileged by birth with the wealth to buy letterpress equipment or job printing out, the time to write, edit, print, and publish free of economic pressure, and the education necessary to knowing how. As the publishers themselves were upper class, so the authors they advanced usually were, or were scions of socio-economic climbers, holding equal allegiance to the status quo. Consider the backgrounds of the Woolfs, Graves, Eliot, Hemingway, Joyce, Nin, Hart Crane, Frost, Cummings, Pound, Lawrence Durrell, F. Scott Fitzgerald, D. H. Lawrence, William Carlos Williams, John Dos Passos, Ford Madox Ford, and for that matter Allen Ginsberg and Lawrence Ferlinghetti, who arrived at the very end of the private press era, or Robert Creeley and Charles Olson, who did likewise. Lawrence excepted, most are of landed, professional parentage, attended expensive private schools, and performed manual labor through personal choice only. Most, including Lawrence, write for a cultural elite, finding readers mostly among their own class—and those actively aspiring to it through education. Working class authors such as Mark Twain, Jack London, Stephen Crane, Upton Sinclair, and John Steinbeck might occasionally self-publish, but only Crane ever crashed elite literary magazine pages, then only rarely. These find most popularity slightly lower on the class scale, among the reading working class. And the small press role in promoting them within their own times was correspondingly incidental.

Comparing small pressmanship to newspaper publishing, we find literature by 1930 roughly where news was in 1830: written, edited, printed, and distributed by and for the few, while the many were as yet uninterested; unable to read even if they were. By 1849 however, Horace Mann's educational reforms brought mass literacy, if not mass literate taste, and a new crop of papers rose to exploit it. The 'golden age' of tabloids fell during the next two decades, led by *Harper's Weekly*, *Frank Leslie's*, and the great eastern dailies later 'sponsoring' the Spanish-American War. These inspired a new writing generation, who, seeking employment, were told by Horace Greeley: "Go west, young man! Go west!"—'west' being his euphemism for 'hell'. But go west they did, along with the Gold Rush, with obsolete handpresses in ox-carts, founding literally hundreds of boomtown weeklies, some of which became today's great western dailies. Others, most notably *The Virginia City Territorial Enterprise*, gave first voice to Twain, Robert Louis Stevenson, Ambrose Bierce, Bret Harte, and late in the era, London. Essentially what had happened was a working class takeover: while the established publications remained in old establishment hands, a new audience inspired new entrepeneurs who eventually created a new establishment atop a pyramid of lesser papers, circulations, and talents. The average subscriber had gone from an educated, landed gentleman farmer to a fifth-grade dropout millhand, miner, or his wife, who likely had even less education than he. It took place within one generation, and represented the birth of all truly popular reading.

The 'golden age' of pulp magazines arrived more or less with the Great Depression and the decline of the tabloids. Printed on newsprint, or woodpulp paper rather than rag bond, pulps ran primarily genre fiction. This gave them far longer saleability than the lurid tabloids, perpetually fighting to be 'firstest with the latest.' Unlike 'news', fiction could not be scooped or supplanted within hours by later breaks. Having longer shelf lives, pulps could of course appear less often than the tabloids while still collecting what odd nickels and dimes Depression era working class readers could afford to spend. By appearing less, the pulps slashed overhead expenses for printing and paper, and simultaneously concentrated advertising, so that each ad carried less editorial matter. Further, most pulps specialized, devoting themselves exclusively to science fiction, detective stories, westerns, crossword puzzles, comics, confessions, or sex. By specializing, pulps could to some degree dodge the competition forcing tabloid budgets up even as income was split again by rivals and newcomers. Through the pulps, and the paperback pocket books that followed some fifteen years later, the working class weaned itself from lurid papers to short stories and novels, formula work to be sure, but still a step toward literature. Recently, we note, the trend is back toward lurid papers, as evidenced by decreasing western and mystery sales per capita while *The National Enquirer* and *The National Tattler* skyrocket. We speculate that this stems from increasing literacy among the lower class, rising into the working class, coupled with increasing sophistication among the old working class, who now read genre nonfiction: how-to, mysticism, and topical material. And genre science fiction daily sets new sales records, perhaps because space rather than the west is our present frontier, hence most obvious dreamland for the tired, bored masses.

Be all this as it may, the pulp magazines sparked a new breed of small press, the fanzine, commonly traced to Ray Palmer's *Comet*, 1930-1933. Fanzines are exactly what the term implies: publications by and for genre fiction fans, generally containing stories and poems from aspiring genre writers, profiles, criticism, and reviews of established genre writers, with a generous smattering of letters to the editor. Like the private presses, fanzines were and are mostly hobbies for the editors. Ray Bradbury's *Futura Fantasia*, 1939-1940, was a developmental step toward his future commercial success, and other fanziners have risen similarly. Artistically, however, most confess second-rate status. As A. B. and Chet Clingan put it in their *Diversifier*, Number 13, "either one (of us) will be the first to admit the tales appearing in our magazine are not of the highest

quality ... we're not a pro market, so you can't expect professional fiction." Accordingly, fanzines too tend to support the publishing establishment. They were, nonetheless, the first working class
literary alternatives, representing the first wave of widespread working class interest in writing, editing, and ultimately printing; commercial printing was as yet beyond working class means. Because
the average fanzine publisher worked from interest in content a-
bove aesthetic pride in appearance, because he held a job forty
hours weekly and could not afford the time hand-setting type requires, and most importantly because he could not afford letterpress equipment in the first place, mimeography, hektography, and
ditto became his principal methods. None were new; Thomas
Edison had invented mimeo in 1878. But because small pressmanship was previously a genteel hobby for the most part, only a few
school literary magazines had used it, and by and large use was confined to classroom and office. One noteworthy exception is
Humphrey Olsen's *Snowy Egret*, of Williamsburg, Kentucky. Concerning "the cultural aspects of natural history", it has been mimeo since 1922. As such it is the oldest non-academic little magazine
active, the oldest mimeo of significance, and among our oldest
working class small press efforts.

Mimeography invaded 'serious' literature on a measureable scale
around 1935, as working class readers grew more sophisticated, discovered Williams, Eliot, Pound, et al, and came to experiment with
poems and prose of their own. At first most submitted to the most
visible magazines and publishing companies, the big slicks and established lines who wanted no one without a reputation. A few
broke through the barriers, finding favor; most settled back into
founding and discovering an increasing variety of hobbyist journals.
Pioneers here were Whitney and Vaida Stewart Montgomery's letterpress *Kaleidograph*, 1929-1959, and Loring Williams' *American
Weave*, 1936-1969; long-lived successors include Clarence Weaver's
Bardic Echoes, 1960-; Jean Calkins' *Jean's Journal*, 1963-1976, recently transferred to another publisher; and Vernon Payne's
Cycloflame, 1963-. Many others come and go in ever-building pro-
fusion. Spiritual descendants of *The Lariat*, these too support the
publishing establishment for the most part, acknowledging inferiority to commercial and academic media. Nevertheless, these too
amplify the working class voice.

By the mid-1950s the working class showed strong signs of dominating, in numbers if not influence. Literary activity from class to class increasingly paralleled, as the early century, upper-class-dominated imagist thrust dissipated into mindless dada and surrealism, exemplified by the equally upper class Beats and Black Mountain school. Ginsberg and Ferlinghetti's City Lights Press, Jonathan Williams' Jargon Press, Robert Creeley's Divers Press, Olson's *Black Mountain Review*, and John Martin's Black Sparrow Press drew commercial and academic attention through the customary fine printing, well placed connections, and well orchestrated publicity stunts. But a working class avant garde closely followed. Leaders were Alan Swallow's *PS*, 1948-1963, and James Boyer May's *Trace*, 1952-1970. Both, significantly, pioneered offset printing as a small press medium, after beginning with letterpress. A third working class leader was *Talisman*, 1952-1959, founded by Robert Greenwood and Newton Baird. Greenwood, sticking with letterpress, continues it today as a book series. But offset was the trend, ever more so into the sixties. Of 311 small presses known to May in his 1960 *International Guide*, 78% still used letterpress, 17% offset, and 5% mimeo, the latter figure discounting fanzines. Of 669 recorded by Len Fulton in the 1973 *International Directory of Little Magazines & Small Presses*, 69% used offset, only 19% letterpress, and 12% mimeo, again discounting most fanzines. Figures today can only be guesstimated, but of over 1,500 listings in Fulton's latest directory, probably 80% are offset, including virtually all publishing frequently.

Like mimeo, offset was not new. Invented in 1906 by Ira Rubel, it had long been used for short runs, a few small newspapers, and even an occasional little magazine. But offset is a dirty process, predicated on water-based wash and oil-based ink not mixing. While cheap and speedy, it at best yields aesthetic results inferior to letterpress, and is more difficult to learn. It correspondingly held little appeal to the upper class dilettantes. Post-war, however, rising labor costs made offset increasingly practical for business use. Offset press manufacturers developed increasingly sophisticated, efficient equipment, and as businesses purchased newer models, relatively late models were sold relatively cheaply. For the first time working class people could afford presses without commercially using them. Press proliferation meanwhile held commerc-

ial printing costs roughly where they were half a century earlier. As
working class income rose, the working class would-be author for
the first time gained a real alternative to commercial publishing.
Today's small press explodes from here. Call it an outgrowth of
the mid-sixties 'mimeo revolution', so-called though mimeo was
scarcely any real revolt, and though no more than 23% of small
presses ever used mimeo according to Fulton's surveys. Call it a
consequence of commercial disinterest in contemporary poetry
and fiction by unknown authors, though this has continued since
Miguel Cervantes had to self-publish *Don Quixote* in 1605. Call it
product of America's first predominantly college-educated generation, though most contemporary small pressmen recoil from academia. Call it what one will, current small pressmanship evolves from
class struggle, representing a proletarian bid to control its own mental destiny. At least at first most small pressmen still support the
publishing establishment, not realizing how antithetical it is to
their long-term purpose. Though frustrated by rejection into founding magazines or presses, most yet nourish hopes of eventual commercial and academic success. The average little magazine, again
according to Fulton's figures, still lasts under four issues, while the
average small book publisher remains active around three years
before turning in other directions. Private presses remain more or
less the rule. Some, like Fred Merkel's Garage Number 3, of Rich-
mond, California, resemble those of fifty years past: Merkel, poet,
painter, and short story writer, works wholly by hand on a variety
of letterpresses. The significant differences between Merkel and
the Trevillions are that he does assay original literature, and that
he is not well-to-do with artistic leanings but a journeyman newspaper printer who chose self-publishing over having children. More
typical are one or two person offset operations, jobbing presswork
but doing all other labor with typewriter, rubber fingers, and stap-
ler. Examples are Gail White's Caryatid Press, of New Orleans, collecting her own poetry; Mort Castle's Eads Street Press, producing
chapbooks by his more talented pupils at Crete-Monee High
School, Illinois; David Greisman's *Abbey*, a little magazine active
since 1970, evolving from ditto; and Dale Donaldson's *Moonbroth*,
an amateur pulp begun in 1969, now appearing from Portland, Oregon. Reaching this point the small pressman, if continuing, typically branches from books into magazines, or vice-versa, still seek-

ing 'respectability' and suspecting the second endeavor may bring it where the first hasn't. Here we have Winnipeg's *Split-Level*, a mostly poetry magazine launched by Harry Peters and Barry Chamish from their Split-Level Press. Split-Level has in fact never owned a press, jobbing three Chamish novels and a mixed anthology of his poems and stories. Here also we get A. D. Winans' *Second Coming*, from San Francisco. Founded in 1972 as an irregular poetry journal, *Second Coming* now does books and chapbooks almost exclusively.

Ultimately, if he sticks with it, the small pressman almost invariably comes to doing his own printing, as a step toward both independence and economy. He may go mimeo, if mobility is important, like John Bennett, whose roving *Vagabond* magazine has appeared that way since 1963, or letterpress if his scale is sufficiently limited, like Merkel. Most likely, however, he goes offset. By this time he has a continuing commitment not only to literature but to alternative publishing as well. He, or she, most probably remains a secretary like White, a teacher like Castle and Chamish, or holds other outside employment. He by this time knows, nevertheless, that small pressmanship is the only viable means for a working class writer holding other than conventional views, writing for other than the commercial marketplace. He understands that while he might arrive in failure, he cannot leave even through artistic success. He may, as Castle has, and Charles Bukowski and Bill Wantling before him, begin turning out pulp under a psuedonymn, reaping financial reward. He may even write a commercial bestseller, winning recognition. But unlike the upper class literary rebel, the working class rebel cannot 'make it' on his own terms. He has no access to the literary elite, the nationally noted opinion makers who mostly attended the schools he could not afford, publish in the magazines he cannot draw serious consideration from, and review those of similar background, connections, and concerns.

In short, by the time he does his own printing the modern small pressman usually is committed to demolishing the publishing establishment, at least as presently constituted. Essentially this means destroying the upper class intelligentsia. Small pressmanship can accordingly be linked to such other movements as the civil rights struggle, the antiwar protests, and feminism. But unlike these, small pressmanship is not a mass movement. To begin with, it does not concern the average citizen. Small pressmanship is by definition a minority activity, each little press or magazine expressing a minority viewpoint concerning what are minority interests already. It is not an obvious activity; unless one looks for inkstains beneath fingernails, the small pressman cannot be told from his more docile neighbor, who watches television, accepting intelligentsia verdicts on what to think or not think. Finally, there is no obvious objective. No one can abruptly grant legal rights, since these already exist within the First Amendment, for large and small alike. No one can end or begin any particular activity that will immediately satisfy most small pressmen. And there are not already small press publications in every home, struggling with slicks, pulps, and the idiot box for equal attention. Nor do many small pressmen crave equal attention, most preferring a few devoted, responsive readers to a large, apathetic 'audience'; if craving the audience, they leave the small press to write genre material.

Apparent disadvantages, these factors actually help promote working class rebellion. Whereas literary representatives of mass movements might be adopted as tokens, appeasing the mob, there are no mobs here. A representative adopted today means nothing to small pressmen starting tomorrow. Once aligned with the intelligentsia, he appears one, no coloration or sexual characteristics misleading newcomers. Intelligentsia representatives may siphon off federal money granted the arts by populist politicians, employing working class taxes toward publishing their own small circulation books and magazines. They may further make academia their private bastion, particularly the more expensive, prestigious, private universities, which in turn produce the professors and become the examples for working class institutions. At all levels academic publications thus reflect intelligentsia attitudes, reviewing primarily books from 'respectable' commercial or institutional presses, while printing mostly authors holding the proper degrees from the right upper class schools. But as this teaches subservience to the aspiring sons and daughters of the nouveau riche white collar class and the blue collar class striving to join it, it intensifies rooted working class antagonism, firing ambition. While working class campuses officially sponsor sterile quarterly imitations of *The Yale Review* and *The Harvard Advocate*, spending thousands on typesetting and perfect binding, their students blast out lively typewriter/offset or mimeographed independent, irregular 'litmags', resembling any others mostly by accident. While the intelligentsia and pseudo-intelligentsia publications reach the same limited readerships, or land on library shelves to go unread, the working class small press-man finds new readers, new means of supporting his efforts, and grows increasingly vociferous in demanding his due. Financial crumbs, with other grudging recognition, may silence some special pests, but those so silenced tend to be more easily satisfied, hence less dangerous, than those not. The most enduring working class little magazines and small presses generally function with little or no grant support and no institutional ties; *Snowy Egret* has had none, and is but one example. Independence rather than commercial or academic acknowledgment becomes our objective. Working class small pressmen, we pursue the working class dream: to be our own owner, our own boss, our own employer. Though anti-capitalism, opposing the traditionally oligarchic wealth/power pyramid, we remain inspired by Horatio Alger and Henry Ford. We want not handouts but freedom from needing them, having to accept them, and sometimes having to beg them. Above all we want no one over us, able to give handouts.

Seeking freedom, we move counter to mass movements. Freedom equalling our right and ability to express individuality, and individuality equalling our capacity for difference, we present no 'front'. We have in COSMEP, the Committee of Small Magazine Editors and Publishers, a sort of combination lobby and trade association roughly equal to a labor union. But because working within any larger body means submerging the very identity we strive for, we give COSMEP little actual power. And rightly so, since unions, gaining power, develop new status quos preserving that power, militating further against the independent voice. Within the new status quo formed by Local 35's sweetheart contract with corporation stockholders, we might enjoy increased pay, and within a COSMEP alliance with the elite-dominated Coordinating Council of Literary Magazines (CCLM), or the equally elitist National Endowment for the Arts (NEA), which channel federal money to small press publications, we might receive increased intelligentsia patronage. But we would lose, in each case, our right to rock the boat, to strike over conditions and raise hell concerning grievances without majority support. To do otherwise would jeopardize security for others, who would swiftly expell us. Having in effect bought into management, a union becomes part and parcel of the establishment. A COSMEP so doing would preserve the intelligentsia its most active members' fight.

This literary class struggle was forseen to some degree by the mostly upper class Marxist editors during the 1930s. While the proletariat itself published fanzines, New Left journals often supported by large private universities and/or foundations speculated on future proletarian rebellion. When the proletariat found its voice, speculation went most often, workers would rise en mass, transforming the United States into a socialist country. The resulting socialist government would of course be guided by the sons and daughters of those already guiding the capitalist government and economy, the children of the rich who were professional students while the masses struggled in the Dustbowl, or did low-paying federal makework. Or, the upper class paradoxically envisioned a supposed classless society with no essential change in class structure. Among the most enduring advocates here is *The Partisan Review*, founded at Rutgers in 1934, edited since 1936 by William Phillips. Phillips, erstwhile defender of the proletariat and revolt against his class, also chaired CCLM from its birth in 1967 into early 1975. And CCLM, year after year granting far more to the wealthy and established than to the relatively new offset and mimeo rebels, is our single most impregnable, conservative, and outright repressive literary institution. While workers and children of workers are welcome as common members, power comes through appointment. Those appointed fall into two categories: those of impeccable upper class credentials, having attended the right universities, formed the right allegiances, and properly avoided working class associations, the majority; and those tokenly representing ethnic minorities, themselves distinctly upper class by economic comparison to most blacks, chicanos, etcetera. The tragedy of William Phillips is that of William Shakespeare's *Coriolanus*, and more particularly that of Bertolt Brecht in Gunter Grass' play-about-the-play, *The Plebians Rehearse the Uprising*. Brecht failed to condemn elitist hypocrisy among the East German Communist rulers in 1952; failed to recognize the would-be burghers before him as the real proletarian uprising, finally seeking their own voices and destinies. Likewise, Phillips failed to condemn hypocritical elitism among his literary cronies; failed to recognize diverse, often apolitical basement-published offsets and mimeos as his long awaited proletarian rebellion. In so failing, Phillips, like Brecht, forfeited his place as Rahab to the proletarian Israel. Rahab, readers recall, was the Canaanite whore helping Joshua bring down Jericho and exterminate its land-owning inhabitants—along with virtually everyone else, just for good measure.

The true impulse behind working class literary rebellion is not Marxism but the American Dream; not the spirit of '17 but of '76; not May Day but the Fourth of July; not either monolithic capitalism or equally monolithic socialism, but basic, individual free enterprise. Pursuing this spirit, the working class evolves yet another small press form never previously seen in numbers and not seen on any significant scale at all since Benjamin Franklin, Andrew Bradford, Isaiah Thomas, and Thomas Paine launched commercial publishing here from humble beginning two hundred years ago: to wit, the independent, one or two person, low readership publishing company. Generally speaking, these come after the self-printing small pressman enjoys relative success with both a magazine and books or chapbooks, finding publishing more pleasurable than working for 'the man', but on his new scale more demanding than he has spare time for. Gambling his life's savings against expected increased publishing income, hoping it will sustain him, he quits his job. Fittingly, Len Fulton leads the current drift in this direction. After founding his *Dust* literary magazine, 1963-1972; Dustbooks, with 25 titles to date; *The Small Press Review*, quarterly 1967-1974, now monthly; *The International Directory of Little Magazines & Small Presses*, annual since 1965; *The Small Press Record of Books in Print*, six editions since 1969, now annual; *The Directory of Small Magazine/Press Editors*, annual since 1970; and helping found COSMEP, publishing various catalogues for it, Fulton writes in Bill Henderson's *Publish-It-Yourself Handbook*, "Something had to give." Then a bio-statistician for the state of California, his choice fell among "the statistics, the publishing, or the nerves." He gave up the statistics, moved from urban Berkeley to rural Paradise, and has survived and expanded on his publishing income ever since.

Other small pressmen of course lack Fulton's virtual monopoly on informational publishing, and further lack the initial capital necessary to launch other surefire profitable ventures. Helping others self-publish through supplying cheap printing and typesetting is therefore a common independent ploy. Authors or sponsors in essence supply the operating capital, the independent supplies his labor, and the product is in some fashion shared. Sometimes this amounts to alternative vanity publishing, but whereas in vanity publishing authors receive frills and promises at exhorbitant rates, the self-publishing author hiring an independent generally gets few frills, fewer promises, and pays less for complete editorial service than he might pay for printing alone at a commercial shop. Triton Press, run by Moses Yanes from Boulder Creek, California, operates in this manner, advertising in *Writer's Digest* to find customers. Besides supporting himself and his family, Yanes publishes *Community of Friends*, a little magazine, and his own collections of Whitmanesque poetry on the proceeds.

Bill Robinson's Border-Mountain Press in Benson, Arizona, and Robert Olmsted's Northwoods Press in Meadows of Dan, Virginia, also print books in this manner. Both also publish cooperatively, however, sharing cash risk, and both occasionally publish under the conventional system. In addition, both run increasingly significant little magazines. Robinson's monthly *Quester,* recently bought from Texas founder Carvin Chastain, has in just a few issues moved from the deathly serious atheist lunatic fringe into raucous anticlerical satire and serious analysis of religious history. Olmsted's semi-monthly *Northwoods Journal*, active since 1973, primarily acquaints newcomers with small pressmanship in general. Contents, mixing fiction, poetry, news, philosophy, and in-house advertising, defy categorization.

My own *Samisdat* is a self-supporting irregular monthly, numbered as a quarterly but producing over twelve issues, books, and chapbooks annually for four years now. Life-partner June Kemp and I both give it full time, freelancing on the side, surviving on roughly $300/month total income. Regular, multi-author issues and our own books are paid for by past issue and book earnings; other individual author issues and chapbooks, while considered and published in the same manner, are author-financed. Authors then take all copies after the first hundred for their own distribution, a system under which many break even and most get sufficient return in both sales and exposure to consider it worthwhile. Proceeds from our hundred return to the regular issue kitty. Except for some underwritten items, we do all our own labor, including printing. Obtaining our first press is what in fact let us go full time. Previously I had worked in the Ketchikan, Alaska pulp mill, been a housepainter and woodcutter, taken various odd jobs, and edited an irregular housing newsletter.

Only a few working class small press people survive on self-financed publishing alone—or augmented, at any rate, only by other self-generated earnings. One such is Mary Balcom, whose Balcom Books in Ketchikan is the only independent publisher in Alaska. Aimed at the tourist trade, her novel and local histories are entirely shop-produced, selling steadily since 1961. Martin Helick supports himself through his Regent Graphic Services, of Swissvale, Pennsylvania. Successfully self-published, with printing and binding jobbed, are three architectural titles and a novel to date. In Scottsdale, Arizona, Paul Freeman edits *One*, a shop-printed fiction magazine distributed through his One Bookstore, formerly Andarth Books.

Independent ambitions sum up the working class rebellion. "All I want," writes Olmsted, "is to be a full time publisher, doing what I want instead of what the school board wants." Until this year Olmsted taught. Robinson flippantly confesses, "I want to be rich. Rich is having one dollar more than I need...If I have ten dollars more, I just spend it on wine or a lid." Neither has any intentions of becoming like the big-timers, of emulating the elite they oppose.

Len Fulton sums up attitudes here in *The Small Press Review*, Number 19: "Hugh Fox (of *Ghost Dance*, a professor) still hopes to educate them (the elite.) Paul Foreman (of Thorp Springs Press, a full-timer) wants to take the novel market away from them. Charlie Potts (of Litmus Press, still a part-timer) thinks we will simply move up through them, and 'the longer we hang on the stronger we get.' I say that any time is a good time to forget about them. Don't buy their books and especially don't sell them any good manuscripts...Mainly I don't think they should matter to us. I think our time and energy too precious to waste so."

In an era of limits imposed by environmental and economic crisis, the modern small pressman brings the publishing class struggle to a close resembling that predicted by Edward Bellamy in *Looking Backward*, 1888. Bellamy, a utopian socialist, nevertheless recognized the importance of free enterprise in motivating human endeavor. He wrote accordingly: "The printing department (of the ideal socialistic state) has no censorial powers. It is bound to print all that is offered it, but prints it only on condition that the author defray the first cost...Of course, if incomes were unequal, as in the old times, this rule would enable only the rich to be authors, but the resources of citizens being equal, it merely measures the strength of the author's motive."

While we have no ideal socialist state, and while we within the working class still lack upper class financial advantages, we find in cheap presses a powerful equalizer. The necessity of self-publishing, with the labor and/or expense involved in doing it, does ultimately measure our motivation. On the positive side, as Helick puts it, "Self-publishing gives the writer the same kind of artistic autonomy that is enjoyed by a painter or a sculptor. He need answer only to his imagination, his energy, and the scope of the raw materials he has chosen to use. The opinions of others are utterly irrelevant until all can see for themselves." Realizing this, and balancing freedom with its inevitable price, we purchase an enduring integrity the upper class cannot match, even when it does yield work of lasting worth.

A quarter of a century remains before we reach Bellamy's projected millennium. By then the intelligentsia may be as invisible as it is irrelevant. Commercial publishing and bestseller psychology will exist, just as television will, in a morass of mindlessness for those seeking escape. Those seeking instead intellectual confrontation shall find accessible a wealth and range of literature from a wealth and range of artist-authors the present system could never bring us, never print and promote in present fashion. All publishers will not be equal, since all energy is not equal, nor all guts, nor all luck, but barring complete destruction of our constitutionally guaranteed press freedom, books and magazines will stand unprecedented opportunity based on quality above inherited connections and slick production. And new writers will likewise. We may have no superstars, since such recognition springs more often from dearth of competition than abundance of it, but any rising will be giants. The struggle shall be among class instead of classes.

[An updated version of this essay is available from Samisdat.*]*

370

Paul Goodman / 1911-1972

THE POLITICS OF BEING QUEER

from *Unmuzzled Ox*, Number 15: 1977
New York City
Editor: Michael Andre

IN ESSESTIAL ways, my homosexual needs have made me a nigger. Most obviously, of course, I have been subject to arbitrary brutality from citizens and the police; but except for being occasionally knocked down, I have gotten off lightly in this respect, since I have a good flair for incipient trouble and I used to be nimble on my feet. What makes me a nigger is that it is not taken for granted that my out-going impulse is my right. Then I have the feeling that it is not my street.

I don't complain that my passes are not accepted; nobody has a claim to be loved (except small children). But I am degraded for making the passes at all, for being myself. Nobody likes to be rejected, but there is a way of rejecting someone that accords him his right to exist and is the next best thing to accepting him. I have rarely enjoyed this treatment.

Allen Ginsberg and I once pointed out to Stokley Carmichael how we were niggers, but he blandly put us down by saying that we could always conceal our disposition and pass. That is, he accorded us the same lack of imagination that one accords niggers; we did not really exist for him. Interestingly, this dialogue was taking place on (British) national TV, that haven of secrecy. More recently, since the formation of the Gay Liberation Front, Huey Newton of the Black Panthers has welcomed homosexuals to the revolution, as equally oppressed.

In general in America, being a queer nigger is economically and professionally not such a disadvantage as being a black nigger, except for a few areas like government service, where there is considerable fear and furtiveness. (In more puritanic regimes, like present day Cuba, being queer is professionally and civilly a bad deal Totalitarian regimes, whether communist or fascist, seem to be inherently puritanic.) But my own experience has been very mixed.

I have been fired three times because of my queer behavior or my claim to the right to it, and these are the only times I have been fired. I was fired from the University of Chicago during the early years of Robert Hutchins; from Manumit School, an offshoot of A. J. Muste's Brookwood Labor College; and from Black Mountain College. These were highly liberal and progressive institutions, and two of them prided themselves on being communities.—Frankly, my experience of radical community is that it does not tolerate my freedom. Nevertheless I am all for community because it is a human thing, only I seem doomed to be left out.

On the other hand, so far as I know, my homosexual acts and the overt claim to them have never disadvantaged me much in more square institutions. I have taught at half a dozen State universities. I am continually invited, often as chief speaker, to conferences of junior high school superintendents, boards of Regents, guidance counsellors, task forces on delinquency, etc., etc. I say what I think is true—often there are sexual topics; I make passes if there is occasion; and I seem to get invited back. I have even sometimes made out—which is more than I can say for conferences of S. D. S. or the Resistance. Maybe the company is so square that it does not believe, or dare to notice, my behavior; or more likely, such professional square people are more worldly (this is our elderly word for "cool") and couldn't care less what you do, so long as they don't have to face anxious parents and yellow press.

As one grows older, homosexual wishes keep one alert to adolescents and young people more than heterosexual wishes do, especially since our society strongly discountenances affairs between older men and girls or older women and boys. And as a male, the homosexual part of one's character is a survival of early adolescence anyway. But needless to say, there is a limit to this bridging of the generation gap. Inexorably I, like other men who hang around the campuses, have found that the succeeding waves of freshmen seem more callow and incommunicable and one stops trying to rob the cradle. Their music leaves me cold. After a while my best contact with the young has gotten to be with the friends of my own grown children, as an advisor in their politics, rather than by my sexual desires. (The death of my son estranged me from the young world altogether.)

On the whole, although I was desperately poor up to a dozen

years ago—I brought up a family on the income of a sharecropper—I don't attribute this to being queer but to my pervasive ineptitude, truculence, and bad luck. In 1945, even the Army rejected me as "Not Military Material" (they had such a stamp) not because I was queer but because I made a nuisance of myself with pacifist action at the examination and also had bad eyes and piles.

Curiously, however, I have been told by Harold Rosenberg and the late Willie Poster that my sexual behavior used to do me damage in precisely the New York literary world. It kept me from being invited to advantageous parties and making contacts to get published. I must believe Harold and Willie because they were unprejudiced observers. What I myself noticed in the 30s and 40s was that I was excluded from the profitable literary circles dominated by Marxists in the 30s and the ex-Marxists in the 40s because I was an anarchist. For example, I was never invited to P. E. N. or the Committee for Cultural Freedom.—When C. C. F. finally got around to me at the end of the 50s, I had to turn them down because they were patently tools of the C. I. A. (I said this in print in '61, but they lied their way out.)

To stay morally alive, a nigger uses various kinds of spite, which is the vitality of the powerless. He may be randomly destructive, since he feels he has no world to lose, and maybe he can prevent the others from enjoying their world. Or he may become an in-group fanatic, feeling that only his own kind are authentic and have soul. There are queers and blacks belonging to both these parties. Queers are "artistic," blacks have "soul." (This is the kind of theory, I am afraid, that is self-disproving; the more you believe it, the stupider you become; it is like trying to prove that you have a sense of humor.) In my own case, however, being a nigger seems to inspire me to want a more elementary humanity, wilder, less structured, more variegated, and where people pay attention to one another. That is, my plight has given energy to my anarchism, utopianism, and Gandhianism. There are blacks in this party too.

My actual political stance is a willed reaction-formation to being a nigger. I act that "the society I live in is mine," the title of one of my books. I regard the President as my public servant whom I pay, and I berate him as a lousy employee. I am more constitutional than the Supreme Court. And in the face of the gross illegitimacy of the Government—with its Vietnam War, military-industrial cabal, and C. I. A.—I come on as an old-fashioned patriot, neither supine nor more revolutionary than is necessary for my modest goals. This is a quixotic position. Sometimes I sound like Cicero.

In their in-group, Gay Society, homosexuals can get to be fantastically snobbish and a-political or reactionary. This is an understandable ego-defense: "You gotta be better than somebody," but its payoff is very limited. When I give talks to the Mattachine Society, my invariable sermon is to ally with all other libertarian groups and libertarian movements, since freedom is indivisible. What we need is not defiant pride and self-consciousness, but social space to live and breathe. The Gay Liberation people have finally gotten the message of indivisible freedom, but they have the usual fanaticism of the Movement.

But there is a positive side. In my observation and experience, queer life has some remarkable political values. It can be profoundly democratizing, throwing together every class and group more than heterosexuality does. Its promiscuity can be a beautiful thing (but be prudent about V. D.)

I have cruised rich, poor, middle class, and petit bourgeois; black, white, yellow, and brown; scholars, jocks, Gentlemanly C's, and dropouts; farmers, seamen, railroad men, heavy industry, light manufacturing, communications, business, and finance; civilians, soldiers, and sailors, and once or twice cops. (But probably for Oedipal reasons, I tend to be sexually anti-semitic, which is a drag.) There is a kind of political meaning, I guess, in the fact that there are so many types of attractive human beings; but what is more significant is that the many functions in which I am professionally and economically engaged are not altogether cut and dried but retain a certain animation and sensuality. H. E. W. in Washington and I. S. 201 in Harlem are not total wastes, though I talk to the wall in both. I have something to occupy me on trains and buses and during the increasingly long waits at airports. At vacation resorts, where people are idiotic because they are on vacation, I have reason to frequent the waiters, the boatmen, the room clerks, who are working for a living. I have something to do at peace demonstrations—I am not inspirited by guitar music—though no doubt the TV files and the F. B. I. with their little cameras have pictures of me groping somebody. The human characteristics that are finally important to me and can win by my lasting friendship are quite simple: health, honesty, not being cruel or resentful, being willing to come across, having either sweetness or character on the face. As I reflect on it now, only gross stupidity, obsessional cleanliness, racial prejudice, insanity, and being habitually drunk or high really put me off.

In most human societies, of course, sexuality has been one more area in which people can be unjust, the rich buying the poor, males abusing females, sahibs using niggers, the adults exploiting the young. But I think this is neurotic and does not give the best satisfaction. It is normal to befriend and respect what gives you pleasure. St. Thomas, who was a grand moral philosopher though a poor metaphysician, says that the chief human use of sex—as distinguished from the natural law of procreation—is to get to know other persons intimately. That has been my experience.

A common criticism of homosexual promiscuity, of course, is that, rather than democracy, it involves an appalling superficiality of human conduct, so that it is a kind of archetype of the inanity of mass urban life. I doubt that this is generally the case, though I don't know; just as, of the crowds who go to art galleries, I don't know who are being spoken to by the art and who are being bewildered further—but at least some are looking for something. A young man or woman worries, "Is he interested in me or just in my skin? If I have sex with him, he will regard me as nothing": I think this distinction is meaningless and disastrous; in fact I have always followed up in exactly the opposite way and many of my lifelong personal loyalties had sexual beginnings. But is this the rule or the exception? Given the usual coldness and fragmentation of community life at present, my hunch is that homosexual promiscuity enriches more lives than it desensitizes. Needless to say, if we had better community, we'd have better sexuality too.

I cannot say that my own promiscuity (or attempts at it) has kept me from being possessively jealous of some of my lovers—more of the women than the men, but both. My experience has not borne out what Freud and Ferenczi seem to promise, that homosexuality diminishes this voracious passion, whose cause I do not understand. But the ridiculous inconstancy and injustice of my attitude have sometimes helped me to laugh at myself and kept me from going overboard.

Sometimes it is sexual hunting that brings me to a place where I meet somebody—e.g. I used to haunt bars on the waterfront; sometimes I am in a place for another reason and incidentally hunt—e.g. I go to the TV studio and make a pass at the cameraman; sometimes these are both of a piece—e.g. I like to play handball and I am sexually interested in fellows who play handball. But these all come to the same thing, for in all situations I think, speak, and act pretty much the same. Apart from ordinary courteous adjustments of vocabulary—but not of syntax, which alters character—I say the same say and do not wear different masks or find myself suddenly with a different personality. Perhaps there are two opposite reasons why I can maintain my integrity: on the one hand, I have a strong enough intellect to see how people are for real in our only world, and to be able to get in touch with them despite differences in background; on the other hand, I am likely so shut in my own preconceptions that I don't even notice glaring real obstacles that prevent communication.

How I do come on hasn't made for much success. Since I don't use my wits or manipulate the situation, I rarely get what I want out of it. Since I don't betray my own values, I am not ingratiating. My artistocratic egalitarianism puts people off unless they are secure enough in themselves to be also aristocratically egalitarian. Yet the fact I am not phony or manipulative has also kept people from disliking or resenting me, and I usually have a good conscience. If I happen to get on with someone, there is not a lot of lies and bullshit to clear away.

Becoming a celebrity in the past few years, however, seems to have hurt me sexually rather than helped me. For instance, decent young collegians who might like me and who used to seek me out, now keep a respectful distance from the distinguished man. Perhaps they are now sure that I *must* be interested in their skin, not in them. And the others who seek me out just because I am well known seem to panic when it becomes clear that I don't care about that at all, and I come on as myself. Of course, a simpler explanation at my worsening luck is that I'm growing older every day, probably uglier, and certainly too tired to try hard.

As a rule I don't believe in poverty and suffering as a way of learning anything, but in my case the hardship and starvation of my inept queer life have usefully simplified my notions of what a good society is. As with any other addict who cannot get an easy fix, they have kept me in close touch with material hunger. So I cannot take the Gross National Product very seriously, nor status and credentials, nor grandiose technological solutions, nor ideological liberation movements. For a starving person, the world has got to come across in kind. It doesn't. I have learned to have very modest goals for society and myself: things like clean air, green grass, children with bright eyes, not being pushed around, useful work that suits one's abilities, plain tasty food, and occasional satisfying nookie.

A happy property of sexual acts, and perhaps especially of homosexual acts, is that they are dirty, like life: as Augustine said, *Inner urinas et feces nascimur*, we're born among the piss and shit. In a society as middle class, orderly, and technological as ours, it's good to break down squeamishness, which is an important factor in what is called racism, as well as in cruelty to children and the sterile exiling of the sick and aged. And the illegal and catch-as-catch-can nature of much homosexual life at present breaks down other conventional attitudes. Although I wish I could have had my parties with less apprehension and more unhurriedly, yet it has been an advantage to learn that the ends of docks, the backs of trucks, back alleys, behind the stairs, abandoned bunkers on the beach, and the washrooms of trains are all adequate samples of all the space there is. For both bad and good homosexual life retains some of the alarm and excitement of childish sexuality.

It is damaging for societies to check any spontaneous vitality. Sometimes it is necessary, but rarely; and certainly not homosexual acts which, so far as I have heard, have never done any harm to anybody. A part of the hostility, paranoia, and automatic competitiveness of our society comes from the inhibition of body contact. But in a very specific way, the ban on homosexuality damages and depersonalizes the educational system. The teacher-student relation is almost always erotic.—The only other healthy psychological motivations are the mother-hen relevant for small children and the professional who needs apprentices, relevant for graduate schools.—If there is fear and to-do that erotic feeling might turn into overt sex, the teacher-student relation lapses or, worse, becomes cold and cruel. And our culture sorely lacks the pedagogic sexual friendships, homosexual, heterosexual, and lesbian, that have starred other cultures. To be sure, a functional sexuality is probably incompatible with our mass school systems. This is one among many reasons why they should be dismantled.

I recall when *Growing Up Absurd* had had a number of glowing reviews, finally one irritated critic, Alfred Kazin, darkly hinted that I wrote about my Puerto Rican delinquents (and called them "lads") because I was queer for them. News. How could I write a perceptive book if I didn't pay attention, and why should I pay attention to something unless, for some reason, it interested me? The motivation of most sociology, whatever it is, tends to produce worse books. I doubt that anybody would say that my observations of delinquent adolescents or of collegians in the Movement have been betrayed by infatuation. But I do care for them.—Of course, *they* might say, "With such a friend, who needs enemies?"

Yet it is true that an evil of the hardship and danger of queer life in our society, as with any situation of scarcity and starvation, is that we become obsessional and one-track-minded about it. I have certainly spent far too many anxious hours of my life fruitlessly cruising, which I might have spent sauntering for other purposes or for nothing at all, pasturing my soul. But I trust that I have had the stamina, or stubbornness, not to let my obsession cloud my honesty. So far as I know, I have never praised a young fellow's bad poem because he was attractive. But of course I am then especially pleased if it is good and I can say so. And best of all, of course, if he is my lover and he shows me something that I can be proud of and push with an editor. Yes, since I began these reflections on a bitter note, let me end them with a happy poem that I like, from *Hawkweed*:

> We have a crazy love affair
> it is wanting each other to be happy.
> Since nobody else cares for that
> we try to see to it ourselves.
>
> Since everybody knows that sex
> is part of love, we make love.
> When that's over, we return
> to shrewdly plotting the other's advantage.

Today you gazed at me, that spell
is why I choose to live on.
God bless you who remind me simply
of the earth and sky and Adam.

I think of such things more than most
but you remind me simply. Man,
you make me proud to be a workman
of the Six Days, practical.

On balance, I don't know whether my choice, or compulsion, of
a bisexual life has made me especially unhappy or only averagely
unhappy. It is obvious that every way of life has its hang-ups, having a father or no father, being married or single, being strongly
sexed or rather sexless, and so forth; but it is hard to judge what
other people's experiences have been, to make a comparison. I have
persistently felt that the world was not made for me, but I have
had good moments. And I have done a lot of work, have brought
up some beautiful children, and have gotten to be 58 years old.

Fred Chappell/Greensboro, North Carolina
A LITTLE HOUYHNHNM IN YOUR LIFE

from *Smart*
Red Clay Books, 1975: Charlotte, North Carolina
Editor: Charleen Swansea

1

WE PARTLY aiding, civilization gets frowzier and frowzier. Already in a country not quite two hundred years old, the cultural life begins to look enervated and shopworn, rather as it must have done at Rome in the years of Diocletian. There is a current and enormously silly soft drink ad on television which advises us to *put a little Yahoo in our lives*, surely the most sardonic monition we are likely to receive in this, the mid-era of Armageddon.

I shall not irritate you with a list of our urgent grievances: pollution, political corruption, dwindling resources of food and energy, and so forth. Each day they impinge upon our consciousness like a jawful of abscessed teeth. And certainly I can propose no solutions to these problems. I am, however, willing to believe that the problems are soluble in the largest sense, and I should like somehow to present an apology for the two areas of thought we ought to consider most likely to aid in solution. I should like to present a fairly formal and elegant apology for the arts and sciences.

2

Well, it ain't going to be elegant and I don't have the means to make it formal.

If I'm not mistaken, it's Joan Crawford who owns that Mountain Dew soft drink and I consider her Yahoo advice with the same stunned bemusement I considered her marital advice in those scores of soppy movies she used to play in. After all, the Mountain Dew motto is no more than a truncated brutalization of the messages of a number of admirable American thinkers and writers. Whitman, Thoreau, Paine, Twain, William James, John Dewey, Theodore Roosevelt, and maybe even Jefferson, could find room in that sleazy advertising slogan, if we cared to elaborate and refine a bit.

There is no need to do this, of course. The likeness in the variegated thinking of these Americans is clear enough. Each of them recognized and to some degree favored, found healthful and refreshing, the wide red streak of barbarism in American society. They proclaimed distrust and detestation of snobbery and preciosity in every form, and each of them possessed a commodity which has become as rare—and possibly as expensive—as sirloin steak: viz., a truly democratic spirit.

(In our time the possession of a democratic spirit is guaranteed to break your health in ten years or less. There seems to be an almost infinite number of public causes to take away your energy. Certainly there are, for practical purposes, an infinite number of individual persons who may make legitimate claims upon your resources.)

But should we not also point out that the barbarism which Whitman, Thoreau, and James recognized, the barbarism they had access to, is not identical with the barbarism we know? For of course it *is* different, and simply to say so is not necessarily to applaud with mindless vigor the Golden Age, with its trolley cars and ole swimmin' holes and real butter from real cows. Any society at any time exhibits a certain amount of scurviness. Huck Finn's pappy has never been improved upon as a model for the malevolent redneck, and the slum life photographs of Jacob Riis have as much sociological point and impact as any NBC White Paper—more, in fact.

But the difference still obtains. Huck's pappy, though he had cronies, never dressed up in some quasi-military outfit, prepared a weird organizational constitution, and handed out rifles to a bunch of sweaty bloodthirsty John Birchers, telling them to make ready for the Great Day. And Riis' immigrants, their faces bleached and pinched, without hope and without hope of hope, had not yet purposefully gone about to create a marginal counter-culture based on the premise that they should never have place in society, not even as factory fodder.

American barbarism still flourishes; it is probably our most conspicuous product, and scores of new varieties have sprung up in the last four or five decades. But for all this, the individualism seems to have gone out of it. Even the rebels seem anxious to ally with others recognizably—sometimes secretly recognizably—as of their own kind. If you wish now to drop out, you can simply choose your own niche, become a Jesus freak, a Hell's Angel, a hippie in a commune, any one or two of a hundred varieties of drug user—whatever you like. For, whatever you like, there is a place waiting and you have only to step into it.

This is merely to say that our barbarism also has become compartmentalized. In a broad sense, the choices are as regulated as they are in the most soporific of bourgeois existences. And the inevitable corollary of this fact is that there are no choices. Once a choice can be foreseen, once a person feels able to pick and choose among a certain number of alternatives, it means that there is no choice at all. When the whole reason for beginning anew, with its onslaught of exhilaration and its vision of limitless horizon, is stymied by foreseeable consequences, something lumpy and metallic and cold plunges *clunk* to the bottom of the soul.

3

The bourgeois on their side are barbarians also, and their barbarism seems no better. It seems worse.

It always does.

4

These two breeds, or sects, of barbarians, counter-culture and bourgeois, are generally regarded as natural enemies. Politically, this is possibly so; to see them so is convenient. But culturally they are akin in at least two respects: each group has a distrust of science, a distrust amounting almost to fear; and each group has a mistaken idea of the aims and purposes of the arts.

As soon as I write down these generalizations—equally obvious, equally enormous—I am aware that qualifications and explanations ought to be made, but as I have little interest or need to make these, I shall trust the reader to arrange them for himself. Or failing that, to throw on them the shovelful of proverbial salt.

But I believe it is known easily enough that those two modes of thought we are pleased to label "radical" and "conservative" still embody the same attitude toward the arts, and more particularly toward what is new in the arts. The radically politicized person views gloomily the making, and even the enjoyment, of all the arts except propaganda. It seems to him a waste of time, effort, psychic force; and supremely he regards it as economic waste. The politically radical individual may well admire an artist's courage, his endurance and perseverance, and his painfully gained expertise. Yet, he thinks, what good is it? What does it *do*? What injustice is rectified, what poverty is alleviated, what new hard knowledge is propounded. In the matter of political efficacy, this misguided man or woman artist may as well have been rolling out mud pies.

And if the products of this art are not easily understood or are subject to the misinterpretation of the uninformed—and we may as well assume that this is going to be the case—the dilemma is so much the worse. For then, not only is the time and effort of the individual maker going to be wasted, but also the time and effort of whatever audience accrues to his work.

If the artist is determined to grovel out his existence in poverty, why should he not do it as easily within the organization, where— if no other work can be found for him—he can hand out leaflets on streetcorners?

There are some few arts the political radical will admire. These are: the culinary (not meaning, of course, Cordon Bleu), the propagandistic, and the forensic. In the latter two, we may often see real accomplishment. In fact, the whole art of American oratory seems to belong almost entirely to radical politicians...

Regarding the bourgeois hatred of art, nothing needs to be said. The theme has been dealt with ably hundreds of times. One has only to list the qualities admired in art by the bourgeois in order to condemn their notion of it. These qualities are: prettiness, the Pollyanna, luxuriousness, triviality. These are the true enemies of art, much more than (as Boccaccio pointed out) fire and sword and the other familiar weapons of ignorance.

To illustrate (unfairly): I am dawdling about the living room, hearing a record of Sonny Boy Williamson singing blues songs when my insurance representative comes to call. "That's interesting music," he says. "You don't get to hear music like that very often." He is not jiving either of us, for he clearly intends to say, Shut off that unearthly racket so we can get down to your premium—or if you have to have music, lay on some Mantovani.—This reaction is clear and predictable.

Even so, when my nineteen-year-old militant-to-the-Afro black friend, Sidi Ahmed el Bakai drops in on Sonny Boy, his comment is, "Hey man, you *really* dig them old whining songs? No way, I can't groove that chittlin music."—His reaction too, though I'm caught off-guard, ought to have been predictable. Both Ahmed and Jefferson Life have managed to alter their physiologies; they have replaced tympanun, malleus, stapes, and cochlea with Doctrine. Doctrine, whether its reaction be defensive or offensive, makes the man. Makes him holier-than-thou because—you dig?—he *knows*. This-here citizen got him a place to stand.

Thus, the unconscious alliance against the arts.

The alliance against the sciences rests on pretty much the same bases.

Our allegorical bourgeois would seem to have little reason to fear or to distrust the sciences, which pervade and delightfully inform every part of his everyday existence, including especially his domestic economy. Always in the background is the perhaps legitimate fear of some sort of automation which will usurp his job, but I'm not at all sure that this is the reason for his almost generic distrust. The truth is that this man in the middle prefers the same qualities in the sciences that he does in the arts. He wants science to be pretty (i. e. comfortable), Pollyanna, contributing to luxury, and trivial. When he reads a science fiction novel, he will probably read Heinlein or Michael Crichton. He will not read Olaf Stapledon or Hal Clement. Assuredly he will not read Jonathan Swift. (Rather too much Yahoo in your life.) When he saw *2001* at Southgate shopping center, he thought the story was completely nutty, but he admired the machines, the furniture, the light show, and maybe the language the characters spoke. His vision of scientists as persons includes the eccentric washing machine repairman in his garage in Trenton, New Jersey, laboring away at the perpetual toothbrush, and it includes also girls in hot pants zipping through the unpronounceable constellations of *Star Trek*; but it does not include a man with a well-gnawed pencil at a grubby desk or a man asleep dreaming of demons dancing in the molecular pattern of the benzine ring.

These examples serve only to underline the nature of bourgeois barbarism: it is a soft barbarism. Its self-indulgence is engendered by, and feeds upon, luxury. It pursues the goal of complacency by means of an aggressive complacency. ("Turn to another channel, Sukie Mae, it makes me sick to watch them long-haired creeps talk.")

And though the life style of the radical individual may be lean and sharp (he doesn't drive a Lincoln or eat lobster), his personal demands of science are probably as soft as his barbarian brother's. ("Hey man, I played 'Black Magic Woman' backwards at 45 and saw God.")–He too is self-indulgent, not because of economic luxury, but out of sheer egoism. His is the complacency of the self-proclaimed rebel; in his heart he knows *we* know he's right.

The radical's larger fear of science issues from his superstitious view of all science as weaponry. When he hears of scientific advance he thinks in terms of defoliant bombs, napalm, and Mace. His instinct tells him that it was Science which invented The Bomb, though even momentary reflection would convince that atomic weapons stand in the exact relationship to the broad aims of science as did the Roman catapult or the poison dagger.

Our two sorts of American barbarian fear science because it is easier to fear than to try to understand. They regard it in the way a distant Nigerian tribesman regards eclipses and comets, as part of an inscrutable yet malevolent weather. This fear is vague and unfocused, but genuine all the same. And this illiterate fear soon systematizes into superstition and then hardens into Doctrine.

5

I don't think I can be persuaded that it is finally in the nature of the human nervous system for Doctrine to suppress and then supplant the information of the senses. I refuse to believe that slogans and mottoes can short-circuit our synapses, that exposure to a bewilderingly complex level of society blinds and deafens us or anesthetizes our normal animal curiosity.

I do believe that we can train ourselves to keep our receptivities fresh, to delight in what is new in our lives and to enjoy what is familiar.

6

Laura Boulton is a famous musicologist who has traveled the world, collecting the music of many nations and cultures. In her autobiography, *The Music Hunter*, she tells of a night in the Belgian Congo, hundreds of miles from any large city, when she tuned in a symphony on her short-wave radio and then sat back to listen.

"I could not at first believe what presently I saw. Forms moved from the darkness into the light of our campfire against the backdrop of dark thorn trees. It was the Bushmen moving softly toward me out of the night, silently, stealthily, with movements usually associated with one animal stalking another. My body grew tense, in anticipation, but I soon realized that what had drawn them from the darkness was the radio several feet distant from me. With a shuffling, soundless dance step they moved circling past me, completely absorbed.

I wondered what they were feeling listening to the music, and as if in answer to my question they began to dance. Perhaps they danced in ancient ritual; perhaps they improvised as they went along. I only know that for me in that stupendous moment they danced to this symphony exactly as it should be danced to, with a profound primeval reverence. It was Beethoven's Ninth, the setting of Schiller's "Ode to Joy," in which he proclaimed the brotherhood of all men everywhere.

The Bushmen danced the Beethoven to the very end. Only when the last notes faded in the air did they turn and like smoke before a gusty wind vanish into the night. Quickly I got up and turned off the radio lest the announcer's voice shatter the beauty of the moment. Alone in the silent night I remembered that Beethoven had once written: 'Let this music go from the heart to the heart.' "

(These Bushmen, you see, have not yet the advantage of Doctrine. Although the music of Beethoven is as alien to them as Cantorian transfinite mathematics is to me, they are able to react to it in humane—civilized—fashion. The soft barbarian on the street corner, busily pushing some alphabetical new drug, cannot do so.

In the Renaissance, the humanists resurrected and proudly espoused this probably-too-familiar line from Terence: *Homo sum; nihil humanum alienum a me puto*. ("I'm a person; whatever touches anyone touches me too.")

7

Although we have already had too many, and certainly we have had too many by the wrong people, it is still possible that a new PR job for the arts and sciences is in order. But this time the

386

grounds for the familiar apologies must be reversed. The arts seem to have been more continuously under attack than the sciences, and those who argue in favor of the arts—being faintly paranoid in the first place—are accustomed immediately to rest their case on ultimate metaphysical grounds which no one will confute merely because it is boring and impractical to try to do so. On the other hand, the person who argues in favor of the sciences almost always argues from immediate utilitarian grounds. Science, he will say, has cured diphtheria and infantile paralysis, it has immeasurably raised the level of food supply, it has established lines of instant communication between nations, and so forth ... Alas, his utilitarian argument is all too easily countered by the man who says, Yes, but it has also poisoned the rivers, disrupted social and mental health; and anyhow what the hell good does it do to cure a disease while Science is lurking about, twiddling its Big Bomb and just aching to explode the planet to dust?

Both science and art are humanist endeavors and surely they share with each other many of their broad purposes. I will list three aims identical between them which I consider pertinent. Science and art intend:

1) To strengthen and remark the brotherhood between man and the universe;
2) To enlighten and broaden our understanding and our sympathies;
3) To enlarge the scope and the breadth of interest of human senses.

I have deliberately chosen—though I do not think it is misrepresentation—identical purposes which are grandiose to the point of ambiguity in order that examples may serve to illustrate the ultimate and the immediate all at once. I ought also to note that although these three enormous goals are set down separately, each one of them includes the others.

8

New technological apparatus designed for purposes of investigation is always merely an extension of human senses. The most complex sort of chemical analysis is merely a mathematical refinement and subtilization of the sense of taste. Mainly it is our eyes and ears which have been monstrously extended and refined. We have the X-ray, the electron microscope, the Skylab cameras; we have radar and sonar and the Geiger counter. Now we can see: the immense raging magnetic storms on the surface of the sun, and the protoplasmic cells clinging and cleaving, spitting out new individuals and mounting new colonies. Now we can hear: dolphins speaking speech together and humpback whales singing motets, and the grand black invisible galaxies muttering as they turn. (These animals and star systems talking in languages not yet broken: *bar-bar-bar-bar . . .*)

Our new senses have presented us with uncountable volumes of information we do not yet understand, but the important thing is that we—some of us, at least—have wanted, have desired ardently to understand. To understand means, in our terms, to interpret; and undoubtedly part of the difficulty in interpreting new information is in the lack of a method by which to humanize it. So very much of this new data seems icily cosmic—how can it impinge upon us as human persons? So much are our senses self-centered that not even science can digest the apparently utterly impersonal.

Perhaps upon this point you will allow me an imprecise analogy. It was first assumed, because the glow-worm had a circumscribed means and area of locomotion and because it seemed to have little or no curiosity, that its sensory equipment (specifically, its vision) must be severely limited. But when Exner, the Viennese scientist, treated the glow-worm eye as if it were a camera, smearing a drop of gelatine behind it and then photographing through it, he was able to pick up a distant line of trees and a church spire. The eye of the glow-worm is extremely receptive, but its nervous system and its memory cannot interpret or retain what they assume is not momentarily urgent to its existence. The glow-worm will always distinguish the objects of its diet; it will never recognize the incomprehensible boot which crushes it.

Thus: ourselves. We have as yet no way to enlarge our circle of understanding so that it may include these masses of information our newly-discovered senses have made available. This is to say, we have discovered facets of the universe towards which our feelings of kinship—brotherhood—have not developed. —And while many scientists aver that our knowledge of the universe is crippled by our habits of anthropomorphism, it is possible that the reverse is true: that we shall have a truer and more intimate knowledge of nature when we have broadened and deepened our anthropomorphic instincts.

For anthropomorphism is not anthropocentrism. The notion that man is at the center of the universe, that the totality was designed for his usage, is foolish and vainglorious. But anthropomorphism is a state of mind inevitable; contort us as we may, we still carry our mortal yardstick out to the stars and the electrons. It will be equally foolish and vainglorious to pretend that we can understand new facts or hypothesize new theorems on some super-computerized, suprahuman level. Anthropomorphism is our largest and soundest means of recognition. The soonest advance in American civil rights came about when minority races were recognized as humankind; the recent breakthroughs in plant and animal research have come about by our at last seeking out those qualities we share in common with plants and animals. This method will, I think, continue valid no matter what subject is under observation: mu mesons, lattice structures of crystals, light rays in superplasms.

In the struggle to anthropomorphize data, attempting to bring our minds closer to their subjects, the best tool is the traditional one of metaphor. Only by comparing subjects—and not merely in their physical measurements and properties, but also in their widest ways of operating and in the strongest impressions they leave upon our understanding—can we make any headway toward appreciating them, either in their kinship or in their otherness. It was useful to the point of necessity for the Greeks and Romans and Shakespeare to have the metaphor of the *body politic*, with its ramifying metaphors of illness, of interdependence of limbs and organs, of supremacy of reason. Earlier in this century it was useful to have the metaphor of the atom as a microcosmic solar system. It turned out that this latter metaphor was inaccurate, but then its very inaccuracy was useful in pointing up new discriminations and contrasts.

Nor are we forever to give allegiance to a metaphor simply because at one time it was pleasing and seemed reasonable. We gave up on the Renaissance metaphor of existence as a Great Chain of Being, and we gave up on the Enlightenment metaphor of the universe as a big Swiss watch, when these proved no longer viable, when they became mere cliches. Metaphorical cliche is the enemy of truth in science just as it is in art. If a scientific metaphor has not freshness, cleanliness, and perhaps a little oddity, it is not likely to be fruitful. I would expect that the same rule of thumb holds for both scientist and artist: if an idea of likenesses comes to them easily, and if it dovetails neatly in every major detail, then it is a product not of observation or intuition, but of laziness and self-indulgence.

So far I have spoken of metaphor only as a means of synthesis, of bringing under a single, and singularly phrased, notion a large number of distinctions, similarities, contrasts, symmetries, assymetries. But metaphor is also a means of discovery. I've spoken of the value of a scientific cliche as a kind of racing chock from which new ideas can depart, but there are also those enlightening metaphors which, at first seeming to belong almost completely to other disciplines, at a later period receive scientific formulation. Almost twenty centuries passed before Uccello worked out mathematically the same laws of perspective by which Kallikrates designed the columns of the Parthenon. When the Curies propounded the formula for radioactive half-life—the idea of a thing vanishing in proportion to its residue—they surely had no notion that ancient Egyptian musicians dampened their lyre strings by the same formula. John Napier in the sixteenth century "invented" the same logarithms by which Roman brass workers flared the bells of imperial trumpets. And to what degree may it be possible that two seminal concepts of modern physics, relativity and simultaneity, owe at least something to Henry James and Marcel Proust?

In sum: metaphor—*after observation*—is the most useful of tools for artist and scientist because it can accumulate and partially control large bodies of observation and impression; because metaphor is manipulable by, and inherent in, the mind; because metaphor is by nature anthropomorphic and aids in defeating the off-putting, momentarily inhumane, faces which nature sometimes presents to us. When we fail to recognize some particle of common humanity in any part of nature, we fail not because the universe is inhumane but because we have accustomed ourselves to a narrow conception of humanity.

9

A necessary reversible corollary: to make a metaphor after observation is only to refute, modify, or extend a pre-existing metaphor. We cannot observe what we cannot recognize, our senses not being sophisticated beyond our human capacities, and we recognize only by means of metaphor. The act of observation begins with the establishment—conscious or unconscious—of a metaphor, if it is only a metaphor from spatial geography: Here am I; there it is, the subject. (Or, more happily: There are you, the subject.)

10

If scientists and artists have at least this little-much in common, why should not they more closely move together to defeat those forces which have already banded against them and which with every succeeding year clamor more insistently and barbarously for darkness? At least four historical personages I know of have uttered, at some point in their lives, this simple formulation: "My purpose is to make you see!" These men were Galileo, Chekhov, Louis Agassiz, and D. W. Griffith.

E. Ethelbert Miller/Washington, D. C.

AN INTERVIEW WITH DENNIS BRUTUS

from *Obsidian*, Volume 1, Number 2: 1975
Fredonia, New York
Editor: Alvin Aubert

(Conducted at the Sixth Pan African Congress, Dar Es Salaam, Tanzania, June 27, 1974)

E. M.: What organization are you representing at the Sixth Pan African Congress?

D. B.: I am a member of the delegation of the African National Congress (ANC) in South Africa. It is the oldest political organization on the continent for blacks. It was formed in the 1890s. It anteceded the formation of the Union of South Africa. It's an organization that has been represented at every Pan African Congress, including the first one. So we've a long history of political awareness. It is now the leading liberation movement, but there are others—the ANC is the oldest. Its leader for a long time was Chief Luthuli, who won the Nobel Peace Prize. He was killed while in banishment, we think, by the South African police. ANC has offices in Lusaka, London, and at the United Nations. It's probably more representative of the people of South Africa than any other organization. It is committed to a revolutionary struggle for a socialist society. But we're not going to impose our will on the people. Our function is to express aspirations of the people. We want a South Africa which is truly free, as well as a free continent of Africa. We want black people all over the world and oppressed people all over the world to achieve their freedom.

E. M.: What is the size of the organization in terms of members?

D. B.: It's hard to say. I was in prison on Robbins Island, a kind of concentration camp. At the time I was there, there were a thousand political prisoners. Those were the leaders of the resistance.

The organization on occasion has been able to rally numbers of ten, twelve thousand for protest demonstrations, for defiance campaigns (similar to your freedom riots in the South) where the people broke the law, and invited the police to arrest them. But the organization is banned. It was banned in 1960 and driven underground. So you can't talk about figures now. Inside South Africa we have cadres working; outside we have people in military camps training as guerrillas. We have had armed clashes with the South African Army, with the Rhodesian Army on the borders and the banks of the Zambesi River. We also fought in Rhodesian territory. But figures are something difficult to talk about, since there is no formal membership inside the country.

E. M.: Tell us something about your life as a political figure and also as an artist.

D. B.: Well, I grew up as most blacks do, in a ghetto, in South Africa. My education was a missionary education by nuns who came from Ireland, Scotland, England or elsewhere. In some ways that was, of course, an advantage because the missionary approach, I believe, was a less racist one than that of the white administration of the State. But in time the State took over all mission schools because it decided that the schools were too liberal. They were encouraging blacks to think that they were the equals of whites. The State said that was bad for the blacks because it created frustrated blacks. Once a man thought he was the equal of a white man, he would begin to think he ought to have the same job as the white man, the same pay as the white man, and the same education. So you needed a new educational system that trained the blacks to believe that they were inferior, which indoctrinated them not only into the acceptance of their inferiority, but into the belief that God had ordained it: that it was the best thing for them, and that it was a permanent state of affairs. There's no society in the world which has attempted systematically to produce slaves both physically and intellectually: educate blacks into the acceptance of their permanent inferiority. Well, I went through that system, but I was fortunate in that much of my education was in the missionary schools before they were taken over by the State. Then from missionary schooling I went to a missionary university run by

393

Catholics, Episcopalians, Presbyterians, Methodists. The year after I completed my degree, the State took over the university as well, because it decided that it was too liberal. I'm fortunate, too, in that I am not a product of the State indoctrination system. I just escaped it.

E. M.: Tell us something about the influences which moved you into the literary realm.

D. B.: When I had finished graduating, I started teaching. I was told I had to teach black kids they were inferior. I was told "they don't need to know European or American history because they're never going to get there—it's none of their business." I refused to accept this. I taught what I thought the kids were ready to learn. I would answer any question they asked, including questions about the political system, and whether or not they were inferior. So it was inevitable that I was served with an order which made it a crime for me to teach. I then became a journalist. Then I got an order which made it a crime for me to write for any paper, and if any paper published me, the editor would go to jail as well. But I went on writing under a false name because they can't always identify who you are, and I wrote poetry mainly for the hell of it.

E. M.: Was the poetry political at this time?

D. B.: No; mainly, I think, sentimental lyrics with an occasional political point. You see, you can't escape your landscape. If you live in the Lake District of England, then you write the kind of poetry Wordsworth wrote. You live in a ghetto, you write ghetto poetry; you can't escape it. But I didn't think much of my own poetry. I still don't have a very high regard for it, but the day the State served me with a new order which made it a crime for me to publish poetry, I got really mad and I said to hell with it. I didn't want to publish, but if they tell me I can't, then I'm going to publish. And I published under a pen name in radical journals and smuggled some of my poetry out which was published in Nigeria. Just at the time it was published, I was arrested for another crime— a very curious one. I had been fighting the white Olympic Committee, trying to get blacks—

E. M.: What year?

D. B.: Sixty-three. I was fighting to get blacks into Olympic
teams because they were faster, they jumped higher, they ran better than the whites. They couldn't get in because they were black.
So I challenged the white system and I said, "if you don't let the
blacks in, we are going to get you expelled from the Olympics because the Olympic charter forbids racism." Sure enough, I did it;
they were kicked out in '64 in Tokyo, '68 in Mexico, '72 in Munich. We've kept them out of the Olympics all these years, and I've
had a great deal to do with it. So, in '63, at a meeting of the white
Olympic Committee, where I had gone to present the case of the
blacks, the Secret Police were tipped off that I was going to be
there and they came out of a cupboard in the wall and arrested
me. I was taken to prison and released on bail, pending sentence.
Whi   waiting to be sentenced I escaped from the country, just
across the border and went into Swaziland. From Swaziland I went
to Mozambique; that was a big mistake. When I got there the Portuguese Secret Police were waiting for me. They arrested me, and
turned me over to the South African Secret Police who took me to
Johannesburg in a car. When I got out of the car with my baggage,
I just put my bags down on the sidewalk and took off. It was 5 o'
clock in the afternoon and the street was crowded. I didn't think
they would shoot me; I was wrong. They shot me at close range in
the back. It was close enough to go right through my body, pene-
trating my gut, my stomach. They never had to take the bullet out
because there was no bullet; it just went clear through me. I was
taken to a hospital and finally sentenced to prison and now had an
extra crime because I had escaped from the police. I was sent to
Robbins Island, which was the worst prison in the country and is
the one for political prisoners—a kind of concentration camp. I
spent 16 months there breaking stones with a hammer.

E. M.: Was there any type of movement outside trying to free you?

D. B.: Oh, yes. It's an interesting question because just last night
I was reminiscing with another South African exile about the people who arrived at the hospital wearing white coats, like ambulance attendants, and with a coffin. They were trying to get me

out of the hospital in the coffin. I had agreed to it, except I was being guarded by six police and the head of the squad came to me and he said, "Look, we've been issued extra bullets tonight, and there are armoured cars patrolling the hospital grounds. We don't know why, but we just want to tell you, it's extra." So I had to send the message with a nurse. When she took my temperature, I wrote a message on the palm of my hand and just let her read it because cops were all around. And she warned them that if they came they would just be shot down. So they gave up. Anyway, I was taken to Robbins Island. I spent my time there. When I came out in '65 I was placed under house arrest for five years. I spent one year like that. I was married; I had kids; I had to earn a living. There's no way you can earn it if you're locked up in a house all day. So I applied for permission for a passport to leave the country. They said to me that they wouldn't give me a passport, but would give me what's called a *one-way exit permit*. This means you sign a promise that if you come back you'll go to prison until they let you out. And they keep that promise. Anytime you come back you go straight to prison.

So I signed that in '66 after a year under house arrest. I came out and went to Britain and worked in England for five years for an International Defense and Aid Fund affiliated with the United Nations for political prisoners, mainly South Africans. I also traveled in Britain, of course, lecturing at the universities about the brutality and the harshness in the prison. I was the first man to come out of Robbins Island alive. No other prisoner at that time had come off the island. So I could give people a rundown on conditions. I did this at the United Nations, before the Red Cross, for the press and television, and did in fact achieve some improvement in the conditions of the other prisoners. But they're still there, and one of my jobs is to try and get them out.

E. M.: Could you make a comparison between the handling of political prisoners in South Africa and America?

D. B.: From what I know of places like Attica, Soledad and other places, there doesn't seem to be much difference. What is interesting (and I don't know if this happens in the States) is that on Robbins Island all the prisoners are black. All the wardens are white.

There is a special group of prisoners who are serving sentences for multiple murder, several rapes or whatever. They're doing life for offenses against criminal law. Those prisoners are used by the wardens to beat up the political prisoners, to assault them sexually, to break their morale. So you have a very clear division between the political and non-political, with the non-political being bribed with marijuana, with money or favors, to sexually assault, beat, break, and sometimes kill the political prisoners.

E. M.: Were you involved in any political struggles to free people who have been arrested in the United States?

D. B.: In the States?

E. M.: Right.

D. B.: Sure. I was involved in the rallies for Angela Davis, for instance. I've been working with the Indians on Wounded Knee, with Chicano groups in Chicago on many issues, Puerto Ricans, others. I worked for political prisoners in Chile, on the campaigns in the Chilean issue. I've been active in opposition to the Greek colonels and their oppression, as well as the American involvement in it. To me, you see, the notion that my struggle is an international struggle is not something I have to theorize about; it's a living thing, my life is an involvement in challenging injustice wherever it might be.

E. M.: Could you tell us about the problems African newspapers must cope with?

D. B.: Let me stick just to South Africa because it's a large issue. First, 99 percent of the press is white-owned, white-controlled. The one percent which is black run is a black front for white control. So there is no real black ownership or black control as you have in the States.

E. M.: Would you say that there is no newspaper vehicle which could be used to arouse support for political prisoners?

D. B.: Right. For one thing, you have to have a vehicle, but for another, if you go get your own duplicating machine and you run off your own thing, you can be arrested and jailed under about 700 different laws. Incitement to hostility, communism, subversion, etc. If you write a slogan you can go to prison under the Terrorism Act. You can be hanged for standing in the street with a placard.

E. M.: There must be some underground papers.

D. B.: Yes, but regrettably very little. I have been urging people. (I broadcast to South Africa, to the underground—we have a radio station in Lusaka. We do an hour every night, broadcasting to the people of South Africa.) I have been urging them that they must not be frustrated by the fact that there are no vehicles or organs at their disposal. They have to go on writing, even if it just circulates by hand within the community. But they've got to go on doing it. But there hasn't been very much, I'm sorry to say. I regret that.

E. M.: This question may deviate, but what are your views on contemporary black poetry, as far as some of the themes and structural problems you might see?

D. B.: You ask such large questions. There are major poets and one can distinguish major trends. But on the other hand, there are trends which are so diversified and so widely scattered that it's difficult to define them. It seems to me that if one looked at the history of black American poetry . . . I must be very careful because this is not my field—my field is African poetry . . .

E. M.: I'm going to ask you a question on that, too.

D. B.: All right. I would say that there was a phase in which people wrote in Western patterns. They rhymed, they scanned; there was a regular stanza structure. I suppose people like Claude McKay belonged to this category. Certainly Countee Cullen, Dunbar, people like that. And then you get a very exciting breakdown, a freeing of rhythm, a freeing of speech and structure—which was not exclusively black because it was happening in European literature.

E. M.: Right.

D. B.:   Now, what was important, of course, was that the blacks like Langston Hughes incorporated speech rhythms and the idioms of the blacks, not merely using black material in terms of black experience, but black diction, black rhythms, so that you get a quite new, different kind of poetry. And it seems to me that the third, a very exciting trend, is the contemporary combination of the rhythms of speech with the rhythms of music, and specifically jazz; a fusion of the two. The tendency is almost always to treat poetry *not* as something on the page. On the page it's nothing. It's the poetry heard that comes alive.

E. M.:   What about the political composition of the poem?

D. B.:   Well, here, I would prefer to say very little. Mainly because I would have to be somewhat critical. All I would say is that I am put off by the rhetoric of a man who says to me, "You gotta off whitey; you gotta get a gun; you gotta make a revolution" and I find him driving around in a Buick, you know, and he's doing pretty well for himself. I think that kind of rhetoric is phony, and I don't believe revolutions are made with words. I think words should try to function like bullets. But it's a lot more than words that's going to change the world.

E. M.:   I agree.

D. B.:   And the guys who settle for words and kid themselves, that if you're a revolutionary poet, you're a revolutionary—that just turns me off.

E. M.:   Could you tell me something about the things in common, as well as the differences, between African writers under the French influence and those under the English?

D. B.:   Again, I think you have raised a very large question, but I would like to stress first the similarities. The writers who come out of the Francophone tradition and who know Breton or Mallarme, or whoever, have experienced a very strong French impact and there's a large French element in their work. On the other hand, those in the Anglophone tradition have all had a very strong English (as opposed to American) influence. The reason is that most professors in African universities have been Englishmen, not Americans, and they know their Wordsworth and their Dickens and their Browning and their Tennyson much better than they know their Walt Whitman or their, shall we say, contemporaries—people like Richard Eberhart or Allen Tate, or anyone like that. So what we have is a very strong British as opposed to American influence. This is reflected in a very conscious concern with form. Writers in Africa are much more interested in form than writers in America. I think the explanations are two. One, the black in America has broken down to free verse consistently. I also think that it may be due to the fact that in Africa the poet is much more of a conscious craftsman than he is in America. I think in America there is a very largely held assumption that if you get it down, if you "tell it like it is," you've done it.

In Africa, we think of poetry as a craft. It's a strategy, it's a method of persuasion. It's a whole lot of things, and you are working at a degree of greater intellectual complexity. Now, some people say, "Oh, this is the African being influenced by the West." It's just not true. Because if you go to the African oral tradition, you see tremendous subtlety, satire, imagery, all kinds of wonderful things in African poetry untouched by the West.

E. M.:   Could you document this with a few names?

D. B.:   Well, I will give you just three poets from South Africa, which is the area I know best. People writing in Zulu, or Xosa. Poets like Mqhayi or Jolobe or a Zulu poet like Vilakari. Now, there is a great poem in which Mqhayi salutes the Prince of Wales. The representative of the Queen of England comes to South Africa as the representative of the great white Queen's civilizing mission. Read on one level, it's a very respectful, almost adoring poem to this representative of this great white civilization. But if you'll read between the lines and if you know the African idiom, it's just making shit out of all that. It's the most superb exaggeration and hyperbole, which makes the whole thing become nonsense. And you realize that this is a man who comes strutting around and for whom the Africans have the deepest contempt. So you see in that kind of subtlety, to say one thing and mean another thing is itself part of the craft, part of the strategy.

E. M.: I think in the American tradition you would find that in some of the spirituals which were sung.

D. B.: Or the slave songs.

E. M.: Right.

D. B.: Go back to the chain gang. You'd find them singing something. For them it means one thing, but the white man may think it means something else.

E. M.: Right. We've talked about poetry in Africa and the United States. What about literature in the West Indies?

D. B.: I think it's far greater than people realize. I don't think it's been given the proper estimate. I'm not thinking of contemporary black writers in the Caribbean, Edward Braithwaite, Calvin John LaRose, people from Trinidad, Jamaica and elsewhere. I think that our debt to the Caribbean influence is far greater than we realize and is not merely in the contemporary field. Of course Claude McKay came from the West Indies. But think of a black like Aime Cesaire, who came from Martinique, went to Paris, and is one of the fathers of negritude. The other one is Leon Damas teaching in Washington—a man I admire greatly. With Senghor, they are the triumvirate which gave birth to negritude. I don't mean contemporary negritude, which has fallen into disrepute. I'm thinking of negritude when it was a vital impulse towards the recovery of black identity and the recovery of black culture. Now it's almost become a servant of neo-colonialism. It's not suspect in America because negritude in America means something quite different to what it means in Africa. Africans distrust negritude because they see how Senghor is still a lackey of the French government and is projecting French values through negritude in Africa. African negritude is distrusted. Negritude in America, I think, is still a valid impulse.

E. M.: Does an African need to be conscious of his negritude?

D. B.: Not in Africa, but maybe in Paris, when he was excluded, having been Frenchified. He wore French clothes, spoke the French language, drank the right French wines, dated French girls. He was in everything but color a Frenchman.

E. M.: Would you say that negritude developed out of alienation?

D. B.: It is a reaction to alienation. A determination to rediscover yourself, when, having adopted a new self, you find that you're still not accepted. Still rejected and therefore, "since when I take this man's culture it doesn't help me to achieve acceptance, I might as well go back and recover my own culture that I abandoned in shame, to satisfy him. I'll go back and recover what I ought to be proud of."

E. M.: Do you see negritude belonging primarily to the intellectual class?

D. B.: I think that's only partly true. I don't think you need to be a member of the elite to be alienated. Therefore, I would be reluctant to say that all those who are proponents of negritude are necessarily elitists or people with colonized minds or intellectuals. You see even the word "intellectual" is dangerous because often in Africa and in America, I think, by intellectual we mean a black or a white who is the product of the Western white system. In time, we will have to produce our own intellectuals. The word "intellectual" ought not to be pejorative. We should not condemn a man as long as he's an intellectual *worker* and he knows he's part of the working people and his function is different. But as of now, we tend to think that only Westernized blacks are intellectuals. I would like to see African intellectuals of great stature emerging.

E. M.: Many of the African writers have problems publishing. How has that been affecting trends and the development of the literature?

D. B.: I think this is a very serious problem. It operates on two levels. One is the problem of simply presses, publishing houses; many of which are branches or subsidiaries of Western enterprises.

402

Longmans has a big branch in Africa. Oxford University Press has a big publishing house, and so it goes on. In a sense one is restricted because the vehicles for publication are not there and the ones that are there are not wholly African-owned. But, of course, we have other problems. For one, literacy. You have a smaller market for reading in English or French. And when you write in Swahili, then you have a very limited market. I don't think we ought to be hung up on the size of a print order. We should settle for small, cheap productions in short runs and then repeat them as the demand increases. One of our very serious problems is that most manuscripts, if they are to be published, must be considered by white Western firms. It is their perspectives which determine whether a work is good or not, whether it is publishable or not. One of the things we might do is establish better links with independent black presses like *Broadside Press*.

E. M.:   Is there a development or movement like that on the Continent, where African writers are trying to get together and publish their own material?

D. B.:   Not quite. What is happening is that there are State publishing houses which at least are independent of Western enterprises. We now have in many African countries a State publishing house and that must horrify many Americans. The notion of State enterprise doesn't scare us because if the State is the expression of the aspirations of the people, then there's no reason why the State should not be willing to publish and make available those people who voice the aspirations of the people. The good old American "free enterprise" notion of conflict between the State and people is a Western one.

E. M.:   How do you see Drama developing in Africa?

D. B.:   Very exciting. If you will look at West Africa there is John Pepper Clark or Wole Soyinka. If you look at Ethiopia you find a dramatist like Gabre Tsegaye-Hedhin, who writes in Amharic. Some South Africans living in exile like Lewis Nkosi; James Ngugi in Kenya. There's a great deal being written and some of it is very good. The exciting element is the reincorporation of elements from

African traditional drama and ritual. In Africa, as in ancient Greece, drama was not something you paid and went to see like the movies. It was religious. It was didactic. It carried the moral values of the society. It instructed the young. It functioned as a part of an initiation ritual. It established community with the dead and the unborn: the African sense of the community of all spirits, living, dead, and unborn, past, present and future. So the reincorporation of these elements into African drama as we reabsorb the existing traditional material which is lying around, which has been neglected, which has been despised, and bringing it back, means that African drama really has something special to give to world drama. I think something which is valid and universally valuable. I think we're doing a lot of exciting things. We need a lot more of the facilities, the financing, the opportunities to develop, but I'm very excited about African drama.

E. M.: In the States for many years, criticism of black literature was in the hands of whites. This is also true as far as African literature is concerned. Do you see African critics increasing?

D. B.: Yes. Not all of them very good. I have seen criticisms of my own work which were misplaced, misconceived, and the publishers have consulted me and I've said, "go ahead and publish." On no account suppress controversy because we need to develop levels of sophisticated criticism. Like James Ngugi's collection of essays, *Homecoming*. Brilliant essays! Peter Nazareth, from Uganda, *The African View of Literature*; Lewis Nkosi's early collection of essays, *Home and Exile*. There's lots more criticism now, but the best criticism, I think, flourishes not in books, but in journals, periodicals, monthlies, quarterlies...

E. M.: Well, do you have those literary outlets?

D. B.: We have them. Some of them are a little suspect; some were funded by the CIA. So we have problems. But there is a growing development of the little review field, and I think that's where the best criticism is written. It's ultimately published in book form. I feel that as of now we haven't shaken off the incubus of European criticism, Western criticism. There's still too many critics in the West who decide what is good and what is bad for Africa. There are not enough African critics. Perhaps among the best is Ezekiel Mphahlele, whose book, *Voices in the Whirlwind*, was severely attacked by the author of the *Black Aesthetic*, Addison Gayle. I still think Zeke's got a great many valuable things to say about literature in Africa and America. But we don't have enough, and we've got to encourage the growth of more writers and critics.

E. M.: What about translation and transaltors?

D. B.: Well, Nyerere, as you know, translated Julius Caesar into Swahili. There has been some done. It's an area that doesn't attract me a great deal so I haven't given it much thought. What I want to see is a strong vernacular tradition developing together with writing in English and French, if you're comfortable in it.

E. M.: What are some of the things that you are doing in the States right now?

D. B.: Well, I do some curious things. One, I teach African literature, which is my main specialty. I also teach courses in British and American literature: Thomas Hardy, Tennyson, Browning, Theodore Dreiser. I think it's important to be able to display that kind of competence, given the prejudices of American academia. You must not be treated as a nigger in a corner with a toy. You must be able to show your ability to move freely on academic levels of scholarship. I teach a graduate seminar on the liberation movements, in the political science department of Northwestern as well as teaching in the English department. But in fact that is only part of my life, because I run the South African Non-Racial Olympic Committee—the body which expelled South Africa from the Olympics. It has now also expelled Rhodesia from the Olympics and is continuing a very active campaign. I will be busy until 1976 when the next Olympics take place in Montreal. South Africans and Rhodesians are going to try to be there again and I'll have to mobilize Canadian and Black-American opposition to throw them out. So that's part of it. But as I said, I work with Greeks on Greek freedom, Chileans on Chilean freedom, Chicanos, the American Indian movement. I speak on many campuses a year just on the liberation struggle in South Africa; radio, television, lectures and occasionally, I write some poetry. So it's a pretty full life.

Joseph Bruchac/Greenfield Center, New York
POETRY IN MODERN AFRICA

from *Greenfield Review*, Volume 1, Number 4: 1971
Greenfield Center, New York
Editor: Joseph Bruchac

One does not react to Africa as Africa is, and this is because so few can react to life as life is.
> —Richard Wright, *Black Power*

1

PEOPLE ARE always trying to categorize the things which come out of Africa. By designating this school as "the only true African writing" or that writer as "the one great African poet" they are able to reduce and deal with a very complex situation. Yet this, though certainly a step forward from the past—since it does admit the existence of African writers and African literature, is equally as deceptive an approach as the old one of assuming that Africa had no indigenous literature and no potential for developing one.

One of the most exciting things about contemporary African poetry—and African writing in general—is that it is so difficult to easily classify or make predictions about. In only two decades it has progressed from simple and imitative lyrics (which usually praised the typical missionary virtues—much as the writing by present day New Guineans does) to a poetry which combines both modernism and ethnic consciousness. And there has been a flood of literature from black Africa in this period unequalled, I feel, by any other part of the world in both impact and subject matter. *The Literature of Africa*, a reader's guide to creative writing by black African authors (edited by Hans M. Zell and Helene Silver with Barbara Abrash and Gideon-Cyrus M. Mutiso, *Africana Press*), lists over 700 books.

The sheer volume of African writing today would be unimpressive if much of it were not truly excellent writing—which it is. Yet much of it, in fact, is still unknown to the reading public of the

Western world. The image of Africa presented to us by the media is almost the same as that of the last seventy years—a land sunk deep in ignorance and savagery. Even documentary movies on other subjects cannot resist the temptation to gratify the reader's expectations about the "Dark" continent. I am thinking in particular of a film about surfing—*The Endless Summer*—and a scene on a supposedly remote beach when the young American heroes looked out at a canoe coming in and: "knowing we were the first white men they had ever seen, we wondered if they were going to eat us." That particular scene was filmed along a section of the Ghanaian coast which has known contact with Europeans for over 400 years. In fact, my wife and I taught at a modern African secondary school only a few hundred yards away from the place where that scene was shot—if one looks closely at the "primitive natives" in the canoe one may notice that one of them is wearing a University of Michigan sweatshirt.

> I do not know when it was, I always confuse childhood
> and Eden
> *As I confuse Life and Death*—a tender bridge
> *unites them*
>
> —Leopold Sedar Senghor

> Such webs as these we build our dreams upon
> To quiver lightly and to fly . . .
>
> —Wole Soyinka

2

Poetry in Africa is as old as the human voice. Although the novel and, to some extent, drama, are Western forms which have been adopted by African writers, poetry has existed in many different forms in Africa. As S. Okechukwu Mezu points out, in the introductory essay printed in his book of poetry *The Tropical Dawn* (Black Academy Press, Buffalo, N. Y.), poetry accompanied nearly every aspect of life in traditional societies and "was conceived as a collective work wherein participate various peoples." Moreover, traditionally very little distinction is made between songs and poetry. Even stories and tales are poetic in form and nature." Praise songs, proverbs, ritual chants, satirical improvisations, even epic poems, all these are part of the heritage of African poetry.

Today, although the novel is by far the most frequently published and the best known form of writing done by black Africans, an overwhelming amount of poetry is being written in Africa. At one time it seemed possible to make clear distinctions between the poets who wrote in French, disciples of *Negritude*, the poetic school founded by Senghor of Senegal, Cesaire and Damas of the Caribbean, and the poets who expressed themselves in the English language, clinging to a more individualistic style of expression. However, although the often quoted remark of Wole Soyinka—that a tiger does not have to proclaim his tigritude—does indicate a difference in poetic theory between the poets of those countries which were formerly colonies of France and England, it has been almost a quarter of a century since Senghor's great anthology of the poetry of Africa and Madagascar was published. A whole generation of poets in both English and French speaking parts of Africa have been influenced by the poetry of both persuasions. The Moore and Beier anthology *Modern Poetry From Africa* has been taught, just to give one example, in Ghanaian schools for half a decade, its translations of Senghor's poetry and the poetry of Diop becoming as well known to students as their own poets Kwesi Brew and Kofi Awoonor (though both Senghor and Ghanaian poets are still much less well known and much more infrequently taught than are such British figures as Keats, Wordsworth and . . . Masefield).

Moreover, most of the subjects of *Negritude*, the evils of colonialism, the beauty of African women, the great heritage of the African past, are frequently the subjects of poems by "English" African poets. It is theory more than practice which divides the "English" African poet from the "French" African poet today. And there are poets in both languages who seem to either transcend or combine such distinctions—to say nothing of the African writers who express themselves in vernacular tongues or Portuguese.

There are some common elements in the contemporary African experience which make it possible to talk of "African" poetry, rather than Ugandan, Ghanaian, Nigerian, South African, etc. All African writers, whether from Cape Coast or Cape Town have the dual and confusing legacies of colonial past and traditional culture. They, or their parents, have seen the introduction of foreign languages, new religions, radically different economic and political systems. They have been educated in an alien literary tradition until it has become their own. Echoes of the Saint James Bible, much less Shakespeare, in the writings of prominent African authors would make more than one doctoral thesis. They have been, to a greater or lesser extent, strangers in their own lands. On the other side, such elements of African culture as respect for the elders and ancestor "worship", communally based systems of government and land tenure, the concept of art as a utilitarian and functional part of society, and the central nature of the drum (in some parts of Africa, languages seem to have been built on the tonality of drum sounds, making it possible to accurately reproduce words with the drum—thus *talking drums*) seem to be Pan-African and provide a strong indigenous tradition for the African poet to draw on. And there *is* an African literary tradition which is pre-European; the oral traditions so rich in mythic and historic detail.

> In spite of your songs of pride
> In spite of the desolate villages of torn Africa
> Hope was preserved in us as in a fortress
> And from the mines of Swaziland to the factories of
> Europe
> Spring will be reborn under our bright steps.
>
> —David Diop

> I am standing above you and tide
> above the noontide,
> Listening to the laughter to waters
> that do not know why ...
>
> —Christopher Okigbo

3

Drawing on the common elements of colonial experience and traditional heritage, the African poet of the next twenty years will undoubtedly explore many of the same themes which have informed the writing of such fine poets of Senghor, Tchicaya U'Tamsi, Gabriel Okara, John Pepper Clark and others. Moreover, most of the poets who have done so much to establish African poetry as great poetry will continue to contribute to its growth. Much of the best African poetry has been published in the last two decades and most of the better known poets are still comparatively young men. Only a few have had the book of their lives closed tragically—as was the case with Christopher Okigbo who was killed three years ago in the Nigerian Civil War while fighting as a Major for the Biafran Army or David Diop who was killed in a plane crash in 1960 at the age of 33.

However, if we expect the poets of Africa to confine themselves rigidly to the treatment of "African" (as the West defines the word) subjects, we are being unfair—and probably fooling ourselves. The background of the present-day African poet is a cosmopolitan one in the largest sense. His education may include such diverse experiences as Mission School, several years abroad in France or England and even (as was the case recently with Okot p'Bitek and Taban Lo Liyong, two young East African writers) a year or so at the University of Iowa Creative Writing Workshop. Leopold Senghor (who is today the President of Senegal) taught French to French students in Paris. Kofi Awoonor teaches in the English Department at Stony Brook, Long Island. Though the African writer, like any other man, will usually find his roots in the culture he was born into, his vision can range as far as any man's. Lenrie Peters, the fine Sierra Leonean poet, gave his first volume of poetry the title *Satellites* (Heinemann, 1967), and includes poems on such diverse subjects as Yevtushenko, the explosion of the Chinese Atom bomb, the death of Churchill and parachuting—as well as ones which have to do with Pan-Africanism and his own city of Freetown.

Modern poetry in Africa began in earnest with the writers of the last two decades. Previous to this, much of the writing done by Africans had something of the self-conscious and overly derivative sound of lines like the following, written by R. E. G. Armattoe, an important pioneer poet in Ghana:

> I once saw a maiden dark and comely,
> Sitting by the wayside, sad and lonely

or like Michael Dei-Anang's:

> Awake, sweet Africa
> Demands thy love
> Thou sleeping heart ...

The fifties and sixties brought a new sound to African poetry, as in the following stanza from Gabriel Okara's amazing poem, "One Night at Victoria Beach", which shows us sea, Aladuras (one of the many Christian sects found in Nigeria), and revellers in bars at the beach in vivid contrast:

> The wind comes rushing from the sea,
> the waves curling like mambas strike
> the sands and recoiling hiss in rage
> washing the Aladuras' feet pressing hard
> on the sand and with eyes fixed hard
> on what only hearts can see, they shouting
> pray, the Aladuras pray; and coming
> from booths behind, compelling highlife
> forces ears; and car lights startle pairs
> arm in arm passing washer words back
> and forth like haggling sellers and buyers—

or as in the concluding lines of Tchicaya U'Tamsi's "Brush-fire":

> I said to you
> my race
> remembers
> the taste of bronze drunk hot.

In the last two decades African writers have learned how to use the languages they have inherited from a colonial past to express their unique double heritage. In so doing they have done what great writers have always done, provided the memorable experience and expanded the borders of perception and human understanding. Whatever happens in modern poetry in Africa in the next twenty years, it seems a safe bet to say that it will be well worth reading.

Felix Pollak/Madison, Wisconsin

TO HOLD WITH THE HARES AND RUN WITH THE HOUNDS: THE LITTLEMAGGER AS LIBRARIAN

from *The Hiram Poetry Review*, Spring/Summer: 1972
Hiram, Ohio
Editor: Hale Chatfield

I WOULD rather write about something more abstract, but having been asked to comment, in my capacity as curator of rare books and little magazines at the library of the University of Wisconsin, on the role played and the problems presented by little magazines in a big library, I will say at the outset that there indeed are problems, and not just one-sided problems either. The relationship between the typical serials librarian and the typical littlemag editor/publisher is an uneasy one at best, and at worst one frought with mutual distrust, animosity, and a multitude of sour gripes. Speaking pretty much from the inside of either camp, I find it easy enough to hold with the hares while running with the hounds—a perfect method of making oneself unpopular with both. But then, I don't even have to do or don't anything to be damned to begin with, for my mere being an "academic" (if you'll pardon the dirty eight-letter word) will put me in the outhouse of a certain faction of professional littlemag outsiders while the onus of "little magazine specialist" alone suffices in some library circles to endow one with an aura of frivolity, bordering on poetry and subversion. So you can see I have nothing to lose by speaking my mind.

To begin with, I fully sympathize with the littlemag editors' usual aversion to invoices-in-triplicate, which to many of them apparently symbolize evil incarnate, everything that they stand *against*. Unfortunately, this moral-philosophical stance is as a rule completely lost on the serials librarian, who has become real liberal in the course of time and is by now usually quite willing to forgive what he imagines to emanate from the single sheet of coffee-stained (or wine-stained?) paper, the backside of a handscribbled poem, that is supposed to pass as an invoice: the fumes of pot, illicit sex, unshampooed long hair, and of blood coagulated around male earrings; the only thing he cannot understand and forgive is that said evil-smelling document was not submitted in triplicate, in the face of all his written instructions, and that it, more often than not, lacks certain small details, like the price of the magazine, its frequency of appearance, and sometimes also an address. At which point I begin to sympathize with the serials librarian, who, after all, has to carry on his business of "setting up" the new mag and, if possible, pay for the subscription, and do the same with a few dozen other mags yet before lunchtime rolls around. What is more understandable, therefore, than that he calls up the curator of rare books who ordered "the crap" in the first place, and gives him a piece of his mind, however little this piece may commend the whole? And what, in the absence of a correct editorial address, is more predictable but that the same curator in due time will receive an irate letter from the editor in question stating that he was being robbed by the motherfucking university in general and the grandmotherfucking curator in particular because he hasn't received any bread *yet*. But provided his letter bears, by a lucky coincidence, a return address, it will, never mind its contents, become the instrument for re-establishing peaceful relations, and all will be well that begins so well.

To that end—or beginning—it is imperative that the idea of conventional business letters be discarded altogether. Here is where the average serials librarian will invariably fall down. This is the point where the alienation gap widens between the members of the same generation and non-communication leads to a complete breakdown of all business relationships, unless somebody sees the light, or there is a go-between, a translator, as it were. I am talking here about the most stubbornly independent, pugnacious, and uncompromising littles, whose non-representation in a large library is a loss to the library as well as to themselves. Where love, ribald indignation, infatuated goofiness, obscene, exuberant humor, and bizarre spelling are proffered and are met with icy New England stares and prefab form letters abounding in impersonal "Dear Sirs" and "Yours of the instant received," no human relationships can, obviously, develop. And while the serials librarian will cry out loud that he doesn't *want* any human relationships to develop, that all he wants to develop is invoices-in-triplicate, the exasperated littlemagger will with a rasping voice advance suggestions as to what the serials librarian can do with his invoices-in-triplicate, averring that the development of human relationships is precisely what he, the littlemagger, is after and the very reason why he is publishing his mag in the first place. And the hell with the subscription money; the serials librarian can shove that the same place where he can shove the invoices-in-triplicate. And with that, only silence can break out, colder than the coldest cold war.

If I sounded anywhere in these remarks as if I felt sorry for myself, I gave the wrong impression. If I now sound as if I were slapping my back, I am giving the wrong impression again. All I am trying to do is report on a real and rather deplorable situation and on my own way of handling it—the only way I know. I carry on a correspondence with littlemag editors that is marvelous and sometimes out of this world and the likes of which has never crossed the desk of the compilers of the *Secretary's Handbook*. And then I translate the gist of this correspondence into serials-librarianese, and everybody appears reasonably happy—or at any rate, the titles and issues keep coming in to maintain the status of Wisconsin's little magazine collection as what I in all modesty believe it to be: the biggest and best English-language littlemag collection in existence. Of course—and perhaps that is what some of my librarian-colleagues find so difficult—one must not have any "dignity" hang-ups. I remember my first letter to Ed Sanders, whom I, in all innocence, addressed as "Dear Mr. Sanders." I received the letter back by return mail with the note, "Dear Felix, cut out that *Mr.* shit— call me Ed." Our relationship improved when I suggested that he change the title of his notoriously famous magazine from *FUCK YOU: A Magazine of the Arts* to *FUCK THEE: A Quaker Journal.* In direct consequence, I like to think, and with the help of some $$$, I hasten to add, Ed later parted with some of his choicest and scarcest items and back issues and we have a full run of this collectors' prize which we cataloged, for the benefit of visiting city fathers, as *F. Y.: A Magazine of the Arts.* (The entering of some of the more vividly titled mags in the public catalog is one of our thorniest problems, for the illiteracy of city fathers is no sure safeguard against discovery: there is always the danger that a student or faculty member may read the catalog card to them.)

Now, having held with the hares most of the time, let me run with the hounds for a stretch. I do have some grievances of my own—and I won't even waste my typewriter ribbon writing about "magazines" that come in boxes filled with objects ranging from someone's beard (or pubic?) hair to cut-outs and pull-outs and pin-ups and pieces of cookies (symbolizing, no doubt, the way the cookie crumbles), etc. Nor will I go into the messes created by the fad of issuing "magazines" in the form of broadsides and fold-ins and fold-outs (usually becoming crushed-ins in transit)—all of which are a pain you know where for the librarian. But this, too, will phase-away and we shall overcome some day. What I do want to raise my voice in protest—no, shhhh. Let me talk like a librarian and make instead a few modest proposals. To wit: What every well-bred little magazine should have, and every ill-bred, feelthy, crappy, crazy, radical, and disgustingly beautiful little magazine too, if it wants to be subscribed to by a public and university library

    1) a title;
    2) a date of issue;
    3) an address.

Those are the essentials. The gravy items, also three, the fringe benefits, are:

    4) name of editor;
    5) frequency (even if fictitious or wishdreaming);
    6) a price (single copy and annual subscription).

If you think I'm breaking down open doors, you are sadly mistaken. The search for a littlemag's name is often one of the most time-consuming, energy-wasting, swear-word-coining occupations of our work. How grateful we would be if it could be found on the front cover, in Roman letters, written from left to right! One mag recently announced its impending birth with the statement, "Each issue will have a different name." You can imagine the happiness of the whole staff. That was just what we'd always been waiting for! Let me share with you a letter that reads, verbatim:

"Thank you for your enquiry about Big Venus, the latest issue of which you would like to receive at the library. I'm not exactly clear which issue it is you wish your sub to begin with—Big Venus began is [*sic*] 1969 with Big Venus, followed by Big Big Venus & then Big Big [*sic*] Venus. Next came Queen Camel, officially Big Venus 4, and the most recent in the series to date. I have copies of each of these issues, and would be grateful if you could tell me whether you want to order a set, or whether in fact it is Queen Camel you require, even though it doesn't bear the title Big Venus. (I presume problems like this are common when dealing with the ephemeral [*sic*] tastes of little magazine editors!)"

You may smile at *Big Venus* and her metamorphoses, no matter how much she contributes to the loss of my hair, but I have in front of me a magazine that looks like a revival of the excellent Canadian magazine *Combustion*, once upon a time edited by the highly respected Raymond Souster. It is titled *Combustion* 15 on the front cover and was, unfortunately, thus recorded by our serials librarian and shelved so by our student assistant. But it wasn't *Combustion* 15 at all. The inside cover disclosed that it was (Victor Coleman's) *Island* Number 6 "edited by Souster as *Combustion* Number 15." Now, as I said, I have the greatest admiration for both editors and their mags, but not all library workers dealing with littlemags can be assumed to be knowledgeable about them. It is true, anyone reading the inside cover could get the correct title of the magazine, but why, pray, put that information on the inside instead of on the outside cover? The answer may well be that littlemags are not being published for libraries—which is at best a half-truth and one of the contradictions with which littlemag editors are apt to wriggle out of tight spots. The fact is not only that the importance of libraries is recognized by most of them by now, for one library subscription is apt to reach, at least, the equivalent of 25 individual subscribers—and also qualitatively a very desirable group of readers, potential and practicing poets and likely future contributors—but the recognition of the importance of library subscription is also attested to by the efforts of littlemag cooperatives, like COSMEP, and organizations like CCLM, to devise schemes of bolstering library subscriptions, among other circulation-increasing projects. This feeling of need, too, is mutual—just as mutual as the disgruntlements described above—and is indicated by an increasing activity of littlemag collecting that is noticeable in college libraries throughout the country. Enlightened head librarians, after all, are prone to differ in outlook from their serials librarians; and the news has gotten around that the relatively new genre, only as old as our century, contains the source materials of modern literature.

Little magazines have thus, as minority voices, an organic function in our public and academic libraries. That function is very different from their function in our society at large, where they constitute, in my view at least, elitist islands in the sea of commercialism and a supermarket civilization that is the death of individuality. This view, I know, will be hotly debated by those who consider "elitist" a dirty word and rejoice in mass (un)culture and see littlemags, quite on the contrary, as the embodiments of pop art. But these, and many related questions, are big subjects in themselves that go far beyond the frame of this particular essay.

Len Fulton with Ellen Ferber/Paradise, California

GREEN SKIES

from *American Odyssey*
Dustbooks, 1975: Paradise, California
Editor: Len Fulton

FROM ITS icewater coast to its dense, deciduous hills, New England is a jut of hard American hide left geographically on its own hook in the North Atlantic. A great white whale still plumbs the seas of its conscience, and the certain slanted light of its afternoon holds still the shadows of Hawthorne, Longfellow and Thoreau. There remains a bleakness here for me, however more fixed in past than present, that oppresses like a winter Sunday. For all the years I knew him, and many before, my father, a Canadian Scot, rassled this grey horned ethic from the Merrimack mill towns to Gloucester on the sea, and far away along the mud-banks of the LaMoille River in northern Vermont. It never made just return to him for his long labors, I always thought, yet to his last day, a bow in his hand, he cherished that hard ground and rooted himself to it. I took the road, it turns out, for both of us.

"Somewhere within a hundred miles," I said to Ellen as we pushed north from Hartford, "I would have to say was home."
"I, too." She looked back toward the New York City we'd just left.

Ah, that was the northeast I knew! You were always within a hundred miles of everything! I recalled a Californian reading my novel *Dark Other Adam Dreaming* in manuscript and commenting that I insisted (oddly) on three miles being such a long way. In California you drive a hundred miles to work; in northern New England in the late forties (the novel's period) you fought each mile of mud-road for a share of your psychesoul.

I had worked here once in northern Connecticut for a tobacco-man, hanging the stalks, six to a lathboard, in long airless rows high up in dusty tobacco sheds. Sometimes we were forty feet above the dirt floor, and the beams we stood on were loose and rolled from underfoot. *What if we fall?* I had wondered to the man working next to me. *You'll grab something before you go too far*, he said with grit on his teeth. It beat cutting the stuff in the fields, which was where I'd started.

We cut a great loop through New England, as if to run backwards through a life that now belonged, for me, in a novel that a year hence (and with a little luck) might scandalize the place. Westfield's one viable bookstore took on copies of *The Grassman*. "My mother will sell them if nothing else," I pointed out. I talked with the proprietor about small press publishing and he grew interested, decided to stock the Directory. Over at the *News Advertiser*, where I'd done my last gig in the region in '58, it was business as usual. A home-town boy you say? Well, leave the book. It was here, fifteen years ago now, that I stood in the town square and watched a young Senator Kennedy come into town in a two-car motorcade. A real estate man I knew introduced Kennedy as "the next President." His partners gave him hell for that afterwards. But it was Jackie's wrinkled skirt that somehow stuck in my memory.

That night in the town of Agawam ten miles away I gave a talk on small press publishing in the local library. The people of Agawam packed the place with body and spirit, and held me long with their interest and kindness. Here was something, I thought, to controvert the seeming melancholia this land brought to me!

In Springfield next day the street struggle reconstituted itself as tooth-and-nail we moved books into three stores at city center and squeezed a promise of review out of Wayne Phaneuff on the *Daily News*. Phaneuff, it turns out, was more interested in California and the West than in my local origins, and I kept that in mind as we pushed deeper into old haunts. In Manchester, New Hampshire, I visited with Joe McQuade of the *Union Leader*, whose oft-infamous publisher William Loeb had given him a book to review. McQuade dug it out of a drawer and showed it to me. "Do you know who this guy is?" Indeed I did! He was a crazy preacher (whose name now escapes) whom I'd many times seen shouting his wares on the Sproul Plaza in Berkeley. Loeb, it seems, has a fascination for the odd while expatiating hard, rightwing causes. Of all the newspapers I visited the *Union Leader* had the toughest security check, though the Omaha *World Herald* ran it a close second, and the *New York Times* has a small army of thugs stationed at its entrance.

Manchester is a dim milltown straddling the Merrimack River, which originates in central New Hampshire, runs south into Massachusetts where it turns abruptly northeast to come into the sea around Newburyport. My grandmother's brother, whom they called "the big Indian of the Merrimack," used to run it via canoe, but like many rivers it invited human intervention because it contemptuously flooded out those old milltowns come each spring. One such town, Lowell, Massachusetts where I was born (as was Kerouac) was damned near converted into mudplain in '36; they say my sisters and I were carried across a bridge over the river as waters licked its underpinnings and the span shuddered. My grandfather refused to leave, ended up on the roof in a fight for his life.

At three points in my life I lived in Manchester, the last to finish high school and put in a year and a half in a bedding factory on Lincoln Street where I learned upholstery and Canadian-American French. It seemed strange to be selling books there, but on the other hand we'd been at it for over four thousand miles and I took to the offensive with ease and objectivity. Two downtown stores stocked the novel, but the city had clearly given way to peripheral shopping malls, and so we made our way to Bedford where such a mall existed. We left eleven *Grassman*s scattered throughout the Manchester area; and months later I learned that an old friend of mine upon hearing of the book went out and bought up every copy he could find (six). If I went back to Manchester right now I could sell more books—but damned if they'll order by mail. There you have the dilemna. By my arithmetic you increase your chances by a factor of forty with a personal visit—something the encyclopaedia publishers have known all along.

We crossed at Kittery and moved deliberately up through seventy miles of Maine's seacoast "vacationland." The names broke in on

421

me like the saltwind: York Beach, Ogunquit, Wells, Kennebunkport, Goose Rocks Beach, Old Orchard, Biddeford-Saco—it was a
gauntlet I'd run many times with my old friend Bob Fay and a
summer newspaper we called the *Tourist Topic* (A Summer Guide
to Maine's Southern Seacoast Splendor"). *It may still be going*, I
thought as we slipped into Kennebunkport where Bob and I had
kept our office. I tried to find that office to prove that the entire
thing had happened, but the building had vanished. The need to
authenticate the past grew: "I remember the day Kenneth Roberts
died. He lived up towards Goose Rocks there, had an interest in
water dowsing, wrote a book called *The Seventh Sense*." Twenty
years is long. "Met Cameron Mitchell in a restaurant right over
there." The restaurant had vanished. I remembered the printing
bills that had mounted against "The Topic" until at last a newspaper publisher from Lewiston up the way owned it all.

A water channel cuts the quaint town asunder and we ate at a
place built over that channel. About a lobster-throw away, across
the tiny square, I visited with the local bookseller and lost a scrap
to mogul publishing by coming on too fast. He was not interested
in small press information if that information was not in the standard trade volumes. "They have everything I want," he said, and
waved me off. If you must challenge, I learned again, do it slowly,
gently.

If I'd had the money I would have bought an Arentz seascape,
partly because of sentiment, mostly because Arentz was the greatest seascape artist I ever saw. I found some of his grand oils once
as far away as Denver, and recklessly wondered how it would be if
he'd been turned loose in the high West.

Heaven and Hell are literary extravaganzas. They are a way of ar-
ranging your character personas along several dimensions in literary form—in time, in morality, in place, etc. If my own persona belonged to a literary character, for instance, Heaven along the *place*
dimension might be Bozeman, or Thunder Basin. Certainly Hell
along that same dimension would be the city of Portland, Maine!

For Portland is the plain meanest town I know, bearing on the absolute front edge of Yankee recalcitrance and visionlessness. I lived in its center for almost two years in a fifth-floor tenement, held more odd jobs than I can count in an effort to squeeze through two years of college, and saw every fraility I possessed magnified in a long, unaltering string of ill-luck. Portland is greying red brick: poverty punished by wintry sleet straight off the awesome Atlantic; it is gaunt factories that were collapsing in '55 when I got there and are now a sort of rubble, nineteen years later; it is the lost "r" in the twanging speech which manifests a lost adventure somewhere in the soul; it is sea-based oil paraphernalia jammed into its waterways, and oil-stink mixed with salt air and tar; it is weathered lobstermen with hands the breadth of a paddle who lean against the pulverizing tide; it is a peninsula with no place to go, so keeps stirring its crumbling ingredients into a vat of Longfellow stew. Ten miles off in any direction Maine is a beautiful land—but Portland festers.

And now, too, it was futile and agonizing. I planted some bio-data with the *Press Herald*, which promised a story, but that information was useless on deaf ears. One storeman was an honest John: "This town doesn't *read*," he said. "Look, I do a hundred a week out front here—and a thousand a week out back." I looked in the back. It was porn. "Tough place," I said, and he grinned. Jones' Bookstore, less than two blocks from where I'd lived, would not take *The Grassman* because its blurb said the author "felt uncomfortable east of the Mississippi." The cycle of madness fed upon itself once more. The *Maine Sunday Telegram* later ran a review titled "Journalist with a Sixgun" and I meanly hoped for the worst for Portland booksellers.

"I've *got* to leave some books in this goddamned town," I bleated to the young bookstore proprietor at the University of Maine. "And you're my last hope. You're also my Alma Mater." The place had changed so since I'd spent two years in study there that I could not locate myself. But the intellectual experience was as fresh as ever, washing as it had the U. S. Army out of my guts. A man named John Jaques had trusted my brain to hold more than anyone had before.

The young proprietor took a mitful of books, but it was only to be a brief break in the weather. When I returned to California a few weeks later the books were waiting marked "refused".

Portland possesses a bright spot for the small presses, however. It is a jobber called Eastern Book Company down on Middle Street along the edge of the red rubble. Like Baker & Taylor (and once Richard Abel), Eastern Book sells mainly to libraries and institutions. I visited with Dan McDonough there, looked over the vast stock of books, and left with the notion that if Eastern Book is all there is here, it is probably enough.

Later that day we sold books up the coast in Falmouth, and moved on into Freeport, home of L. L. Bean—and yet another of my late-fifties haunts. My friend Bob and I had abandoned the Kennebrunkport office once the tourist summer was over down on the coast, and had come to a small letterpress newspaper plant here, he to run a paper called the Lisbon Enterprise, I one called the Freeport Press. They were tiny, bootstrap weeklies with circulations of a thousand or so, and in perhaps too young and swift an instant we killed them both and replaced them with one big tabloid called The Weekly News. We fought ignorance, our own mostly, and one brutal snowstorm upon the other until by spring we were looking for any high, warm   ground that life could give. I thought briefly that old Mister Bean might save us, with a full page ad a week and some endorsement, but he was a Yankee trader who dealt in hard goods, and did not chase another's fate up the icy alleys of chance.

Bean's of course, when Ellen and I pulled into Freeport, was flourishing with cars from as far away as British Columbia in the parking lot. The cold quonset hut where we'd printed those miserable weeklies was mercifully gone, like the Kennebunkport office. Maine and I had scrubbed each clean of the other!

For awhile an awful silence stormed my heart. Ellen read aloud from Curt Johnson's novel *Nobody's Perfect* (whose title I swear I suggested to him in a letter in 1969) and the comical, outrageous Mr. Schoenebatic and his friends gradually raised the spirit of this bookjourney back to its old, high plain. Ellen, to defend her ground here a moment, does not share my achromatic sentience of

New England Territory. "It is the only place I know," she says, "where the trees grow a canopy over the roads so that the sky is green. When I see New England I see green."

For a spell we rode that green highway across New England's northern reaches. Some of the names were unlikely—Lisbon, Paris, Norway, Berlin—but some were apple pie: Gorham, Randolph, Lancaster, Danville—where (she's right) the sky *is* green, and the close-fitting hills are studded with white pine, hemlock, maple, and punctuated white with those incredible birches that cluster in small blizzards for mile upon mile. You drive with care for the old road twists and the mind entangles itself into the snake-tight thickets, follows up the gorges and breaks free along the top of the wind.

We crossed the Connecticut and came down into the Green Mountains in a driving rain. At the Moose, the Passumpsic and the Winooski the storm's electricity had locked itself to the water to make a midnight show of unarguable dominion. It broke along our front as we came, and it cracked down our backtrail as we went—and we took care to know just how water and greenness came to this land. Next day in Monpelier it was still raining. We sold books at the Bear Pond, a nice and unexpected find, and tracked the Winooski to Burlington.

I first came to this northcountry in 1947 when my father uprooted us from a rather suburban life in Sudbury, Massachusetts. He would be a farmer, he thought, and beat the coming recession. It was a boyhood dream to him, born of the smoke and grime of the milltowns. The farm had a hundred cows, a 1600-bucket sugarbush, and what seemed to me then to be an endlessly isolated wilderness. In an instant, or almost, I was transformed from suburban to primitive, from slouch to worker. And when, three or four years later, we lost the place to economic vagaries, I did not know how to deposit money in a city bank—but I could drive a team, operate a dump rake without sliding into its teeth, boil sap to syrup, put manure to a winter field, and survive the damndest snowstorm the north could deliver.

That northcountry is gone now, of course. The great highway we

rode up to Burlington told much of it, for it slammed across the
hills like a new, straight tyne with no accord to the land's true and
wrinkled face. The old roads, now untravelled which I could see below and far away were losing their crumbling surfaces to history, a
history of psychic seasons of work; of a pleasure-pain principle
that announced itself as fast and as true as the taste of fresh fall
blackberries—or chokecherries; of tools that were as vital a part of
life as food—the side-rake, tedder, pung, front-pan, pulsator, hay-
fork (not a pitchfork), stone bolt, eveners, trace-chains, peevee and
so on; of horses weighing 1800 pounds, shod to walk on ice; of
weathered old barns in full function, topless silos, houses with tiny
upper windows tucked under the eaves; and of cow dung plastered
along those serpentine roads marking them off in time forever
from the smooth and faceless highway we now traversed.

In the late forties Burlington was a cow-town where you went to
get your teeth fixed or buy farm equipment or sell milk. Now it
was international. You could get Greek food on Church Street.
You could see cars on the UVM campus from anywhere in the universe. The town too tried to emphasize a kind of quaintness, not
unlike in fact the rest of the state, which was seeing its rather ordinary old qualities achieve a worth on the New York auction
blocks. I had to forgive myself for the notion that much of it all
was skin-deep—like the master highways that carved Vermont into
saleable quarters.

At the Burlington Free Press I visited with Barbara Vonbruns
who promised a short mention (she came through within a month,
too). We then ran into coffee breaks and forenoon absenteeism of
every imaginable sort until we finally gave up and dropped into a
restaurant ourselves to wait them out. While waiting for service,
Ellen decided to try for more addresses from a phonebook, and
was instructed that there was a public telephone in the back. After
two cups of coffee I grew itchy after her whereabouts and arose to
investigate, but just then she returned, full of fluster and hate. To
get to the telephone she'd had to climb across a piano, then
through a clothes rack with fifteen jackets on it—then there was
no light.
  "How'd you see?"

She looked incredulous. "There was a *candle* going in back of all that!"

At the Little Professor Book Center a poet named Tinker Green was the manager. He took one look at the Directory and asked if I was "with Dustbooks or something." He'd used the Directory for years—and needless to say that saved me some words! What was important there, though, was why Green had not thought to stock the Directory before my visit—underscoring once again the importance of personal contact.

The University of Vermont Bookstore also took some Directories, and we left about a dozen *Grassman*s in Burlington on the basis of the promised Vonbruns review. We then drove northeast through Essex, Essex Junction, Jericho, Underhill, Cambridge Junction and into Jeffersonville, where I deposited a copy of the novel in the public library, a one-roomer centrally heated with a pot-bellied wood stove. The librarian, it turned out, lived on a section of what had been my father's farm.

"That was the one gap in the history of that land we couldn't fill," she said, and seemed to want me to stay and talk longer. But I had some gaps of myself to fill, and spent the rest of the daylight reviewing landmarks and reconstructing events now a quarter of a century old. Ellen, who has been working with me editing the novel about this place, *Dark Other Adam Dreaming*, was beautifully patient with my insistence on remembering. Finally, as the rain slowed and the light began to fade we slipped up through Smuggler's Notch and wound down into Stowe, a ski-town of moneyed quaintness. Even in the forties it had been so, with the great mountain, Mansfield, standing behind it, dividing the wealthy skiers in the south from the struggling farmers in the north.

The next day, after getting lost on a dirt road trying to find Bellows Falls, we drove back into New Hampshire, sold books in Keene, and visited an old Wyoming friend who now teaches at Franklin Pierce College in Rindge. About half way down from Keene to Rindge lies a mountain called Monadnock, jutting about three thousand feet into the southern New Hampshire sky. During the '38 hurricane I lived at the foot of that mountain.

Then we turned west again, driving out of the past.

GRAPHICS

Renee Barkan/New York City
from *Zone*, Number 1: 1977/Brooklyn, New York
Editors: Peter Cherches; Dennis DeForge; Jay Heller; Stephen Lackow

John Cavanagh / New York City
from *Tamarisk*, Number 4: 1977 / Philadelphia
Editors: Dennis Barone & Deborah Ducoff-Barone

Wiley B. Perry / Birmingham, Alabama
from *Aura*, Volume 3, Number 1: 1976 / Birmingham, Alabama
Editor: Steven Ford Brown

Faith Echtermeyer / Saint Helena, California
from *Gallimaufry*, Number 2: 1973 / Arlington, Virginia
Editor: Mary MacArthur

Jane Miller/Champaign, Illinois
from *Me Too*, Number 3: 1976/Iowa City, Iowa & New York City
Editors: Mary Stroh & Patty Markert

433

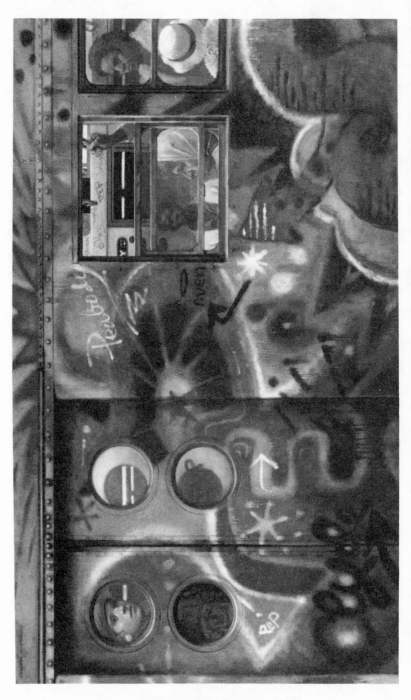

Colleen Browning/New York City
from *Painted Bride Quarterly*, Volume 4, Number 2: 1976/Philadelphia
Editors: Louise Simons & R. Daniel Evans

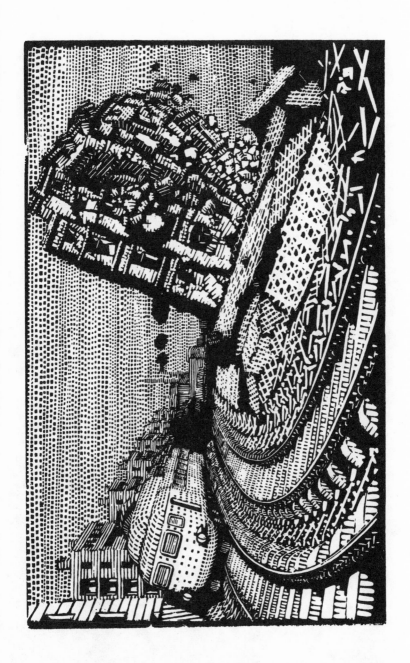

Palle Nielson / Denmark
from *Late Day*, Curbstone Press: 1976 / Willimantic, Connecticut
Editors: Alexander Taylor & Judith Doyle

435

Larence Shustak / whereabouts unknown
from *Trace*: 1968 / Hollywood, California
Editor: James Boyer May

Barbara Hawkins/Lawrence, Kansas
from *Sunday Clothes*, Volume 1, Number 3: 1971/Hermosa, South Dakota
Editor: Linda Hasselstrom

Owen Seumptewa/Oraibi, Arizona
from *Sun Tracks*: Spring 1977/Tucson, Arizona
Editors: Carol Kirk; Ray Armstrong; Faith Seota; Larry Evers

438

Mark Aronoff/Marysville, California
from *Heirs*, Volume 6, Number 1: 1975-76
Editors: Alfred D. Garcia; Jill Immerman; Ernest J. Oswald

Bil Paul/San Mateo, California
from *Second Coming*, Volume 2, Numbers 4 & 5: 1973/San Francisco
Editor: A. D. Winans

440

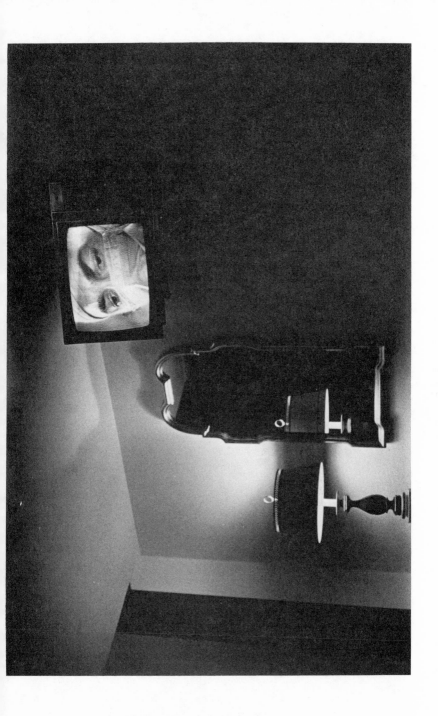

Jim Wallace / San Francisco
from *Combinations*, Number 2: 1976 / Greenfield Center, New York
Editor: Mary Ann Lynch

R. C. Gorman / Taos, New Mexico
from *Sunday Clothes*, Volume 1, Number 1: 1971 / Hermosa, South Dakota
Editor: Linda Hasselstrom

Rolando Mercado / Sun Valley, California
from *Contemporary Quarterly*, Volume 2, Number 2: 1977 / Los Angeles
Editor: Ken Atchity

Ena Swansea Whisnant / Sullivans Island, North Carolina
from *Vanishing Species*, Red Clay Books: 1975 / Charlotte, North Carolina
Editor: Charleen Swansea

Russel Lockwood/Brooklyn, New York
from *Grub Street*, Number 5: 1977/Somerville, Massachusetts
Editors: Alan Ball; Pat Russell; et al

Greg Laska / Elyria, Ohio
from *Firelands Arts Review*, Volume V: 1976 / Huron, Ohio
Editor: Joel Rudinger

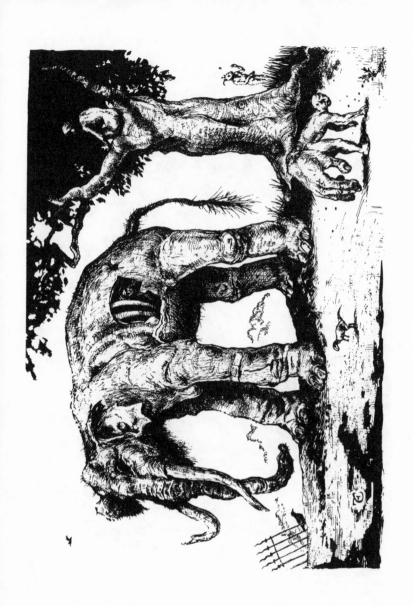

Tom Chalkley / Baltimore
from *Gargoyle*, Number 2: 1976 / Chevy Chase, Maryland
Editors: Richard Peabody; John Elsberg; Gretchen Johnsen

447

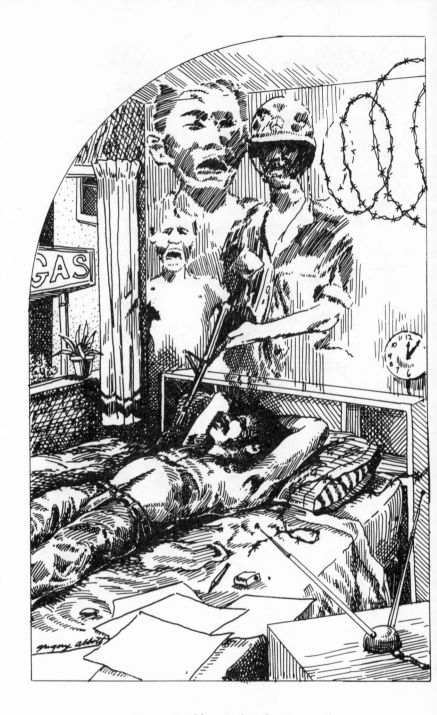

Gregory L. Abbott / Salt Lake City, Utah
from *Demilitarized Zones*, East River Anthology: 1976 / Montclair, New Jersey
Editors: Jan Barry & W. D. Ehrhart

448

Author / Visual Artist
&
Press / Magazine

AUTOBIOGRAPHICAL NOTES

AUTHOR AUTOBIOGRAPHICAL NOTES

Note: Where authors are deceased, notes were taken from biographical sources or from information supplied by individuals. In some cases we either could not contact authors or they did not supply biographical information; in those cases we either took information from other sources or entered only their names in this list.

Due to deadline demands, those notes received late are entered at the end of this list, and not in alphabetical order.

The editors of this anthology apologize for any credits not given. Because our notes are based mostly on what was supplied by the authors, they may not be complete. Also, consideration should be given to the fact this anthology had its beginnings over two-and-a-half years ago.

The editors refer the reader to the following sources for additional information concerning authors and presses/magazines: Small Press Record Of Books In Print; International Directory Of Little Magazines And Small Presses; Directory Of Small Magazine/Press Editors And Publishers *(all from Dustbooks in Paradise, California). The reader may also consult his/her librarian for other sources such as* Contemporary Authors, Books In Print *and so on.*

*   *   *   *   *   *   *

ABBOTT, GREGORY. Born 1945 in Saint George, Utah. Is half owner of Abbott Interior Design. Has done murals for ten years. Presently lives and works in Salt Lake City, Utah. Has traveled in Vietnam, Japan, Hong Kong, New York.   Has published in Utah Holiday magazine; Improvement Era; Coast magazine; Art Week. Some exhibitions: Chautaqua Exhibition of American Art Award (New York); Rutgers National Drawing (Rutgers University); Davidson National Print and Drawing Show, Purchase Award (Stowe Gallery, North Carolina); One Man Show (Lawson Galleries, San Francisco); Special Guest Artist (6th Annual Bishop Art Show, California).

ADAMS, JOHN. Born 1930 in Zillah, Washington. Is presently Professor of Medieval English at Washington State University at Pullman.   "The sense of time and place contain the essence of experience."   Has traveled in England. Major publications: TWO PLUS TWO EQUALS MINUS FOUR (novel, Macmillan); AN ESSAY ON BREWING, ETC.; BEEKEEPING: THE GENTLE CRAFT; BACKYARD POULTRY (all from Doubleday).

ALEIXANDRE, VICENTE. Born 1899 in Malaga, Spain. Lives in Madrid. Is going blind, but writing. Has been a poet since 1928. In 1977 he was awarded the Nobel Prize for Literature for his TWENTY POEMS OF VICENTE ALEIXANDRE from Seventies Press. Other publications include LA DE-STRUCCION O EL AMOR (Signo, Madrid, 1944); SOMBRA DEL PARAISO (Adan, Madrid, 1944); HISTORIA DEL CORAZON (Espasa Calpe, Madrid, 1954); POEMAS DE LA CONSUMACION (Plaza & Janes, Barcelona, 1968); and many more.

ARONOFF, MARK: see end of this listing.

ASSED, NAGIB: see end of this listing.

BALL, BO. Born 1937 in Davenport, Virginia; presently living and teaching in Decatur, Georgia, at Agnes Scott College. His stories have appeared in Chicago Review; Prairie Schooner; Southern Humanities Review; Roanoke Review; Box 749.

BARAKA, AMIRI. Born 1934 in Newark, New Jersey. Is presently in Newark working on "arts & politics." Has been assistant professor of African Studies at the State University of New York at Stoney Brook, New York.   Philosophy: "Marxist-Leninist, see Mao's 'Yenan Forum on Arts and Literature.' "   His books include SELECTED POETRY, and SELECTED PLAYS AND PROSE, both from William Morrow Publishers. The poem in this anthology appeared in SELECTED POETRY as well as the nominating periodical, Contemporary Quarterly.   The editors refer the reader to Lorenzo Thomas' "Baraka In Newark" in this anthology, for an in-depth portrait.

BARKAN, RENEE. Born 1952 in Fort Benning, Georgia.   Work experiences include "every shit job in the book and a few that aren't!" She's presently living and working in New York City when not traveling. She spends her summers in Vermont.   "My most recent trip was last year. I spent a month traveling through the Yucatan photographing ruins in Chichen-Itza, Uxmal, Tulum, etc. Being an Army brat I have traveled and lived in many places throughout the USA and Europe—I have made two cross-country trips on my own and have also traveled extensively through Europe though I am most familiar with Paris, Barcelona, and Ibiza. I have lived in five states and two countries all before the age of 10."

BATKI, JOHN: see end of this listing.

BENNETT, JOHN: see Vagabond Press in the press/magazine listing.

BERRIGAN, TED. Born 1934 in Providence, Rhode Island. Is presently teaching at Stevens Technical College in New York City. He was a core faculty member at Naropa Institute from 1975-1980.   He's traveled in Korea, Japan, England, France, Italy, Mexico, The Netherlands, Germany, Switzerland, Canada, and Luxemburg. Philosophy: "American pragmatic confusionism. Constant and cocky."

"Crystal" also appeared in RED WAGON, Yellow Press; "Things To Do In Providence" also appeared in Chicago, and Paris Review. Other books include MANY HAPPY RETURNS; IN THE EARLY MORNING RAIN; SO GOING AROUND CITIES: New and Selected Poems, 1958-1980.

BIRKBECK, BIG JOHN. Born 1930 in Mason City, Iowa. Makes a living as a technical illustrator and has for the past 15 years, in Iowa City, Iowa. "Spent first part of life doing everything I shouldn't have. Blew three careers: Military, Industrial, Academic. In danger of blowing present one, but in control of the situation. Have always employed the oral tradition of storytelling even in childhood. Impossible to capture tone, gestures, manner on paper, but try to, in form of poetry, stories. Love to draw cartoons and do watercolour paintings for fun, and spend most of my leisure time reading just about anything between cheap pulp porn on through Tolstoy, Nabokov, Twain, Orwell, and so many others it would be tedious to list them. John Berryman is my boss." Publications include TWELVE-PLUS TWO; DONNELLY'S BEVERAGE; FRANCE POEMS, as well as poems, stories and drawings in The Iowa City Reading Series Magazine; The New Pioneer; People Watcher; The Iowa City Press-Citizen; The Daily Iowan; The Des Moines Register; The Salvador Dali Fan Club.

BLAZEK, DOUGLAS: see Ole, in press/magazine listing.

BLY, ROBERT: see The Seventies, in press/magazine listing.

BOND, RUSKIN. Born of English parents in India. Has lived for the last several years in Mussoorie, a hill station in the Himalayas. He writes that he "cannot stay away from the mountains for very long" and elsewhere says, "... Once you have lived in the mountains, you belong to them, and must come back again and again. There is no escape." In recent years he has written frequently for The Christian Science Monitor (London) and Blackwood's Magazine. He has written several books for children; in 1958 his novelTHE ROOM ON THE ROOF was awarded the John Llewellyn Rhys Prize (London). He's had two short story collections published in India and other stories or essays have been included in WORLD'S BEST CONTEMPORARY SHORT STORIES (Ace Books, New York); The Lady; Short Story International; The National Observer.

BOYLE, MARTIN III: see end of this listing.

BROWNING, COLLEEN: see end of this listing.

BRUCHAC, JOSEPH: see The Greenfield Review, in press/magazine listing.

BUKOWSKI, CHARLES. Born 1920 in Andernach, Germany. Following that bit of information on the back cover of his COLD DOGS IN THE COURT-YARD (Chicago, 1965) is "... something to do with the war. Old man American soldier. Brought his German wife and me over here in 1922 and the land was gifted with a hardmouth poet. Meaning me. I stood around a lot as a kid and I didn't learn much. I am still in the process. Went to Los Angeles City College for two years—journalism, art and diddling; only the latter has held water for me. I didn't go to the war.

"In my 20's, I thought I was a short story writer and I starved and lived in little rooms and wrote hundreds of short stories, 5 or 6 a week, sending them to the Atlantic Monthly and Harper's, and, naturally, they all came back running and punched in the mouth. I finally landed one in the old Story Magazine, the one with the orange cover. Then, I said to hell with it and got drunk for ten years. Then I started writing again and this time poetry. Had luck. Five books of collected poetry: FLOWER, FIST AND BESTIAL WAIL; LONGSHOT POEMS FOR BROKE PLAYERS; RUN WITH THE HUNTED; IT CATCHES MY HEART IN ITS HANDS, and CRUCIFIX IN A DEATH HAND.... and now, COLD DOGS.... and they have their bones!"

Travel: Germany, France, Canada, Mexico. Presently lives in San Pedro, California. Neither Bukowski nor Black Sparrow have a record of where the poems in this anthology appeared prior to the Black Sparrow books. BS thinks that "If We Take" was not previously published. Besides MOCKINGBIRD WISH ME LUCK, from which these poems were nominated, Bukowski has many other books, among them THE DAYS RUN AWAY LIKE WILD HORSES OVER THE HILLS (Black Sparrow Press); the ones listed by him above; POEMS WRITTEN BEFORE JUMPING OUT OF AN 8 STOREY WINDOW; ERECTIONS, EJACULATIONS, EXHIBITIONS AND GENERAL TALES OF ORDINARY MADNESS; MAYBE TOMORROW. He's written a screenplay, "Barfly."

BUMPUS, JERRY. Born 1937 in Mount Vernon, Illinois. He teaches at San Diego State University and lives with his wife, a World War II historian, and two daughters who are divers aboard the retired U.S. Navy destroyer "Lester." "My aesthetics: bringing in the world is the objective—the language, craft, art serve to charge the reading experience with the tension, exhilaration, dignity, sublimity which burn in us during those rare moments when we become aware that truth is not only coming down *now* but that it has been constantly present, just under the skin of things." He's published about 100 short stories, and 20 or so have been anthologized in Foley's BEST AMERICAN SHORT STORIES; THE O. HENRY PRIZE; THE SECRET LIFE OF OUR TIMES (Doubleday); CUTTING EDGES (Holt, Rinehart & Winston), and THE PUSHCART PRIZE, where the story in this anthology also appeared. A novel, ANACONDA (1967) was published by December Press. A short story collection, THINGS IN PLACE (1975) is available from the Fiction Collective. The Carpenter Press is publishing another collection of his stories.

CARVER, RAYMOND. Born 1939. He is presently living in Syracuse, New York and is a Professor of English at Syracuse University. The story appearing in this anthology also appeared in BEST LITTLE MAGAZINE FICTION, 1971 (New York University Press). He's also been anthologized in (among others) THE BEST AMERICAN SHORT STORIES (Houghton-Mifflin, 1967); SHORT STORIES FROM THE LITERARY MAGAZINES (Scott, Foresman, 1971); NEW VOICES IN AMERICAN POETRY (Winthrop Publishing Company, 1973); PRIZE STORIES: THE O. HENRY AWARDS (Doubleday, 1973, 1974, 1976); ALL OUR SECRETS ARE THE SAME: NEW FICTION FROM ESQUIRE (W.W. Norton, 1976); THE PUSHCART PRIZE: BEST OF THE SMALL PRESSES, 1976, 1979). His books include WINTER INSOMNIA (poems, Kayak Press, 1970); AT NIGHT THE SALMON MOVE (poems, Capra Press, 1976); WILL YOU PLEASE BE QUIET, PLEASE? (stories, McGraw-Hill, 1976); FURIOUS SEASONS (stories, Capra Press, 1977). His awards include a National Book Award nomination in fiction, 1977, for WILL YOU PLEASE BE QUIET, PLEASE? and a Guggenheim Memorial Fellowship, 1979-1980. He was founding editor of Quarry West magazine.

CASTILLO, OTTO RENE. Born 1936 in Quezaltenango, Guatemala. At the age of 17 he was already a student leader and was exiled that same year, 1954, for the first time. His short adult life was laced with exile and imprisonment although he also managed to study law at the University of Guatemala, do graduate work at Leipzig, Germany, and publish several books of poetry. Early in 1966 he incorporated himself definitively in the F.A.R. (Revolutionary Armed Forces) under the command of Cesar Montes. In March 1967, after 15 days of eating only roots and weeds, he and a girl with whom he was standing guard were wounded in an ambush by the military. They were captured and tortured for four days, after which they were burned alive. Members of both families and friends who went to the scene of the death to try to recover the bodies found only pieces of hair and charred disjointed bones, testifying to the extent of the fractures and other tortures suffered by both fighters. Otto Rene, aside from the example of his fight and life, left several books of poetry among which VAMANOS PATRIA A CAMINAR (from which this poem is taken) is the best known.

CAVANAGH, JOHN. Born 1952 in Englewood, New Jersey. Is presently a photo-researcher at Magnum Photos, Inc. in New York City. He's been a free-lance photographer, graphic arts pressman, dishwasher, custom printer and writer. "Ambiguity leaves room for psychic material to enter. The photograph must deal with reality, i.e. physical fact, which can express emotional content. In short, less is more, more or less. Life is essentially bizarre." He's traveled in Canada, Baja, San Francisco, Los Angeles and Colorado. His work has appeared in Modern Photography, and Soho Weekly News, and was exhibited in Rockland County Council on Arts Show; Small Works Exhibit of 80 Washington Square East Galleries; Fashion Moda Gallery (Bronx, New York).

CELINO & STEFF—THE GREATS. "I got the sheaf of poems from a friend who got it from a friend, etc. It was some summer session with kids somewhere." *—Dick Bakken, editor who nominated their work.*

CHALKLEY, TOM. Born 1955 in South Bend, Indiana. Presently lives in Baltimore where he works as a free-lance illustrator, chiefly for public interest periodicals. Is a lead singer in The Reason, a Rock 'n Roll band. "Cooked chicken two months at Gino's. I've pasted up about 300 minor newspapers in Washington, D.C. area (including Duckpin Bowler, and Mothers of Twins); have done editorial cartoons for County Courier, a rural newspaper. My goal, ultimately, is to create art that has power as propaganda and legitimacy as art, in whatever medium. I've pretty much forsaken surrealism as a luxury of a bygone age—it's okay for other folks. Present struggle has moral rewards and is remunerative. As to Art..." He's been to Xalapa, Mexico; Grinnell, Iowa and Seattle, Washington ("great train ride"). "Formerly given to astral voyages but in recent years stick to Greyhound." He also had work in NOTHING CAN BE DONE, EVERYTHING IS POSSIBLE by Byron Kennard, 1980.

CHAPPELL, FRED. Born 1936 in Canton, North Carolina. Is presently an English professor at the University of North Carolina at Greensboro. He's married and has one son. Received his B.A. and M.A. at Duke University. In addition to publication of the essay which appears in this anthology, in SMART, he has to his credit IT IS TIME, LORD; THE INKLING; DAGON; THE WORLD BETWEEN THE EYES; THE GAUDY PLACE; RIVER; BLOOD-FIRE; WIND MOUNTAIN (all books). Awards include: Rockefeller; National Institute of Arts and Letters; Roanoke-Chowan Poetry Award; Prix du Meilleur (Academie Francaise); Sir Walter Raleigh Prize. Philosophy: " ' Work a little every day, without hope and without despair.'—Isak Dinesen"

CLIFTON, MERRITT: see Samisdat in the press/magazine listing.

COHAN, TONY: see Acrobat Books in the press/magazine listing.

CREELEY, ROBERT. Born 1926 in Arlington, Massachusetts. Presently in Buffalo, New York where he teaches at State University of New York. Otherwise he lives in Placitas, New Mexico. Author of the collections of poetry FOR LOVE; PIECES; LATER; and of prose THE GOLD DIGGERS; THE ISLAND (a novel)and MABEL—A STORY, in which the piece in this anthology, nominated by Unmuzzled Ox, later appeared.

ELLIOTT, PATRICIA. 1917-1977. Born in Saskatoon, Saskatchewan. She studied music with Marjorie Wilson and received her LRSM from London, England. Graduated from the University of Saskatchewan with a Bachelor of Music degree. Studied piano with Rudolf Ganz in Chicago. In her work she combined poetry, art and music. "She had a great feeling for friendship, and that bond I think came from where life was raw, and the imagination had room to grow."—Art Cuelho, editor of Black Jack.

EVERHARD, JAMES P. Born 1946 in Dayton, Ohio. Is currently Graduation Evaluator at George Washington University and is starting his M.A. in English. He's bagged groceries, unloaded trucks, been in the Navy and done cafeteria work. "I came out gaily and poetically at the old Mass Transit writer's open readings in Washington, D.C. in 1975." Ideals: "Leftist-liberal tendencies, with wide-sweeping anarchistic exuberances. I like words to do what they want to do and I like them to do what I want them to do and I like them to do what you like them to do. My credo is pleasure with responsibility. Make it all count. My favorite poet of all times is Rainer Maria Rilke who's taught me everything I know (just about) about angels. I also like Robert Duncan for his values. Gary Snyder for his desires. Stephen Dunn for his wild circus needs. Denise Levertov for all the things she does with poetry that I can't. Evelyn Thorne, editor of Epos, who taught me most of all I know. And all those Spanish poets and New York poets who turned me on to Anguish and Awe of the Mundane. Finally Robert Bly and St. Geraud, James Tate and James Wright, our best Chinese poets. My one poetic credo is read everyone and steal 'em blind. But do it with style." He's had poetry in Hanging Loose; Fag Rag; Iowa Review; Epos; Mouth of the Dragon and other magazines. Books include LANDSCAPES AND DISTANCES: POETRY OF VIRGINIA (anthology from University of Virginia Press).

FERBER, ELLEN: see Dustbooks, in the press/magazine listing.

FERLINGHETTI: see end of this listing.

FERNANDEZ, RAMON. Translator's note: Ramon Fernandez was born in the small coastal village of Casalona on April 20, 1923, of peasant stock. Of his childhood very little is known. A close friend of his, Pedro Gonzales, writes 'At an early age his soul was captured by the sea. Again and again in the early hours I would find him on the rocky pinnacle near Casalona, gazing trance-like at the distant horizon. About his work he said little. On one occasion, however, I remember him saying "I look back through my poems as if they were not mine. As if they belonged purely to space and time. A voice? Say that Space assumed one to hypnotize Time.' " Three slender volumes of Fernandez's poems have appeared in Spanish, all privately printed in Madrid: UNKNOWN WORKS (1946); TURNIPS (1949); WHERE DID THE CARBON SLEEP THAT IT AWOKE SO BLACK (1956). *Editor's note: Ramon Fernandez is a heteronym of Darrell Gray's.*

FIELD, EDWARD. Born 1924 in Brooklyn, New York. Presently lives in New York City and working on an historical novel. Philosophy: "It [writing] is a useful thing to do." Work expériences include being a farmer's helper, warehouseman, summer theater actor and machinist, and teaching poetry at Eckerd College, the Poetry Center—YMHA (New York), Hofstra College and Sarah

Lawrence. Travel: "all the way to Afghanistan." Major publications include STAND UP, FRIEND, WITH ME (Grove Press, 1963); VARIETY PHOTO-PLAYS (Grove, 1967; reprinted by Maelstrom); A FULL HEART (Sheep Meadow, 1977); ESKIMO SONGS AND STORIES (Delacorte, 1973); A GEOGRAPHY OF POETS (Bantam, 1979).

FULTON, LEN: see Dustbooks, in the press/magazine listing.

GARDNER, ISABELLA. Born 1915 in Newton, Massachusetts. Presently resides in the Hotel Chelsea in New York City and is working on a book of new poems. She's acted professionally for several years, was assistant, then associate editor of Poetry "under the aegis" of Karl Shapiro, taught poetry seminars two years for YMHA [New York], had many readings at home and abroad. "I write what I must when I can." Travel includes several visits to England, Ireland, France, Italy, and Greece and to the Carribean island of Saint Martin. Major publications include BIRTHDAYS FROM THE OCEAN; UN ALTRA INFANZIA (poems selected and translated into Italian by Alfredo Rizzardi); THE LOOKING GLASS; WEST OF CHILDHOOD; THAT WAS THEN.

GILDNER, GARY. Born 1938 in West Branch, Michigan. Graduated from Michigan State University in 1960 and received an M.A. from there in 1961, in comparative literature. His first poem appeared in his book THE RUNNER (University of Pittsburgh Press,1978); three other books from Pittsburgh are FIRST PRACTICE (1969); DIGGING FOR INDIANS (1971); NAILS (1975). Unicorn Press brought out a limited edition sequence, LETTERS FROM VICKSBURG in 1976. He's been anthologized in, among others, A GEOGRAPHY OF POETS (Bantam, 1979).

GLEN, EMILIE. Born 1937 in Fredonia, New York. She is presently living in New York City where she acts in off-Broadway plays and does free-lance writing. She has served on the editorial staff of The New Yorker. Philosophy: "Art is life. Do I write? Do I breathe? Yes I write, I breathe." She has traveled in Europe, England, Greece, Canada and the United States. Her poetry has been anthologized in New Directions; NEW VOICES; THE GOLDEN YEARS; IN TIME OF REVOLUTION and POEMS FROM THE HILLS. Her stories have appeared in BEST AMERICAN SHORT STORIES and BEST ARTICLES AND SHORT STORIES; poems have appeared in France, Switzerland, Germany, Italy, Sicily, The Philippines, The Argentine, England, Canada, New Zealand, Australia, Sweden and India; translations have appeared in, among others, Moderne; La Voix des Poetes; Trapani Nuova; she's had poems in The Nation; New York Quarterly; The North Stone Review; The Christian Science Monitor; Folio; Prairie Schooner; Weid; Confrontation; Vagabond and other magazines; she has a book of poetry, A HERO SOMEWHAT.

The poem which appears in this anthology, nominated by Second Coming, first appeared in The Miscellany.

GOEDICKE, PATRICIA. Born 1931 in Boston. Since 1971 she and her 2nd husband, novelist, short story writer and poet Leonard Wallace Robinson have been living and writing in San Miguel de Allende "enjoying its beauty and serenity" and giving occasional workshops in and around the Instituto Allende. She grew up in Hanover, New Hampshire, graduated from Middlebury College in 1953, spent the next 15 years working in publishing and getting an M.A. in Creative Writing at Ohio University as well as teaching there and at Hunter College. She met her second husband in 1968. Some of her poetry books include BETWEEN OCEANS (Harcourt, Brace, 1968); FOR THE FOUR CORNERS (Ithaca House, 1976); CROSSING THE SAME RIVER (The University of Massachusetts Press, 1980). She has been anthologized in THE TREASURY OF AMERICAN POETRY (Doubleday, 1978); THE ARDIS ANTHOLOGY OF NEW AMERICAN POETRY (Ardis Press, 1977); SINCE FEELING IS FIRST (New Letters, 1976).

GOODMAN, PAUL. 1911-1972. Born in New York City. Received his doctorate in humanities from the University of Chicago and taught and lectured at various schools, including Sarah Lawrence and Black Mountain College. A novelist, social commentator, poet, literary critic and psychologist, he was consistently controversial and thought-provoking. Goodman's writings have appeared widely, and his best-known books include GROWING UP ABSURD; THE EMPIRE CITY; COMPULSORY MIS-EDUCATION; GESTALT THERAPY. The essay in this anthology, nominated from Unmuzzled Ox, first appeared in WIN (November 1969) and was reprinted in NATURE HEALS: The Psychological Essays of Paul Goodman, edited by Taylor Stoebur (Free Life Editions).

GORMAN, R.C.: see end of this listing.

GRAY, DARRELL: see Suction, in the press/magazine listing.

GYLLENHAAL, LIZA. Born 1953 in Cleveland, Ohio. "The plight of American poetry is American academe: the treadmill of making a living by teaching what one loves best, but not necessarily teaches well. I made a decision after getting a B.A. at Iowa [University of Iowa, Iowa City] and seeing how the workshop world operates to get the hell out of it and into the real world. I work nine to five and then come home and write, and read, and write. Some kind of integrity is salvaged for me this way. The best minds of our generation are being destroyed by the universities." She has a background in copywriting, editing, and graphics for New York publishing firms; freelance writing for major trade houses. Is presently advertising manager of Columbia University Press. She's traveled all over the U.S. as far west as Lincoln, Nebraska. Also, "lots of time in Florida. Studied junior year abroad in Wales with Welsh poet Raymond Garlick. Since then have traveled back to France and parts of the Continent."

HAWKINS, BARBARA. Born 1947 in Columbia, Missouri. She is presently living in Lawrence, Kansas, where she earns a living by being a substitute rural mail carrier once a week. She taught at the University of Missouri while working on her master's, and has been an aid in mental hospitals, worked in various fast food "joints", worked at Orange Julius in Hollywood and shoveled manure. Philosophy: "never stop working". She's traveled within the U.S. and Mexico. The painting appearing in this anthology, nominated from Sunday Clothes (Lame Johnny Press), also appeared in Gail Shen's Chinatown in Columbia, Missouri. Her works have appeared in shows at Park Central Gallery (Springfield, Missouri); Jewish Community Center (Kansas City, Missouri); Kansas Watercolor Society Juried Show (Wichita); Douglas Drake Gallery (Kansas City, Kansas); Women Artists, Paperworks 1979 (University of Kansas, Lawrence).

HERNANDEZ, MIGUEL. 1910-1942. Spanish peasant poet, largely self-educated and influenced during the Spanish Civil War by his friends Aleixandre and Neruda and by his experiences as a Republican volunteer. Many of his poems were meant to be recited to the fighting troops. Apart from four satirical one-act plays, "Teatro en La Guerra"(1937),he wrote the more traditional verse drama, "El Labrador de MasAire"(1937),before the tragic post-war years. He was kept in prison in Alicante where he died of tuberculosis. Later, more tragic war poems appear in EL HOMBRE ACECHA (1939) and CANIONERO Y ROMANCERO DE AUSENCIAS (1938-41) in the manner of the old songbooks, and dwell on his separation from his wife and son.

HILTON, DAVID. Born 1938 in Oakland, California. He is presently in Baltimore where he's been teaching English ("a heavy load of freshman composition") at Anne Arundel Community College in nearby Arnold since 1971. "My writing is getting plainer, moving from sparse to sparser maybe. I seem unable to 'make things up'. I like to get down, in the most precise language I can manage, what is directly before my senses and sentiments. To illustrate, the elegant perpetual-motion machines of an Ashbery or Charles Wright are impossible for me to make. Rube Goldberg pretty much exhausted that line of work. Solipsism may be a fact of our existence, but as the stuff of current magazine verse it's a drag: flashy wardrope *sans* emperor. I like real toads—and real gardens, too. And I have no doubt at all that they're out there, and that I'm here, and that the seeming separation is in fact a realm of connection." He was in the Army for two years, worked several years in factories, and worked ten years in "low-level academia." He has traveled widely in the U.S. "as continental drift brought me from California to Maryland." In the summer of 1978 he toured England and Ireland for six weeks. "Ireland especially a joy." Major publications: HULADANCE (The Crossing Press, 1976) and THE CANDLEFLAME (Toothpaste Press, 1976). His poetry has appeared in Poetry (Chicago); Poetry Northwest; New Letters; BRIGHT MOMENTS: A Collection of Jazz Poetry (Abraxas Press, 1980); THE ACTUALIST ANTHOLOGY (The Spirit That Moves Us, 1977).

HOLLO, ANSELM. Born 1934 in Helsinki, Finland. Presently teaching in Virginia. He has been a journalist, a broadcaster for the BBC in London and a translator. He's traveled western and northern Europe and the U.S. Books include MAYA (Cape/Grossman, London & New York, 1970); SOJOURNER MICROCOSMS (Blue Wind Press, Berkeley, 1977); HEAVY JARS (Toothpaste Press, West Branch, Iowa, 1977); FINITE CONTINUED (Blue Wind, 1980); WITH RUTH IN MIND (Station Hill, Barrytown, 1980).

HOLUB, MIROSLAV. Born 1923 in Pizen, Czechoslovakia. He is a distinguished research chemist and is regarded as the leading Czech poet of his generation. His first poems appeared in a periodical in 1947 and his first collection in 1958. His books translated into English include SELECTED POEMS published by Penguin in their series, Modern European Poets, 1967, and ALTHOUGH published by Grossman, Cape Editions. He has participated in several international poetry reading festivals. He's married, with one son.

HONGO, GARRETT KAORU. Born 1951 in Hilo, Hawaii. He's presently a teaching assistant in literature and completing an MFA in Creative Writing (poetry) at the University of California at Irvine. Work experience includes poet-in-residence for the Seattle Arts Commission; Director of the Asian Exclusion Act (a Seattle-based Asian American theater group); meter-reader for the Los Angeles Department of Water and Power; gardener's apprentice. He's traveled to Japan on a Thomas J. Watson Fellowship in 1973-74. His book of poetry, with Alan Chory Lau and Lawson Fusao Inada, THE BUDDHA BANDITS DOWN HIGHWAY 99 is from Buddhahead Press, Irvine, California, 1978. He's published poetry in Poetry in Amerasia Journal; Antaeus; Bachy; Bamboo Ridge; Greenfield Review; Harvard Magazine; Hawaii Review; The New Yorker. Philosophy: "Towards an Impure Poetry" by Pablo Neruda; "Essay on Historiography" by Ssu-ma Ch'ien; "A Flower Does Not Talk" by Shibayama Rushi.

HYDE, LEWIS. Born 1945 in Boston, Massachusetts. Is presently living in Watertown, Massachusetts and working on a prose book THE GIFT ("variously described as 'an economy of the imagination' and 'about poetry and money.'") Was a graduate student, teacher, alcoholism counselor, writer and social science researcher. The poem he translated in this anthology, nominated from Seventies Press, originally appeared in American Poetry Review. Major publications include A LONGING FOR THE LIGHT: Selected Poems of Vicente Aleixandre (Harper & Row, 1979); "Alcohol & Poetry: John Berryman & the Booze Talking" (monograph, 1977); THE GIFT: Poetry and the Erotic Life of Property (forthcoming from Houghton-Mifflin).

JACOBSEN, ROLF. Born 1907 in Oslo, Norway. He's a journalist. He matriculated at Oslo, 1926. Married 1940, and has two sons. Some collections of his poems: JORD & JERN, 1933; FJERNTOG, 1951; BREV TIL LYSET, 1960; HEADLINES, 1969. Translations of his poems are included in anthologies in English, German, French, Russian, Dutch and Romanian. Some awards: Gyldendal's Jubilee Legacy, 1961; Dobloug Prize, Swedish Academy, 1968; Onskedikt Prize, Norwegian Broadcasting, 1979.

JONAS, STEVE. 1927-1970. (Biographical note by John Wieners, 1975): "Stephen Robert Jonas Jones was raised in Atlantean Georgia, attended Boston Universities. He worked in the U.S. Armored Services, studied under officers of U.S. Department of Army. Armory history includes among these offices LOVE, THE POEM, THE SEA & OTHER PIECES EXAMINED BY STEVE JONAS (for Michael Farmer, USN), White Rabbit Press, San Francisco, 1956; TRANSMUTATIONS (Ferry Press, London, 1968); SELECTED POEMS (Stone Soup Press, Boston, 1973). He also became involved with racial insurrectionists' compositions. Temptations to earlier condemnations, among these, towards godly anarchism, staunch witless assumptions. His experiences of a hereafter took place upon the dinner time of the second month in the first year of this decade (1970); his final resting place is Mt. Hope Cemetery, Jamaica Plain, Massachusetts."

JOZSEF, ATTILA. (This information is taken from Jozsef's Curriculum Vitae (1937) and a Chronology, both in ATTILA JOZSEF: Selected Poems and Texts): "I was born in Budapest [Hungary] in 1905 ... My father ... left the country when I was three years old, and I was sent to live with foster-parents ... I even started working as a swineherd, like most poor children in the village of Ocsod ... When I was seven years old, my mother ... brought me back to Budapest ... [She] supported us—me and my two sisters—by doing washing and housework ... I skipped school and played in the streets. In the third-grade reader, however, I found some interesting stories about King Attila and so I threw myself into reading. These stories about the King of the Huns interested me not only because my name was Attila but also because my foster-parents at Ocsod used to call me Steve [they believed there was no such name as Attila] ... I believe the discovery of the tales about Attila had a decisive influence on all my ambitions from then on; in the last analysis it was perhaps this that led me to literature. This was the experience that turned me into a person who thinks, one who listens to the opinions of others, but examines them critically in his own mind; someone who resigns himself to being called Steve until it is proved that his name is Attila, as he himself had thought all along.

"... there were times when I stepped into the line in front of a food store at nine in the evening, only to be told, when my turn came up at eight in the morning, that the cooking lard was all gone. ... My mother died in 1919 at Christmas time. ... I served on the tugs Vihar, Torok, and Tatar of the Atlantica Ocean Shipping Co. ... I tutored at Mezohegyes to earn my room and board [at the Demke boarding school]. I finished the sixth year of gymnasium with excellent grades, despite the fact that, due to adolescent problems, I had several times tried to commit suicide, ... my first poems appeared at this time; Nyugat published some of my poems written at the age of seventeen. They took me for a prodigy; actually I was just an orphan.

"After the sixth year of gymnasium I left school because I was lonely and had nothing to do ... " Jozsef was urged by two teachers to take the exam for his graduation certificate, and graduated a year ahead of his classmates. At about that time he was prosecuted for blasphemy in one of his poems, and was acquitted by the High Court. He was a crop-watchman and field-hand, a book salesman and a clerk in a bank. He passed his teaching exams at Szeged University with distinction, but his examiner in Hungarian philology said he would not allow him to become a secondary school teacher because "The kind of person who writes this sort of poem [one which appeared in Szeged, a periodical] is not to be trusted with the education of the future generation." The poem, "With A Pure Heart" became famous. He attended the University at Vienna, at twenty, and then the Sorbonne. He returned to Budapest and the university there but didn't take his teacher's diploma because he felt he wouldn't get a job teaching anyhow. "Then I was overtaken by a succession of such unexpected blows that, however toughened I was by life, I simply could not go on.... I left my job, since I realized I could not stay on as a burden... Since then I have been living on my writing. I am the editor of Szep Szo, a literary and critical periodical." Books: BEGGAR OF BEAUTY (1922); THAT'S NOT ME SHOUTING (1925); FATHERLESS AND MOTHERLESS (1929); his fourth volume (poems and Villon-translations) is confiscated and Jozsef prosecuted, after which he begins psychoanalytic treatment; NIGHT IN THE SLUMS (1932) BEAR DANCE (1934, new and selected poems).

In a 1937 meeting with Thomas Mann, police prevent him from a public reading of his poem welcoming Mann. On April 11, 1937 he was sentenced to lifelong correction in a workhouse, on counts of sedition, espionage, betrayal of secrets, indecent exposure, penal idleness, constant creation of scandals and pathological prevarication. On November 4 his sisters take him to Balatonszarszo. On December 3 he threw himself under the wheels of a freight train.

KABIR. Died 1518. Indian poet and Hindu sectarian reformer. The little that is known of his life derives mainly from traditions handed down by his sect. His poetry is the expression of his religious eclecticism. He's believed to have taught only orally, and the canon of his works is uncertain. Three collections written in a mixture of Hindi dialects are generally considered authentic: the BIJAK ('Account Book'); a collection in the Sikh ADI GRANTH and the GRANTHA-VALI ('Collected Writings'). KABIR POEMS, translated by Robert Bly, is from The Seventies Press.

KESSLER, STEPHEN. Born 1947 in Los Angeles. He's lived for several years in the Santa Cruz mountains. "Imaginative writing in this country is the farming of language, the act of restoring to our speech its native nutritive values by way of attention to and cultivation of its natural music. Electronic folklore need not be ignored. I write between firewood and radio." Kessler learned Spanish in high school, has traveled in Spain, worked as a journalist, and cooks with garlic. His poems, translations and articles have appeared in numerous literary magazines and alternative newspapers, and in the following books and chapbooks of poetry: NOSTALGIA OF THE FORTUNETELLER (Kayak Books); POEM TO WALT DISNEY (ManRoot Books); DESTRUCTION OR LOVE (translations from the Spanish of Vicente Aleixandre; Green Horse Press); BEAUTY FATIGUE (Alcatraz Editions); HOMAGE TO NERUDA (translations of eight Chilean poets, Editorial Puelche); he is also the editor of ALCATRAZ/an assemblage (Alcatraz Editions).

KOERTGE, RONALD. Born 1940 in Olney, Illinois. He's been a writing teacher at Pasadena City College since 1965. Philosophy: "Do the work." Major publications: THE BOOGIEMAN (novel, W. W. Norton, 1980); and the books of poetry SEX OBJECT (Little Caesar Press); 12 PHOTOGRAPHS OF YELLOWSTONE (Red Hill Press); THE FATHER POEMS (Sumac Press); more.

KOOSER, TED: see New Salt Creek Reader, in the press/magazine listing.

KORNBLUM, ALLAN: see Toothpaste Press, in the press/magazine listing.

KORNBLUM, CINDA: see Toothpaste Press, in the press/magazine listing.

KRYSS, T. L. Born 1948 in Cleveland, Ohio. Present location and work: "Cleveland, dispatcher. Hobbies—none. Disease—baseball. Electric shock therapy—three kids, wife, two cats, dog." He has been a stockboy, mailboy, orderly, and "mangler in laundry." He's traveled "in San Francisco, Sacramento and Sandusky." Major publications include MUSIC IN THE WINEPRESS, PARROTS IN THE FLAMES (Vagabond Press, 1975); SUNFLOWER RIVER (Deadangel Press, 1972); KRULIK KSIEGA (Ayizan Press, circa 1969); he was anthologized in NEW AMERICAN AND CANADIAN POETRY (Beacon Press, 1971).

LALLY, MICHAEL. Born 1942 in Orange, New Jersey. Is presently in New York City "where I continue to write my own works, free lance other writing and act in movies while raising two kids." He's been a handyman, dishwasher, recreational therapist in a mental institution, college instructor, bookstore clerk, book reviewer for the Washington Post, editor, and a film actor ("so far only in 'B' horror films"). Philosophy: "to write 'poetry' that never depends on the traditional poetic devices for its impact and that is true to the language and experience of my life and imagination." He's traveled all the 48 continental states throughout the late 50's and 60's, and Puerto Rico, Italy, Spain, France and England in 1974. The poem in this anthology, nominated by Z Press, also appeared in chapbook form from Wyrd Press, and in the anthology NONE OF THE ABOVE. Major publications include ROCKY DIES YELLOW (Blue Wind Press); CATCH MY BREATH (Salt Lick Press); JUST LET ME DO IT (Vehicle Editions); DUES (Stone Wall Press); NONE OF THE ABOVE (editor; Crossing Press). His work has also appeared in Partisan Review; American Review; Gum; others.

LASKA, GREG. Elyria, Ohio. Unable to get further information.

LIFSHIN, LYN. Born 1945 in Burlington, Vermont. She's presently in Niskayuga, New York, teaching, editing and writing. "In the Eskimo language, 'to

breathe' and 'to make a poem' are the same." Her books include BLACK AP-
PLES (Crossing Press); OFFERED BY OWNER (Slohm Association); UPSTATE
MADONNA (Crossing Press); LEANING SOUTH (Red Dust Press); TANGLED
VINES (Beacon Press).

LOCKWOOD, RUSSEL: see end of this listing.

LONG, DAVID. Born 1948. Has worked a number of years in Montana's Poets
and Writers in Schools program. The poem which appears in this anthology,
nominated by Porch, also appears in his EARLY RETURNS from Jawbone
Press (Seattle, 1979). He has an unpublished manuscript of stories, SALVAGE
RIGHTS.

LOPATE, PHILLIP. Born 1943. Grew up in Brooklyn, New York where he attended Eastern District High School in the Williamsburgh section, and graduated from Columbia University in 1964. He has traveled in Europe, Morocco,
California and Mexico, always returning to New York City to live and work.
Since 1969 he has taught children to do their own creative writing, filmmaking,
theater and comic books, under the auspices of the Teachers & Writers Collabo-
rative. His experiences there formed the basis of his education book BEING
WITH CHILDREN. His poetry has appeared in The World; the Village Voice;
the Yale Literary Review; Z; Sun; Liberation and others. A special issue of Blue
Pig magazine was devoted to his poems. His fiction has been published in The
Paris Review; Columbia Review; in an anthology A CINCH; and was selected
for THE BEST AMERICAN SHORT STORIES OF 1974. He has also written
on film for The Thousand Eyes; Moviegoer; Cinemabook; The Herald; Pacific
Film Archives; collections of his poems, THE DAILY ROUND and THE EYES
DON'T ALWAYS WANT TO STAY OPEN are from Sun Press; a novel, CON-
FESSIONS OF SUMMER is from Doubleday, 1979.

LORCA, FEDERICO GARCIA. 1898-1936. Spanish poet and dramatist and a
talented musician. His first book (prose) IMPRESSIONES Y PAISAJES was
published in 1918. His first plays were produced in the 1920s. In 1929, after
the public success of the volume of verse ROMANCERO GITANO (Gypsy Bal-
lads), he left Spain to visit New York and Cuba. On his return he co-directed
La Barraca, a government-sponsored student theatrical company that toured th
country, and in 1933 he visited Argentina. Just after the outbreak of the Civil
War, he was executed by Nationalist partisans and his body thrown into an unmarked grave. Most famous of his lyrical and partially surrealist plays in transla
tion are "La Zapatera Prodigioss" ("The Shoemaker's Prodigal Wife"),"Bodas
de Sangre" ("Blood Wedding"), "Yerma" and "La Casa de Bernarda Alba"
("The House of Bernarda Alba"). Selections of his poetry have been translated
and published in book form by Robert Bly and others.

MACEY, LEE: see end of this listing.

MAGORIAN, JAMES. Born 1942 in Palisade, Nebraska. Is presently located in Helena, Montana where he's writing poetry and exploring ghost towns. The poem that appears in this anthology, nominated by Scarecrow Press, also appeared in Samisdat. Some of his books: ALMOST NOON (The Ibis Press, Chicago, 1969); THE RED, WHITE, AND BLUE BUS (The Berkeley-Samisdat Press, 1975); PIANO TUNING AT MIDNIGHT (Laughing Bear Press, Woodinville, Washington, 1979); REVENGE (Samisdat, Richford, Vermont, 1979); SCHOOL DAZE (Peradam Publishing House, Urbana, Illinois, 1978—one of his children's books).

McDANIEL, SANDRA: no information available.

MERCADO, ROLANDO: see end of this listing.

MILLER, CHUCK. Born 1939 in Kenney, Illinois. He is currently in Iowa City, Iowa after having completed his first novel. He's been a teacher, social worker, tutor and laborer. Philosophy: "To return to some more primitive personal basis of art and in this way to speak out directly." He's traveled in Mexico, Europe, and Canada. Major publications: OXIDES; HOOKAH; 1000 SMILING CRETINS; THIN WIRE OF MYSELF (all poetry).

MILLER, E. ETHELBERT. Born 1950 in New York City. Presently Director of the Afro-American Resource Center, Howard University, Washington, D.C. Was formerly Research Associate, Institute for the Arts and Humanities, Howard University. "I write because my father lived a silent life and my mother was afraid... " Travel includes Africa, the U. S. S. R. and Cuba. Major publications include MIGRANT WORKER (1978); WOMEN SURVIVING MASSACRES AND MEN (editor, 1977); SYNERGY (1975).

MILLER, JANE. Born 1954 in Connecticut. She is presently a teaching assistant in elementary drawing and expects to receive her MFA in 1980 from the University of Illinois, Champaign. "My approach to my work is one of investigation of a subject and a statement about each particular inquiry. Subject to my scrutiny, personal perception, a visual idea is cemented from internal, and later external points of view. The idea is developed, the physical process begins. This battle, a play between the spirit (the idea) and the physical (the media) is a personal forum that is the subject of my intent." She was a Museum Technician from 1976-77 and Assistant Art Gallery Manager from 1977-78. She's traveled in England, Scotland, Lebanon, Jordan, Egypt and Malta. Some exhibitions include the competitions, Print Club 55th Exhibition (Philadelphia 1979); Charlotte Printmakers Society (North Carolina 1979); Boston Printmakers 32nd National Exhibition (DeCordova Museum, Lincoln, Massachusetts; Juror: Gabor Peterdi, 1979). Some group shows include Illinois in Washington (Sarah Spurgeon Gallery, Central, Washington, 1979) and Iowa Print Group Exhibitions I and II (Iowa City, 1976-77). Publications in which her works have appeared include WINDCHIMES by Ann Brownscombe (poems handset and printed with one cover illustration, 1978) and MOON DOG by Tony Hoagland (poems handset and printed, including five wood engravings, 1977).

MULAC, JIM. Born 1942 in Berwyn, Illinois. Owns Jim's Used Books & Records in Iowa City, home of many poetry and fiction readings. Worked in the past as a small city news reporter and a solo piano player, plus many short-term jobs. Has lived for months or years in Boston, Chicago, the San Francisco Bay Area, New Orleans, the Mississippi Valley. No major publications, a scattering of poetry and prose published in midwestern little mags. "Would like to see more writing about people struggling with this world which nobody owns in the real reality. Will keep trying to understand and write about this myself."

NATHAN, LEONARD. Born 1924 in Los Angeles. He's been an instructor in the Department of Rhetoric at the University of California at Berkeley since 1960. He was an instructor at Modesto Junior College from 1954-60. "My hope is to be clear, true, and good listening." He traveled in Mexico from 1962 to 1963, and India from 1966-67, and in England and France during World War II. His books include DEAR BLOOD (Pittsburg Press, 1980); RETURNING YOUR CALL (Princeton, 1975; nominated for a National Book Award, awarded a Commonwealth Medal for Poetry); THE TEACHINGS OF GRANDFATHER FOX (Ithaca, 1976); THE DAY THE PERFECT SPEAKERS LEFT (Wesleyan, 1969); GLAD AND SORRY SEASONS (Random House, 1963).

NERUDA, PABLO. 1904-1973. He was born Ricardo Eliezer Neftali Reyes y Basoalto, in Parral, Chile, to a railroad worker. Neruda wrote in 1954 that "we come upon poetry a step at a time, among the beings and things of this world: nothing is taken away without adding to the sum of all that exists in a blind extension of love." He was not fond of English and American poets who have worked predominantly in the symbolist tradition, and called them "too purely intellectual for the Latin American sensibility. It seemed to us a limitation that they could never deal directly with the world they lived in... Somewhere after the turn of the century, our modernism and yours parted company. You might say that we were retarded in not pursuing French symbolism to its logical conclusions. But then again someone might say that your most influential poets dropped the burden of being human and socially alert, dropped it too easily. As a young man in the early twenties my gods were Walt Whitman and Ruben Dario." Tempered by reason, intelligence, wit and humor, his poetry is nevertheless "committed to the satisfaction of man's emotional needs, and not his discursive intelligence," said Luis Monguio.

A list of his publications may easily be found (in Contemporary Authors—Permanent Series, where these notes were found), and since they are numerous, we will only list ESPANA EN EL CORAZON: HIMNO A LAS GLORIAS DEL PUEBLO EN 'A GUERRA (poetry), first printed by Spanish Republican soldiers on the battle front, Ercilla, 1937 (second edition 1938). Neruda's books have been translated into Italian, Russian, German, French, Swedish, Esperanto, and at least eighteen other languages.

Some honors he's received: Premio Municipal de Literatura (Chile), 1944; Premio Nacional de Literatura (Chile), 1945; International Peace Prize, 1950; Lenin and Stalin Peace Prize, 1953; the Nobel Prize in Literature, 1971.

He was a member of the central committee of the Chilean Communist Party. He traveled to Burma, Ceylon and Java as the Chilean consul, visiting China, Japan and Indo-China. During the early 1930s he was consul in Buenos Aires, Siam, Cambodia, Anam and Madrid. He helped Spanish refugees in Paris in 1939, and from there was sent to the Chilean Embassy in Mexico City where he was consul from 1941-44. When he returned to Chile he was elected to the Senate as a Communist. He wrote letters from 1947-49 charging President Gonzalez Videla with selling out to the United States, and carried his case to the Chilean Supreme Court, which upheld Videla's position. He escaped to Mexico and also traveled in Italy, France, USSR and Red China. He returned to Chile in 1953 after the victory of the anti-Videla forces. He was a member of the World Peace Council from 1950-73, came to New York for the PEN Congress in 1966, and was the Chilean ambassador to France from 1971-72.

NETTELBECK, F.A. Born 1950 in Chicago. Is presently a junk dealer in Santa Cruz, California. Was formerly a janitor, house painter, and "criminal." Philosophy: "Observe/relate." Travel includes the entire U.S. and Mexico and Canada. Major publications include DESTROY ALL MONSTERS (Konglomerati Press, 1976); CURIOS (Quark Press, 1976); SPECTATOR (Drivel Press, 1977); BUG DEATH (Alcatraz Editions, 1979).

NIELSON, PALLE. Born 1920 in Copenhagen, Denmark. One of Denmark's leading graphic artists. He has exhibited world-wide, and won the Premio Giornalista Italiana at the Venice Biennale in 1958 and has since become professor of graphic arts at the Academy in Copenhagen. His work is represented in the U.S. at the Museum of Modern Art in New York.

PERRY, WILEY B. Born 1933 in Rome, Georgia. Presently lives in Birmingham, Alabama where he's president of Photonics, Ltd. (photographic specialists). Philosophy: "Getting there is all the fun!" He's been a sports editor and photographer for the Cedartown, Georgia Daily Standard; photographer and writer for the Rome, Georgia News-Tribune; staff photographer for the Atlanta Journal-Constitution; photographer and manager of photographic services for Emory University in Atlanta; manager of photographic data retrieval in Los Alamos, New Mexico Scientific Laboratory; production manager, motion picture and still photography for Storer Studios in Atlanta; manager of photographic department for Obata Design in Saint Louis, Missouri. Lived in Atlanta, Saint Louis and Albuquerque. Extensive travel in Midwest, South. Major publications: Sports Illustrated; Jet; Ebony; Together Magazine; Amerika Illustrated (U.S. Information Agency Publication); Atlanta Magazine.

The photo in this anthology missed publication in Life by two hours.

POLACKOVA, KACA: biographical note not supplied.

POLLAK, FELIX. Born 1909 in Vienna, Austria. Presently retired in Madison, Wisconsin. Was Curator of Rare Books at the Memorial Library at the University of Wisconsin in Madison. His essay which appears in this anthology also appeared in (along with the nominating Hiram Poetry Review), Camels Coming and the COSMEP Newsletter. Books include THE CASTLE AND THE FLAW (Elizabeth Press, 1963); SAY WHEN (Juniper Press, 1969); GINKGO (Elizabeth Press, 1973); SUBJECT TO CHANGE (Juniper Press, 1978). Philosophy: "Art for Art's sake."

POTTS, CHARLES: see Litmus, Inc., in the press/magazine listing.

PRUITT, BILL. Born 1948 in Saint Louis, Missouri. Is presently manager of the Genessee Co-op Foodstore in Rochester, N.Y. He's been a groundskeeper, loading dock receiver, hospital courier, librarian and construction laborer. "I want to give a voice to that which most needs to be said." He's been to Montreal, Lawrence, Iowa, Florida, Niagara, East Saint Louis, Mobile, Tulsa, Mount Desert Island, Estes Park, Duluth, Buffalo, California and Missouri. His poem, nominated by Allegany Poetry, also appeared in RAVINE STREET (White Pine Press, Buffalo, New York). Other work has appeared in Poetry Now; Niagara Magazine; ON TURTLE'S BACK (New York state anthology).

PURCELL, CHARLES: unable to locate for biographical information.

RANDALL, MARGARET. (Note from Richard Morris) Originally from New York. Edited the noted bilingual literary magazine El Corno Emplumado in Mexico City with Sergio Mondragon during the 1960s. A widely published poet as well as editor and translator, she is currently living in exile in Cuba.

RAY, DAVID: see New Letters, in the press/magazine listing.

REA, SUSAN IRENE. Born 1945 in Reading, Pennsylvania. She's taught at Community College of Philadelphia and Drexel University. She's traveled to Switzerland, England, and cross-country in Canada. Her work has appeared in Ponchartrain Review; Choice; Intro 10; California Quarterly; Ploughshares.

REYNOLDS, LOUISE: see The New Renaissance, in the press/magazine listing.

RILKE, RAINER MARIA. 1875-1926. One of the greatest lyric poets of the German language. He dedicated his life to poetry as to a religious vocation. Widely traveled, he met Tolstoy in Russia (1900), worked as a secretary to Rodin in Paris (1905-6). He corresponded with numerous acquaintances including Valery, whose work he translated along with the work of Gide and others. Married only briefly, he spent his last years in almost continual solitude in a medieval tower, little bigger than a hermit's cell, at Muzot (Valais), where his last two works of poetry, SONNETS TO ORPHEUS and DUINO ELEGIES were completed, dictated nearly in their entirety in a few days and nights. These works and selections of his earlier poems are available in English translations along with THE NOTEBOOKS OF MALTE LAURIDS BRIGGE and a number of volumes of correspondence.

ROBERTS, ANDREW: see end of this listing.

SCHECTER, BARRY. Born 1948 in Chicago. Is presently a composition instructor at the University of Illinois, Chicago Circle. Formerly a postal worker, cab driver and receiving clerk. Travel: "I adhere to the philosophy of Peter Kostakis: 'The best night out is a night at home.' " His work has appeared in Paris Review; Chicago Review; Chelsea; FIFTEEN CHICAGO POETS; The Chicago Daily News; he is the author of THE GRAND ET CET'RA. Philosophy: "I don't know."

SCULLY, JAMES. Born 1937 in New Haven, Connecticut. Presently resides in Willimantic, Connecticut. Books of poetry: THE MARCHES; AVENUE OF THE AMERICAS; SANTIAGO POEMS; SCRAP BOOK. He co-translated PROMETHEUS BOUND (with C.J. Herington); QUECHUA PEOPLES POETRY (with Maria A. Proser) and DE REPENTE/ALL OF A SUDDEN (with Maria A. Proser and Arlene Scully). He's received fellowships from the Ingram Merrill Foundation, the Guggenheim Foundation and the National Endowment for the Arts.

SEUMPTEWA, OWEN. Born 1946 in Bellemont, Arizona. Is presently Director of Education of the Hopi Tribe in Oraibi, Arizona. He is himself a Hopi Indian. Previous work includes Coordinator of the Hopi program for Northland Pioneer College, manpower specialist for the University of Utah, Assistant Director of Health Professions for the Hopi Tribe, and Assistant Director of the Learning Resource Center for the Navajo Community College. He received his BFA in 1976 with an educational media filmstrip on Native American culture. His work has appeared in several issues of Sun Tracks, and in Scholastic News Pilot, Scholastic News Ranger, Professional Magazine of the Elementary Grades, and Southwest Indian Tribes. He's traveled coast to coast throughout the U.S.

SHUSTAK, LARENCE: see end of this listing.

SKLAR, MORTY: see The Spirit That Moves Us, in the press/magazine listing.

SMITH, ED. Born 1941 in Foochow, China. He is presently a reverend in Iowa City, Iowa. He's also been a cabdriver. He's traveled in Vietnam, Burma and China. Major publications include THE FLUTES OF GAMA and GOING, both from Litmus, Inc.

STAFFORD, WILLIAM EDGAR. Born 1914 in Hutchinson, Kansas. He's worked in sugar been fields, construction, an oil refinery, the Forest Service, Church World Service; taught high school in California and college in Iowa,

California, Kansas, Indiana, Washington, Alaska, Ohio and Oregon. He was poetry consultant for The Library of Congress; a member of the Literature Commission of the National Endowment for the Arts and Literature Committee for The National Council of Teachers of English; lecturer on literature for the USIA in Egypt, India, Bangladesh, Pakistan, Iran and Nepal. He received his B.A. and M.A. at the University of Kansas, and his PhD at the University of Iowa. "Married, four children, Fellowship of Reconciliation, MLA, ECTE, AAUP, biker, photographer and reader." Publications include the books of poetry TRAVELING THROUGH THE DARK; ALLEGIANCES; SOMEDAY, MAYBE; STORIES THAT COULD BE TRUE; NEW AND COLLECTED POEMS—all from Harper & Row, and other collections of poetry from Perishable Press and others, and the books of prose WRITING THE AUSTRALIAN CRAWL (Views on the Writers Vocation; University of Michigan Press); FRIENDS TO THIS GROUND (National Council of Teachers of English); DOWN IN MY HEART, an account of serving as a conscientious objector in World War II (Church of the Brethren Press).

STROH, MARY: see Me Too, in the press/magazine listing.

THOMAS, LORENZO. Born 1944 in Panama, Republica de Panama. He's presently in Arkansas, Oklahoma, Louisiana and Texas doing research, writing and teaching. He is a writer-in-residence, Arkansas Arts Council, and formerly at Texas Southern University; was an artist-in-the-schools for the State Arts Council of Oklahoma, and formerly (also) for the Texas Commission on the Arts and Humanities; has done free-lance advertising and magazine features. He travels "all the time." "My effort in both 'creative' and critical writings is to investigate the multicultural dimensions of contemporary American life . . . a rich dimension despite the persistently *mono*cultural prejudices and discriminations that yet dominate the United States." Major publications include CHANCES ARE FEW (Blue Wind Press, 1979) and appearances in JAMBALAYA: Four Poets (Reed Cannon & Johnson, 1975); NONE OF THE ABOVE (editor, Michael Lally; Crossing Press, 1977). He's also published critical articles in numerous historical and literary journals.

THOMPSON, JEAN. Born 1950 in Chicago. Presently teaches creative writing at the University of Illinois. The story in this anthology, nominated by Fiction International, also appeared in the anthology ITINERARY ONE: FICTION (Bowling Green State University Press, Ohio, 1974). Other work has appeared in Ascent; Ploughshares; Descant; Kansas Quarterly and Mademoiselle, among other places. Her collected short stories THE GASOLINE WARS will be published in the University of Illinois short fiction series, 1980.

VALLEJO, CESAR. 1892-1938. Born in the small town of Santiago de Chuco in northern Peru. According to the poet, both his parents were the children of the union of a priest and an Indian woman. Despite the fact that the family was not well-off, Vallejo was able to attend Trujillo University and he also attended the University of San Marcos in Lima for a short time. His first collection LOS HERALDOS NEGROS (The Black Riders) appeared in 1918. In 1920 he was arrested in his home town and accused of being implicated in some political disturbances. Although apparently innocent, he was imprisoned for several months. His second collection TRILCE (1922), refers to this experience, and is one of the most rigorously experimental volumes in modern literature. In 1923, Vallejo went to Paris where, except for short periods spent in Spain, he was to remain for the rest of his life. He lived in Paris in great penury and seems to have earned his money mainly by writing for the press. For many years he wrote little poetry, but as his sympathies became increasingly left-wing he turned to other forms of literature. He made two short trips to Russia in 1928 and 1929. In 1930 he was expelled from France for his political activities and lived for a short time in Madrid, where he published a novel of social protest set in Peru, EL TUNGSTENO, and wrote a number of left-wing plays. In 1933 he was back in Paris but again left for Spain at the beginning of the Civil War. He began writing poetry again intensively, but his remaining poetry was published after his death: POEMAS HUMANOS (Human Poems) and ESPANA, APARTA DE MI ESTE CADIZ (Spain, Take Thou This Cup From Me). His work has been translated in book form by Clayton Eshleman, Robert Bly, David Smith and James A. Wright.

VENTURA, MICHAEL. Born 1945 in New York City. He worked in NYC as a printer, and while attending Bard College he worked as a gardener and sold vacuum cleaners. He also worked on the Austin Sun and is now working on the L.A. Weekly as a film reviewer and writer. Major publications include RAGS (Austin Sun Press, 1976) and THE MOLLYHAWK POEMS (Wings Press, Houston, 1977).

WALLACE, JIM: unable to locate for biographical notes.

WANTLING, WILLIAM: see end of this listing.

WHISNANT, ENA SWANSEA.Born 1956 in Charlotte, North Carolina. Is presently a painter-photographer and designer for Red Clay Books. Was formerly a television news photographer for ABC-TV, a teacher of optical printing techniques at the University Film Study Center at MIT, and an assistant recording engineer in the Systems Complex for Performing Arts at the University of South Florida at Tampa Bay. "I do not believe that fine art and mass marketing are mutually exclusive." She's traveled in Europe and West Africa. She had a one-woman show, Reverential Paintings of Africa, in 1979 in Charlotte.

WILD, PETER. Is presently in the English Department at the University of Arizona in Tucson. His books include COCHISE (Doubleday, 1973); THE CLONING (Doubleday, 1974); CHIHUAHUA (Doubleday, 1976); WILDERNESS (New Rivers Press, 1980).

WRIGHT, JAMES A. 1927-1980. Born in Martins Ferry, Ohio. Left widow Edith Anne Runk and two sons. His last job was Professor of English at Hunter College of the City University of New York. He served in the U.S. Army. Some awards he received include Fullbright Fellow in Austria, 1952-53; Eunice Tietjens Memorial Prize, 1955; Kenyon Review fellowship in poetry, 1958; National Institute of Arts and Letters grant in literature, 1959; Ohiona Book Award, 1960, for SAINT JUDAS; Oscar Blumenthal Award from Poetry magazine, 1968; Guggenheim fellowship; Pulitzer Prize in poetry, 1972. Some of his books of poetry: THE GREEN WALL (Yale University Press, 1957); THE BRANCH WILL NOT BREAK (Wesleyan University Press, 1963); TWENTY POEMS OF CESAR VALLEJO (translator, The Sixties Press, 1964); TWENTY POEMS OF PABLO NERUDA (translator with Robert Bly, The Sixties Press, 1968); COLLECTED POEMS (Wesleyan University Press, 1971); TWO CITIZENS (Farrar, Straus, 1973). He's been anthologized in HEARTLAND, edited by Lucien Stryk (Northern Illinois University Press, 1967); others.

ZIETLOW, E. R. Presently an Associate Professor in English at the University o' Victoria, Victoria, British Columbia. Grew up in the ranch country near Scenic on the edge of the South Dakota Badlands. He completed his B.A. at Dakota Wesleyan University in the fifties before serving with the U.S. Army in Germany. Upon his return, he studied creative writing at Boston University with New England novelist Gerald Warner Brace. In the sixties he received the degree of Doctor of Philosophy from the University of Washington.

The following are people for whom information was either obtained too late for inclusion in alphabetical order, or not obtained at all.

ARONOFF, MARK: unable to obtain information.

ASSED, NAGIB: unable to obtain information.

BATKI, JOHN. Born 1942 in Hungary. Presently living in Lower Manhattan, New York where he is working on translations from Gyula Krudy. Approach to his art: "Teach, move, amuse." Major publications: THE MAD SHOEMAKER (poems); FALLING UPWARDS (poems); ATTILA JOZSEF: POEMS & TEXT (translation). He was a lecturer at Harvard from 1975-78.

BROWNING, COLLEEN: unable to obtain information.

CUMMINGS, DARCY. Born 1937 in Philadelphia. Presently living in Cherry Hill, New Jersey, and teaching at the University of Pennsylvania (where she is a graduate student) and at Rutgers University and the Philadelphia College of Art The poem which appears in this anthology, nominated from The Smith, also appeared in Pennsylvania Review, and is one of a series called "Songs for a Stone Baby." "My tastes for poetry are eclectic. I write about people, sometimes in very formal stanzas. Most of my work is narrative or dramatic monologue, but I wish I could write a surrealist poem. I got a very late start writing poetry and now my youngest child is going to college, and I'm going to write as much as I can." Her poems have appeared in Graham House Review; Intro II; Pennsylvania Gazette and other places. Travel: "Someday I'm going to go everywhere."

ECHTERMEYER, FAITH: unable to obtain information.

FERLINGHETTI, LAWRENCE. Born "1919 or 1920, probably in Yonkers, New York, perhaps in the Virgin Islands or in Paris, France." Is co-owner of City Lights Books in San Francisco, established 1953 (the first all-paperbound bookstore in the country). He's founder of City Lights Books and sole editor of it (from 1955, with the Pocket Poets Series. Was arrested in San Francisco in 1956 for publishing and distributing Allen Ginsberg's allegedly obscene HOWL. Arrested 1968 and placed in the Santa Rita Rehabilitation Center for "blocking the entrance to war at Oakland Army Induction Center." He was a commanding officer during Normandy invasion, World War II.

"Populist Manifesto," which appears in this anthology (nominated from Nitty Gritty), also appeared in the Granite State Independence (a small town newspaper—its first appearance); the Los Angeles Times; The New York Times; The Chicago Review; Sol Tide and many other places. It was translated into Spanish, Italian, French, and published in the anarchist Antigruppo (Sicily) and the Revista de Bellas Artes (Mexico City). Some books: PICTURES OF THE GONE WORLD (City Lights, 1955); A CONEY ISLAND OF THE MIND (New Directions, 1958); HER (novel, New Directions, 1960); BEATITUDE ANTHOLOGY (City Lights, 1960); and many more. The editors refer the reader to sources such as Contemporary Authors (from which these notes were taken) for documentation of a long and varied career. Ferlinghetti was a leader in the American poetry revival in San Francisco in the fifties, a movement whose primary purpose was to bring poetry back to the people.

GORMAN, R.C. No personal information received. He owns the Navajo Gallery in Taos, New Mexico, where he lives. Some one-man exhibitions: Coffee Gallery (San Francisco, 1963); Museum of Indian Arts (San Francisco, 1966); van Straaten Gallery (Chicago, 1976); Musee Municipal de St. Paul (France, 1979); Bayard Gallery (New York, 1979). A 30-minute film of him was aired nationally over Public Broadcasting Service Stations in 1976. He has a long list of selected collections and book/magazine appearances.

LOCKWOOD, RUSSEL: unable to obtain information.

MERCADO, ROLANDO: unable to obtain information.

PAUL, BIL. Born 1943 in Trempealeau County, Wisconsin. Lives and works in San Mateo, California. He's a part-time letter carrier, and operates Alchemist/ Light Publishing, which has produced THE TRI-X CHRONICLES (a photo collection of the 60's); CROSSING THE U.S.A. THE SHORT WAY: Bicycling A Mississippi River Route (a guidebook); MAILMEN'S DOG STORIES (a collection of stories written by mailmen across the U.S.) "My approach to art was once highly idealistic. Now it is a healthier mixture of idealism and capitalism." "My international travel was mostly via the Army (see the world out of the back of a deuce-and-a-half). Germany, France, Vietnam, Thailand, Laos, Maylaysia, Indonesia, Mexico. I see a lot of the American countryside on long bike trips. I'm starting to write a novel. I photograph constantly."

ROBERTS, ANDREW: unable to obtain information.

SHUSTAK, LARENCE: unable to obtain information.

WANTLING, WILLIAM. 1933-1974. Born in Peoria, Illinois. Served in the Marine Corps in Korea. Was married, with two sons. Was formerly a factory worker, surveyor, zoo-keeper, teacher, writer on electronics, inmate at San Quentin State Penitentiary (1958-63). "I vacillate from spare, realistic free verse to mysticism, which employs rhyme and Welsh 'Cynghanedd.' " Wantling was an "underground" American writer who had an establishment success in England. Some books: THE SEARCH (edited by Kirby Congdon; Hors Commerce Press, 1964); HEROIN HAIKUS (Fenian Head Center Press, 1964); DOWN, OFF AND OUT (Mimeo Press, 1966); THE SOURCE (Dustbooks, 1967); PENGUIN MODERN POETS 12 (with Alan Jackson and Jeff Nuttall; 1968); 10,000 RPM AND DIGGIN IT, YEAH (Second Aeon Publications, 1973); YOUNG AND TENDER (novel; Bee Line Books, 1969); SICK FLY (Second Aeon, 1970).

PRESS/MAGAZINE AUTOBIOGRAPHICAL NOTES

Note: Due to deadline demands, those notes received late are entered at the end of this list, and not in alphabetical order.

The editors of this anthology refer the reader to the following sources for additional information concerning presses/magazines and authors: Small Press Record Of Books In Print; International Directory Of Little Magazines And Small Presses; Directory Of Small Magazine/Press Editors And Publishers *(all from Dustbooks in Paradise, California). The reader may also consult his/her librarian for other sources such as* Books In Print, Contemporary Authors *and so on.*

*   *   *   *   *   *   *

ACROBAT BOOKS. Editors: Tony Cohan and Gordon Beam. Founded 1975 in Los Angeles. Major publications include: NINE SHIPS; OUTLAW VISIONS; STREET WRITERS, and RECORD PRODUCER'S HANDBOOK. Aspirations: "Quality books."

Tony Cohan. Born 1939 in New York City. Attended Browning School in New York, public school in California, and Stanford University; received B.A. in English from the University of California in 1961. He's lived in Europe, North Africa and Japan. He is the author of NINE SHIPS (1975) and OUTLAW VISIONS (1977), both from Acrobat Books. He has also written articles for the Los Angeles Free Press, an article "Architecture" for the Aspen Design Conference in 1970, and other articles. He's written the script for "Fire Myth" (30-minute film, National Endowment for the Humanities,1974) and for "Sailor" (a feature film screenplay, optioned, Columbia Pictures,1974). He has also written record liner notes and done advertising for dozens of films and records. He was editor for the University of California Press and edited/published STREET WRITERS and OUTLAW VISIONS and other books. He composed the score for his film "Fire Myth" and nine songs as lyricist with Chick Corea. He has played and performed with Bud Powell, Dexter Gordon, Memphis Slim, Ry Cooder, Lowell George and Ravi Shankar, among many others. He's produced hundreds of television and radio spots, multi-media presentations and records, and demo tapes for film and record companies.

ALDEBARAN REVIEW. Editor: John Oliver Simon. Founded in 1968 in Berkeley, California. Aldebaran Review "has always been a vehicle for printing poetry the editor feels close to, migrating from mags thru chapbooks toward occasional anthologies." Major publications include: FREEDOM'S IN SIGHT by Alta (1969); LITTLE LORD SHIVA by Charles Potts (1969); CITY OF BUDS & FLOWERS: a poet's eye view of Berkeley (1977); THE CAGED COLLECTIVE: a documentary anthology of the life and death of the Folsom

Prison Creative Writer's Workshop (1978), and A RAINDROP HAS HER TO DO HER WORK: poems from California Poets In The Schools (1979).

John Oliver Simon was born in 1942 in New York City. He received his B.A. from Swarthmore College (Highest Honors, Phi Beta Kappa) and his M.A. from the University of California at Berkeley. He's published nine chapbooks of poems and RATTLESNAKE GRASS: selected shorter poems (Hanging Loose Press, 1978). He has completed "an epic narrative science-fiction poem," "Seedstone." He is working as Statewide Coordinator for California Poets In The Schools. He's lived in Berkeley since 1964 and has two daughters.

ALLY PRESS was founded in 1973 and takes its name from THE TEACHINGS OF DON JUAN: "An ally is a power capable of carrying a man beyond the boundaries of himself. This is how an ally can reveal matters no human being could." Ally has published small poetry collections by Robert Bly, Ted Kooser, Norbert Krapf, Susan Fromberg Schaeffer and Englishman Martin Booth. No public monies are used in these productions in deference to the opinion that there should be no government.

Paul Feroe, editor of Ally Press, was born 1951. He makes his living as a commercial printer after short-lived careers in reporting and banking. He graduated from Saint Olaf College in Minnesota and worked in Denver five years before moving to Saint Paul. Having taken classes from a German Master bookbinder, he handcases the limited editions of the Ally chapbooks.

ALLEGANY POETRY. Edited by Ford F. Ruggieri and Helen Ruggieri. Helen is poetry editor and Ford is fiction editor as well as printer (they do the entire process themselves, except binding). Published four issues and featured regional (mostly upper New York state) poets Robert Lax, John Logan, Lyn Lifshin, David Lunde, John Leax, Gerald McCarthy and many more. "By 1977 it became difficult to maintain the regional status and a new magazine, Uroboros, was started, which included fiction, essays, and reviews as well as poetry and graphics. Allegany Mountain Press also publishes the Rebis Chapbook Series and Uroboros Books—full length, paperbound volumes of poetry. Rebis includes WAITING TO DISAPPEAR by Douglas Carlson, WATER by Steve Lewandowski, SKIN OF DOUBT by Paul Grillo and others. Uroboros Books include MOTHERING by Judith Kerman, THE WOMEN'S HOUSE by Arlene Stone, THE POETESS by Helen Ruggieri and others.

ASPECT. Present staff: Edward J. Hogan, co-editor/publisher, and co-editors Ronna Johnson, Christine Lamb, Susan Lloyd McGarry, Paul McGovern and Miriam Sagan. About fifteen others have co-edited the magazine during the past eight years, three of whom, Jeffrey Schwartz, Ellen Schwartz, and Carol Trowbridge should especially be mentioned. Aspect began "as an unaffiliated and impossibly obscure monthly of undergraduate writing. The first issue, March 1969, was xeroxed in 12 copies, 13 pages, typed, and stapled in the upper lefthand corner." From 1970-72, the magazine's main stresses were political commentary (particularly anti-war criticism) and poetry. Its circulation was still under 100. In 1973-74, Aspect evolved into a collectively-edited literary magazine. "Our most steadfast aim has been to find and publish exceptional work by writers who deserve to be better known. We have consciously opposed the trickle-down theory of litmag publishing success: to publish a few 'names' in each issue, pushing it on that basis and hoping some of the benefit of readership will be shared by the other contributors. Present circulation is 1200."

AURA. Editor: Steven Ford Brown. Founded 1975 in Birmingham, Alabama by Bart Paugh and Steven Ford Brown, as Aura Literary/Arts Review. It ceased publication in May 1978 and Thunder Mountain Review began in May 1979 under the editorship of SFB.   "Thunder Mountain Review and Thunder City Press both try to fill the vacuum that was created out of the demise of Aura. I want to publish the best material I can find with a particular emphasis on the avant garde and surrealism. I am particularly interested in translations right now and the magazine is publishing a great deal in the way of translations."   Major publications include the books of poetry JAWBONE: Portraits Of Contemporary Poets (D. C. Berry, 1978); WINTER NIGHT (Georg Trakl, translated by David J. Black, 1979); THE BLUE MAN (Susan Fromberg Schaeffer, 1980); SHABBY LOVE (M. R. Doty, 1980) and A DRIFT OF SWINE (Ed Ochester, 1980).

BkMk PRESS. Editor: Dan Jaffe.   "We try to publish new people and give them a start . . . we did one of Angela Jackson's first books. We publish well-known people who haven't received the attention they deserve—such as John Knopfle. We publish middle-of-the-country people but don't limit ourselves to that. We're eclectic." Founded 1971 in Kansas City, Missouri.   Major publications: CENTRAL STANDARD TIME, Dave Etter (new and selected poems); THE BODY AND THE BODY'S GUEST, Tom McAfee; LATE HARVEST, an anthology of Plains and Prairie poets, edited by Robert Killoren; DUST DANCERS, Jack Anderson; LYRICS AND LAMENTS, translations from Hebrew and Yiddish, by Howard Schwartz.

BLACK JACK. Editor: Art Cuelho. Founded 1973 in Billings, Montana; is presently located in Big Timber, Montana.   Aspirations: "To publish the best western and rural poems and stories in America. To select certain writers and poets who have depth in this type of literature and feature them."   Major publications: FATHER ME HOME, WINDS; IN THE PEOPLE IN THE LAND; THE AMERICAN HOBO; VALLEY GRAPEVINE and OKIE FACES AND IRISH EYES.

CAMELS COMING. Editor: Richard Morris. Founded 1965 in Albuquerque, New Mexico.   Major publications include THE ECOLOGICAL SUICIDE BUS by Hugh Fox, and RENO, NEVADA by Richard Morris, from Camels Coming Press.   The last issue of Camels Coming magazine appeared in 1968. The last Camels Coming Press chapbook appeared in 1972. Camels Coming Newsletter still comes out once every two years or so from San Francisco.

Richard Morris is Coordinator of COSMEP (Committee of Small Magazine Editors and Publishers... soon to change its name to The Independent Publisher). His most recent book, THE END OF THE WORLD, is from Anchor Press/Doubleday.

CHICAGO. Editor: Alice Notley. Founded 1972 in Chicago. Ceased publication 1974. "I [A. N.] wanted to educate myself, get through a couple of pregnancies, do the best magazine in America, if possible, and publish a large number of works per poet in each issue." Major publications include THE END OF THE FAR WEST by Frank O'Hara.

COMBINATIONS. Editor: Mary Ann Lynch. Founded 1976 in Greenfield Center, New York. "Combinations exists to showcase the photographic work that is being created today, emphasizing works that demonstrate intelligence, vision and a mastery of appropriate craft or technique, regardless of style or genre. It is devoted to the growth of photography as a creative medium and to increased communication among active photographers throughout the world. Its pages also feature poetry, short works of fiction, and articles and interviews pertaining to photography. To accomplish this, we are working towards coming out on a regular quarterly basis in our current format (44 pages plus cover, 8½ x 11 coated stock), and as soon as finances permit, will begin the production of chapbooks featuring the works of one to three individuals at a time. In publishing poetry in each issue we hope to offer a continuing exploration of the relationship between these two art forms—poetry and photography—and to create a context which will bridge both literary and photographic interests. We no longer have a consideration fee as a requisite for submitting work."

CONTEMPORARY QUARTERLY: POETRY AND ART. Editor: John D. Engle. Founded 1976 in Los Angeles, fathered by the California State Poetry Quarterly, which was begun 1973. Kenneth Atchity was editor through CQ 10. "CQ's single criterion is excellence, the guiding editorial principle eclectic, in that CQ provides a forum for all eloquent contemporary voices. We encourage the submission of poems of any length as well as graphic art and photographs."
   Kenneth Atchity has published four books, including HOMER'S ILIAD: THE SHIELD OF MEMORY and a book of poetry, SLEEPING WITH AN ELEPHANT.
   John D. Engle has published articles and reviews in Notes On Contemporary Literature; the Journal Of Irish Literature; America; and elsewhere.

CURBSTONE PRESS. Editors: Alexander Taylor and Judith Doyle. An incorporated, non-profit publishing and printing house founded by Alexander Taylor 1975. "Our primary goal is to publish important works of poets and translators which might not ordinarily find a voice in the commercial publishing channels. We have a bias toward poetry of the left that rises above political invective. As of 1979, our primary emphasis has been on publishing the works of younger American poets and the translations of some Danish and

Latin-American writers. Among the American writers Curbstone Press has published are Margaret Gibson, Joan Joffe Hall, Marion Metivier, Richard Schaaf, Victor Kaplan and Thomas Churchill. We have published the first books in English by the Danish poets Klaus Rifbjerg, Ole Sarvig, Jorgen Gustava Brandt and Henrik Nordbrandt. QUECHUA PEOPLES POETRY, a volume of contemporary, oral folk poetry of the Quechua Indians around Bolivia, was published in the Fall of 1977, and the poems of the Chilean, Teresa de Jesus, DE REPENTE/ALL OF A SUDDEN, has recently been completed in a bilingual edition. QUECHUA PEOPLES POETRY was a finalist in the Islands and Continents translation award, 1978, and THE RIFT ZONE was a finalist for the William Carlos Williams prize in 1979."

DECEMBER PRESS. Editors: Curt Johnson and Robert Wilson. "December magazine was founded in 1958 by four dissident Writers Workshop members (Iowa City): Louis Vaczek, the Trissells, Richard Schechner, given by them after several issues to Jeff Marks, poet, given by Marks in 1962 to Curt Johnson, who—with Robert Wilson—continues to publish the magazine (and December Press books) to the present day." The press is presently located in Chicago. Major publications include: ANACONDA by Jerry Bumpus, THE BONNY-CLABBER by George Chambers, THE FORBIDDEN WRITINGS OF LEE WALLEK; YOUNG IN ILLINOIS by Robert Wilson and DESTINY NEWS by Robert Fox. Raymond Carver's book of short stories, WILL YOU PLEASE BE QUIET, PLEASE, the title story of which, among others in the volume, first appeared in December mag, was nominated for a National Book Award in 1977.

"Robert Wilson and Curt Johnson are long-time Midwesterners and writer-editors—all three."

DUSTBOOKS. Founder/editor/publisher: Len Fulton; associate editor: Ellen Ferber. Founded 1963 in Berkeley, California; presently located in Paradise, California. Major publications include: INTERNATIONAL DIRECTORY OF LITTLE MAGAZINES AND SMALL PRESSES; SMALL PRESS RECORD OF BOOKS IN PRINT; Small Press Review (monthly); AGAINST NATURE: WILDERNESS POEMS by Judith McCombs, and GUIDE TO WOMEN'S PUBLISHING.

Len Fulton was born 1934 in Lowell, Massachusetts ("me and Kerouac"). He's been an author since 1963. Philosophy: "Psychogeometric". Travels 15,000-20,000 miles per year in the U. S. Some publications include THE GRASSMAN (novel); DARK OTHER ADAM DREAMING (novel) and AMERICAN ODYSSEY (travelogue).

Ellen Ferber was born 1939 in Brooklyn, New York. She's presently an associate professor at California State University at Chico and resides in Paradise. She's been a teacher at the University of Connecticut, the University of Puerto Rico, Trinity College and California State U. since 1973. "Sound is meaning; language is lovely; technique is discovery; words are things." Travel: "Cross-country, bookseeling, book-fairing. Bicycled through Pyrenees before

10-speeds." Some publications: chapters in AMERICAN ODDYSEY and "The Art of Literary Publishing" (co-author with Len Fulton), Pushcart Press.

EAST RIVER ANTHOLOGY. Editors: Jan Barry and W. D. Ehrhart. Founded 1975 in Brooklyn, New York; presently located in Montclair, New Jersey. Major publications: DEMILITARIZED ZONES: VETERANS AFTER VIETNAM (1976) and PEACE IS OUR PROFESSION: POEMS AND PASSAGES OF WAR PROTEST (1980). "The press is a non-profit forum for writings from the Indochina war experience, seeking to aid the process of peace and freedom through nonviolent action."

Jan Barry, a poet and journalist, resigned from a military career after a war tour in Vietnam. He was co-editor of WINNING HEARTS AND MINDS: WAR POEMS BY VIETNAM VETERANS (1st Casualty Press/McGraw-Hill, 1972) and DEMILITARIZED ZONES.

THE FAULT. Editor: Terrence McMahon. Founded 1971 in Fremont, California; is located presently in Union City, California. "I've published over 1500 pages of work in the magazine, in addition to the 25 books by different authors and artists, and from all this work the editors of this anthology decided to select a single photo to represent my press. I would like to make it perfectly clear to my past contributors, that it was not my choice—I love you all equally." *Editors' note: EDITOR'S CHOICE is based on nominations made by editors of publications such as The Fault. It was Terrence McMahon's responsibility to nominate work from his press. He said he didn't want to. We asked him again, saying we couldn't possibly read all the books and magazines published. He again said he didn't want to.*

FICTION INTERNATIONAL. Editor/publisher: Joe David Bellamy. The magazine founded 1973 in Canton, New York. "Our aim is to publish as much good fiction as possible and to provide a forum for reviewing fiction, criticizing it, and simply talking about it. We are one of the few magazines concentrating on fiction to this extent: that is, committed to publishing fiction as well as reviewing it, and interested in considering what fiction is and should be about. During the last two years, we have also begun a program of book publishing, focusing on collections of stories by one author." Contributors have included Jerry Bumpus, Russell Banks, Joyce Carol Oates, David Madden, Alvin Greenberg, Clark Blaise, Rosellen Brown, Gary Gildner, Ishmael Reed, Tess Gallagher, Raymond Federman, Clarence Major, Robert Bly, Mary Peterson, C. E. Poverman, Gary Snyder, William Matthews, Howard McCord, Jerome Klinkowitz, Jerzy Kosinski and others. Books include LIVING ALONE by Robley Wilson, Jr. and TRANQUILITY BASE AND OTHER STORIES by Asa Baber.

Joe David Bellamy was born 1941 in Cincinnati. He attended Duke University, Antioch College (B.A.1964), University of Iowa Writers Workshop (M.F.A. 1969). His books include APOCALYPSE (Lippencott,1972), THE NEW FICTION (Illinois, 1974), OLYMPIC GOLD MEDALIST (North Ameri-

FIRELANDS ARTS REVIEW. Executive editor: Joel Rudinger. Started in 1972 as Mixer Magazine, name changed to Mixer: Firelands Arts Review, which name was maintained until 1979 when changed to Firelands Review. "It started as a way to create a scholarship program in the arts for Ohio students, and still maintains that function, under the auspices of the Rudinger Foundation."

Joel Rudinger is presently associate professor of English and Humanities at the Firelands College, and editor and publisher of the Cambric Press. He began editing as poetry editor for the Polar Star, the student newspaper at the University of Alaska around 1962-63. He received an M.A. from the Fairbanks campus of the University of Alaska, then went on to the University of Iowa where he received his MFA in 1966. After a year teaching at Indiana State University he went on to complete a PhD in American Literature and Folklore at Bowling Green State University.

GARGOYLE (Paycock Press) was started in May 1976 by Russell Cox, Paul Pasquarella and Richard Peabody. "We started out of frustration at our own inability to get published and planned to print our own work, but the word spread and before too long we were deluged with manuscripts. There have been 13 issues. The staff has been fluid, but I [Richard Peabody] have been sole owner/publisher since issue 5 when Cox followed Pasquarella into retirement. Current fiction editor is John Elsberg; poetry editor is Gretchen Johnson." Gargoyle publishes fiction, poetry, graphics and reviews. The most recent issue (1979) is a 208 page perfectbound volume of fiction. "We've recently published interviews with Allen Ginsberg and novelist John Gardner. I'm an Anglophile, so the magazine tends to publish work by British poets and artists such as Michael and Frances Horovitz, Pete Brown, Tina Fulker, David Ward and Dave Slater. Recent contributors include: Janine Pommy Vega, Ann Darr, Linda Pastan, Ron Androla, Larry Eigner, George Myers, Jr., Wolfgang Hildesheimer, David McAleavey, Linda McCloud and Steven Ford Brown." Two books published in 1979: THE LOVE LETTER HACK (fiction) by Michael Brondoli and I'M IN LOVE WITH THE MORTON SALT GIRL (Richard Peabody).

GAY SUNSHINE PRESS. Editor/publisher: Winston Leyland. "Gay Sunshine Press was founded in 1970 to publish cultural, literary, political material by Gay people. During the first five years of its existence it published only the tabloid cultural journal, Gay Sunshine. In order to publish we are dependent in part on the generosity of Gay people who believe in the kind of catalytic publishing we are doing."

THE GREENFIELD REVIEW. Editor: Joseph Bruchac. Began publishing 1970. "In the more than eight years since our first issue, The Greenfield Review has published what we feel to be some of the finest poetry being written in America today, by both new and established writers. In addition, we have always opened our pages to work in translation and, through special issues and regular issues alike, to the new poetry being written in English by non-Western poets." Volume 7, Numbers 1 & 2, THE AMERICAN MICROCOSM, co-edited by Michael Hogan and Joseph Bruchac, is devoted to prison writing. Some books published: LEAD US FORTH FROM PRISON by James Lewisohn; THE HOUSE BY THE SEA by Kofi Awoonor (composed in prison in Ghana); MAN SPIRIT by Ted Tomeo Palmanteer and Ron Rogers (poems, drawings and stories by two Native American writers); NUMEROUS AVALANCHES AT THE POINT OF INTERSECTION by Geraldine Kudaka; AFTERMATH, edited by Roger Weaver and Joseph Bruchac (an anthology of poems in English from Africa, Asia and the Caribbean).

Joseph Bruchac was born in 1942 in Saratoga Springs, New York. He is also presently working for Skidmore, running a prison program, and "in the Adirondack foothills in the house I grew up in, built by my grandfather." He was a teacher in Ghana, an English instructor at Skidmore College, and has been Director of the Skidmore College Program at Great Meadow Correctional Facility since 1974. He's traveled throughout the U.S. and in West Africa, Puerto Rico, and Haiti. "I believe that art makes a difference, that writing can be a way of maintaining a balance, that the writer has a great responsibility—not just to himself or herself, but to the Earth." Books include THE DREAMS OF JESSE BROWN (novel from Cold Mountain Press); ENTERING ONONDAGA AND OTHER POEMS (Cold Mountain Press); THE GOOD MESSAGE OF HANDSOME LAKE (Unicorn Press); STONE GIANTS AND FLYING HEADS (Iroquois folktales from The Crossing Press) and HOW TO START AND SUSTAIN A LITERARY MAGAZINE (Provision House).

GRUB STREET. Editors: Alan Ball, Pat Russell, et al. Founded 1969 in Bronx, New York. Aspiration: "To publish and promote accessible poetry and fiction." Present location is Somerville, Massachusetts.

HAMPDEN-SYDNEY REVIEW. Editor: Tom O'Grady. Founded 1975 in Hampden-Sydney, Virginia by Tom O'Grady and Michael Egan. Aspiration: "To publish new and established writers—the best poetry that comes across my desk."

HIRAM POETRY REVIEW. Co-editors: David Fratus and Carol Donley. Founded 1967 in Hiram, Ohio. Original editor was Hale Chatfield. Aspiration: "To publish excellent poetry, especially that of previously unpublished writers."

HOLLOW SPRING PRESS. Poetry editor/publisher for Hollow Spring Review of Poetry: Alexander Harvey. Founded 1975 in Berkshire, Massachusetts. Present location is Chester, Massachusetts. "Hollow Spring Press seeks to publish new and emerging writers as well as established, in fine letterpress chapbooks, and strives to present the best in contemporary writing in the Press' magazine, The Hollow Spring Review of Poetry." Other press publications

482

include MONTHS AND SEASONS (Oriental style poems) by Alexander Harvey and TOWARD MORNING/SWIMMERS by Elaine Terranova.

HOO-DOO (BlackSeries). General editor: Ahmos Zu-Bolton; associate editors: Harryette Mullen, Jerry Ward and E. Ethelbert Miller. Founded 1973 and first published by Energy BlackSouth Press. It has had offices in DeRidder, Louisiana, Washington, D.C. and Houston, Texas. "The Hoo-Doo (BlackSeries) magazine is a multi-cultural series, projected as a 13-volume mini-anthology (13 being the exit and emerging number in the hoodoo rituals practiced mostly in the deepsouthlands)." The series is currently published by Energy Earth Communications, Inc. and is located on the Galveston Island in the Gulf of Mexico.

INTERNATIONAL WRITING PROGRAM. Editors: Paul Engle and Hualing Nieh Engle. Founded 1971 in Iowa City, Iowa. "One of the most curious aspects of this century has been the way in which powerful heads of states with armies, secret police and the press at their disposal have been frightened by helpless poets, whose only resource was the powerful and beautiful words of language. We believe that in the dangerous 20th century people of good mind and good will must translate or die. People talking to each other (poetry is the highest form of talk) are not fighting each other. We believe that translating poetry, that insight into the emotionalized ideas of men and women is an honor, a privilege, and one of the toughest jobs offered to the human race." The International Writing Program tries to translate from all languages, but especially the more obscure ones. Each year the IWP brings writers to Iowa City from all around the world, to live, write and interact for a period of three-four months. Some books: EARTH ERECT by Vasco Popa (Yugoslavia); THE STILL UNBORN ABOUT THE DEAD by Nichita Stanescu (Romania); THE WAR IS OVER by Evegny Vinokurov (Russia); WRITING FROM THE WORLD (anthology); THE SELECTED POEMS OF AGNES NEMESNAGY (Hungary).

INVISIBLE CITY. Editors: Paul Vangelisti and John McBride. Fairfax, California. Invisible City is a tabloid magazine of poetry, visuals, and statements published by Red Hill Press. Red Hill Press has published American editions of titles from Edizioni Geiger, including Adriano Spatola's VARIOUS DEVICES and ZEROGLYPHICS. A manual of Italian poetry and visual poetry, 1960-1980, edited by Adriano Spatola, will be available later in 1980.

JAM TO-DAY. Editors: Don Stanford (who also designs the mag, does typesetting and makeup, and chooses graphics), Judith Stanford and Floyd Stuart. Presently located in Northfield, Vermont. "Jam To-day publishes poetry, reviews and, beginning with the 1980 issue, fiction. The editors are concerned more with quality (as defined by their biases) than with quantity, and so only seven issues have appeared since the magazine began in 1973. Rather than issuing a formally stated literary aesthetic, the editors feel that the magazine itself is the best statement of what they think is good poetry and fiction. Jam To-day is independent, not affiliated with any institution. Contributors are paid—not

much, but something. Money is, perhaps unavoidably, the dominant standard
of value in our society, and poetry and fiction are worth at least something.
At least to some people. The editors make a positive effort to be open to new
voices. Older, better-known voices are welcome, too. Some better known poets
appearing in issues 1-7 are Douglas Blazek, Tom Disch, John Engels, Ron
Koertge, Denise Levertov, Dick Lourie, Tom McKeown, Robert Peters and
Marge Piercy.

Don Stanford works for MIT Press in Cambridge, Massachusetts. Judith
Stanford teaches English and women's studies at Merrimack College in North
Andover and at Northern Essex Community College in Haverhill. Floyd Stuart
is a poet and Associate Professor of English at Norwich University, Northfield,
Vermont.

LAME JOHNNY PRESS. Editor: Linda M. Hasselstrom. Sunday Clothes, which
preceded Lame Johnny Press, was begun in 1971, "six years and about
$20,000 of my own money and perhaps that much in individual contributions
and grants later. It began as Sunday Clothes: A Magazine of the Fine Arts,
gradually dropped the "fine" and began concentrating on grass roots work
from a loosely defined 'Great Plains.' I moved from a slick professional design
to a more folksy design, as the art and writing progressed—but the quality of
work consistently went up. I moved from reviewing major press publications
to reviewing almost all small press work—as I discovered the small presses, and
became one. My vision of the magazine was (as my press vision still is) to publish writing from those resident in the Great Plains or working out of it, that
reflects the best we are able to do; in a way to define what it is that makes us
live/work/play here." Some books: Craig Volk's MATE COME HEAL ME;
MOUNTAINS (a manuscript on farm activism in South Dakota in the 1930s);
THE BOOK BOOK (a "how-to" book) by Linda M. Hasselstrom; NEXT-YEAR
COUNTRY: ONE WOMAN'S VIEW by Alma Phillip (photographs).

"I [Linda M. Hasselstrom] was raised on the Great Plains, on a ranch near
Hermosa, South Dakota; my press is there; recently married (my name's the
same); I divide my time between the ranch and our home in Spearfish, or my
husband's tipi."

LITMUS, INC. Editor/publisher: Charles Potts. Presently located in Walla
Walla, Washington. [no date of origin given, but we believe it was around
1967 ... we also believe Litmus was situated in Salt Lake City for a good
stretch] Litmus has published 18 first editions, including works by Charles
Bukowski, Richard Krech, Jo Merrill, Kell Robertson, Karen Waring, Peter
Koch, David Hiatt, and first books by Andy Clausen, Mike Finley, Charles
Foster, Charley George, Edward Smith, Greg Stewart and Nolan Palmer. Lit-
mus has also published critical articles, essays, and reviews on the works of
Gene Marine, Robert Creeley, Hayden Carruth, Charles Bukowski, Robert Bly,
Thomas McGrath, Henry Ebel, Gerald Locklin, Stanley Crouch, John Weiners,
Charles Olson and many others. Litmus sponsored seven festivals and readings
from 1967-1976, and hosted "Oasis", a half-hour weekly broadcast of poetry

and contemporary literature on KUER in Salt Lake City, national public radio for Utah, with Charles Potts as host.

Charles Potts was born 1943 in Idaho Falls, Idaho. He is married to Judith Silverman and has one child, Emily Karen, who was born 1977. He received a B.A. in English from Idaho State University in 1965. He has been a farm laborer, college student, ski lift operator, bartender, mimeo operator, warehouse manager, import executive, computer operator, typesetter, real estate salesman, landlord and weatherization supervisor. He's traveled in Mexico, El Salvador, Guatemala and Canada. Philosophy: "Reductivism: whereby the essence of the subject matter is reduced to the most succinct representation, as differentiated 180 degrees from minimalism." Some books: ROCKY MOUNTAIN MAN (selected poems, The Smith, 1978); VALGA KRUSA (psychological autobiography, Litmus Inc., 1977); TH GOLDEN CALF (Litmus, 1975); THE LITMUS PAPERS (Gunrunner, Milwaukee, 1969); LITTLE LORD SHIVA (Noh Directions—Aldebaran Review, Berkeley, 1969); BLUES FROM THURSTON COUNTY (Grande Ronde, Folsom, California, 1966); A RITE TO THE BODY (forthcoming). Some anthologies he's appeared in: THE FACE OF POETRY (Gallimaufry, 1977); ELEVEN YOUNG POETS (The Smith 17, 1975); DO YOU WANT TO BE IN OUR ZOO TOO (Zoo Press, 1966). He coedited a symposium issue of Margins on THE MAXIMUS POEMS VOLUME III by Charles Olson.

MAGAZINE. Editor: Kirby Congdon. "Interim Books is named to cover that interval or interim of time between a poet's original anonymity and his later recognition by the more commercial houses. Magazine was begun because I did not like what anyone else was doing, and subsequent issues were published to cover areas I felt were taboo or otherwise neglected. To date there are five issues, 1964-1972."

MANROOT. Editors: Paul Mariah and Richard Tagett. Founded 1969, Bay Area/South San Francisco. Major publications: THE JACK SPICER ISSUE (ManRoot Number 10); THIS LIGHT WILL SPREAD: SELECTED POEMS 1960-1975 by Paul Mariah; HYMNS TO HERMES by James Broughton; THE POET AS ICE SKATER by Robert Peters; THE POEMS OF JEAN GENET, edited by Paul Mariah. Aspirations: "To publish fine contemporary poetry, with occasional pieces from the past. We have published 11 issues of ManRoot and 27 books by living Americans, the majority of which are gay. We are not an exclusively gay press. Though we are almost exclusively a poetry press. Monies are too tight in this recession so we are only doing 2 or 3 books a year."

Paul Mariah lead a poets and writers workshop in San Francisco for five years. He was one of the four coordinators for the newly released Kinsey study, Indiana University, 1969-70. With Sally Gearhart he was President of the Council on Religion and the Homosexual, 1971-73.

ME TOO. Founded 1973 by Barbara Sablove as a mimeographed edition of mostly Actualist poets living in or around Iowa City, Me Too was then edited by Patricia Markert and Mary Stroh and included poems by Allan Kornblum, Joseph Gastiger, Barbara Sablove and K.L. Deal. These issues were published yearly, and while the last one appeared in 1977, another may appear. "The best thing we can say about the idea of keeping a small press going is what William Carlos Williams said: 'To me it [the little magazine] is one magazine, not several. It is a continuous magazine, the only one I know with an absolute freedom of editorial policy and a succession of proprietorships that follows a democratic rule.' In choosing the poets who appear in Me Too, what it came down to was who was saying most in the best possible way."

Patty Markert lives and works in New York City. She's an editor for McGraw-Hill.

Mary Stroh was born 1949 in Chicago. She is presently in Iowa City working with the Energy Conservation Program at the University of Iowa and "writing writing writing." She has been a car hop, waitress, cook, dishwasher, clerk-typist, secretary, receptionist, computer terminal operator, printer (multilith, AB Dick, letterpress), paper cutter, day-care worker, fine arts sales, communications analyst, etc. Has traveled all over the U.S. Philosophy: " 'What the hell Jane, do it yourself!' " She has been published in NEW POETS: WOMEN (anthology) and Iowa Woman.

MODERN POETRY IN TRANSLATION. Editor: Daniel Weissbort. Founded in London, England 1965 by Weissbort and Ted Hughes. Presently located in Iowa City and London. Aspirations: "To open lines of communication between contemporary cultures. To promote awareness and appreciation of the scholarly and inspirational art of translation."

NEW LETTERS. Editor: David Ray. Founded as a continuation of The University Review (founded 1934) in Kansas City, Missouri. Aspirations: "To present the finest writing available, with special attention given to neglected work (see our special issue on Jack Conroy) and work by writers who have not received attention due them." Major issues of the magazine include SINCE FEELING IS FIRST (anthology of contemporary American poetry); TWO NOVELS by Natalie L.M. Petesch; FICTION OMNIBUS, with photos by Lewis W. Hine; THE WRITINGS OF PAUL GOODMAN; AFRICAN AND CARRIBEAN WRITING, with Chinua Achebe and Wilson Harris.

David Ray was born 1932 in Sepulpa, Oklahoma and presently lives in Kansas City, Missouri "in an upstairs yellow room with a rug worn thin as Persia itself." He has been a social worker and a free-lance and ghost writer. He lived in Europe from 1966-69 on a University of Vienna fellowship and has traveled in Mexico. "Poetry merely expresses life, day to day, its simplicity and ecstasy, and more celebration than lament. Basically I am a Platonist in that I feel the poet is more or less mad and, when tuned in, in touch with the higher realities, the permanent forms, the noumena. I am also, when I am not a poet, a Platonist in that I fear the irrationality of poetry (at least, of poets), and I'd probably opt for some controls other poets would detest—the price we pay for freedom seems absurd at times, I'd have the handguns picked up tomorrow if I had the chance, and I'd probably shoot some TV producers. I'd agree with Shelley that poets should be the "unacknowledged legislators of the world." But in order to do that poets would have to agree to some rules. I get the impression that most poets today are genuine anarchists, but not in the Shelleyan sense. I have never felt cozy in or been with any real warmth admitted into their circles. I feel just as alienated from them as from people in the streets, probably more so." David Ray has a book of stories, THE MULBERRIES OF MINGO; among his books of poetry are X-RAYS; DRAGGING THE MAIN; GATHERING FIREWOOD; THE TRAMP'S CUP and THE FARM IN CALABRIA & OTHER POEMS.

THE NEW RENAISSANCE. Co-editor/publisher: Harry Jackel; co-editor: Louise T. Reynolds. Presently located in Arlington, Massachusetts. "the new renaissance began in the fall of 1968. Sylvia Shirley was to have been co-editor but her sudden death delayed the inauguration of the magazine and early promotion of it as well. The idea of tnr grew out of a desire for a) continuity and stability of a little magazine (we were determined to publish, regardless of reception, success, etc., three full volumes before even considering disbanding) in order to provide both writers and readers with a viable publication; b) pay all writers and visual artists for their work because we believe the artist, no less than the craftsman or other worker, is worthy of his hire and because we believe that only through a monetary payment can we exhibit our respect for art —we have followed this policy at considerable personal sacrifice since the magazine is not capitalized and exists only by sales and my own donation of one week's net salary out of every six paychecks; c) offer an open submission policy to writers all over the world who have something to say, who say it with style or grace, and who speak in a personalized voice (now qualified by the writer's purchase of a single issue); and d) publish a magazine that has an international consciousness and which offers the literate reader a sense of being a citizen of the whole world, fully aware of the human predicament, interested in the social and political issues of our time, and thoroughly and completely convinced of the meaning and importance of the arts to mankind.

"What we look for in manuscripts is for the language to leap off the page and, in fiction particularly, for the 'shock of recognition' (Edmund Wilson's phrase) from the artist who has articulated something we've always known."

Harry Jackel lives and works in New York City. He has taken on the full editorial responsibilities his late wife, Sylvia Shirley, would have had.

Louise T. Reynolds has worked for newspapers and commercial magazines in New York City, for radio and TV in Boston, for theatrical producers in New York City, and for Gambit, Inc., publishers, in Boston, a small commercial publishing house that grew out of Houghton-Mifflin and which distributed through that firm. She writes fiction and non-fiction.

NEW SALT CREEK READER. Editor: Ted Kooser. Founded 1967 in Lincoln, Nebraska. The last publication of NSCR appeared in 1975.

Ted Kooser was born 1939 in Ames, Iowa. He lives in Lincoln, Nebraska, where he is employed as an underwriter in the home office of a Lincoln-based insurance company. He is married, and has one son, Jeff, from a prior marriage. He graduated from Iowa State University in 1962, and entered graduate school in English at the University of Nebraska in 1963. He dropped out after one year to take the job in the Lincoln insurance company. He is also the editor and publisher of Windflower Press, a small publishing concern specializing in poetry. In 1976 he was awarded a writing fellowship by the National Endowment for the Arts. The poem which appears in this anthology first appeared in SHOOTING A FARMHOUSE (Ally Press, 1975) and was reprinted in his SURE SIGNS: NEW & SELECTED POEMS (University of Pittsburgh Press, 1980). Other books: TWENTY POEMS (Best Cellar Press, 1973); A LOCAL HABITATION & A NAME (Solo Press, 1974); VOYAGES TO THE INLAND SEA VI (with Harley Elliott; Center for Contemporary Poetry, University of Wisconsin, 1976); OLD MARRIAGE AND NEW (Cold Mountain Press, 1978); HATCHER (an illustrated novella, Windflower Press, 1978).

NITTY GRITTY: see end of this listing.

OBSIDIAN. Editor: Alvin Aubert. Founded 1975 at State University College, Fredonia, New York. Presently located in the English Department, Wayne State University, Detroit. "Obsidian's aim is to publish the best contemporary writing in English by and about Black writers worldwide: poetry, fiction, critical articles, interviews, short plays, bibliographies."

OLE: see end of this listing.

OUT THERE. Co-director and editor: Rose Lesniak; co-director: Andrea Kirsch; special editor: Barbara Barg; advisor: Felix D'Arienzo. "Out There Press grew out of the Apocalypse Poetry Association at Northeastern Illinois University in Chicago in 1975. The founder was Neil Hackman. The magazine was passed on to myself [Rose Lesniak] soon after, as well as directorship of the association. We have published many volumes of poetry, funded poetry readings, donated our time in teaching at community centers and just recently completed a Poetry In Performance tape, an educational TV pilot of poets reading and performing their works throughout various locations in New York City. The goals of our non-profit organization are to provide the community and audience with the best American contemporary poetry and poets, as well as provide outlets for poets to be read and seen. We are into all types of styles and sensibilities. We are against oppressive poetry and sexist writings."

PAINTED BRIDE QUARTERLY. Editor: Kate Britt. Founded 1973 in Philadelphia by Louise Simons and R. Daniel Evans. Major publications include SHIT PISS BLOOD & BRAINS by John Giorno, and WOMAN EXPLORER by Lynn Lonidier.

PENTAGRAM PRESS. Editor: Michael Tarachow. Founded 1974, and has since issued over twenty-five titles, from Diane Wakoski's 8-page FABLE to Tom Montag's 258-page collected essays and reviews, CONCERN/S. Beginning with mainly offset collections of poetry in Milwaukee, Wisconsin, Pentagram moved to Markesan, a town of 1,100, on the Grand River. It's acquired an 1892 Chandler and Price 10 x 15 letterpress, and will be doing handset letter-pressed collections of poems. At work now on MAIZE by Gil Ott. The book marks its first attempt at integrating graphics with poetry. Pentagram has published or will publish, Theodore Enslin, Cid Gorman, Ted Kooser, Bill Kloefkorn, William Matthews, Tom Bridwell, Marilyn Kitchell, Marty Rosenblum, Harley Elliott, John Judson and others. In January 1979, as the mimeo arm of Pentagram, it founded Hawk-Wind, a magazine of poetry and commentary. "With an AM 1250 press due in soon (co-owner, Tom Montag), and with my [Michael Tarachow] bookbinding and typesetting knowledge, we will have a complete printshop capacity under one (uninsulated but also un-leaky) roof."

POETRY &. Editor/publisher: JoAnn Castagna; art editor: Sara Counts; and Barbara Mackowiak. "Poetry & was inclusive (tried to cover the entire Chicago area as far as news was concerned, and published poets from all over the U.S.) and inexpensive (only 25¢). We also tried—and achieved—regularity of publication (24 issues in 2 years)." Poetry & did a Poetry & Postcards Series 1 & 2. The last publication of Poetry & was Azimuth (1979), a Small Press review journal.

POETRY NEWSLETTER. Editor: Richard O'Connell. Founded 1971 in the Department of English at Temple University in Philadelphia. Philosophy: "The poetry is the news."

POETRY NOW: see end of this listing.

PORCH. Editor: James Cervantes. Founded 1977 at Arizona State University. Published by Porch Publications, which also has a chapbook series and initiated the Inland Boat pamphlet series in Spring 1979. "We publish the best contemporary poetry that comes our way, as well as intelligent reviews." Porch has published work by Michael Burkard, Robert Hedin, Norman Dubie, Danny Rendleman, Mary Ruefle, James Bertolino, Pamela Stewart, Tess Gallagher, Laura Jensen, Greg Simon, Jeanie Thompson, Roger Weingarten, Rachel Hadas and others. Its chapbook series includes ODALISQUE IN WHITE by Norman Dubie; FERRY ALL THE WAY UP by Katherine Kane and the forthcoming FROM SHEEPSHEAD, FROM PAUMANOK by Frank Graziano; DREAM-WORK by Lorrie Goldensohn. The Inland Boat pamphlet series for 1979 includes "Touchwood" by Cynthia Hogue; "Elkin Pond" by Sherod Santos; "The Rabbi's Daughter" by Peggy Gifford; "In My Brother's House" by Mick Fedullo; "Casa de Luz" by Paul Cook, and others.

James Cervantes presently teaches creative writing at Arizona State University. His work has been published in CutBank, Panjandrum, Cincinnati Poetry

Review and raccoon, and is forthcoming in Ironwood and New Letters. His first collection, THE YEAR IS APPROACHING SNOW, will be published by W. D. Hoffstadt & Sons.

Greg Simon (Northwest editor and review editor) has published in American Poetry Review, The New Yorker and other magazines.

RED CLAY BOOKS. Editor: Charleen Swansea. Founded 1963 in Charlotte, North Carolina, where it's "still going strong!" The editor aspires to "The discovery of new voices! We publish primarily first books of poetry and we market them nationally. We aim to do for new writers what conglomerate publishing will no longer do—read their manuscripts, give criticism and get new work out to a national market." Major publications include LOVE STORIES BY NEW WOMEN, edited by Charleen Swansea; VANISHING SPECIES, poems by Chuck Sullivan; LOVERS AND AGNOSTICS, poems by Kelly Cherry; BLACK BLUES AND SHINY SONGS, poems by Tommy Scott Young; HORSE, HORSE, TYGER, TYGER, poems by Heather Miller; ANOTHER LIGHT, poems by Marion Cannon.

RIVER BOTTOM. Founded in 1973 by R. Chris Halla with a chapbook by himself and another Oshkosh, Wisconsin poet, Dale David. The press name at that time was Broken Arrow, but that was changed immediately after publication of the chapbook. "It is interesting to note that David's poem, River Bottom, was written for the volume, rather than the volume being named for the poem." Publication of the magazine and the broadsides (Baseball, Floating, and Nickle Times) began in 1974 with Halla as editor and Bill Weitenbeck and Janet Halla as assistant editors. (Weitenbeck left midway through 1975 and Gary Busha joined as co-editor early in 1975). Since 1973, River Bottom has published 10 issues and chapbooks, nine postcards, one pamphlet and over 20 broadsides. There have been almost 100 contributors. In addition to subscriptions and single copy sales, hundreds of copies have been given to high school and university teachers to pass out in their classes. Many copies have also been given to various small press and other libraries. Publication was aided with one $600 grant from CCLM in 1976. River Bottom has been a member of CCLM and COSMEP. It was begun in Oshkosh in 1973, moved to Milwaukee for three months in 1977 and then to the village of Iola, Wisconsin from which the last issue was published in autumn of 1977. A five-year index was published in 1978.

ROUGH LIFE PRESS. Editors: Kenton Marks, Mary McComb and John Selby. Founded 1976 in Los Angeles. Last publication was in 1978. The press is now defunct. Aspiration: "To print the best poetry there is. (was?)" Major publications include NO PLACE FAST by F. A. Nettelbeck; HOUSES by Karen Hine; TEENAGE DEATH LUST by Peter Fenton. *An ironic note: According to F.A. Nettelbeck, who supplied us with the press information, Kenton Marks was stabbed to death since the press made their Editor's Choice nominations. The reader is referred to the poem in this volume, by Nettelbeck.*

SALTED FEATHERS. Editor/publisher: Dick Bakken. "... launched in 1964 in the heyday of the 'mimeo revolution' " by Bakken, Lee Altman and Wilbur Braden, who worked together on the first few issues. "Salted Feathers was a first or early publisher of many enduring writers," with a roster that includes Howard McCord, Dave Kelly, Keith Abbott, Diane Wakoski, James Hazard, John Logan, Carole Berge, Charles Bukowski, Carlos Reyes, Gary Snyder and Sandra McPherson. Publications include: MIRACLE FINGER: A Book of Works by Children Ages Two to Fifteen, with notes by parent and teacher poets (Dick Bakken, Philip Dow, Gwen Head, Sandra McPherson, Primus St. John and others, edited by Dick Bakken, 1975) and HUNGRY!, a document of 1964-65 Bengali "Hungry Generation" obscene poetry bust (includes essays by guest editor Howard McCord, Jyotirmoy Datta, Allen Ginsberg, others, edited by DB, 1967, now out-of-print. Miracle Finger and complete original sets of the magazine are available from DB c/o E. 14622 Valley Way, Spokane, Washington 99216.

Dick Bakken was born in Montana in 1941 and grew up in the Pacific Northwest. In 1970 he resigned his position as a tenured English professor to devote his full energies to poetry. He has traveled coast to coast organizing poetry centers and festivals. Until now he has consistently refused to publish—other than with his voice—any of his poems but a few very short ones, such as those that have appeared in St. Andrews Review. A book of poetry is forthcoming from Lynx House.

SAMISDAT. "Vietnam vet and war-resistor Tom Suddick and I [Merritt Clifton] founded Samisdat in '73, as The Berkeley Samisdat Review. Transferred from Berkeley to San Jose, it grew from out-and-out sociopathy into a concerted assault on Big Brotherism—first in literature, then in North American society in general. June Kemp joined us in 1976, and in 1977 we moved to Brigham, Quebec. Our stories and poems concern the culture of the future, the gradual but inevitable and inexorable trend toward self-reliance, conservation, live-and-let-live libertarian politics, and Transcendentalist philosophy. Our authors, like ourselves, tend to be disaffected outlaws, those aware both that Horatio Alger was a kiss-ass and that Karl Marx and Mao Tse Tung were just Billy Grahams with a slightly different religion. We publish at least a dozen issues and chapbooks per year, with the emphasis on fiction, but including non-fiction and poetry as well. Regulars include Kurt Nimmo, Mark Phillips, Brock Dethier, Gary Metras, Miriam Sagan, Rita Rosenfield, Margaret Kingery and Jo Schaper, among others."

Merritt Clifton was born 1953 in Oakland, California. "Broke into print as journalist, Berkeley, California, '67-'70. Founded Samisdat in '73, and it's been my chief occupation and support since late '74. Either ran or helped run numerous other litmags and small presses in San Jose, '70-'77. Married June Kemp, of Brigham, Quebec, in '76, and now live and work there, dividing time equally between creative endeavors and environmental/investigative journalism for The Sherbrooke Record, and Townships Sun, the region's only major English-language newspapers. Am going after river pollution, nukes, and the acid rain problem in particular. Personal beliefs: anarcho/libertarian. Lifestyle: back-to-the-earth, self-reliant, irreverent. Past occupations: reporter, editor, photographer, house-painter, pulp mill hand, janitor, security guard, stagehand, carpenter, fireman, and semi-pro ballplayer." Books include the novels BETRAYAL (1979); A BASEBALL CLASSIC (1978); 24 x 12 (1975). Poetry: VINDICTMENT (1977); FROM THE GOLAN HEIGHTS (1974). Non-fiction: RELATIVE BASEBALL (1979); THE SAMISDAT METHOD: A GUIDE TO DO-IT-YOURSELF OFFSET PRINTING (1978). Miscellany: THREE OF A KIND (short stories/poems/essays, 1979) and TWO FROM ARMAGGEDON (short stories, 1976). All of these are from Samisdat, though 24 x 12 is due in reprint from Mudborn of Santa Barbara, and others are scheduled by Dustbooks and Border-Mountain.

SCARECROW BOOKS (now known as Poor Souls Press/Scaramouche Books). Editor: Paul Fericano. "Scarecrow Books had its very humble beginnings in 1974. Its policy then, as now, was to publish the works of creative individuals —both young and old, established and aspiring—solely on the quality of the work submitted and not on the name or reputation of any one poet or writer. There was already too much of that going on, and a lot of good writing—especially humor and satire—was being ignored. Scarecrow Books published two magazines from 1974-1977: Crow's Nest (annual) and The West Conscious Review (three times a year). The magazine and press managed to remain truly independent, relying on the editor/publisher's own resources and steering clear of any government assistance. This was done by choice. It urged self-reliance for other presses and mags, and still does.

"Because of alleged trademark infringement charged by Scarecrow Press of New Jersey (a non-literary publisher), Scarecrow Books was forced to change its name in 1978. It is now know as Poor Souls Press/Scaramouche Books.

"If one is to remember the contributions Scarecrow Books made to the literary community during this decade, STOOGISM—a satirical movement ridiculing the mindless Seventies—would have to be at the top of the list." Authors they have published include Leon Spiro, A.D. Winans, Ann Menebroker, Ben Hiatt, Steven Ford Brown, Joan Colby, Ronald Koertge, William Packard, Steve Sneyd, Paula Jackson and many others. Books include ORG-1 by A.D. Winans; PASSPORT by Leon Spiro; IF I DON'T FIND PLEASURE I WILL DIE by Roger Langton; CANCER QUIZ by Paul Fericano. The works of 18 different poets appear on "Poets-Cards."

SEAMARK PRESS. Editors: Kay Amert and Howard Zimmon. Founded 1968 in Iowa City, Iowa. Major publications include OXIDES by Chuck Miller; EASY WRECKAGE by Ken McCullough; ODD WEATHER by Scott Wright; RANDOM by Howard Zimmon.

SECOND COMING. Editor: A.D. Winans. Founded 1971 in San Francisco. "Second Coming was created with the intention of maintaining and expanding on the true spirit of the early 60's when poets wrote for the people and not

each other and the masses were not looked down upon as being too dull to understand poetry but instead were sought out as the future audience of new
wave poetry." Major publications include CALIFORNIA BICENTENNIAL
POETS ANTHOLOGY (1976); 19 + 1: An Anthology of San Francisco Poetry
(1978); 7 ON STYLE by William Wantling (1977); FURTHER ADVENTURES
OF CRAZY JOHN by A.D. Winans (1979); DARK SMOKE by Pancho Aguila
(1977).

THE SEVENTIES. Editor: Robert Bly. Founded in the 1950s, with The Fifties,
followed by The Sixties; The Eighties will continue.   Major publications in-
clude TWENTY POEMS OF GEORG TRAKL, 1961, translated by Bly and
James A. Wright; TWENTY POEMS OF CESAR VALLEJO, translated by *
James A. Wright, 1963; TWENTY POEMS OF PABLO NERUDA, 1965, trans-
lated by Robert Bly and James A. Wright; TWENTY POEMS OF TOMAS
TRANSTROMER, 1970, translated by Robert Bly; A POETRY READING
AGAINST THE VIETNAM WAR, 1967, co-edited by Bly and David Ray.
"I publish mainly European poets in translation early in their careers, before
the big publishers will do them."
    Robert Bly: "I've avoided teaching and spend most of my time in Madison
or in the woods of northern Minnesota."   Last book published is THIS TREE
WILL BE HERE FOR A THOUSAND YEARS, 1979, Harper & Row. In 1980,
from University of Michigan Press: TALKING ALL MORNING: COLLECTED
CONVERSATIONS & INTERVIEWS; from Sierra Club: NEWS OF THE UNI-
VERSE: POEMS OF TWO-FOLD CONSCIOUSNESS (an anthology of nature
poems from the Eighteenth Century to the present).
    *The Vallejo book was edited by John Knoepfle, and translators are several,
tho not mentioned in The Cumulative Book Index.

THE SIXTIES: see The Seventies, above.

THE SMITH: see end of this listing.
*(SOUTH DAKOTA REVIEW is out of place: it follows the following entry.)
THE SPIRIT THAT MOVES US. Editor/publisher: Morty Sklar. Founded
1975 in Iowa City with the first issue of the literary periodical, The Spirit That
Moves Us.   From the outset I looked for work, including translations, from all
around the U. S., in any style as long as it had heart, guts, honesty, energy and
skill. I've published poetry, fiction, essays, interviews and artwork by such di-
verse talents as Chuck Miller (in this anthology), Atukwei Okai (Ghana), Marge
Piercy, Alberto Rios, Bessie Head (Botswana, South Africa), Ahmos Zu-Bolton,
Allan Kornblum, Constantin Toiu (Romania), Anselm Hollo, Charles Potts,
Barbara Holland, Warren Woessner, Lucien Stryk, Brown Miller, Attila Jozsef
(Hungary), Harley Elliott, Wolfgang Kohlhaase (East Germany), Joan Colby,
Mark Vinz, David Ray, John Sjoberg, Catherine Doty, Emery George, Rod
Tulloss and many many others.   Major publications: THE POEM YOU ASKED
FOR by Marianne Wolfe, 1977; THE ACTUALIST ANTHOLOGY, co-edited by
Darrell Gray and Morty Sklar, 1977; THE FARM IN CALABRIA & OTHER

POEMS by David Ray, 1979/80; CROSS-FERTILIZATION: THE HUMAN
SPIRIT AS PLACE, edited by Morty Sklar, 1980; and of course, this antholo-
gy, EDITOR'S CHOICE. Forthcoming is a new-and-selected poetry book by
Chuck Miller, as yet untitled. Both THE ACTUALIST ANTHOLOGY and
THE POEM YOU ASKED FOR were listed as "Best Titles" in Library Journal.
The magazine has been "Highly recommended" by Library Journal and well-
reviewed in several Small Press journals.

The Spirit That Moves us was begun and continues for several reasons,
among them my having found only one or two works I liked very much in
issues of magazines and books, and wanting to publish publications full of
works I liked very much. The Spirit That Moves Us is a non-profit, IRS tax-
exempt organization which also has published "Poetry-With-Drawings In The
Buses", and presents open as well as featured poetry and fiction readings, and
maintains "little magazines" racks in Iowa City.

Morty Sklar: I was born 1935 in New York City and lived there until 1971
when I came to Iowa City, not for the university (which I ultimately did attend for the purpose of cashing in on my G. I. Bill Educational Program), but
because someone I met at the National Poetry Festival in Allendale, Michigan
in 1971 said it was a nice place to live. I became turned on by and involved
with the non-university community of writers here: Allan & Cinda Kornblum,
Anselm Hollo, Chuck Miller, Jim Mulac, George Mattingly, Dave Morice,
Josephine Clare, John Sjoberg and many others who were writing, living, loving
and publishing such magazines as Toothpaste (the original, mimeo publication
of the now letterpress Toothpaste Press), Gum, Search For Tomorrow, P. F.
Flyer, Suction and others.

In New York City I floundered thru the Sixties as a heroin junkie until 1966
when I was saved by the example and guidance of Victor Biondo, an ex-junkie.
Victor and other ex-addicts, along with myself and other junkies began
Phoenix House, a therapeutic community for addicts in New York City. I graduated from it in 1969, took my first poetry workshop (after defensively writing in isolation for 3 years) with Isabella Gardner in 1971. Her workshop is
the best I've seen and should be a model for workshops: all the members (12)
were individual in style and approach, whether beginners or involved for
awhile, and Isabella's approach was unacademic and nurturing.

I'm a veteran of the Korean War (but saw battle only in the regimentation
of the army here in the U.S.), and have worked as a hardware clerk for my
father, a waiter, busdriver and drug counselor, among other things. Books:
THE NIGHT WE STOOD UP FOR OUR RIGHTS: Poems 1969-1975 (Toothpaste Press, 1977); THE FIRST POEM (Snapper Press, 1977); RIVERSIDE
(Emmess Press, 1974). The first was listed as a "Best Title" in Library Journal.
I'm halfway thru a first novel (interrupted by Editor's Choice). I'm engaged
to be engaged to Shelley Sterling, a found poem.

SOUTH DAKOTA REVIEW (and Dakota Press). Editor: John Milton. Founded at the University of South Dakota in Vermillion: South Dakota Review in
1963, and Dakota Press in 1969. Aspirations: SDR—"to maintain emphasis

on the literature of the American West, to occasionally promote regional literature, to publish quality fiction and poetry that is not faddish." Dakota Press—
"Generally, a devotion to regional material, including Indians." Major publications include AMERICAN INDIAN SPEAKS and AMERICAN INDIAN II,
from both the press and SDR; SAM PECKINPAH: MASTER OF VIOLENCE
and THE LITERATURE OF SOUTH DAKOTA, from the press.

*(THE SPIRIT THAT MOVES US is out of place: it precedes South Dakota Review.)

SUCTION. Editor: Darrell Gray. Founded 1969 in Iowa City; now located in
Oakland, California. "Suction is the magazine of the Actualist Movement in the
Arts. It appears only when the editor has collected enough good material to just-
ify a new issue. The next issue will feature predominantly 'heterogenic' poems—
that is, poems written in personae. We shall include classics such as Fernando
Pessoa (Portuguese); Ogar Mu (created by Anselm Hollo); Dirac Jislerav (created by George Chambers); Phillipe Mignon (created by Darrell Gray); Frank W.
Lewis (created by Dave Hilton). Publication date is scheduled for September 15,
1980. (Also to be included are heterogenic poets in Andrei Codrescu's
LICENSE TO CARRY A GUN. This issue will be an attempt to avoid ego-
centered poetry.)

Darrell Gray was born 1945 in Sacramento, California and grew up in Walnut, Kansas. "A Euell Gibbons-type childhood, then back to California for
high school and college. Back to the Midwest (Iowa) for two years duty on the
USS Prairie Schooner which houses the Famous Poet's School, a singularly en-
igmatic vessel that always seems on the verge of 'going somewhere.' MFA with
honorable discharge in 1969." He has been "a postoffice worker, part-time car-
wrecker, gravedigger, encyclopedia salesman, high school teacher, and a consultant for the National Prune Advisory Board." He is presently living in Oakland, California, "casting a line in the ocean for my limit of soluble fish."
Philosophy: "Art is an unpredictable guy, so I approach him with caution and
a generous supply of wine."

Besides being editor of Suction, he was co-editor of THE ACTUALIST
ANTHOLOGY (The Spirit That Moves Us Press, 1977) and author of the fol-
lowing books: THE EXCUSES (Abraxas Press, 1970); THE BEAUTIES OF
TRAVEL (Doones Press, 1970); SOMETHING SWIMS OUT (Blue Wind Press,
1972); SCATTERED BRAINS (The Toothpaste Press, 1974); ESSAYS AND
DISSOLUTIONS (Abraxas Press, 1977); THE PLAIN THAT BECAME A
MOUNTAIN (Tendon Press, 1977); others.

SUNDAY CLOTHES: see Lame Johnny Press.

SUN TRACKS. Editors: Carol Kirk, Roy Armstrong, Faith Seota and Larry
Evers. Founded 1971 in Tucson, Arizona. "We are interested in 1) promoting
literary expression and appreciation among all Indian peoples and 2) promoting understanding and appreciation of this country's native literary heritage."

TAMARISK. Editors: Dennis Barone and Deborah Ducoff-Barone. "Tamarisk
grew out of Apocalypse. Apocalypse was begun in 1975 by Tom Smith and

Dennis Barone. We thought we could drag in the contemporary where even the modern was shunned. We didn't know what we were doing: Accepting poems without being familiar with the author's body of work; printing big names (in our minds) as just that—advertisement—to sell, which we wouldn't do anyway. The most valuable lesson an editor can learn is when not to come out with an issue. Apocalypse ceased after one issue. The following year Tamarisk—having small scalelike leaves and clusters of pink flowers (a bouquet)—under the editorship of Dennis Barone and Deborah Ducoff-Barone published UNUSUAL GIFTS, a first collection of poems by Bruce Daryl Barone. In 1977 a chapbook by Ron Atkinson with drawings by Cormac Tully was published. The Winter 1978 issue of Tamarisk was yet another beginning. By then we realized that 'A continuous attempt at definition seems to be not what makes us different, but what *will* make us different.' "

Recent single artist issues are THE NEW LESSONS by Barry Schwabsky and VAPOR LOCK by Bill Wilson. Future single artist issues will feature John Cavanagh, John Cline and John Smyth. Their work always appears in the regular issues. After twenty issues, like Origin, Kulcher and Caterpillar, we will cease publication and move on to something else.

Dennis Barone was born in Teaneck, New Jersey. A graduate of Bard College, he is currently working towards a PhD in American Civilization at the University of Pennsylvania. His major research interest is rhetoric in colonial America. His poems, fiction, essays and interviews have appeared in Triquarterly, Some Other Magazine and others.

Deborah Ducoff-Barone was born in Rahway, New Jersey. A graduate of Bard College, she also holds an M.A. in Material Culture from the University of Pennsylvania. Her interests are business concerns of early Philadelphia, early iron making in colonial America and visual documentation and presentation of historical archaeology.

TOOTHPASTE PRESS. Editors/publishers: Allan and Cinda Kornblum. Founded 1970 in Iowa City; presently located in West Branch, Iowa. Five most recent books: COUNTRIES by Anne Waldman; GONE SAILING by Helen Adam; QUICKSAND THROUGH THE HOURGLASS by Dave Morice; YOUNG ANGER by Rose Lesniak; LITTLE MYSTERIES by Ken Mikolowski.

Cinda Kornblum was born 1950 in Newton, Iowa. She's been doing clerical work in the University of Iowa Department of Surgery since 1972. She has had one book of her poems published, BANDWAGON (Toothpaste Press), and her work has appeared in THE ACTUALIST ANTHOLOGY (The Spirit That Moves Us Press), In The Light, and PUSHCART PRIZE I I. A book of her poems is forthcoming from Toothpaste in 1981. "I'd rather write the poems first and figure out *why* later. I hope to live to be 80 or 90." The poem which appears in this anthology has also appeared in The Spirit That Moves Us.

Allan Kornblum was born in New York City 1949. He attended elementary school in Chelsea, Massachusetts, and high school in Wilmington, Delaware. He spent three years moving from N.Y.U. to Boston to New Hampshire, to the Lower East Side of New York City and the Saint Marks Poetry Project. During this time he worked in a screen/storm-window assembly line, in outdoor maintenance, at the postoffice, as an usher at Filmore East, as a flower shop clerk, an order clerk in a clothing factory, and made shoe-box tops in a shoe factory. Then he came to Iowa, settled down, and married Cinda Wormley in 1972. They have one girl, Annabel Patience, who was born in March 1979. "The Beats, Black Mountain, and the New York School have influenced my writing, along with Iowa City contemporaries, Iowa Writers Workshop rebels mostly. Harry Duncan, Kim Merker, Al Buck, Kay Amert, Howard Zimmon and Tom Miller have influenced my printing directly. I have never met Noel Young, Graham Mackintosh, Holbrook Teeter, Clifford Burke, but I have admired their work from afar. I hope to write more poems and print more books until I die ... I'm just another person, cup of coffee in hand, looking around, telling a few stories now and then." Major publications: AWKWARD SONG (Toothpaste Press, 1980); THE SALAD BUSHES (Seamark Press, 1975); GOOD MORNING: 14 SONNETS (J Stone Press, 1975), co-authored with Darrell Gray. The poem which appears in this anthology also appears in Saloma and AWKWARD SONG.

TRACE: see end of this listing.

UNMUZZLED OX. Editors: Michael Andre and Erika Rothenberg. Founded 1971 in New York City and Kingston, Canada. "As the author's chair was empty, we sat in it, assuming all authority. Poets are the best authors. And here their business is to examine not the individual, but the species, to remark general properties and large appearances. Audacious! The Poets imagine all knowledge; and thus their Encyclopedia contains everything worth knowing or imagining. Everything? The Poet, of course, does not number the streaks of the tulip, or describe the different shades of the verdure forest. Everything is seen as a part of the whole." Major publications: EARTH EGG by Gregory Corso; TROPICALISM by Kenward Elmslie; JOB SPEAKS by David Rosenberg; THE POETS ENCYCLOPEDIA, edited by Michael and Erika Rothenberg. *

Erika Rothenberg is a sculptor. She worked in advertising, did commercials for Coca Cola and The New York Times and made enough to stake the sculpture for years.

Michael Andre: "My mother's father wrote and edited small town newspapers in Canada and England. He was a traveling salesman of the word, a circuit rider of the news. As well as leaving newspapers behind, he left at least two families behind—including my mother's. I never met the man. In grammar school I played football and hockey. I decided instead of being a star athlete, I'd be a sports writer. I got my mother's typewriter, and would use carbon paper to produce a sporting magazine in an edition of five. I was about eight. My first 'novel'—my only novel, as a matter of fact—was begun about then, and was really a scrapbook of writing and clippings from magazines and newspapers. I went to a local Jesuit high school. The Jesuits confiscated my copy of Neitzche's ANTICHRIST and a general warning was issued to all students to beware of punk atheists. The summer of 1968 I became a film critic for The Montreal Gazette, then decided at the end of the summer to get a Master's degree at the

University of Chicago. In Chicago I learned about New York. My friends at Chicago were poets, and we read together, published together and were written up by the end of the year as "The New Chicago School." Meanwhile, I was reading art criticism and contemporary poetry, and they all seemed to be talking about the New York School. I got a doctorate from Columbia, joined the editorial board of The Little Magazine, and started writing art criticism for Art News. I met Erika Rothenberg in 1972. She re-designed the magazine. We got married. In 1978 I published a full-length collection called STUDYING THE GROUND FOR HOLES."

* "Unmuzzled Ox is a magazine with uncompromising articles and art by Daniel Berrigan and Joe Brainard and Sol LeWitt and Romare Bearden, the daybooks and personal work of writers of style like Robert Creeley, James Wright, Anne Waldman and Carolee Schneemann, and interviews—chats, really —with many people who seem to have something to say: Gary Snyder, Andy Warhol, Kate Millet, Pierre Trudeau, Djuna Barnes, Phil Glass, Robert Duncan and James Joyce."

VAGABOND. Editor: John Bennett. Founded 1966 in Munich, Germany; presently located in Ellensburg, Washington. "Hit hard, cut deep, pull out, regroup, disappear and hit again." Major publications include SIX POETS (Masarik, John Thomas, Menebroker, Lifshin, Koertge, Penfold; drawings by Bukowski); THE WORMS ARE SINGING (Jerry Bumpus); LACE AND A BOBBITT (Curt Johnson, novella); MUSIC IN THE WINEPRESS, PARROTS IN THE FLAMES (T.L. Kryss, poetry); THE VAGABOND ANTHOLOGY (the first decade of Vagabond magazine).

John Bennett was born 1938 in Brooklyn, New York. Besides editing Vagabond, he is also washing windows in Ellensburg, Washington. He has traveled "lots" and had many work experiences. His books include THE ADVENTURES OF ACHILLES JONES (novel, Thorp Springs Press); THE NIGHT OF THE GREAT BUTCHER (short stories, December Press); THE PARTY TO END ALL PARTIES (short stories, Fault Press); WHIPLASH ON THE COUCH (stories and poems, Duck Down Press).

WEST BRANCH. Editors: Robert Taylor and Karl Patten. Founded 1977 in Lewisburg, Pennsylvania. Aspiration: "To publish the best poetry and fiction being written today."

Karl Patten's poems appear widely in literary journals. He teaches courses in film and poetry at Bucknell.

Robert Taylor teaches the fiction workshops at Bucknell and publishes fiction "here and there."

WINDOW: see end of this listing.

YELLOW PRESS . Co-editors/-directors: Richard Friedman, Peter Kostakis and Darlene Pearlstein. Founded 1972 in Chicago. Publishes Milk Quarterly. "We look for the most tricky, imaginative and light-footed work (regardless of "school") with which we have become acquainted." Major publications: STRAIGHT by Richard Friedman; 15 CHICAGO POETS; RED WAGON by Ted Berrigan; ALICE ORDERED ME TO BE MADE by Alice Notley; CARAPACE by Henry Kanabus; NEW AND SELECTED POEMS by Paul Carroll.

Z PRESS: see end of this listing.

ZONEPRESS. Editors: Peter Cherches, Dennis DeForge, Jay Heller and Stephen Lackow. "The editors of Zone are writers, teachers, typesetters, bums and Brooklynites all." Major publications: LOCAL: AN ANTHOLOGY OF THE SUBWAY EXPERIENCE (1977); HERE AT THE DOOR by Janine Pommy Vega (1978); A THIRD SUMMARY by Harry Roskolenko. "Zone/ Zonepress is extremely eclectic."

The following are presses or magazines for which information was either obtained too late for inclusion in alphabetical order, or not obtained directly (in the latter case, information was taken from the International Directory Of Little Magazines And Small Presses).

BLACK SPARROW PRESS. Editor: John Martin. Founded 1966 in Los Angeles; present location is Santa Barbara, California. "... publishes avant-garde American poetry and prose." Major publications: POST OFFICE by Charles Bukowski (1971); THE MAGELLANIC CLOUDS by Diane Wakoski (1970); BURNING IN WATER by Charles Bukowski (1974); COLLECTED STORIES by Paul Bowles (1979); THE COMPLETE CORRESPONDENCE of Charles Olson and Robert Creeley (1980).

John Martin says he is "Elitist and opinionated."

GALLIMAUFRY. Editors: Mary MacArthur & Jonis Agee, fiction; Mary Mackey, plays. Founded 1973. Now defunct (location at time of nomination of work for this anthology was Arlington, Virginia). "Primarily fiction with special interest in work by women, though not limited to same... art, photos, criticism, reviews, parts-of-novels, collages, concrete art." [14th edition of the International Directory of Little Magazines and Small Presses]

HEIRS. Editors: Alfred D. Garcia; Jill Immerman; Ernest J. Oswald. Founded 1968 in San Francisco. The periodical is published in English/Spanish/Chinese. Aspiration: "Quality and variety." Some contributors: John Morita, Bruce Hutchinson, Dan Georgakas, Kenneth Lee, Luciano Mezzetta, Dadaland, Lorraine Tong, Andre Codrescu, Sandra Case, Buriel Clay II, Jessica Hagedorn. Books: PREPARING THE GROUND by Gary Gach (1977); FAREWELL TO THE COAST by Allejandro Murguia (1980)

NITTY GRITTY. (Goldermood Rainbow Press) Editor: Bill Wilkins. Founded 1974 in Pasco, Washington. Articles, commentary, fiction, poetry, art, cartoons, interviews, satire, criticism, reviews, letters, concrete art.

OLE. (Open Skull Press) Editor: Douglas Blazek. Founded 1964 in Bensenville, Illinois. Now defunct (last publication 1970). Aspiration: "To publish a type of poetry that arises from a closer contact with daily experience, the inglorious and glorious wallowing in the truth of physical detail (hopefully with the concomitant dropping of a rope ladder to enlightenment, or some such result that betters our living)." Some books: CONFESSIONS OF A MAN INSANE ENOUGH TO LIVE WITH BEASTS by Charles Bukowski; ALL THE ASSHOLES IN THE WORLD by Charles Bukowski; DOWN, OFF & OUT by William Wantling; WHY IS THE HOUSE DISSOLVING? by Lyn Lifshin; RED LADY by d.a. levy.

Douglas Blazek was born 1941 in Chicago. Presently lives in Sacramento, California in an "overstuffed chair in garage/grunting out biography better forgotten." The poem which appears in this anthology (nominated from Poetry Now) also appeared in Vagabond and the Vagabond Anthology, as well as in EXERCISES IN MEMORIZING MYSELF. He's done odd jobs, worked in supermarkets and factories. Other books: ALL GODS MUST LEARN TO KILL (Analecta Press, 1968); SKULL JUICES (Two Windows, 1970); FLUX & REFLUX (Oyez, 1970); EDIBLE FIRE (Morgan Press, 1978). Aspiration: "To develop the infra-red visions of life into something tangible, something that can be used like a hammer & saw within our psyche to make a better house." He's made "one long trip from Chicago through Southwest to California—Laid down the carpet in front of myself as I went & rolled it up seemingly for good upon reaching Sacramento."

POETRY NOW. Editor: E.V. Griffith. Founded 1973 in Eureka, California. It publishes in newspaper format, "the best work available in all moulds." Each issue has a poet "profile." The "review" section contains selections from books of poets. A section entitled "Other Men's Flowers" contains reprints from other magazines/presses. Poetry Now Press will issue its first titles in 1981-82.

THE SMITH. Editor: Harry Smith. Founded 1964 in New York City. Philosophy: "Generalist." Publications include the periodicals The Smith; NEWSArt; The Scene; and several dozen books of poetry, fiction, drama, and essays. Two recent titles are THE CHACKAMAS by Jana Harris, and FOREVER AND EVER AND A WEDNESDAY by Menke Katz.

Harry Smith says he is "frequently compared to Zeus and Orson Welles."

TRACE. Editor: James Boyer May & "too many to list, from year to year." Founded 1952 in Hollywood, California. Ceased publication in 1970. "My name is known to the strangest people—and many others of more sane mind. I have been translated into fourteen languages." Aspiration: "To aid new writers, artists."

Z PRESS. Editor: Kenward Elmslie. Founded 1973 in Calais, Vermont. The literary periodical (annual) is issued as Z; ZZ; ZZZ; and so on. Some contributors have been: Terrence Winch, Keith Abbott, Tim Dlugos, Michael Brownstein, Tony Towle, Pat Nolan, Frank O'Hara, Kenneth Koch. From the press (partial list): MILTIE IS A HACKIE by Edwin Denby, 1973; A NEST OF NINNIES by John Ashberry, 1975; TROPICALISM by Kenward Elmslie, 1975; TWELVE POSTCARDS by Joe Brainard, 1976; THE HOME BOOK by James Schuyler, 1977.

Editors Morty Sklar & Jim Mulac
(see Autobiographical Notes)
photo by Shelley Sterling